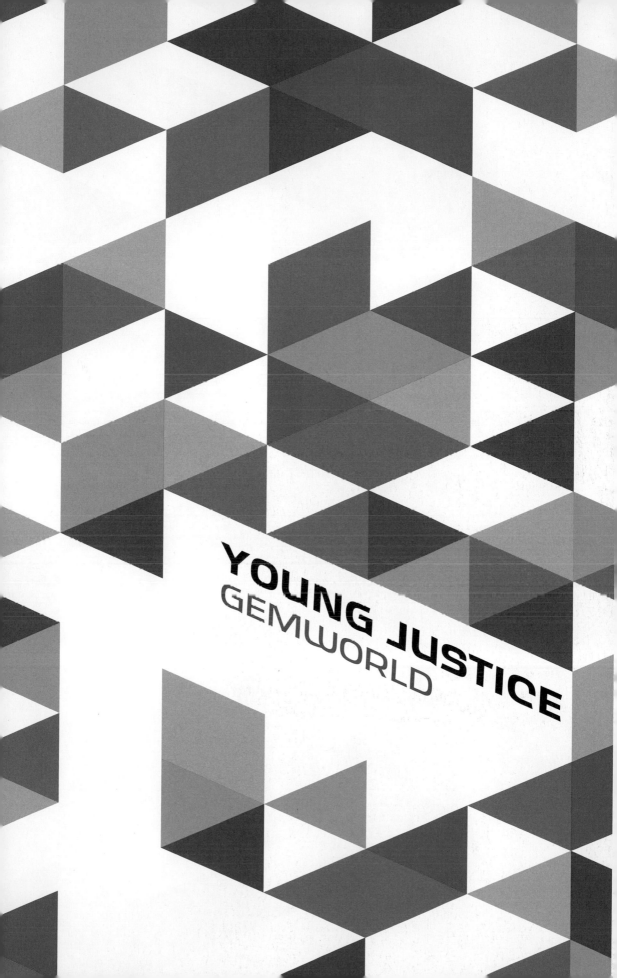

YOUNG JUSTICE
GEMWORLD

YOUNG JUSTICE

GEMWORLD

BRIAN MICHAEL BENDIS
writer

PATRICK GLEASON
JOHN TIMMS
EMANUELA LUPACCHINO
KRIS ANKA
VIKTOR BOGDANOVIC
EVAN "DOC" SHANER
RAY McCARTHY
JONATHAN GLAPION
artists

ALEJANDRO SANCHEZ
GABE ELTAEB
ALEX SINCLAIR
CHRIS SOTOMAYOR
HI-FI
colorists

JOSH REED
WES ABBOTT
CARLOS M. MANGUAL
letterers

PATRICK GLEASON
& ALEJANDRO SANCHEZ
collection cover artists

SUPERMAN created by JERRY SIEGEL and JOE SHUSTER
SUPERBOY created by JERRY SIEGEL
By special arrangement with the Jerry Siegel family

MIKE COTTON, ANDY KHOURI Editors – Original Series
JESSICA CHEN, BRITTANY HOLZHERR Associate Editors – Original Series
JEB WOODARD Group Editor – Collected Editions
ALEX GALER Editor – Collected Edition
STEVE COOK Design Director – Books
MONIQUE NARBONETA Publication Design
ERIN VANOVER Publication Production

BOB HARRAS Senior VP – Editor-in-Chief, DC Comics
PAT McCALLUM Executive Editor, DC Comics

JIM LEE Publisher & Chief Creative Officer
DAN DiDIO Publisher
BOBBIE CHASE VP – New Publishing Initiatives & Talent Development
DON FALLETTI VP – Manufacturing Operations & Workflow Management
LAWRENCE GANEM VP – Talent Services
ALISON GILL Senior VP – Manufacturing & Operations
HANK KANALZ Senior VP – Publishing Strategy & Support Services
NICK J. NAPOLITANO VP – Manufacturing Administration & Design
DAN MIRON VP – Publishing Operations
NANCY SPEARS VP – Sales
MICHELE R. WELLS VP & Executive Editor, Young Reader

YOUNG JUSTICE VOL. 1: GEMWORLD

DC Comics, 2900 West Alameda Ave., Burbank, CA 91505
Printed by LSC Communications, Kendallville, IN, USA. 8/23/2019. First Printing.
ISBN: 978-1-4012-9253-9

Library of Congress Cataloging-in-Publication Data is available.

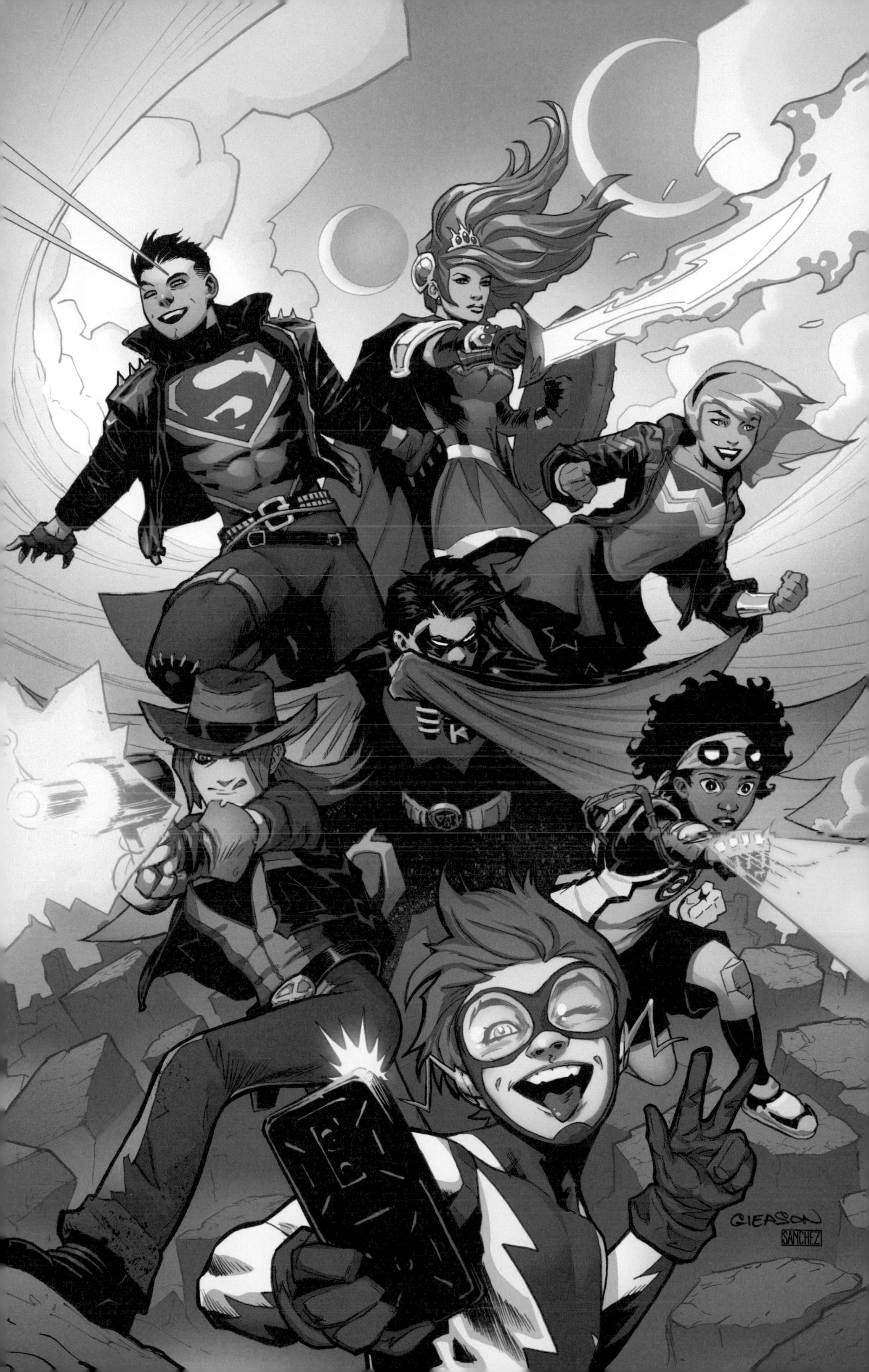
GLEASON
SÁNCHEZ

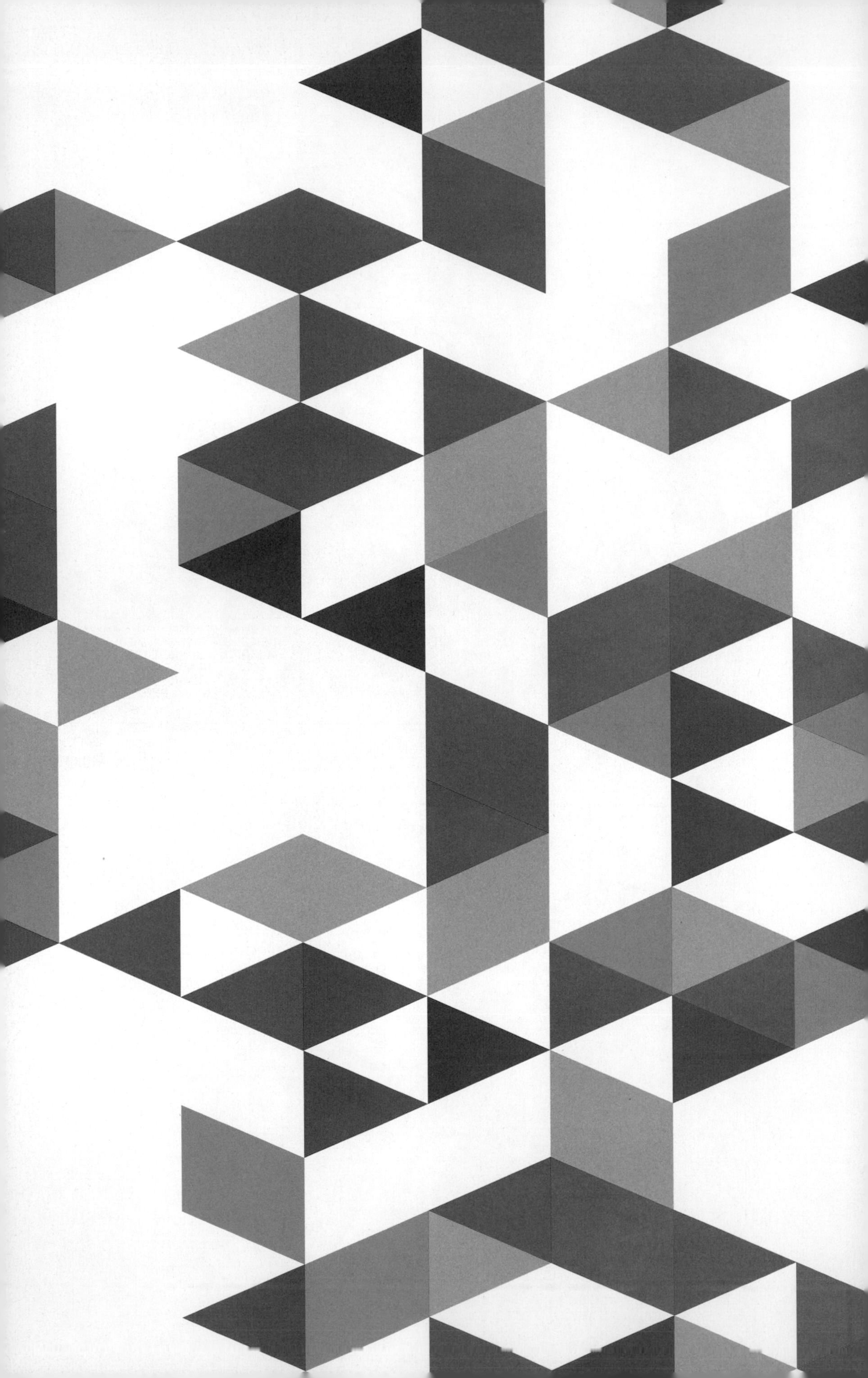

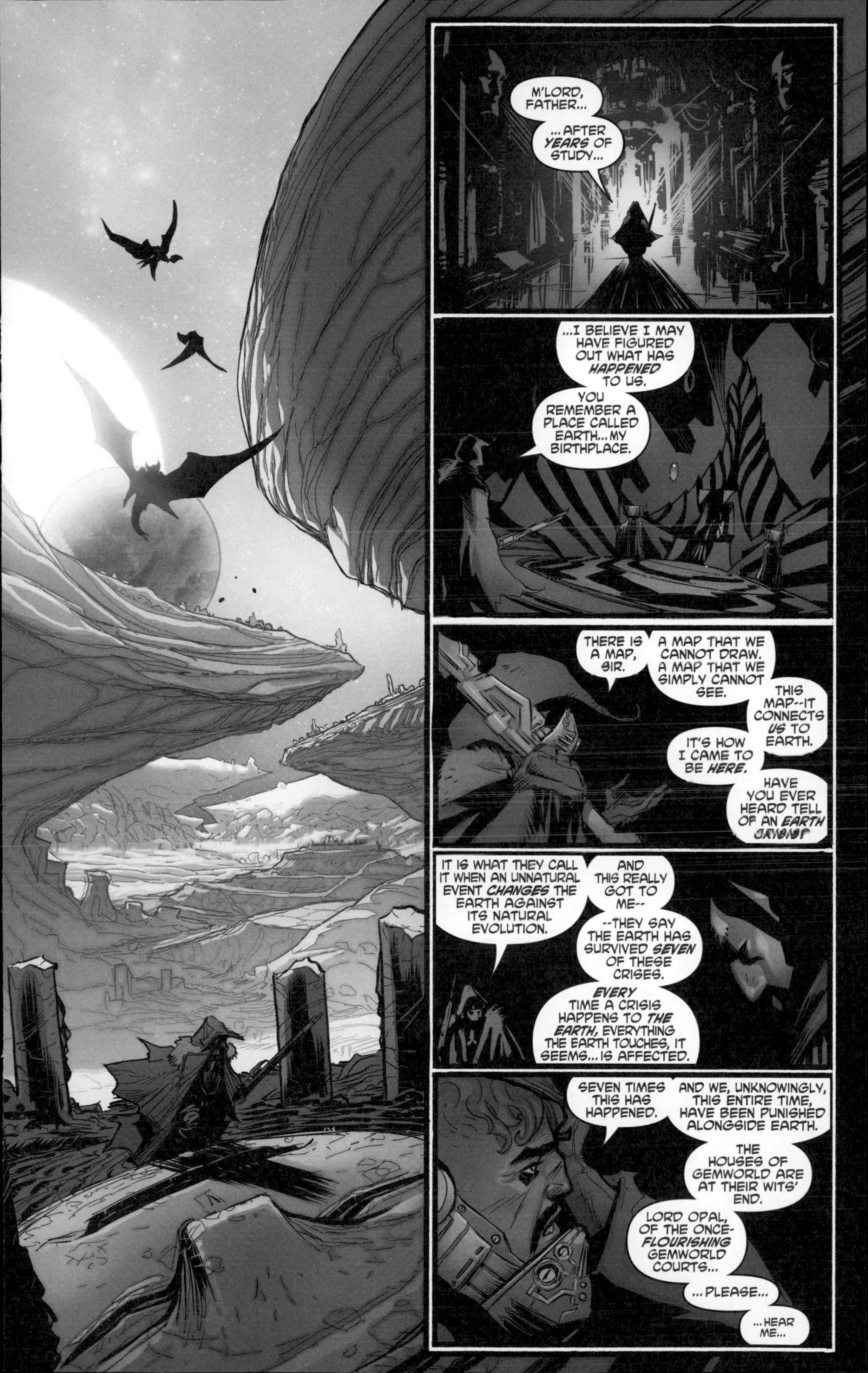
M'LORD, FATHER...
...AFTER YEARS OF STUDY...
...I BELIEVE I MAY HAVE FIGURED OUT WHAT HAS HAPPENED TO US.
YOU REMEMBER A PLACE CALLED EARTH... MY BIRTHPLACE.
THERE IS A MAP, SIR.
A MAP THAT WE CANNOT DRAW. A MAP THAT WE SIMPLY CANNOT SEE.
THIS MAP--IT CONNECTS US TO EARTH.
IT'S HOW I CAME TO BE HERE.
HAVE YOU EVER HEARD TELL OF AN EARTH
IT IS WHAT THEY CALL IT WHEN AN UNNATURAL EVENT CHANGES THE EARTH AGAINST ITS NATURAL EVOLUTION.
AND THIS REALLY GOT TO ME--
--THEY SAY THE EARTH HAS SURVIVED SEVEN OF THESE CRISES.
EVERY TIME A CRISIS HAPPENS TO THE EARTH, EVERYTHING THE EARTH TOUCHES, IT SEEMS... IS AFFECTED.
SEVEN TIMES THIS HAS HAPPENED.
AND WE, UNKNOWINGLY, THIS ENTIRE TIME, HAVE BEEN PUNISHED ALONGSIDE EARTH.
THE HOUSES OF GEMWORLD ARE AT THEIR WITS' END.
LORD OPAL, OF THE ONCE-FLOURISHING GEMWORLD COURTS...
...PLEASE...
...HEAR ME...

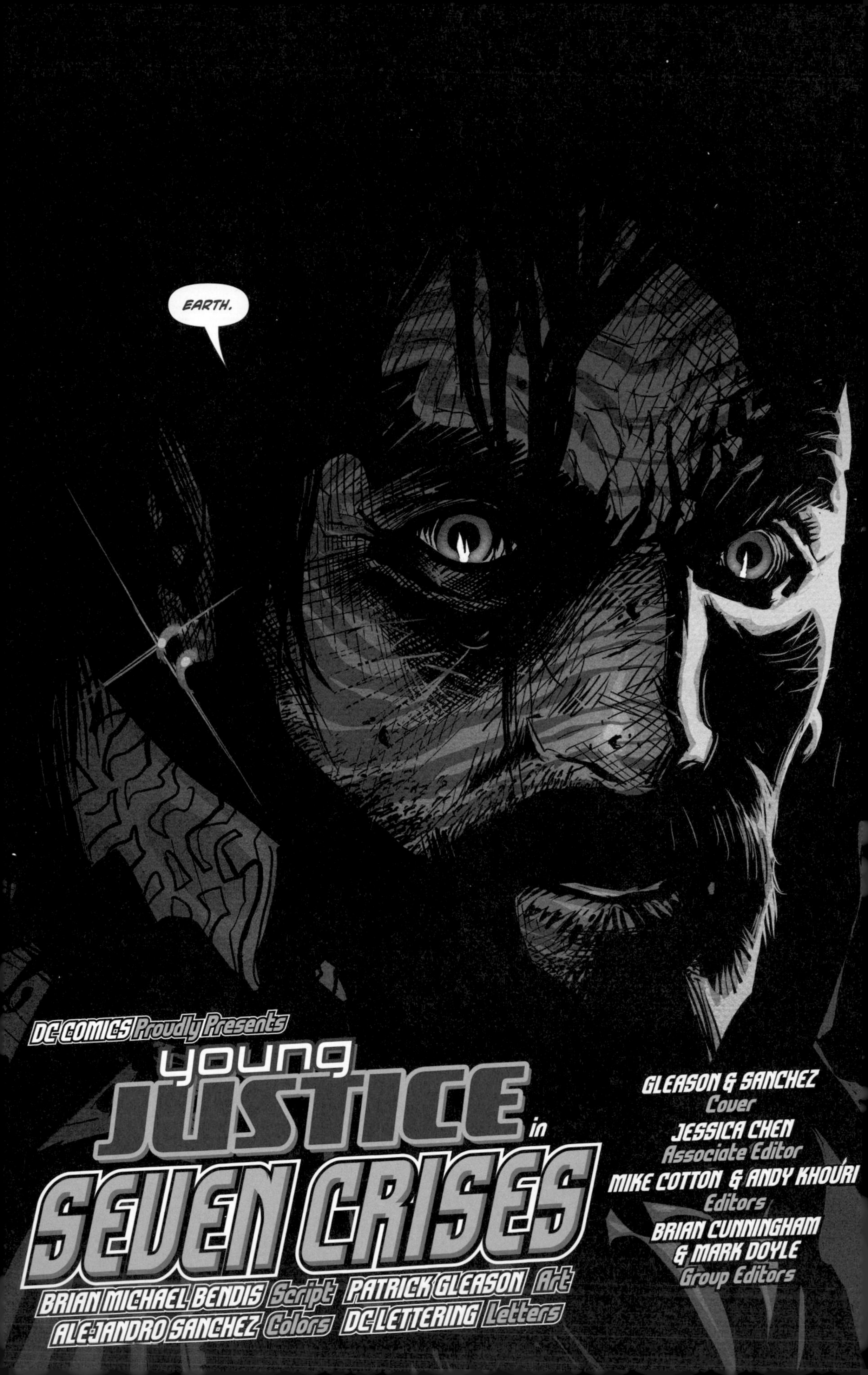
EARTH.
DC COMICS Proudly Presents
YOUNG JUSTICE in
SEVEN CRISES
BRIAN MICHAEL BENDIS Script PATRICK GLEASON Art
ALEJANDRO SANCHEZ Colors DC LETTERING Letters
GLEASON & SANCHEZ Cover
JESSICA CHEN Associate Editor
MIKE COTTON & ANDY KHOURI Editors
BRIAN CUNNINGHAM & MARK DOYLE Group Editors

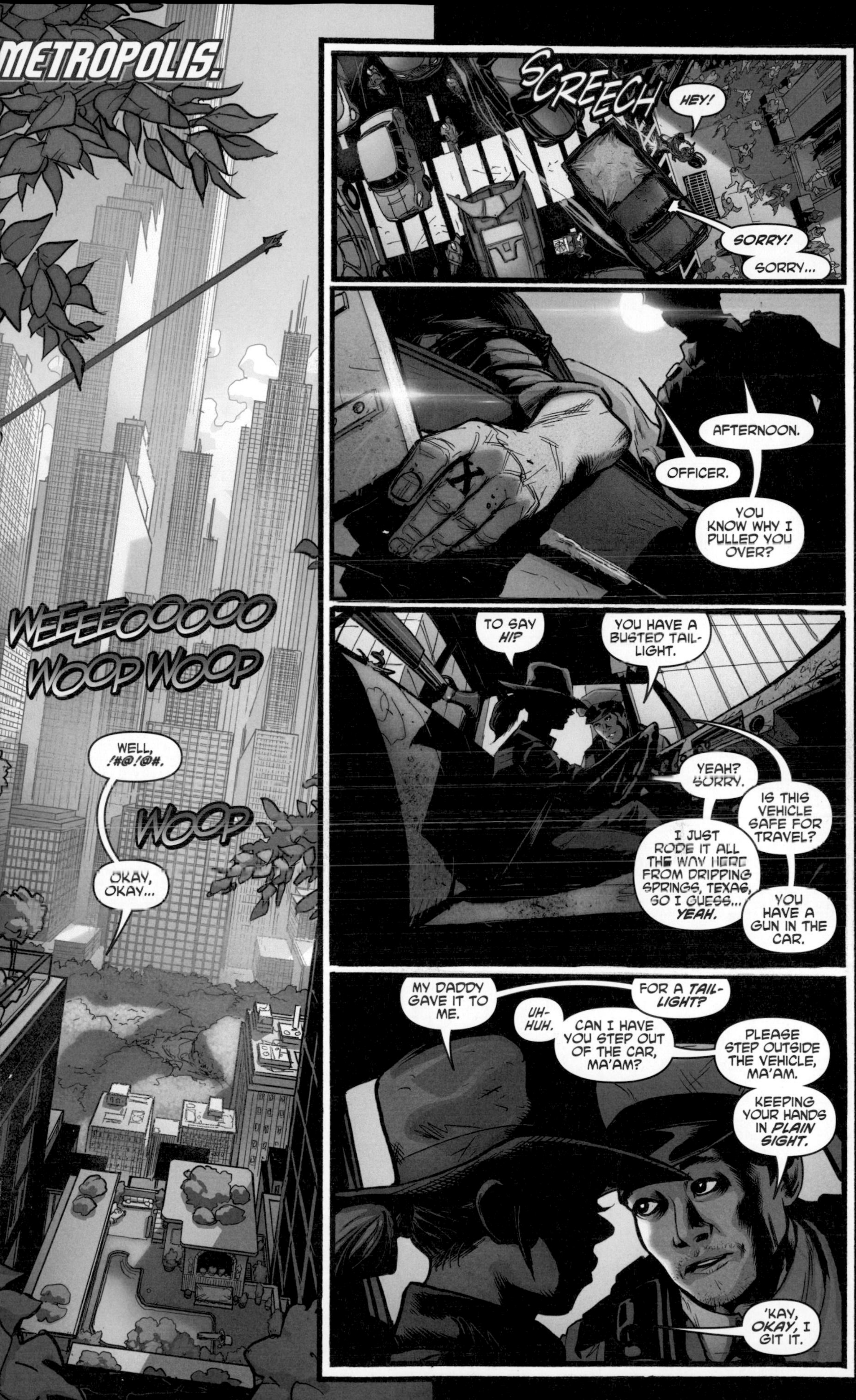
METROPOLIS.
WEEEEOOOOOO
WOOP WOOP
WELL, !#@!@#.
WOOP
OKAY, OKAY...
SCREECH
HEY!
SORRY!
SORRY...
AFTERNOON.
OFFICER.
YOU KNOW WHY I PULLED YOU OVER?
TO SAY HI?
YOU HAVE A BUSTED TAIL-LIGHT.
YEAH? SORRY.
I JUST RODE IT ALL THE WAY HERE FROM DRIPPING SPRINGS, TEXAS, SO I GUESS... YEAH.
IS THIS VEHICLE SAFE FOR TRAVEL?
YOU HAVE A GUN IN THE CAR.
MY DADDY GAVE IT TO ME.
FOR A TAIL-LIGHT?
UH-HUH.
CAN I HAVE YOU STEP OUT OF THE CAR, MA'AM?
PLEASE STEP OUTSIDE THE VEHICLE, MA'AM.
KEEPING YOUR HANDS IN PLAIN SIGHT.
'KAY, OKAY, I GIT IT.

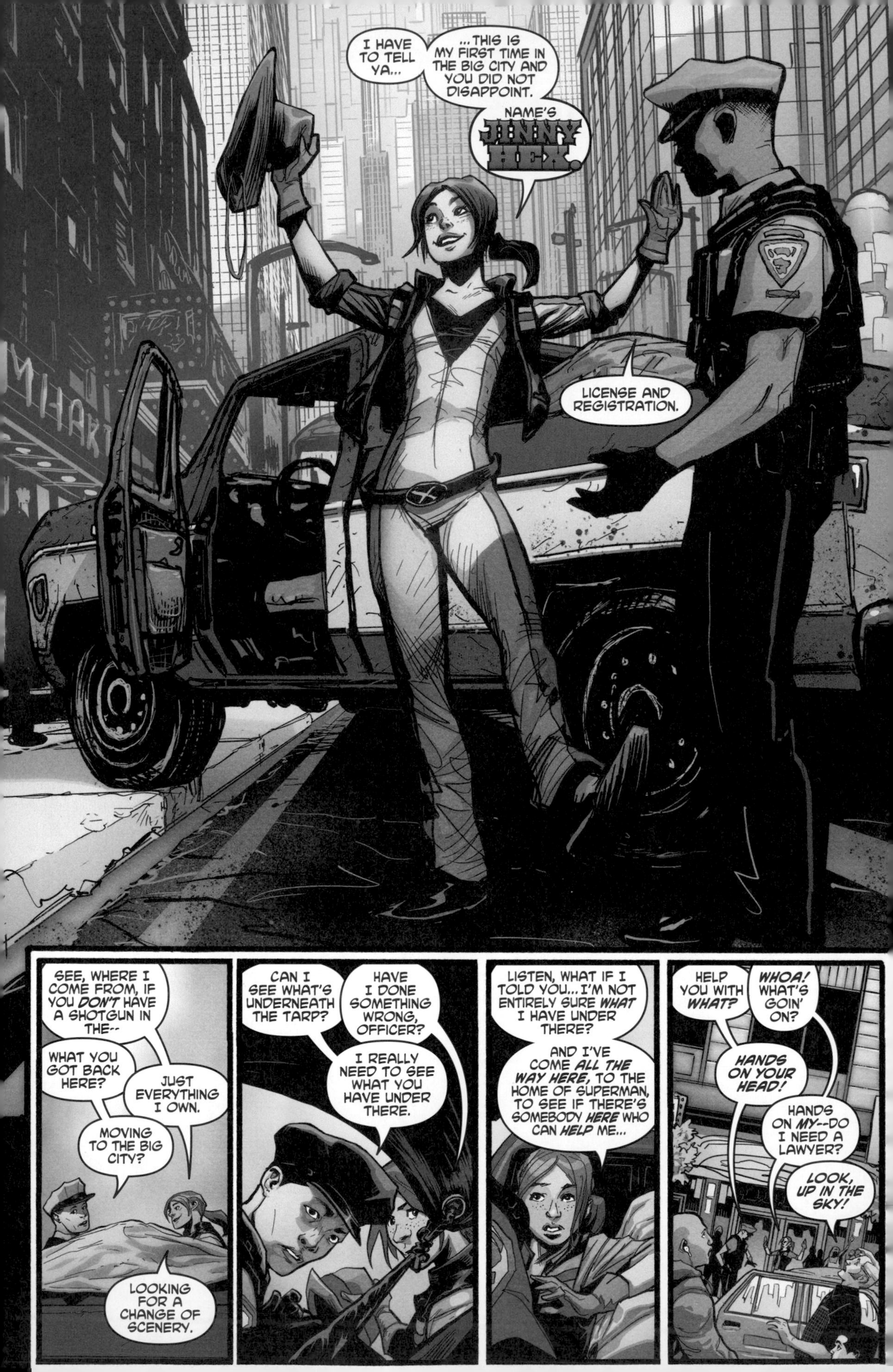
I HAVE TO TELL YA...
...THIS IS MY FIRST TIME IN THE BIG CITY AND YOU DID NOT DISAPPOINT.
NAME'S JINNY HEX.
LICENSE AND REGISTRATION.
SEE, WHERE I COME FROM, IF YOU *DON'T* HAVE A SHOTGUN IN THE--
WHAT YOU GOT BACK HERE?
JUST EVERYTHING I OWN.
MOVING TO THE BIG CITY?
LOOKING FOR A CHANGE OF SCENERY.
CAN I SEE WHAT'S UNDERNEATH THE TARP?
HAVE I DONE SOMETHING WRONG, OFFICER?
I REALLY NEED TO SEE WHAT YOU HAVE UNDER THERE.
LISTEN, WHAT IF I TOLD YOU... I'M NOT ENTIRELY SURE *WHAT* I HAVE UNDER THERE?
AND I'VE COME *ALL THE WAY HERE*, TO THE HOME OF SUPERMAN, TO SEE IF THERE'S SOMEBODY *HERE* WHO CAN *HELP* ME...
HELP YOU WITH *WHAT?*
WHOA! WHAT'S GOIN' ON?
HANDS ON YOUR HEAD!
HANDS ON *MY*--DO I NEED A LAWYER?
LOOK, UP IN THE SKY!

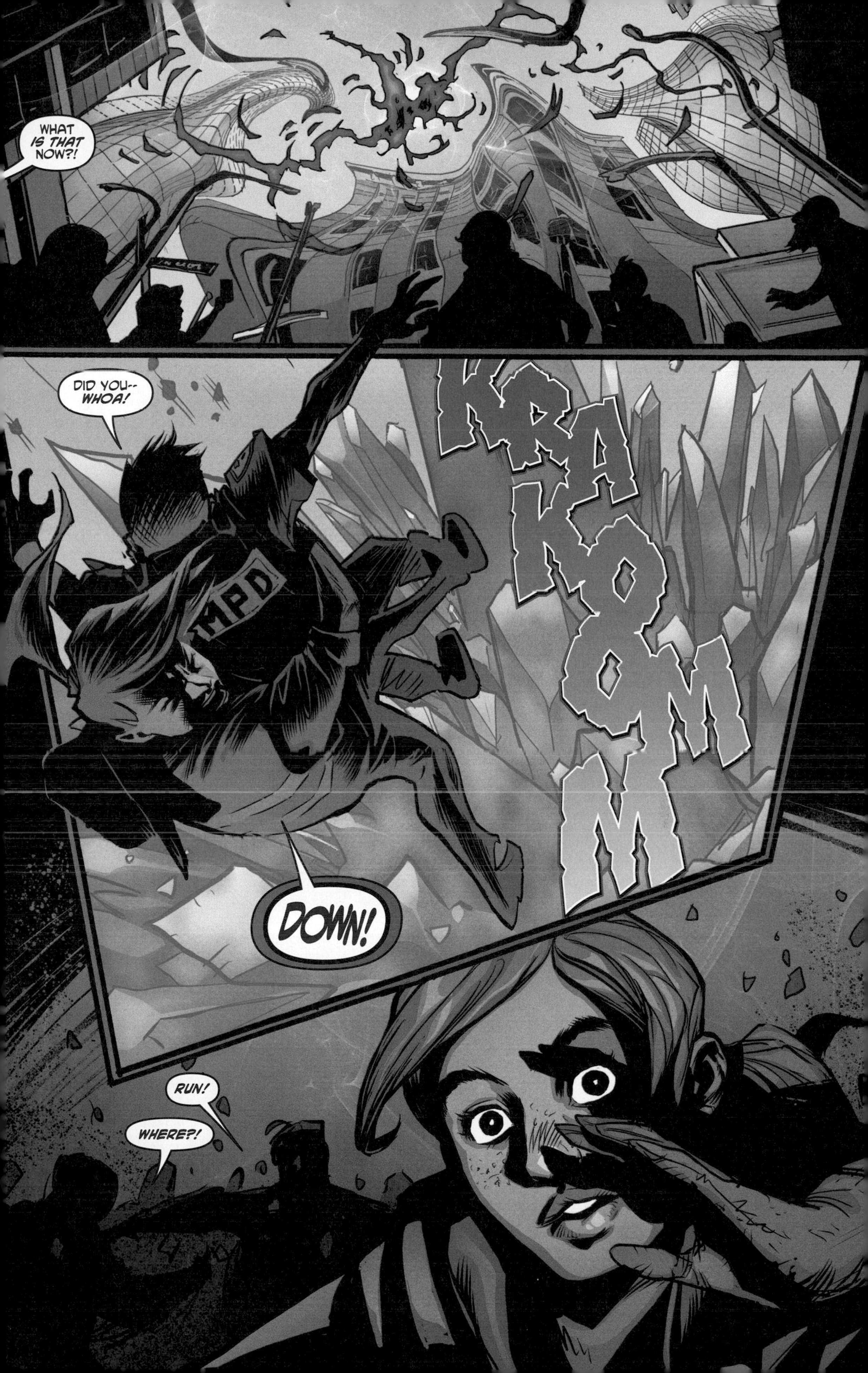
WHAT IS THAT NOW?!
DID YOU-- WHOA!
KRAKOOMM
DOWN!
RUN!
WHERE?!
MPD

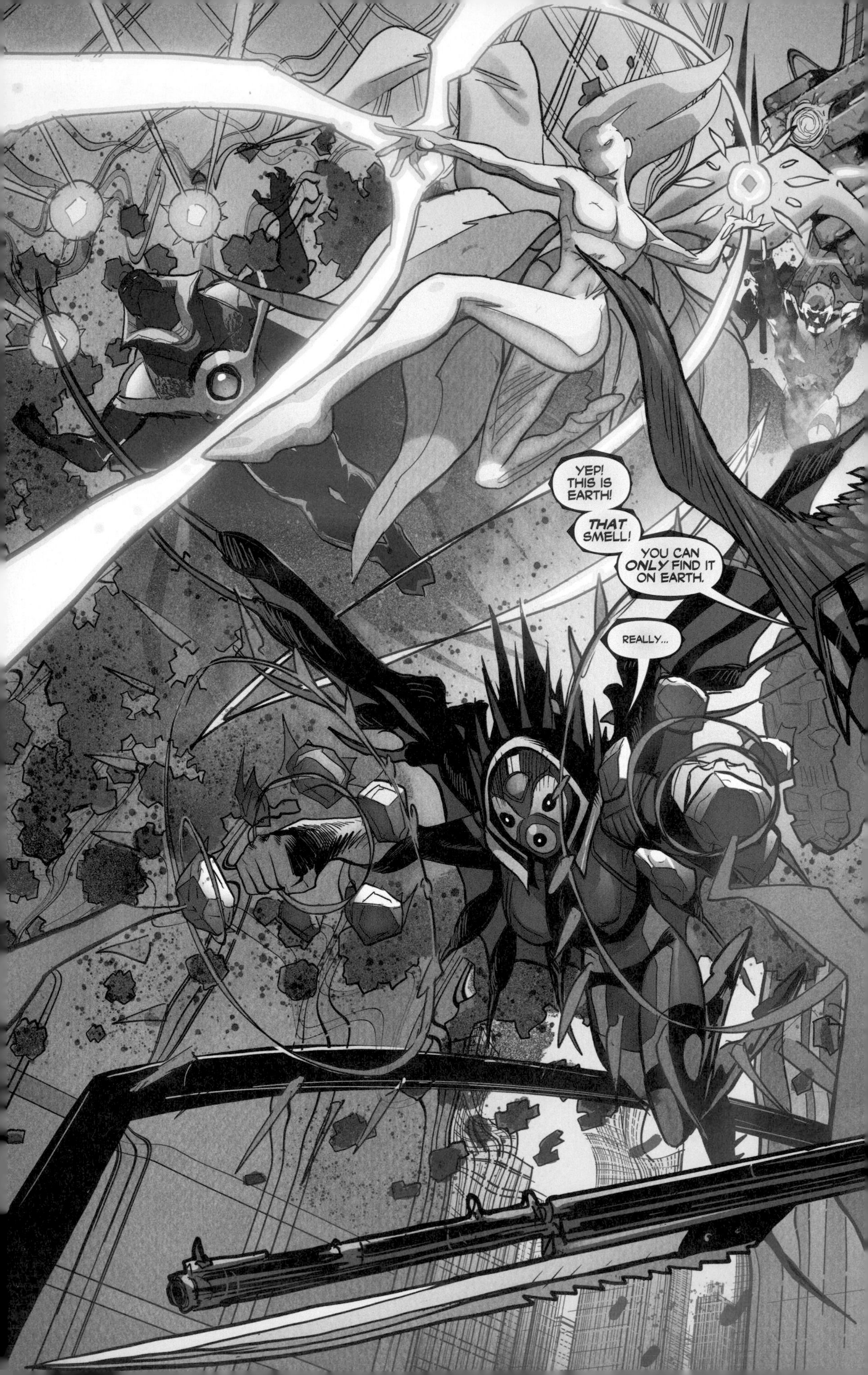
YEP! THIS IS EARTH!
THAT SMELL!
YOU CAN ONLY FIND IT ON EARTH.
REALLY...

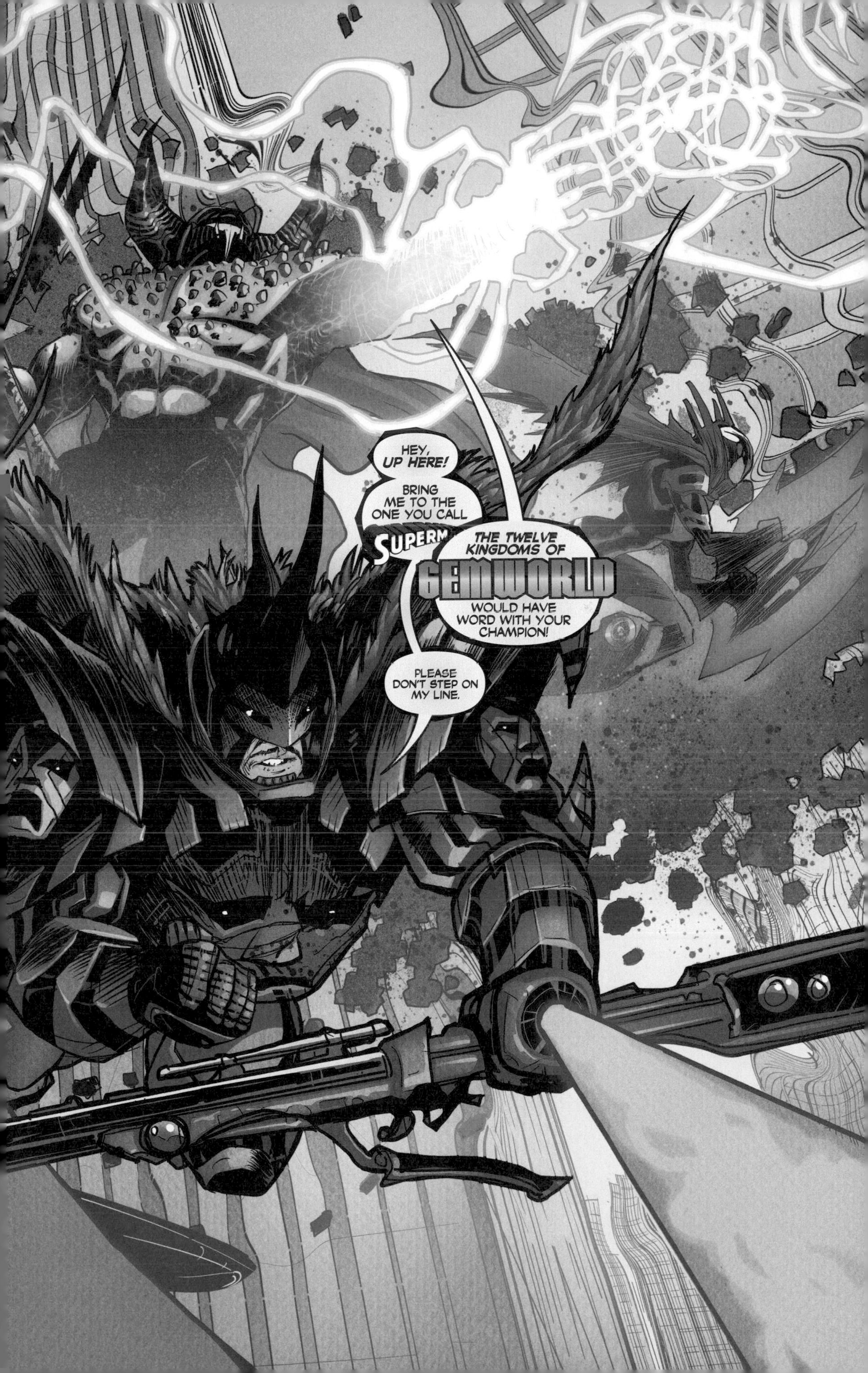
HEY, UP HERE!
BRING ME TO THE ONE YOU CALL SUPERM
THE TWELVE KINGDOMS OF GEMWORLD WOULD HAVE WORD WITH YOUR CHAMPION!
PLEASE DON'T STEP ON MY LINE.

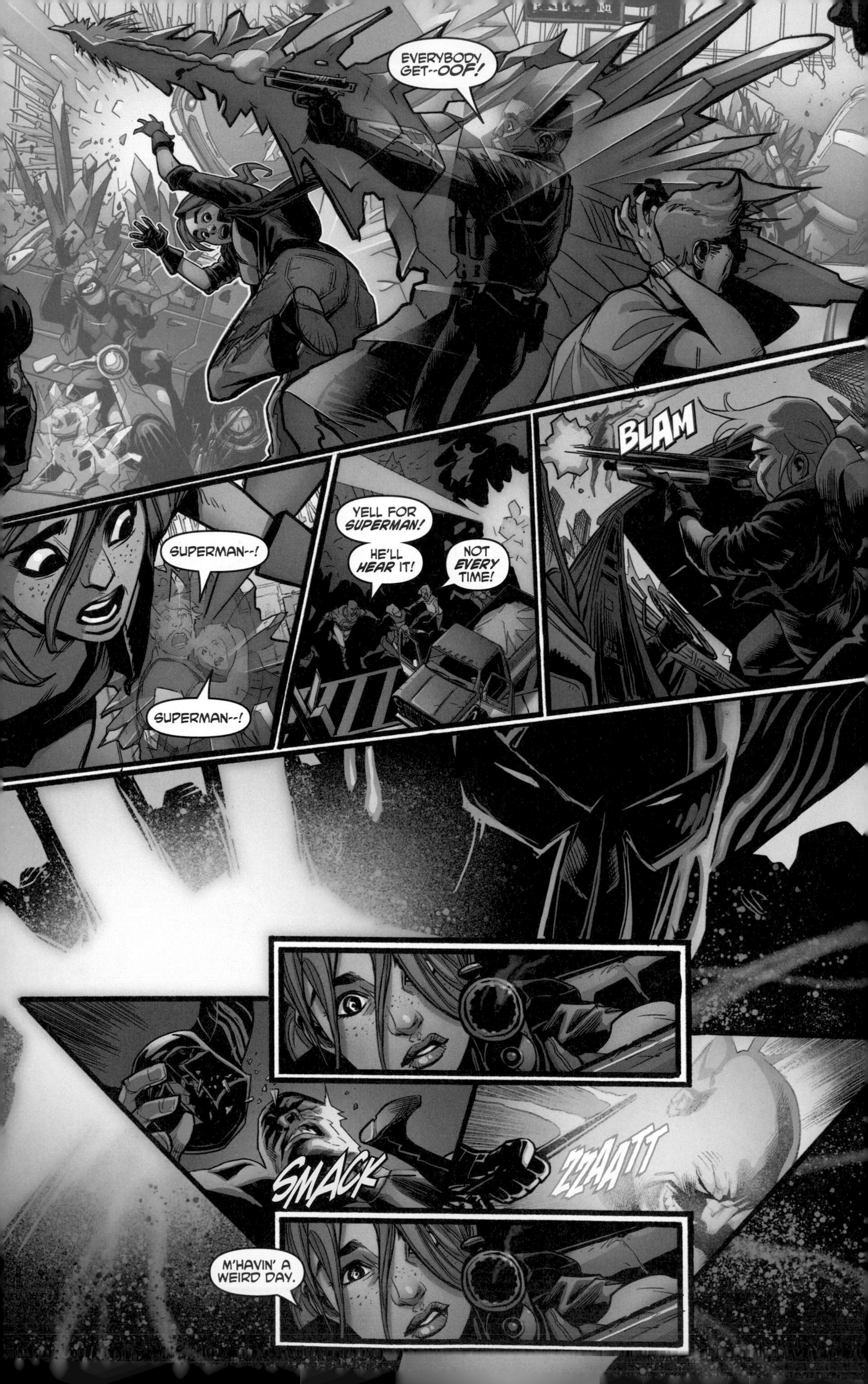
EVERYBODY GET--OOF!
BLAM
SUPERMAN--!
SUPERMAN--!
YELL FOR SUPERMAN!
HE'LL HEAR IT!
NOT EVERY TIME!
SMACK
ZZAATT
M'HAVIN' A WEIRD DAY.

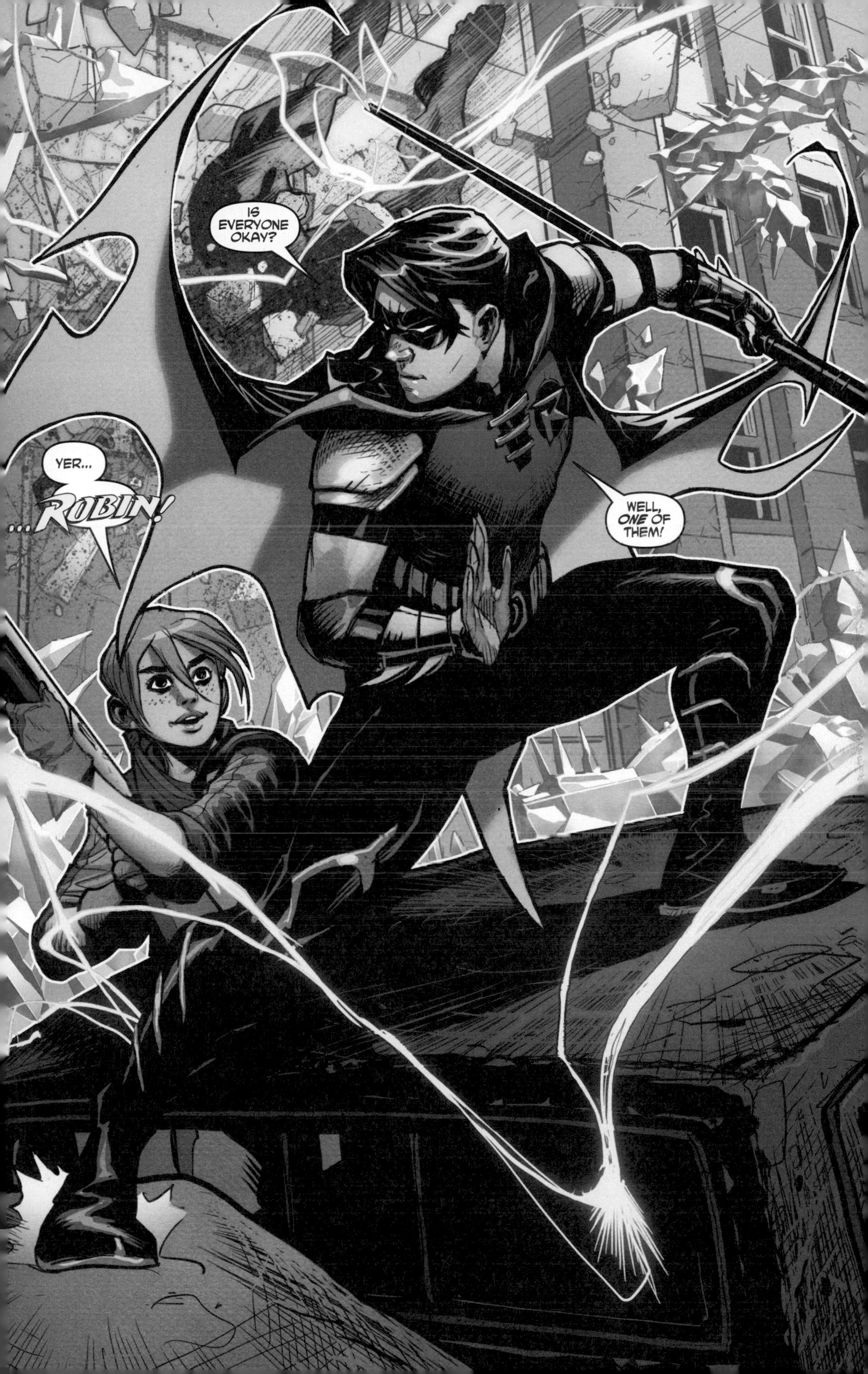
IS EVERYONE OKAY?
YER... ...ROBIN!
WELL, ONE OF THEM!

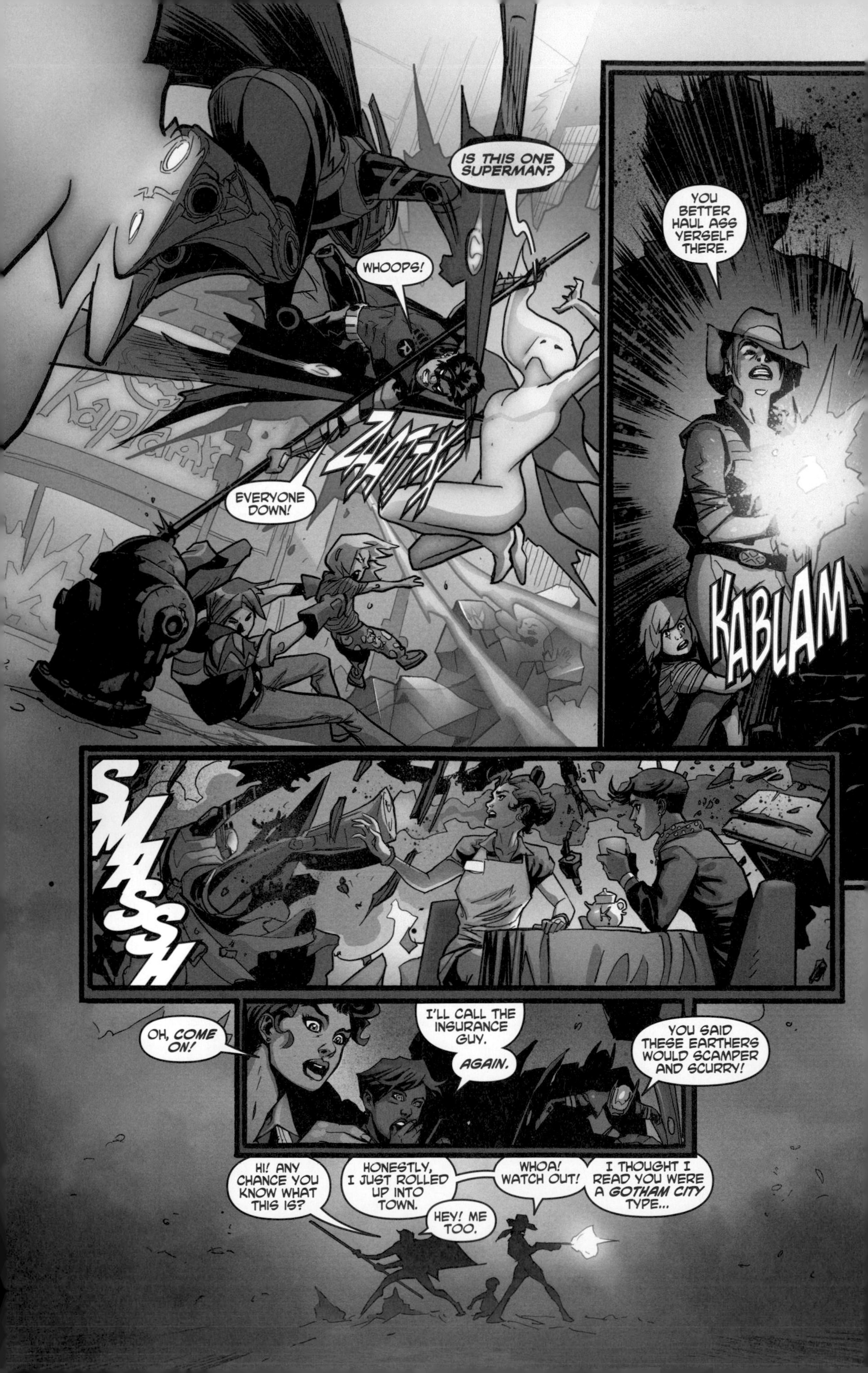
IS THIS ONE SUPERMAN?
WHOOPS!
ZZATTX
EVERYONE DOWN!
YOU BETTER HAUL ASS YERSELF THERE.
KABLAM
SMASSH
OH, COME ON!
I'LL CALL THE INSURANCE GUY.
AGAIN.
YOU SAID THESE EARTHERS WOULD SCAMPER AND SCURRY!
HI! ANY CHANCE YOU KNOW WHAT THIS IS?
HONESTLY, I JUST ROLLED UP INTO TOWN.
HEY! ME TOO.
WHOA! WATCH OUT!
I THOUGHT I READ YOU WERE A GOTHAM CITY TYPE...

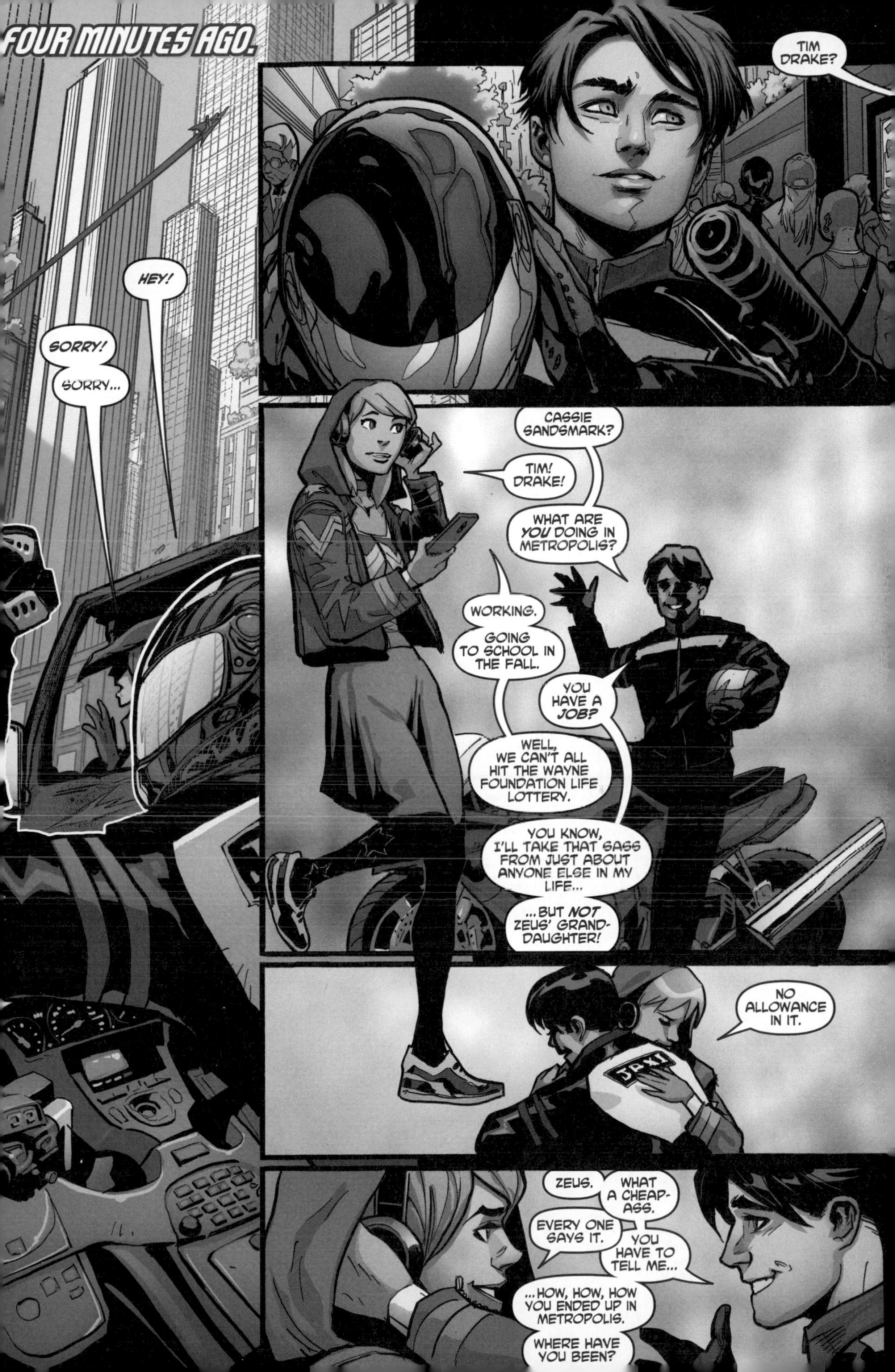
FOUR MINUTES AGO.
HEY!
SORRY!
SORRY...
TIM DRAKE?
CASSIE SANDSMARK?
TIM! DRAKE!
WHAT ARE YOU DOING IN METROPOLIS?
WORKING.
GOING TO SCHOOL IN THE FALL.
YOU HAVE A JOB?
WELL, WE CAN'T ALL HIT THE WAYNE FOUNDATION LIFE LOTTERY.
YOU KNOW, I'LL TAKE THAT SASS FROM JUST ABOUT ANYONE ELSE IN MY LIFE...
...BUT NOT ZEUS' GRAND-DAUGHTER!
NO ALLOWANCE IN IT.
ZEUS.
WHAT A CHEAP-ASS.
EVERY ONE SAYS IT.
YOU HAVE TO TELL ME...
...HOW, HOW, HOW YOU ENDED UP IN METROPOLIS.
WHERE HAVE YOU BEEN?

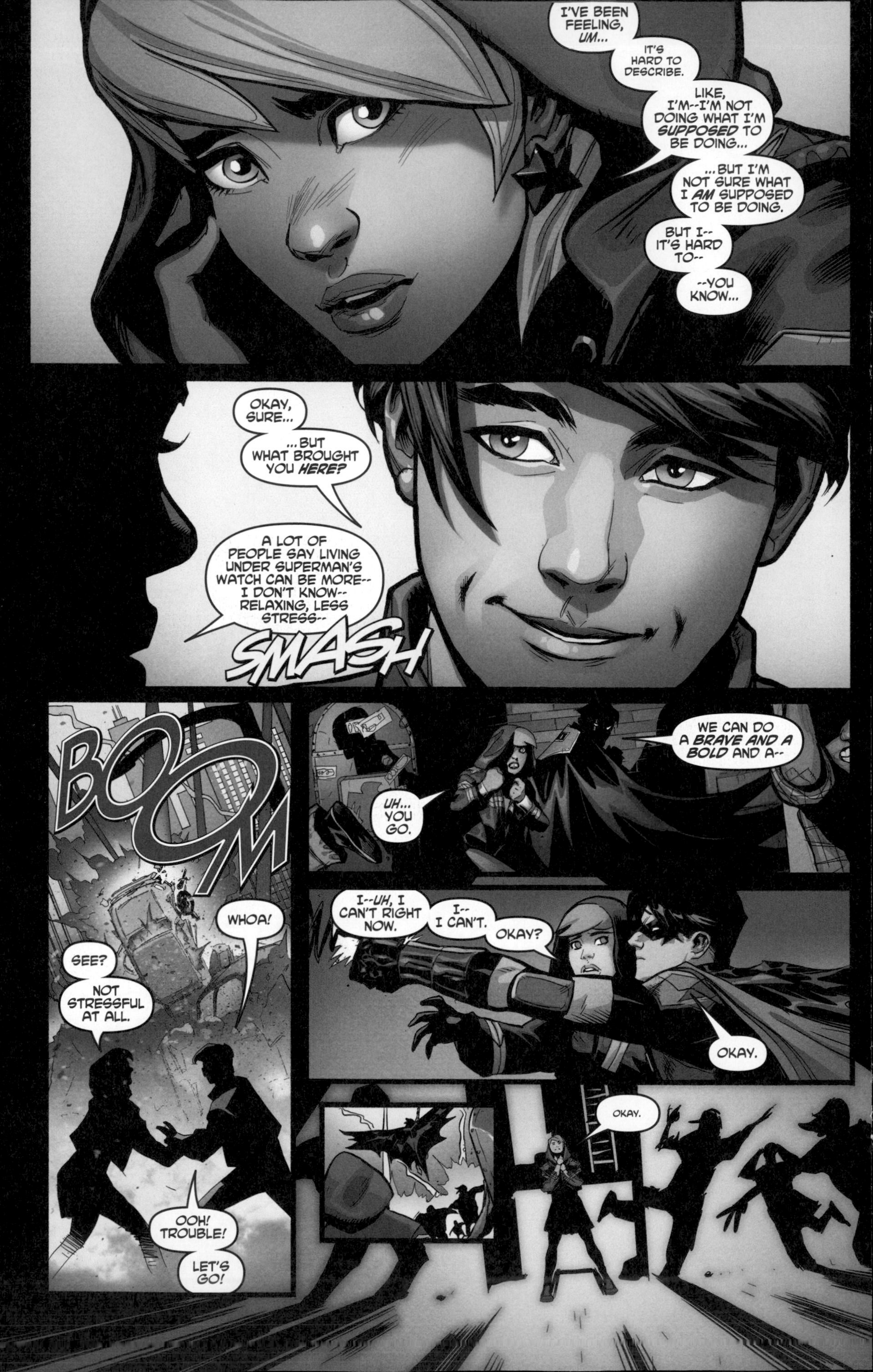
I'VE BEEN FEELING, UM...
IT'S HARD TO DESCRIBE.
LIKE, I'M--I'M NOT DOING WHAT I'M SUPPOSED TO BE DOING...
...BUT I'M NOT SURE WHAT I AM SUPPOSED TO BE DOING.
BUT I-- IT'S HARD TO--
--YOU KNOW...
OKAY, SURE...
...BUT WHAT BROUGHT YOU HERE?
A LOT OF PEOPLE SAY LIVING UNDER SUPERMAN'S WATCH CAN BE MORE-- I DON'T KNOW-- RELAXING, LESS STRESS--
SMASH
BOOM
WHOA!
SEE?
NOT STRESSFUL AT ALL.
OOH! TROUBLE!
LET'S GO!
WE CAN DO A BRAVE AND A BOLD AND A--
UH... YOU GO.
I--UH, I CAN'T RIGHT NOW.
I-- I CAN'T.
OKAY?
OKAY.
OKAY.

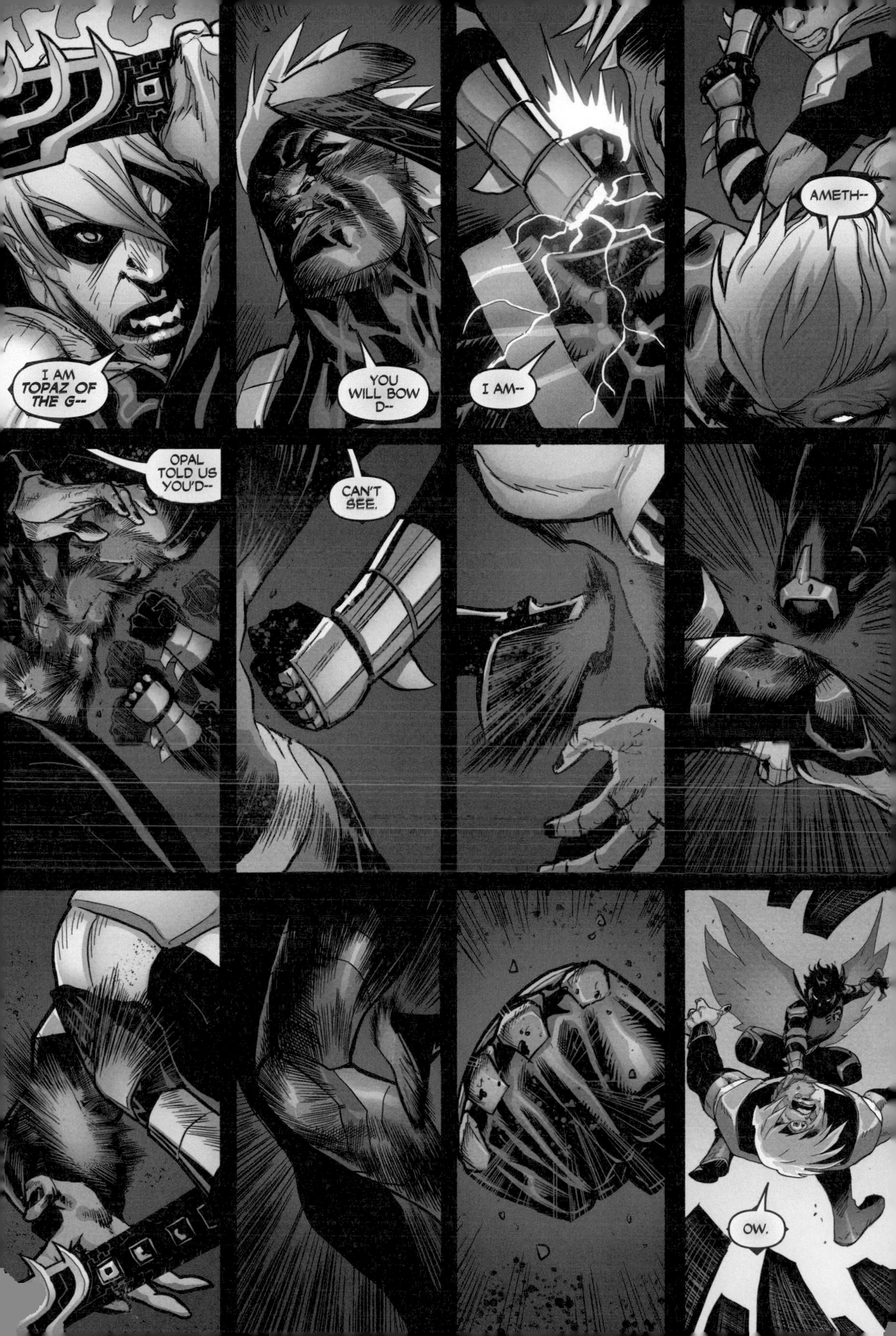
I AM *TOPAZ* OF THE G--
YOU WILL BOW D--
I AM--
AMETH--
OPAL TOLD US YOU'D--
CAN'T SEE.
OW.

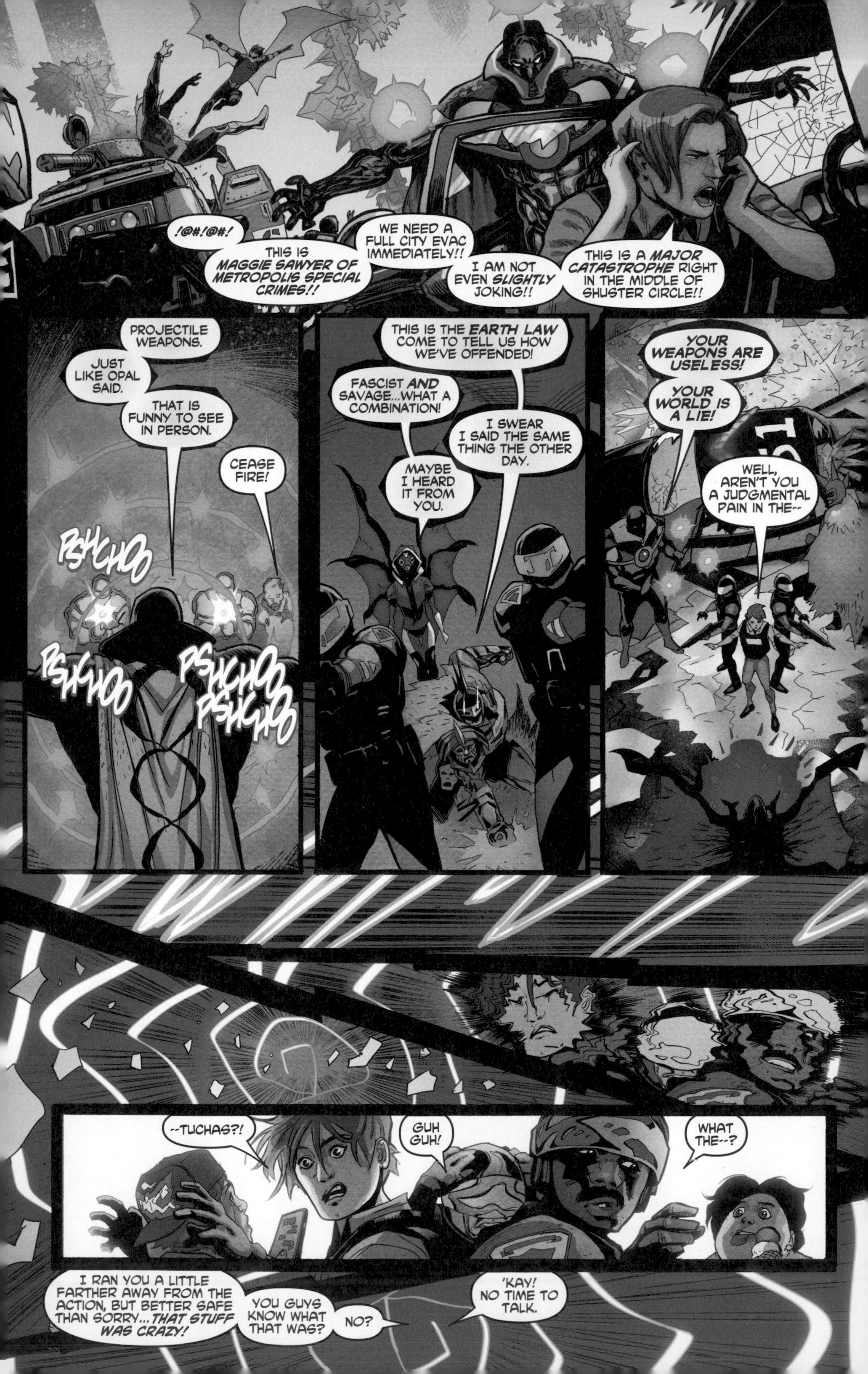
!@#!@#!
THIS IS MAGGIE SAWYER OF METROPOLIS SPECIAL CRIMES!!
WE NEED A FULL CITY EVAC IMMEDIATELY!!
I AM NOT EVEN SLIGHTLY JOKING!!
THIS IS A MAJOR CATASTROPHE RIGHT IN THE MIDDLE OF SHUSTER CIRCLE!!
PROJECTILE WEAPONS.
JUST LIKE OPAL SAID.
THAT IS FUNNY TO SEE IN PERSON.
CEASE FIRE!
PSHCHOO
PSHCHOO
PSHCHOO PSHCHOO
THIS IS THE EARTH LAW COME TO TELL US HOW WE'VE OFFENDED!
FASCIST AND SAVAGE...WHAT A COMBINATION!
I SWEAR I SAID THE SAME THING THE OTHER DAY.
MAYBE I HEARD IT FROM YOU.
YOUR WEAPONS ARE USELESS!
YOUR WORLD IS A LIE!
WELL, AREN'T YOU A JUDGMENTAL PAIN IN THE--
--TUCHAS?!
GUH GUH!
WHAT THE--?
I RAN YOU A LITTLE FARTHER AWAY FROM THE ACTION, BUT BETTER SAFE THAN SORRY...THAT STUFF WAS CRAZY!
YOU GUYS KNOW WHAT THAT WAS?
NO?
'KAY! NO TIME TO TALK.

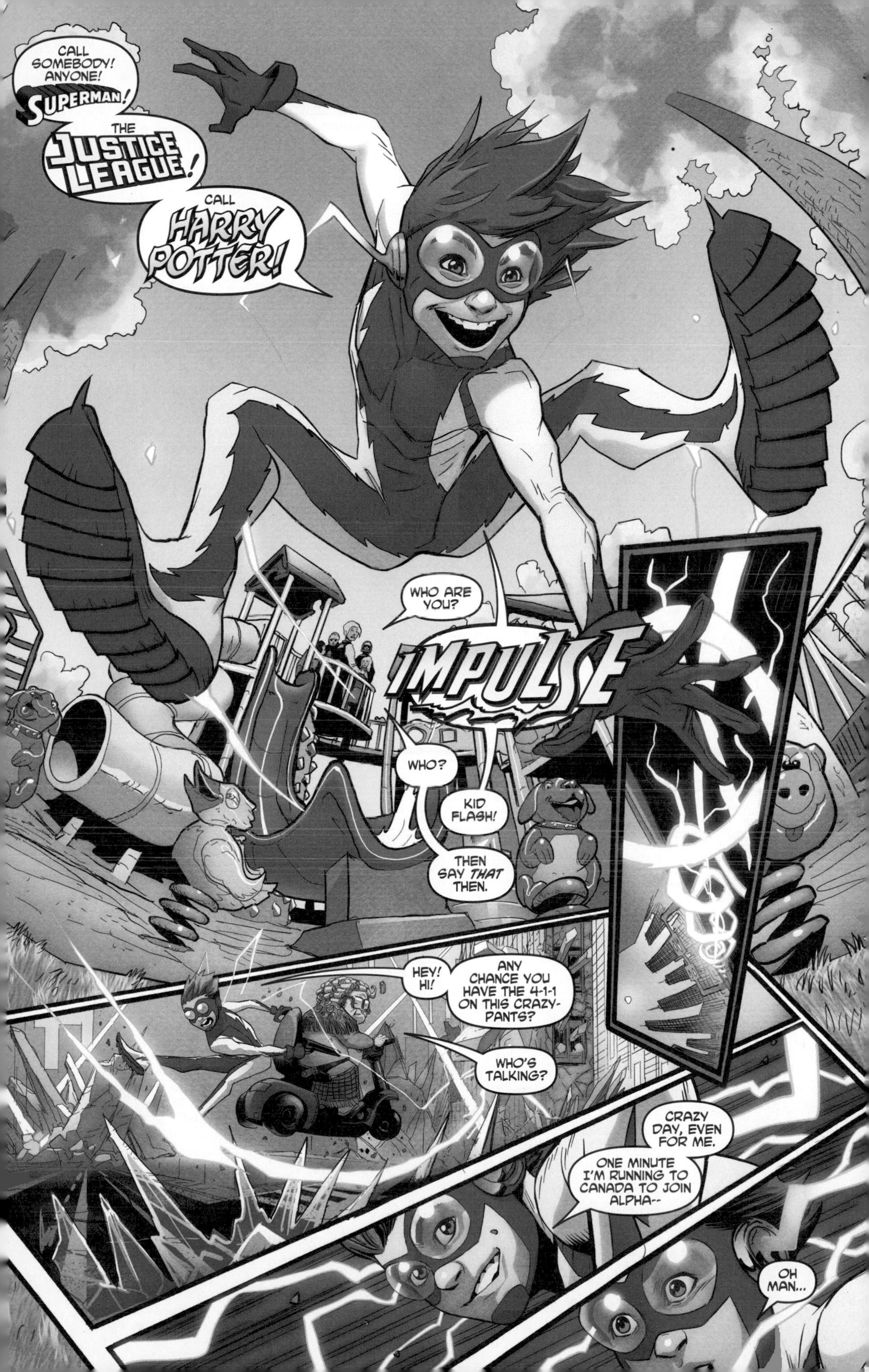
CALL SOMEBODY! ANYONE! SUPERMAN!
THE JUSTICE LEAGUE!
CALL HARRY POTTER!
WHO ARE YOU?
IMPULSE
WHO?
KID FLASH!
THEN SAY THAT THEN.
HEY! HI!
ANY CHANCE YOU HAVE THE 4-1-1 ON THIS CRAZY-PANTS?
WHO'S TALKING?
CRAZY DAY, EVEN FOR ME.
ONE MINUTE I'M RUNNING TO CANADA TO JOIN ALPHA--
OH MAN...

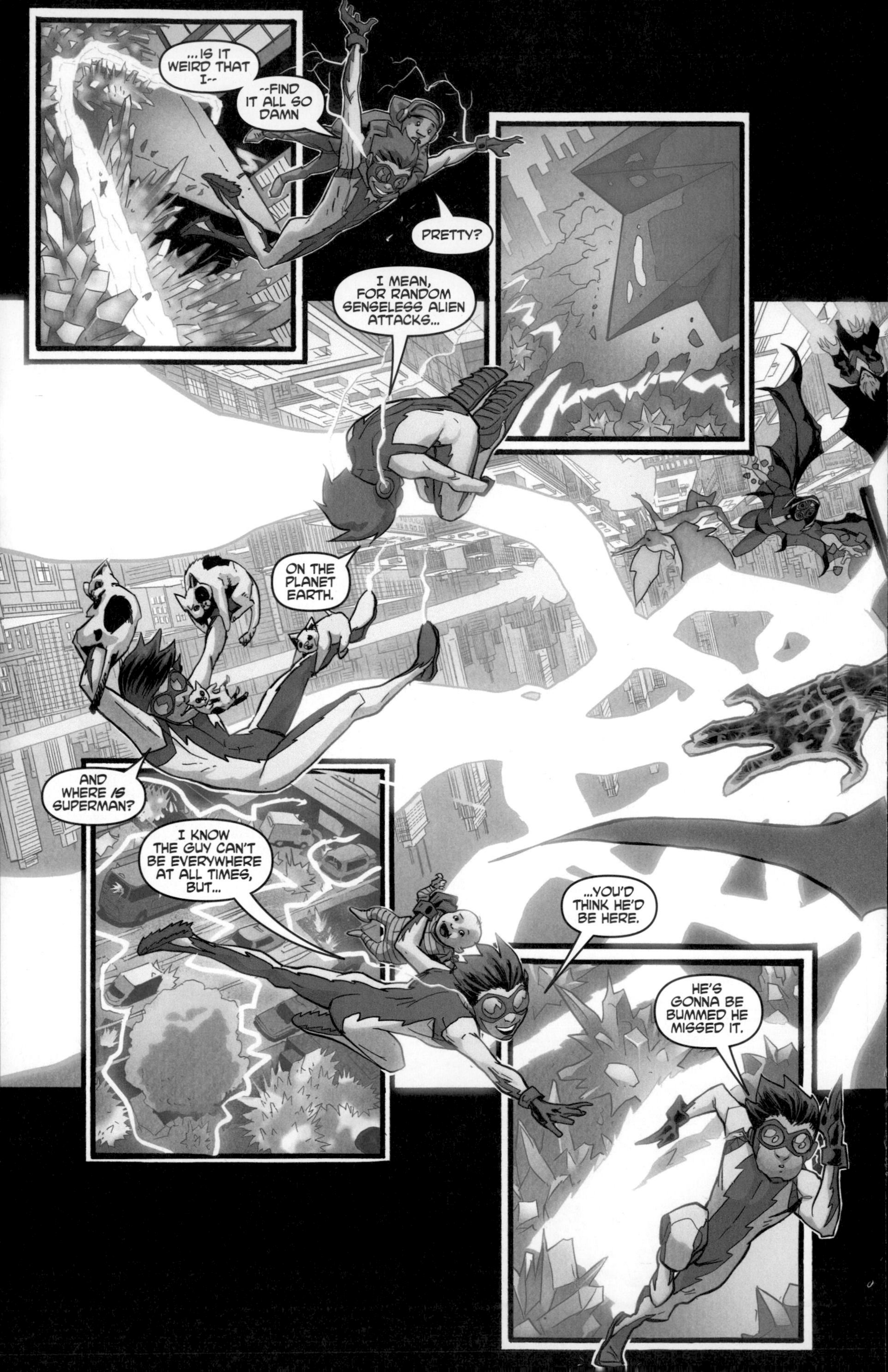
...IS IT WEIRD THAT I--
--FIND IT ALL SO DAMN
PRETTY?
I MEAN, FOR RANDOM SENSELESS ALIEN ATTACKS...
ON THE PLANET EARTH.
AND WHERE *IS* SUPERMAN?
I KNOW THE GUY CAN'T BE EVERYWHERE AT ALL TIMES, BUT...
...YOU'D THINK HE'D BE HERE.
HE'S GONNA BE BUMMED HE MISSED IT.

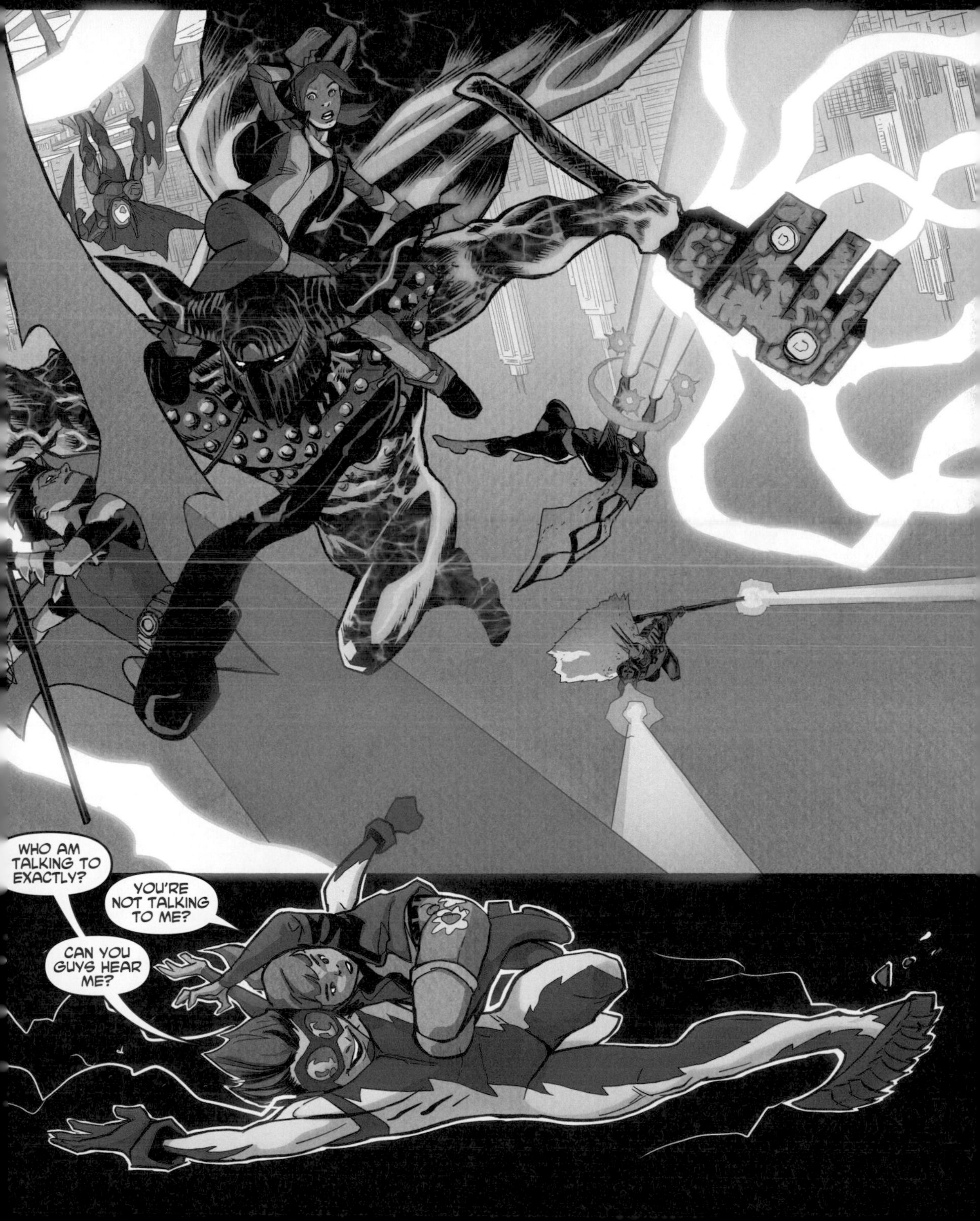
WHO AM TALKING TO EXACTLY?
YOU'RE NOT TALKING TO ME?
CAN YOU GUYS HEAR ME?

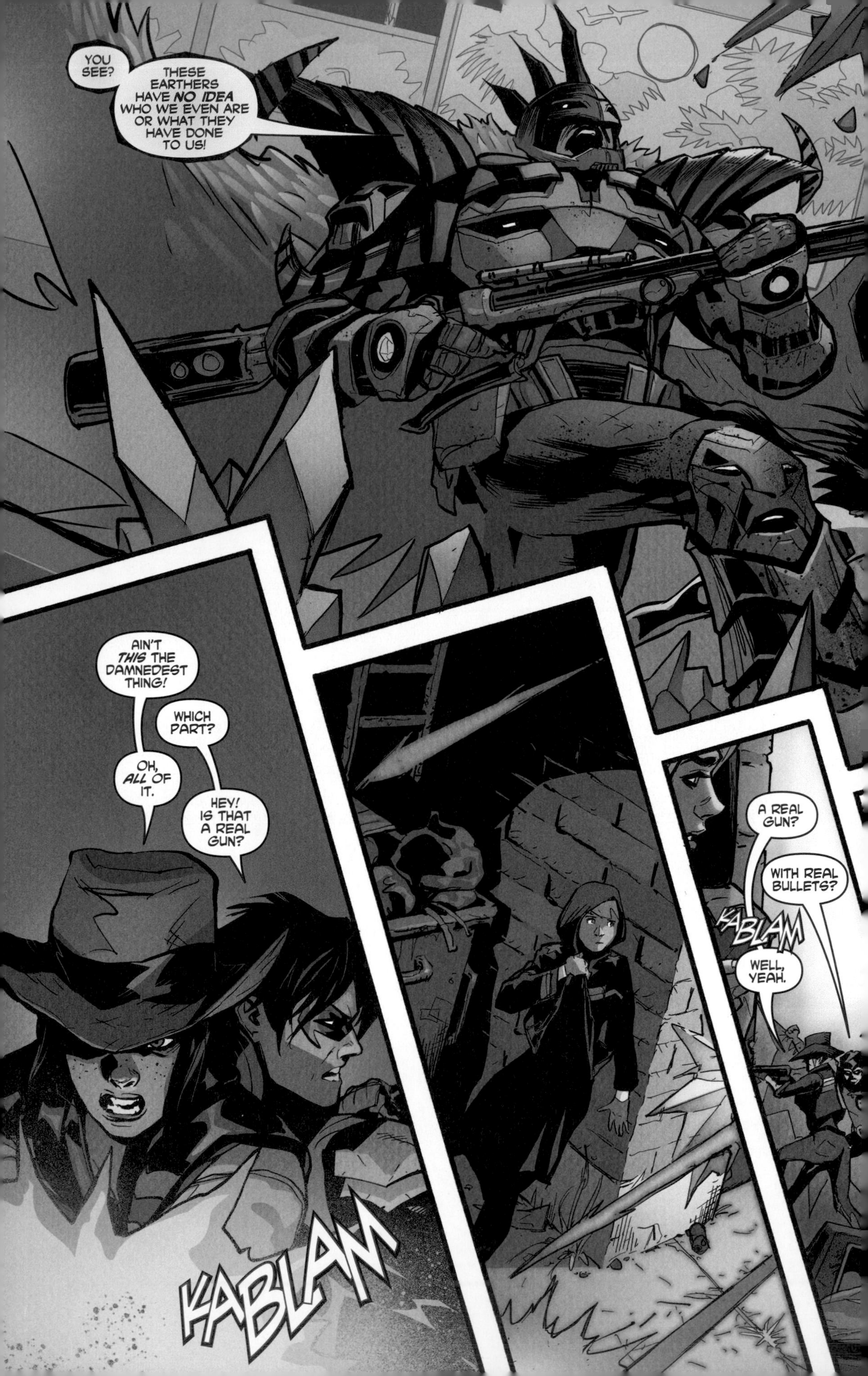
YOU SEE?
THESE EARTHERS HAVE NO IDEA WHO WE EVEN ARE OR WHAT THEY HAVE DONE TO US!
AIN'T THIS THE DAMNEDEST THING!
WHICH PART?
OH, ALL OF IT.
HEY! IS THAT A REAL GUN?
KABLAM
A REAL GUN?
WITH REAL BULLETS?
KABLAM
WELL, YEAH.

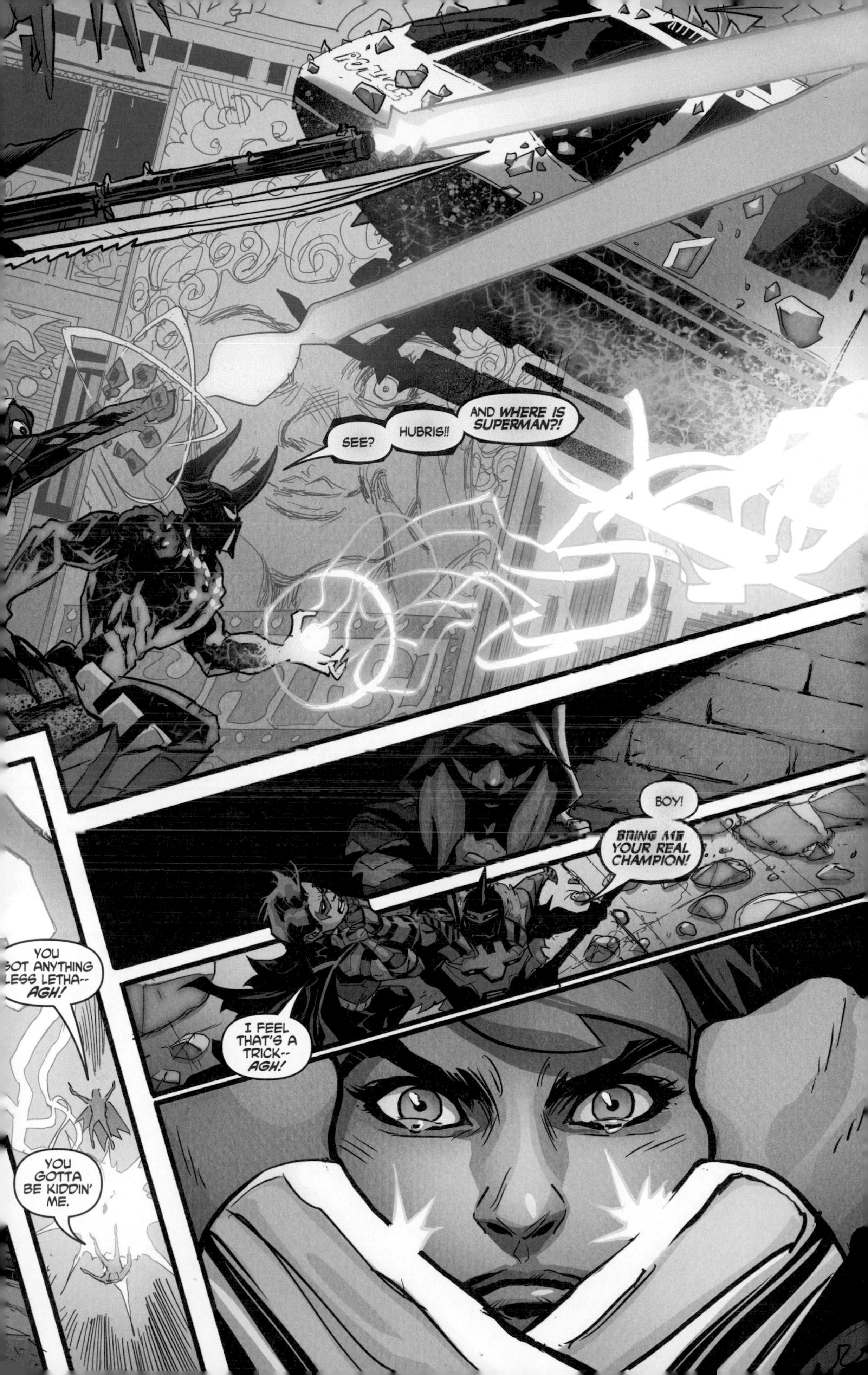
SEE?
HUBRIS!!
AND WHERE IS SUPERMAN?!
BOY!
BRING ME YOUR REAL CHAMPION!
YOU GOT ANYTHING LESS LETHA-- AGH!
I FEEL THAT'S A TRICK-- AGH!
YOU GOTTA BE KIDDIN' ME.

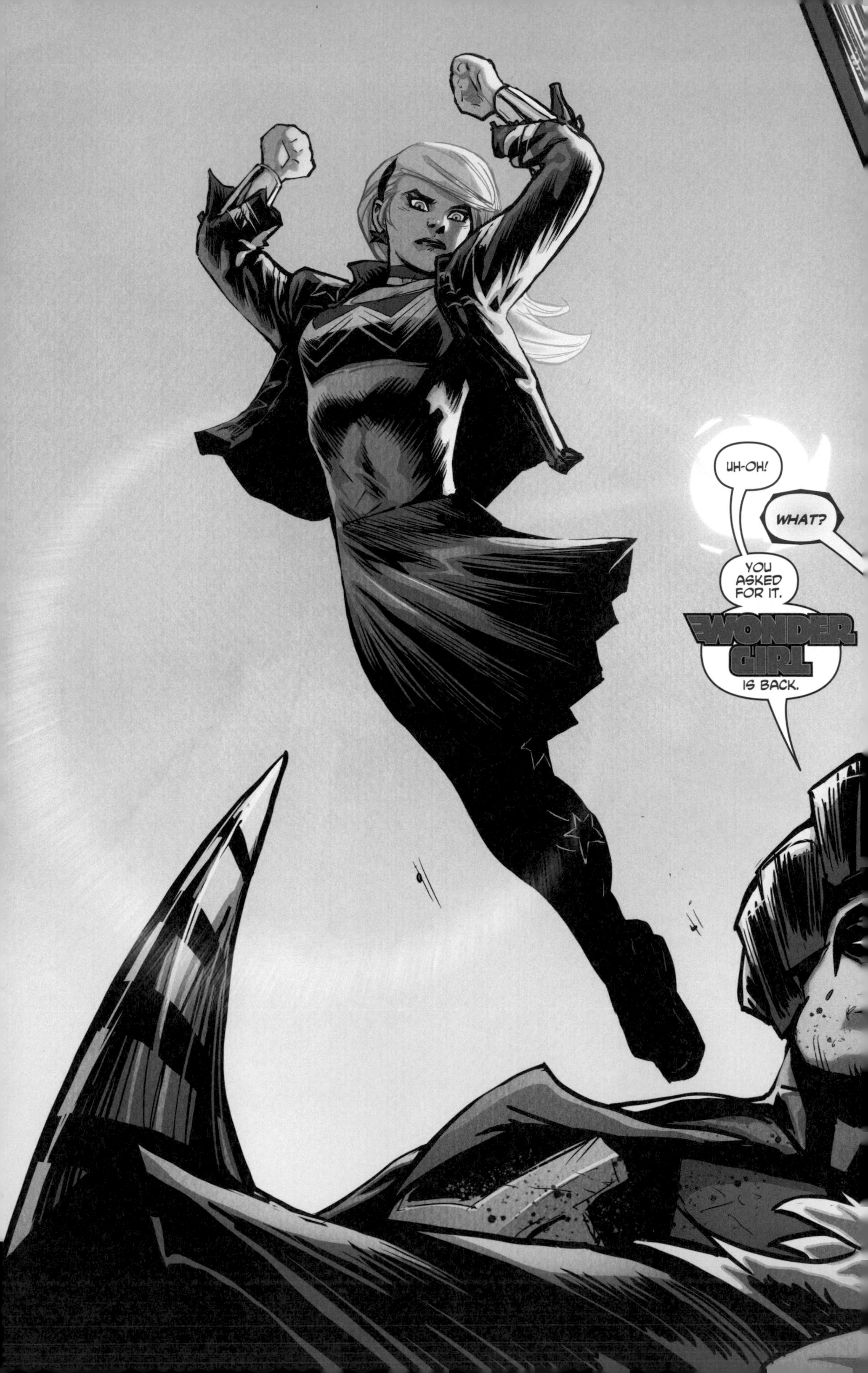
UH-OH!
WHAT?
YOU ASKED FOR IT.
WONDER GIRL IS BACK.

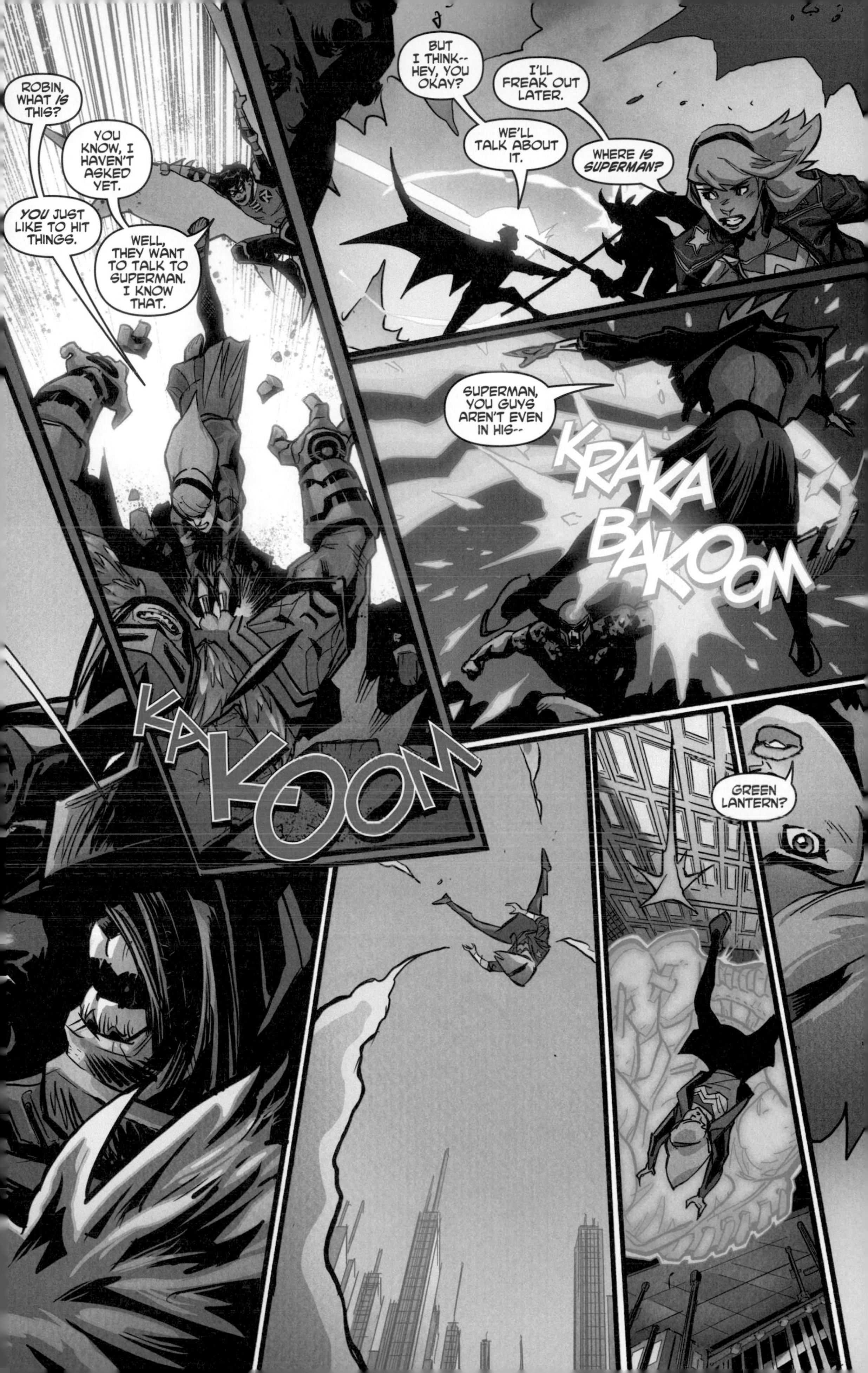
ROBIN, WHAT *IS* THIS?
YOU KNOW, I HAVEN'T ASKED YET.
YOU JUST LIKE TO HIT THINGS.
WELL, THEY WANT TO TALK TO SUPERMAN. I KNOW THAT.
BUT I THINK-- HEY, YOU OKAY?
I'LL FREAK OUT LATER.
WE'LL TALK ABOUT IT.
WHERE *IS* *SUPERMAN*?
SUPERMAN, YOU GUYS AREN'T EVEN IN HIS--
KRAKA BAKOOM
KAKOOM
GREEN LANTERN?

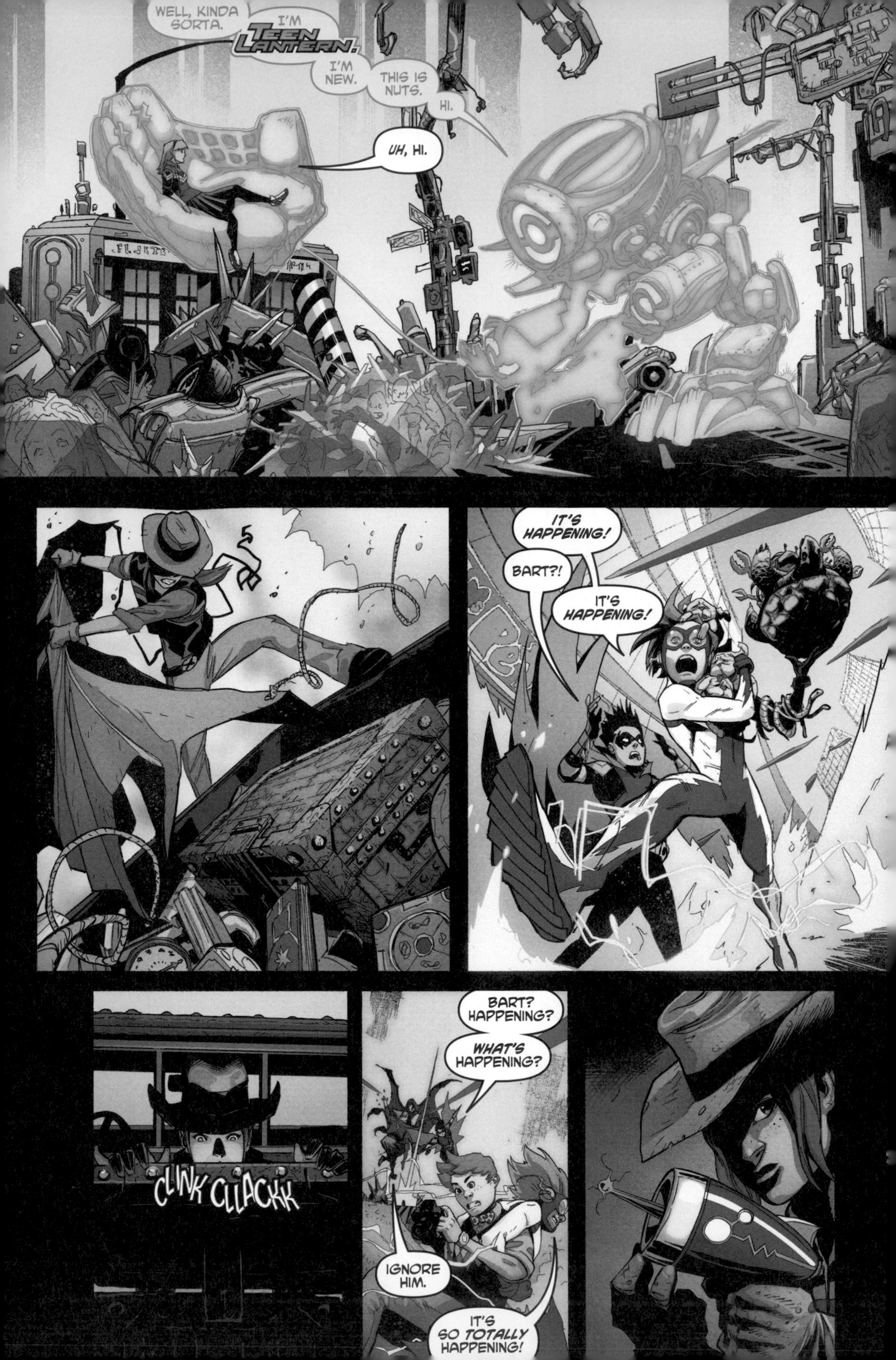

WELL, KINDA SORTA.
I'M TEEN LANTERN.
I'M NEW.
THIS IS NUTS.
HI.
UH, HI.
IT'S HAPPENING!
BART?!
IT'S HAPPENING!
CLINK CLLACKK
BART? HAPPENING?
WHAT'S HAPPENING?
IGNORE HIM.
IT'S SO TOTALLY HAPPENING!

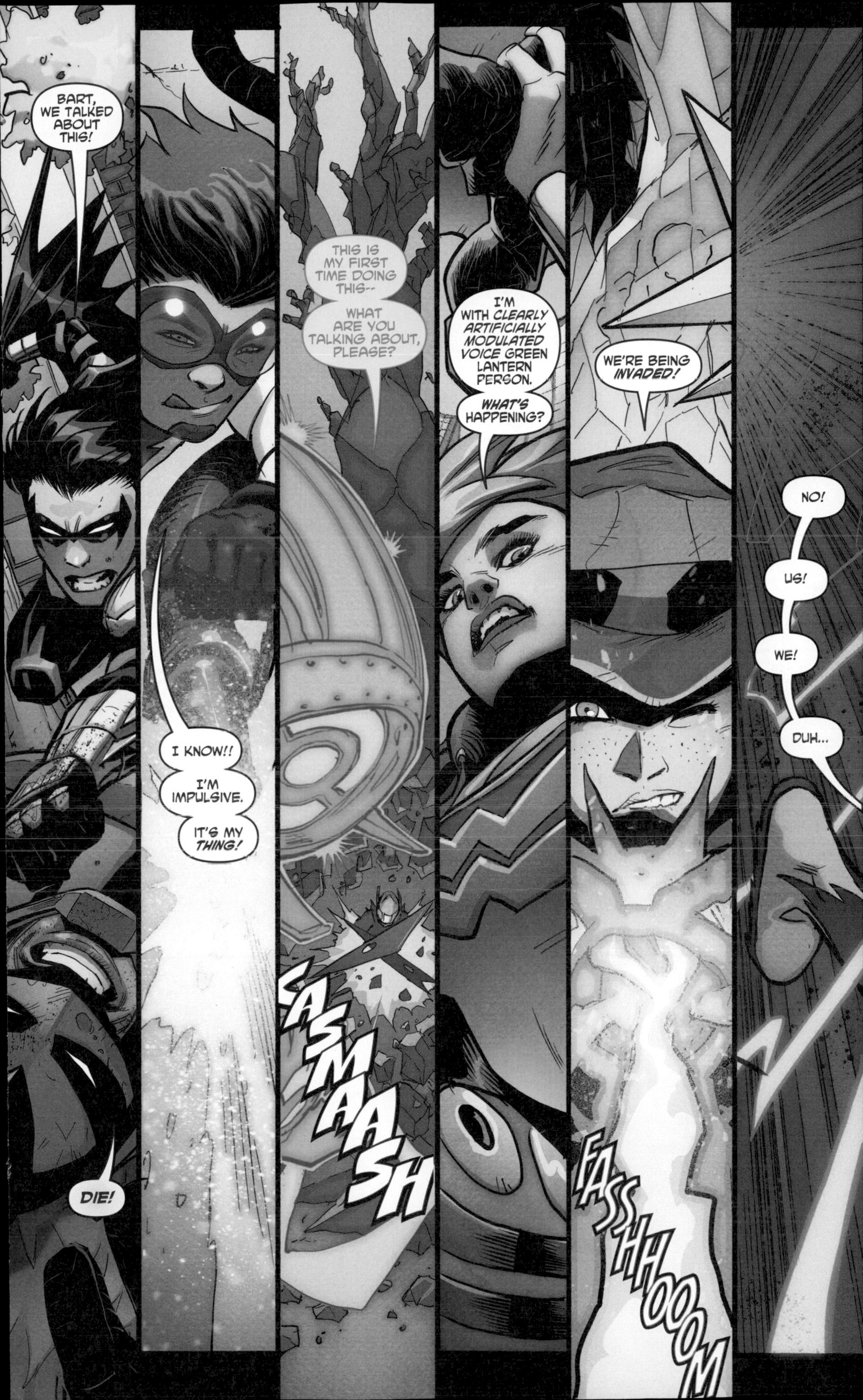
BART, WE TALKED ABOUT THIS!
I KNOW!!
I'M IMPULSIVE.
IT'S MY THING!
DIE!
THIS IS MY FIRST TIME DOING THIS--
WHAT ARE YOU TALKING ABOUT, PLEASE?
CASMAASH
I'M WITH CLEARLY ARTIFICIALLY MODULATED VOICE GREEN LANTERN PERSON.
WHAT'S HAPPENING?
WE'RE BEING INVADED!
FASSHHOOOM
NO!
US!
WE!
DUH...

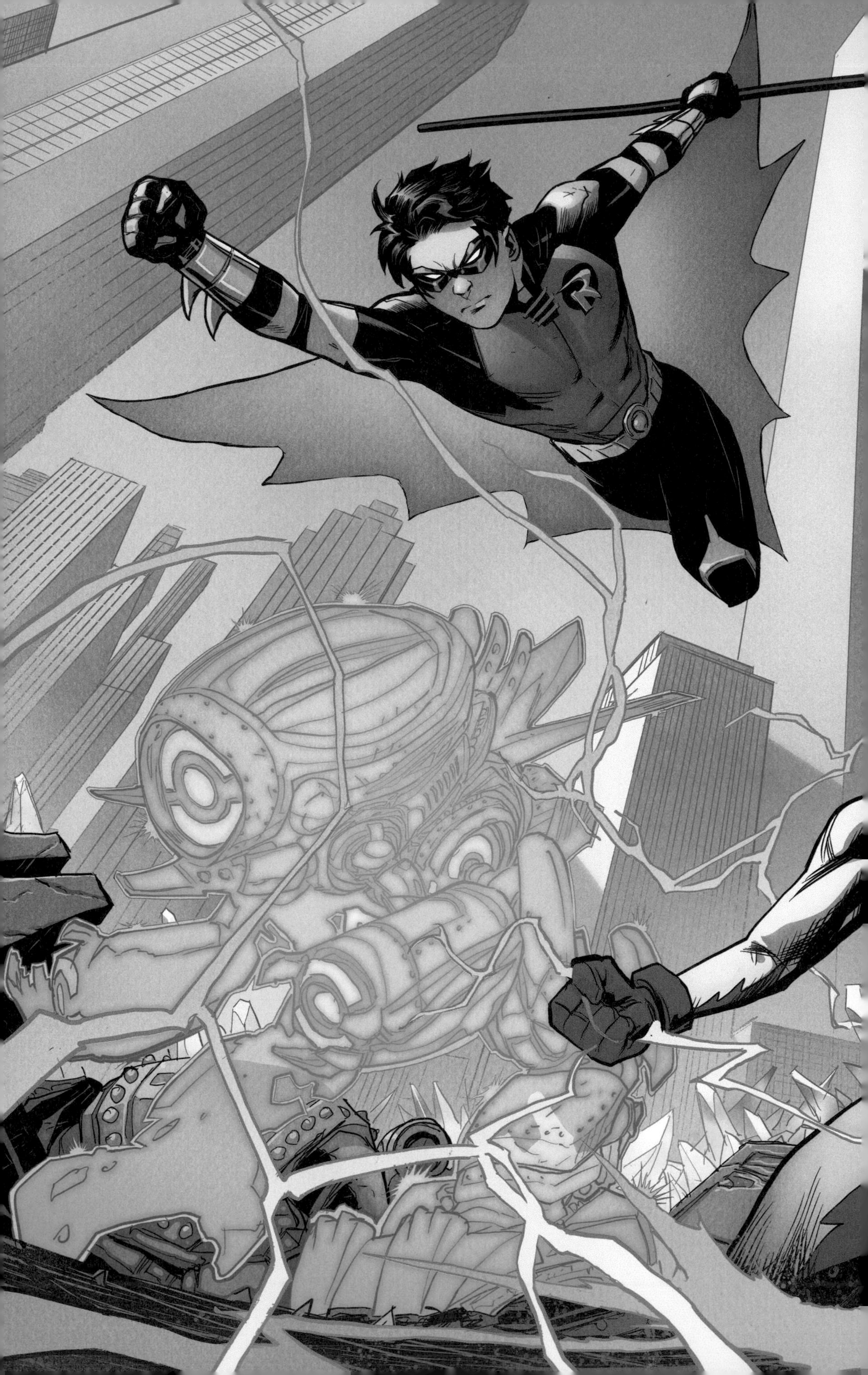

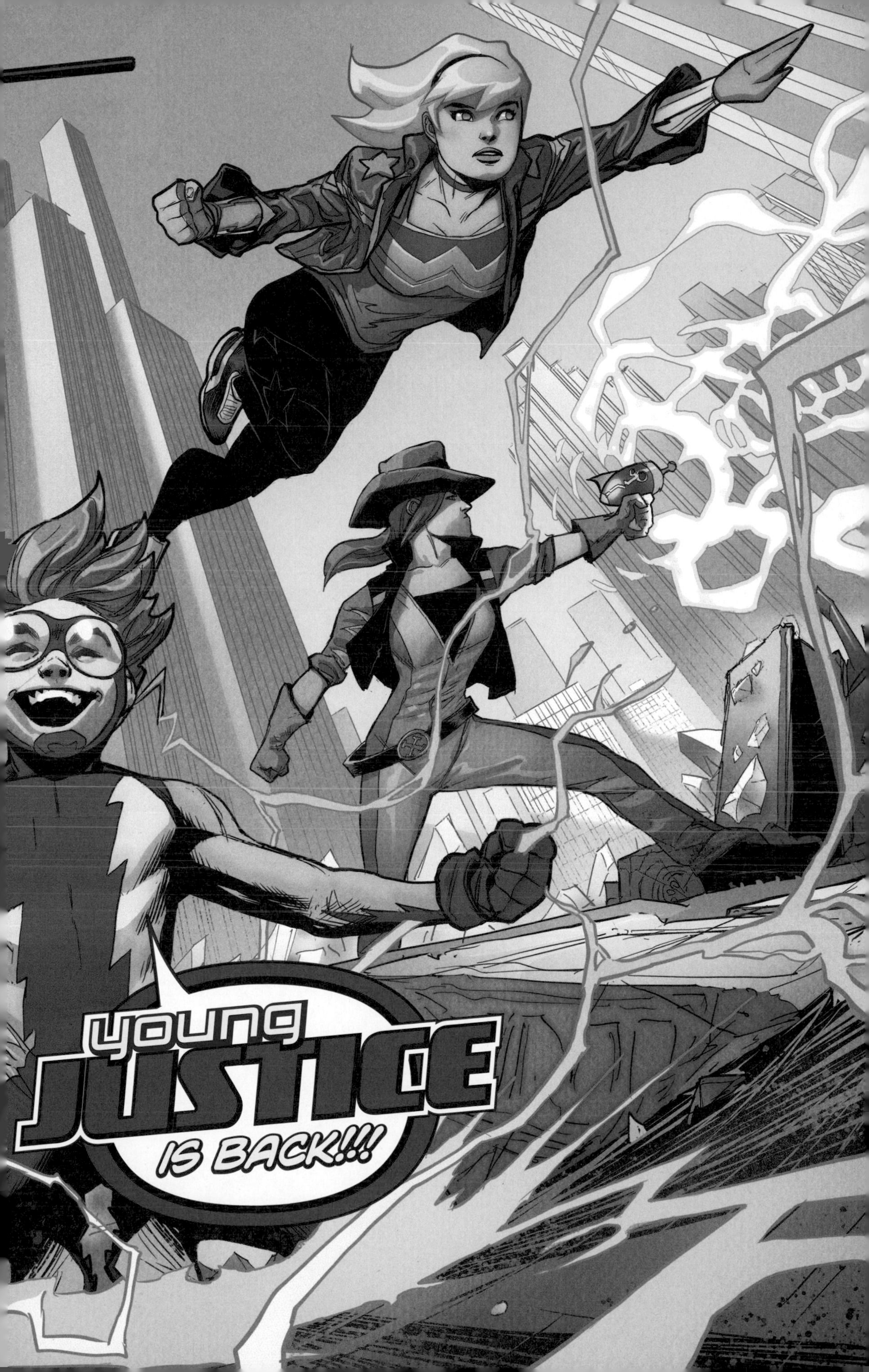
YOUNG JUSTICE IS BACK!!!

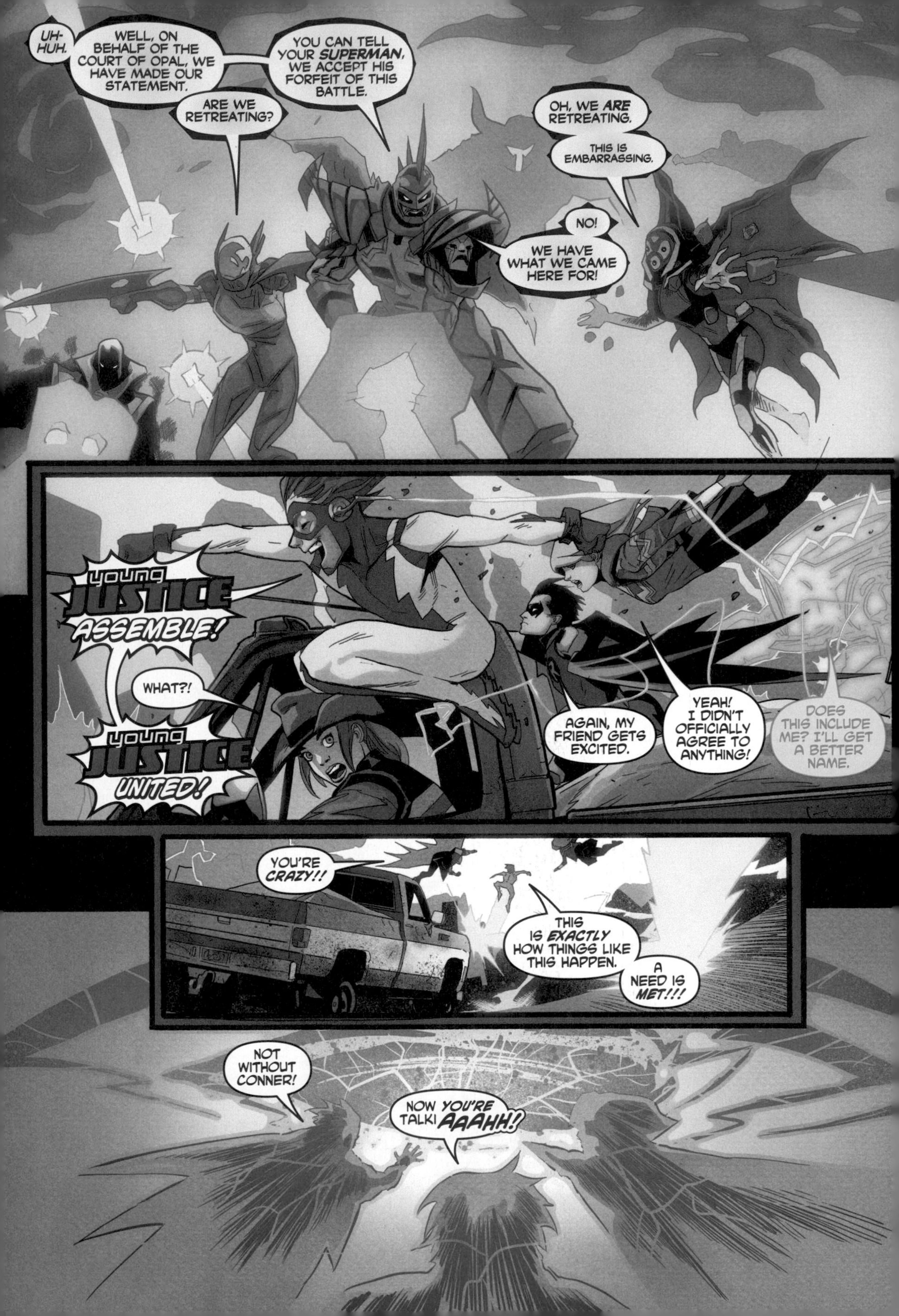
UH-HUH.
WELL, ON BEHALF OF THE COURT OF OPAL, WE HAVE MADE OUR STATEMENT.
ARE WE RETREATING?
YOU CAN TELL YOUR SUPERMAN, WE ACCEPT HIS FORFEIT OF THIS BATTLE.
OH, WE ARE RETREATING.
THIS IS EMBARRASSING.
NO!
WE HAVE WHAT WE CAME HERE FOR!
YOUNG JUSTICE ASSEMBLE!
WHAT?!
YOUNG JUSTICE UNITED!
AGAIN, MY FRIEND GETS EXCITED.
YEAH! I DIDN'T OFFICIALLY AGREE TO ANYTHING!
DOES THIS INCLUDE ME? I'LL GET A BETTER NAME.
YOU'RE CRAZY!!
THIS IS EXACTLY HOW THINGS LIKE THIS HAPPEN.
A NEED IS MET!!!
NOT WITHOUT CONNER!
NOW YOU'RE TALKIAAAHH!

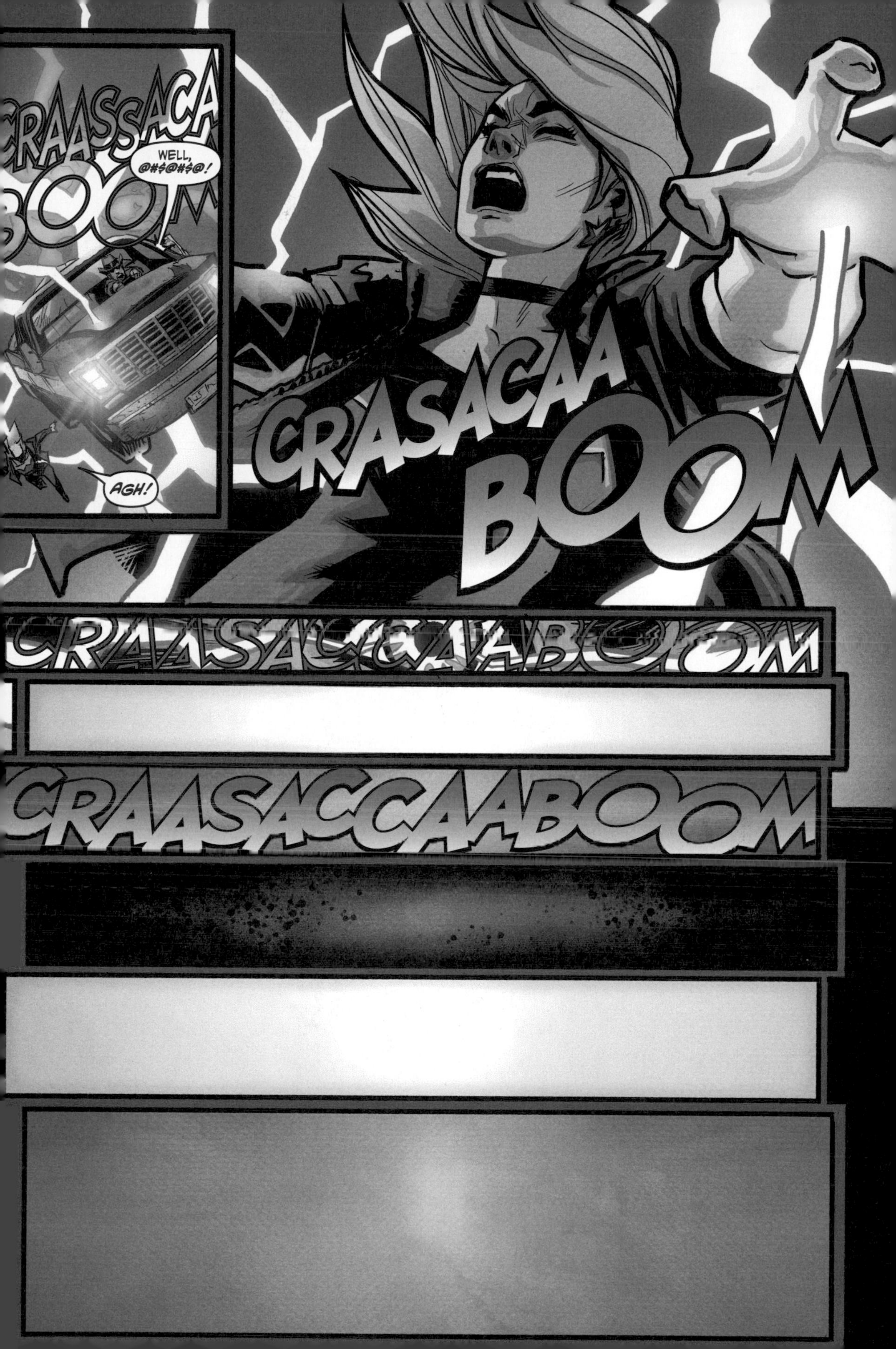
CRAASSACA BOOM
WELL, @#$@#$@!
AGH!
CRASACAA BOOM
CRAASACCAABOOM
CRAASACCAABOOM

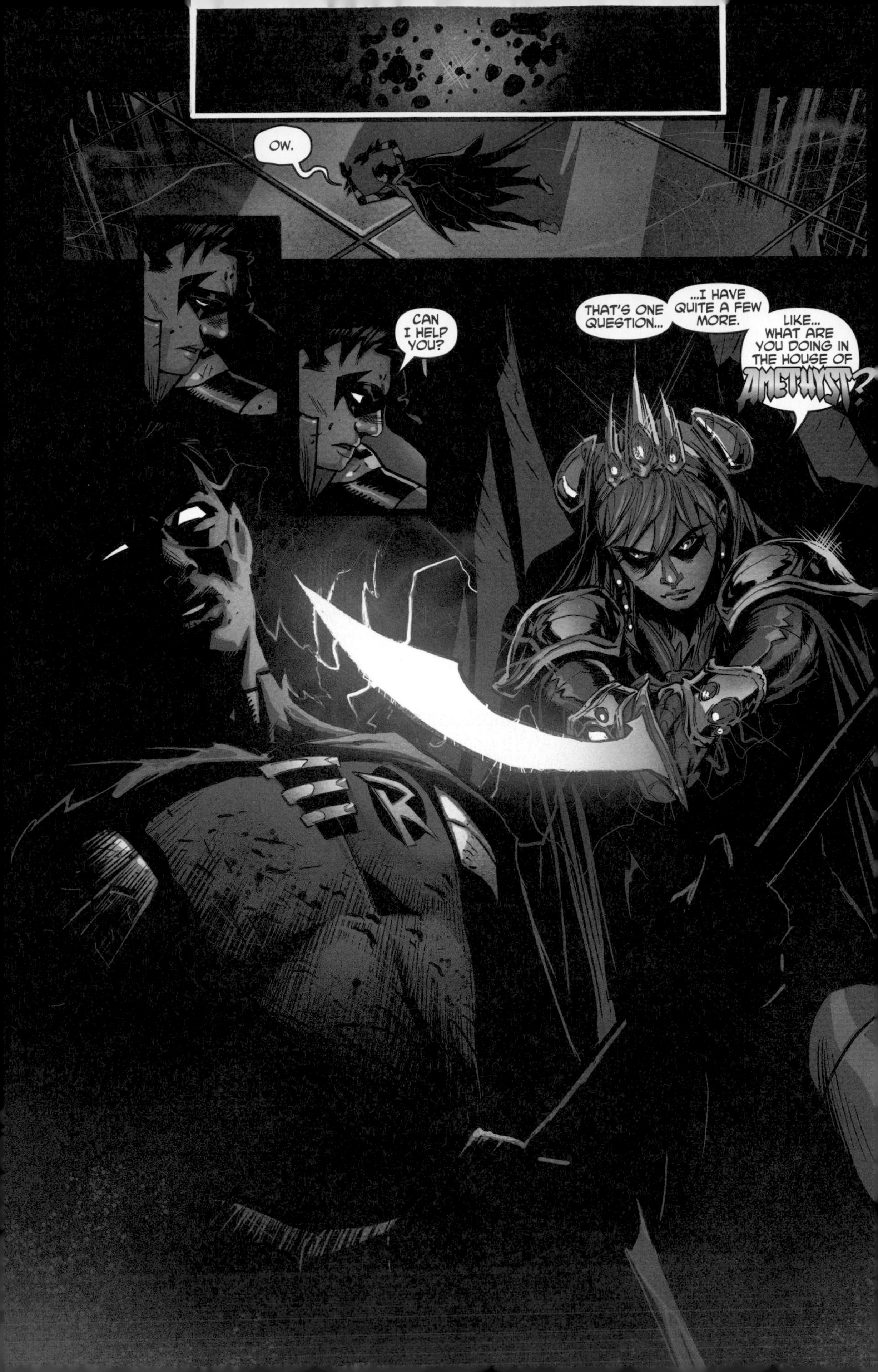
OW.
CAN I HELP YOU?
THAT'S ONE QUESTION...
...I HAVE QUITE A FEW MORE.
LIKE... WHAT ARE YOU DOING IN THE HOUSE OF AMETHYST?

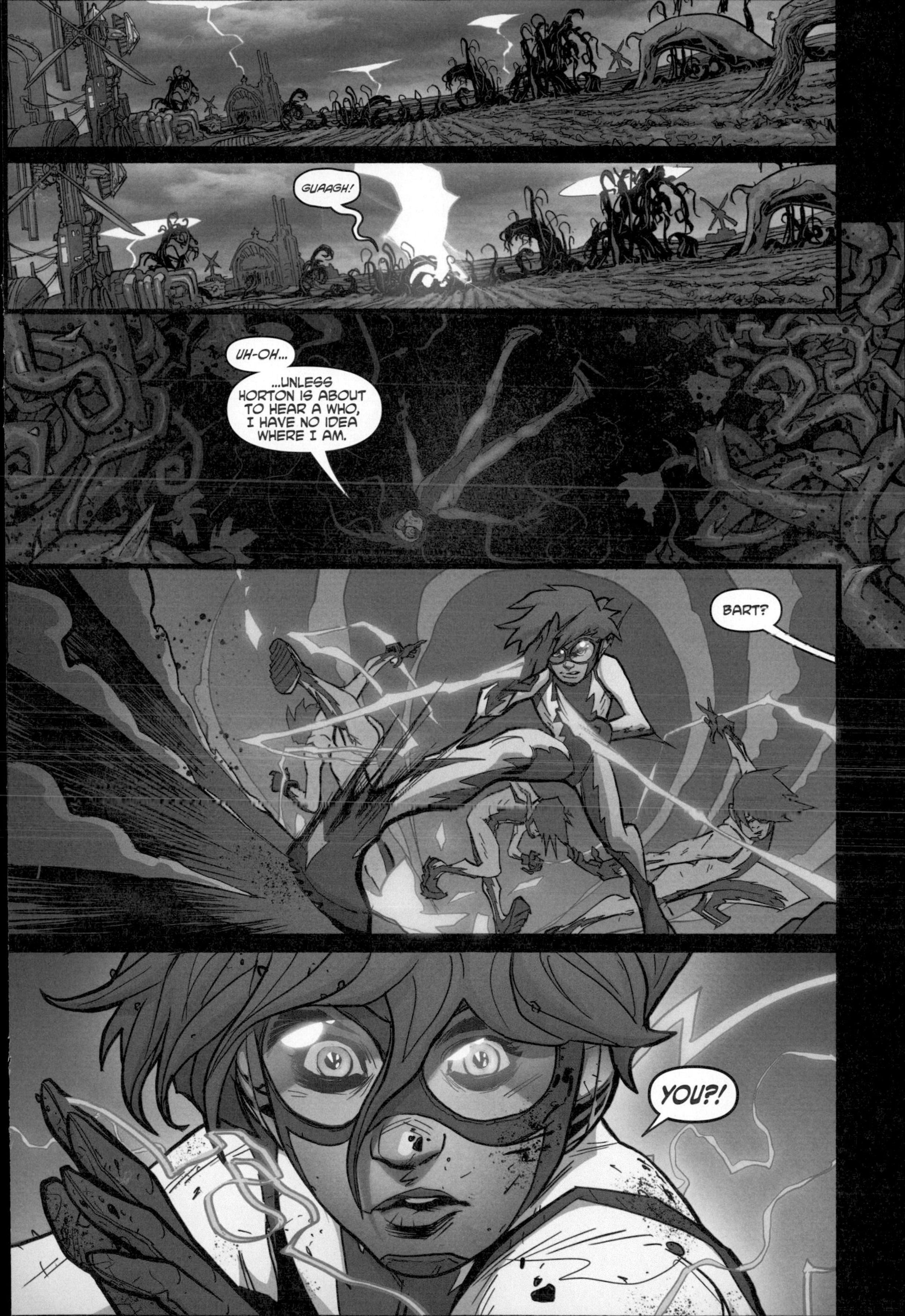
GUAAGH!
UH-OH...
...UNLESS HORTON IS ABOUT TO HEAR A WHO, I HAVE NO IDEA WHERE I AM.
BART?
YOU?!

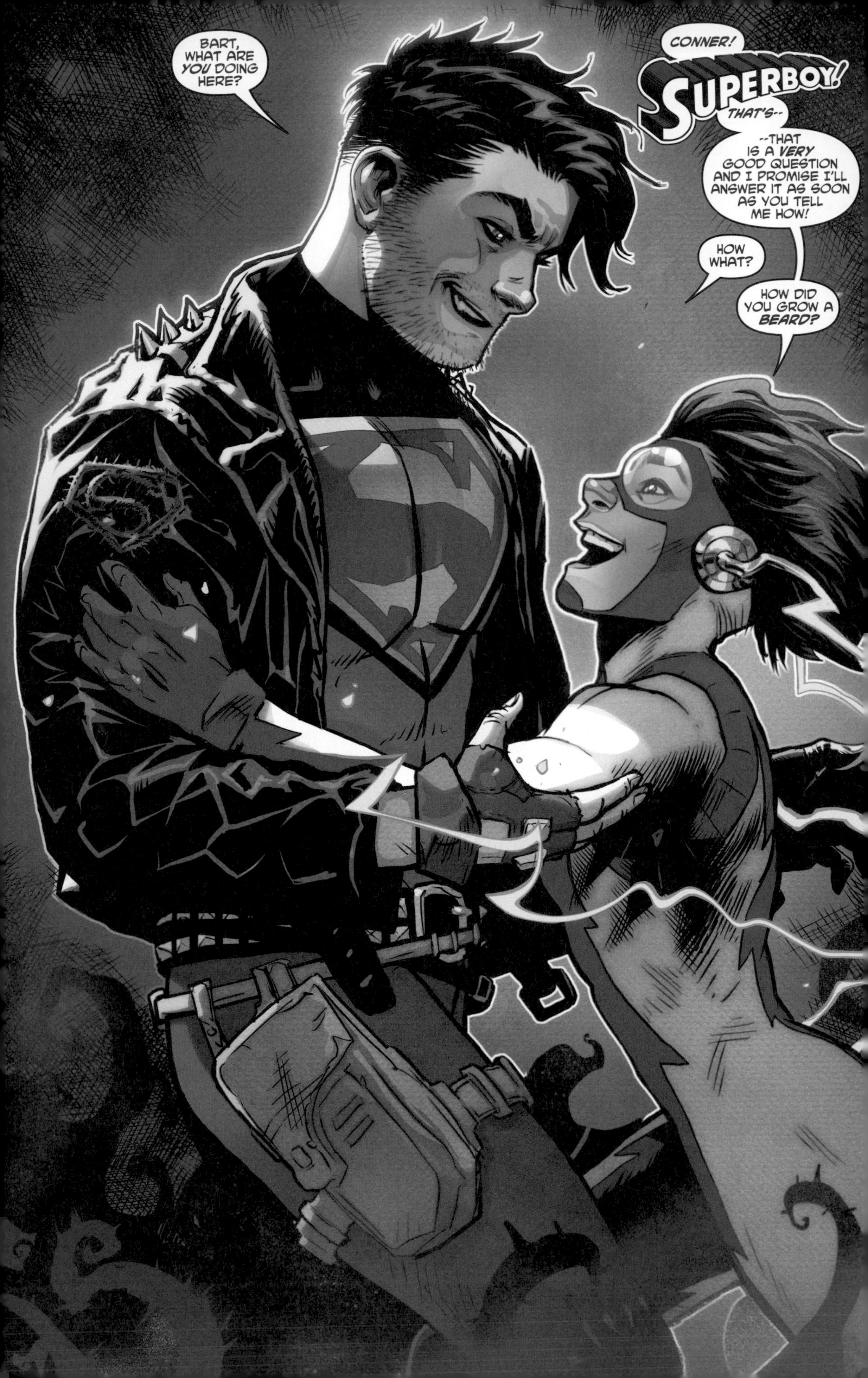
CONNER!
SUPERBOY!
THAT'S--
BART, WHAT ARE YOU DOING HERE?
--THAT IS A VERY GOOD QUESTION AND I PROMISE I'LL ANSWER IT AS SOON AS YOU TELL ME HOW!
HOW WHAT?
HOW DID YOU GROW A BEARD?

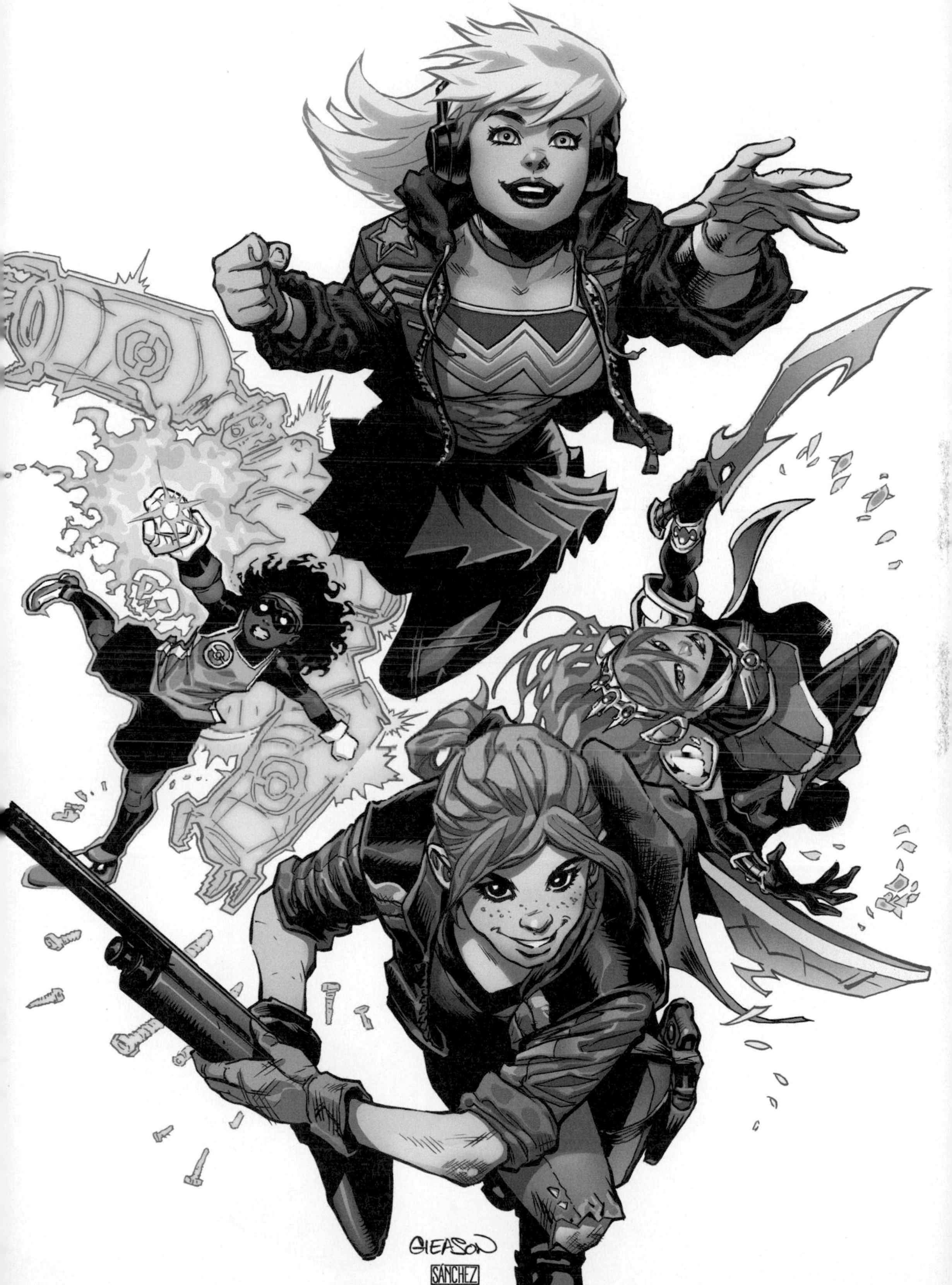
GLEASON
SÁNCHEZ

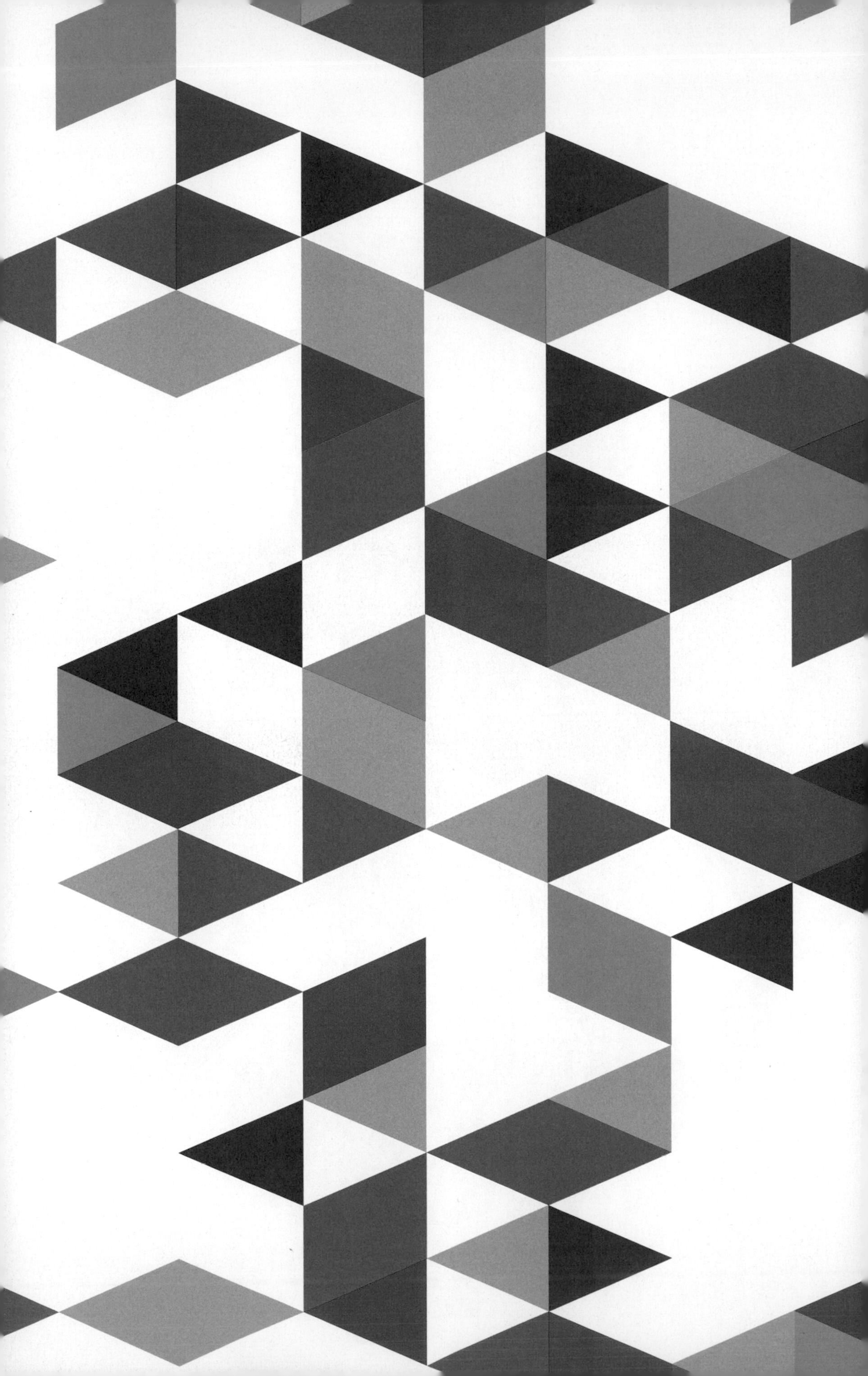

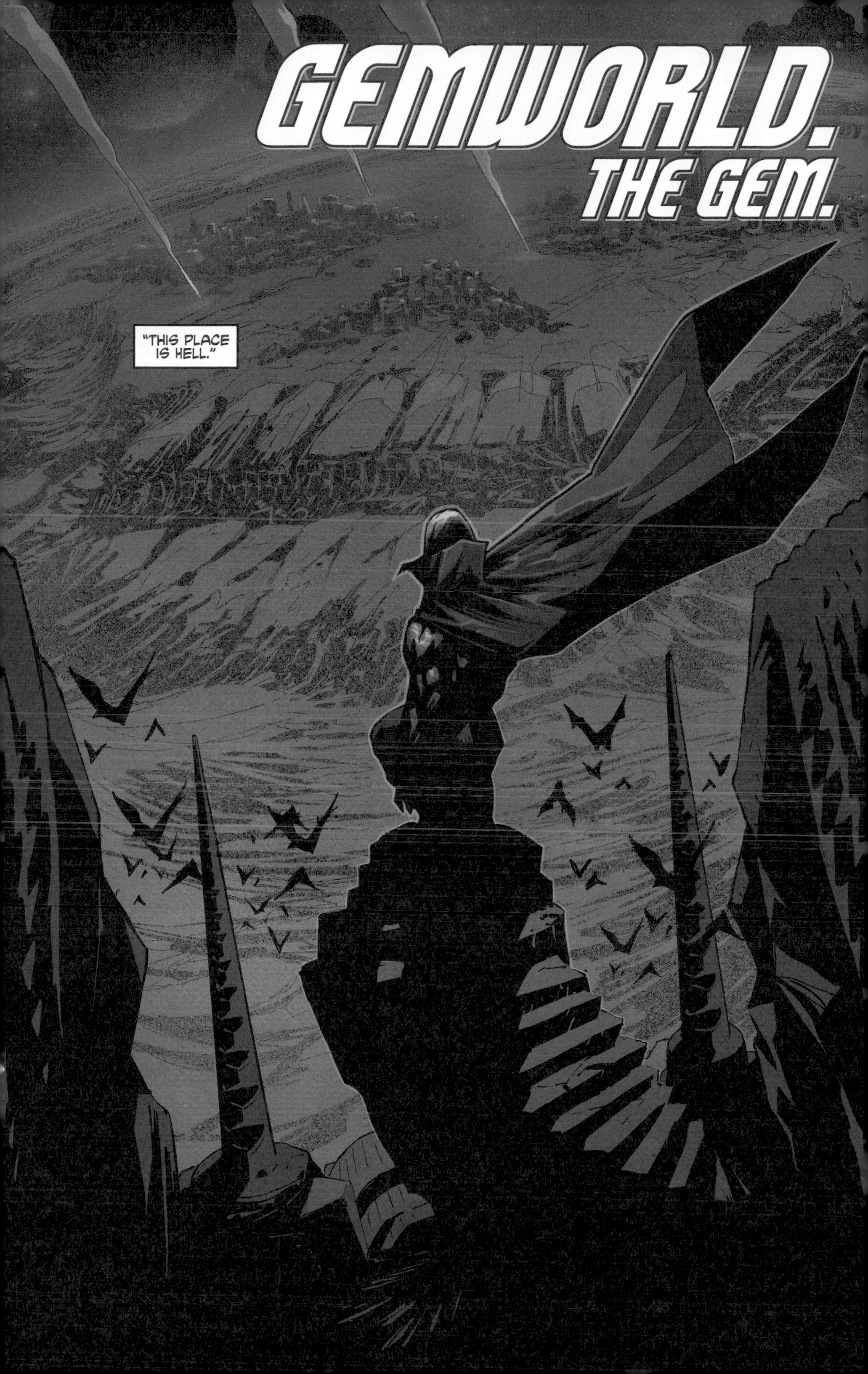
GEMWORLD.
THE GEM.
"THIS PLACE IS HELL."

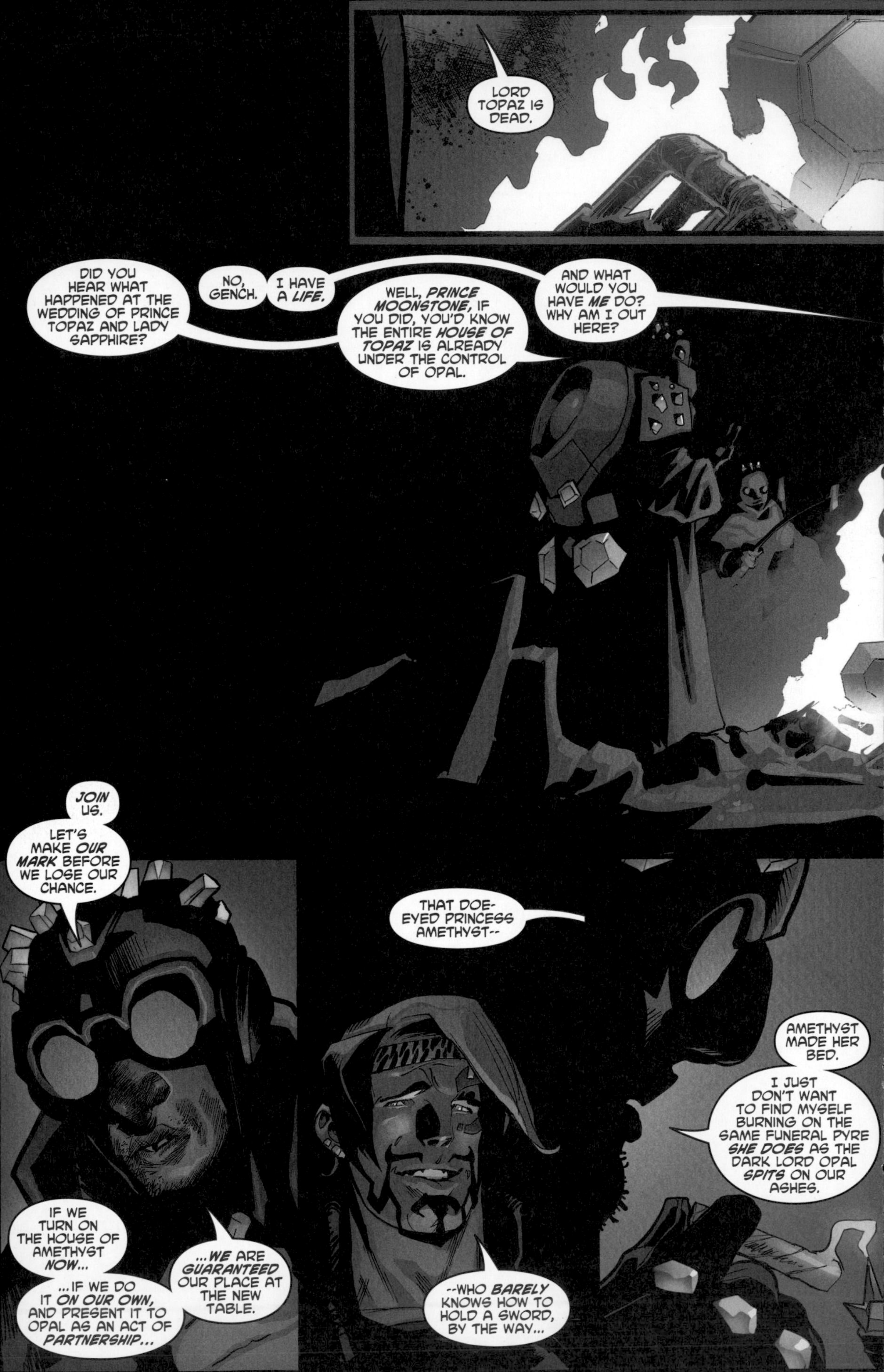
LORD TOPAZ IS DEAD.
DID YOU HEAR WHAT HAPPENED AT THE WEDDING OF PRINCE TOPAZ AND LADY SAPPHIRE?
NO, GENCH.
I HAVE A *LIFE.*
WELL, *PRINCE MOONSTONE,* IF YOU DID, YOU'D KNOW THE ENTIRE *HOUSE OF TOPAZ* IS ALREADY UNDER THE CONTROL OF OPAL.
AND WHAT WOULD YOU HAVE *ME* DO? WHY AM I OUT HERE?
JOIN US.
LET'S MAKE *OUR MARK* BEFORE WE LOSE OUR CHANCE.
IF WE TURN ON THE HOUSE OF AMETHYST *NOW*...
...IF WE DO IT *ON OUR OWN,* AND PRESENT IT TO OPAL AS AN ACT OF *PARTNERSHIP*...
...*WE* ARE *GUARANTEED* OUR PLACE AT THE NEW TABLE.
THAT DOE-EYED PRINCESS AMETHYST--
--WHO *BARELY* KNOWS HOW TO HOLD A SWORD, BY THE WAY...
AMETHYST MADE HER BED.
I JUST DON'T WANT TO FIND MYSELF BURNING ON THE SAME FUNERAL PYRE *SHE DOES* AS THE DARK LORD OPAL *SPITS* ON OUR ASHES.

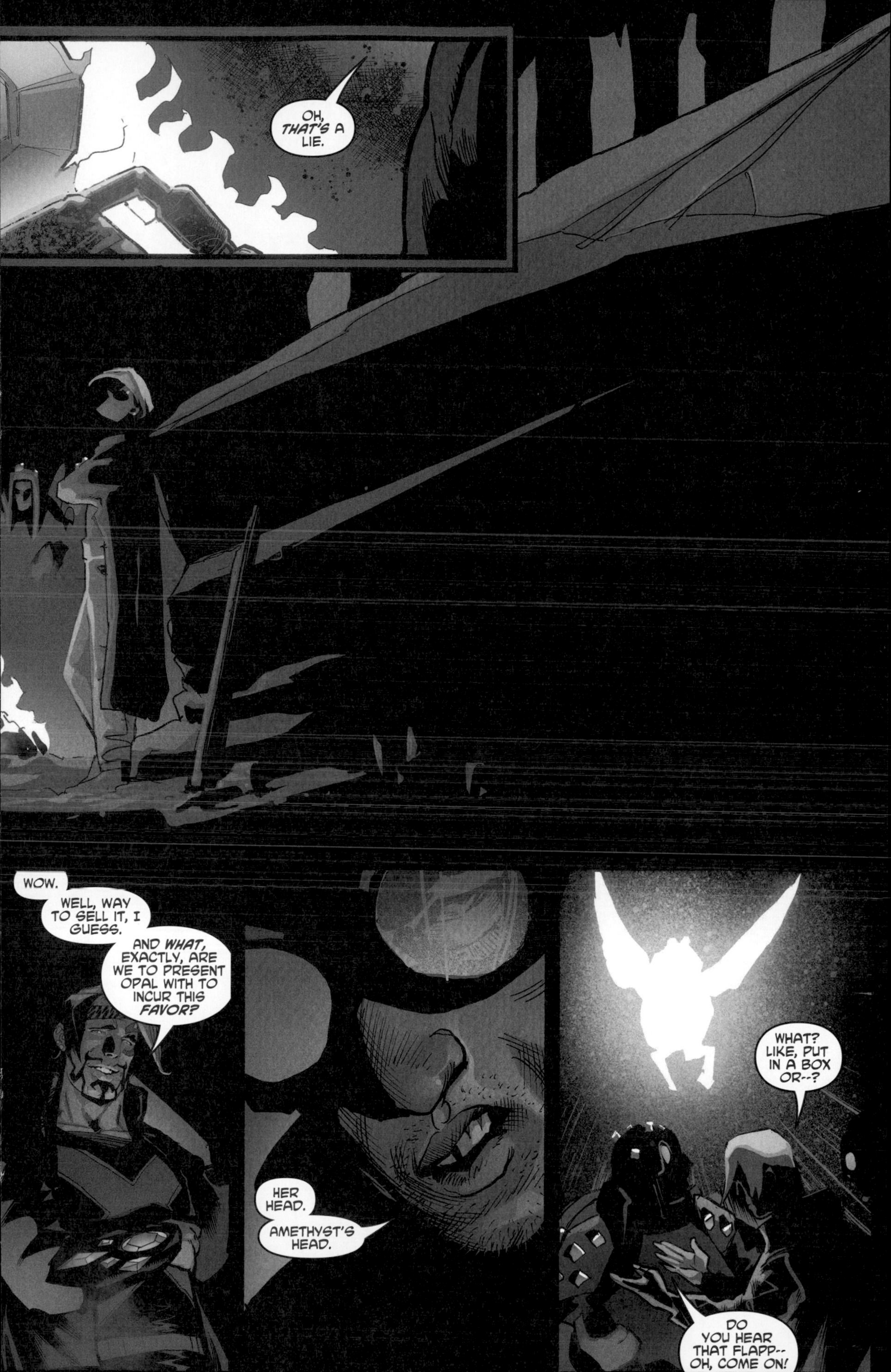
OH, THAT'S A LIE.
WOW.
WELL, WAY TO SELL IT, I GUESS.
AND WHAT, EXACTLY, ARE WE TO PRESENT OPAL WITH TO INCUR THIS FAVOR?
HER HEAD.
AMETHYST'S HEAD.
WHAT? LIKE, PUT IN A BOX OR--?
DO YOU HEAR THAT FLAPP-- OH, COME ON!

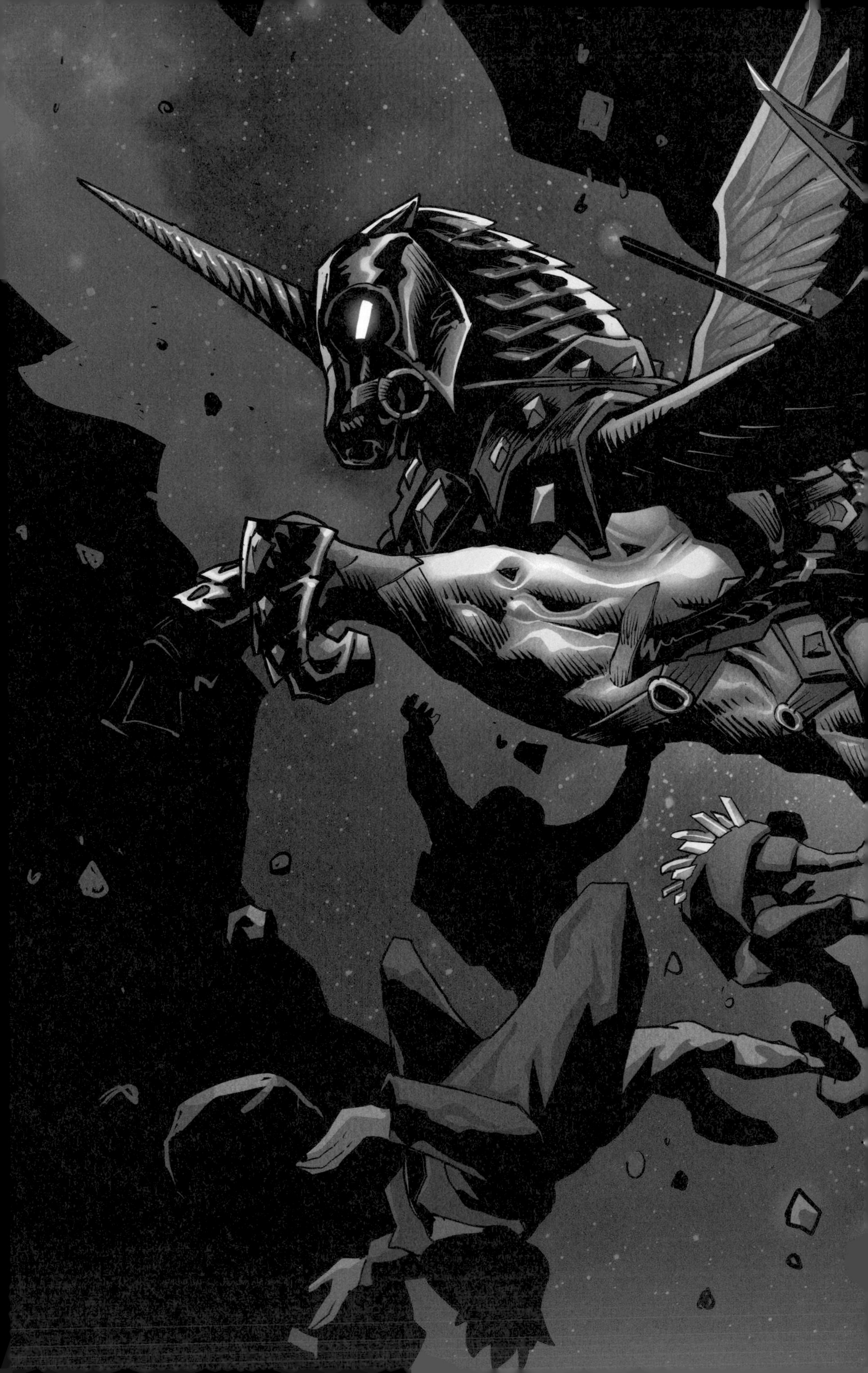

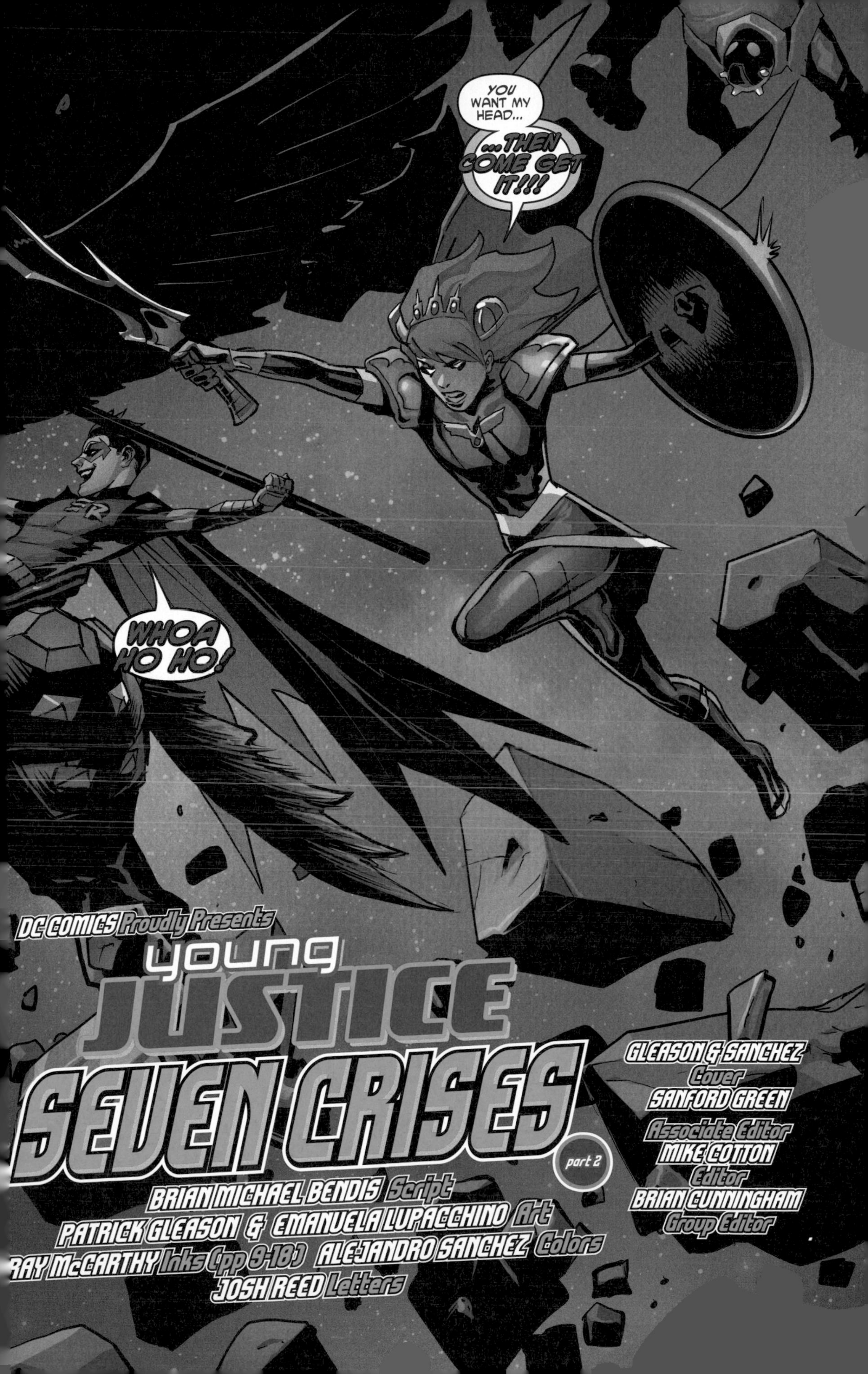
YOU WANT MY HEAD...
...THEN COME GET IT!!!
WHOA HO HO!
DC COMICS Proudly Presents
YOUNG JUSTICE
SEVEN CRISES
part 2
BRIAN MICHAEL BENDIS Script
PATRICK GLEASON & EMANUELA LUPACCHINO Art
RAY McCARTHY Inks (pp 8-18) ALEJANDRO SANCHEZ Colors
JOSH REED Letters
GLEASON & SANCHEZ Cover
SANFORD GREEN Associate Editor
MIKE COTTON Editor
BRIAN CUNNINGHAM Group Editor

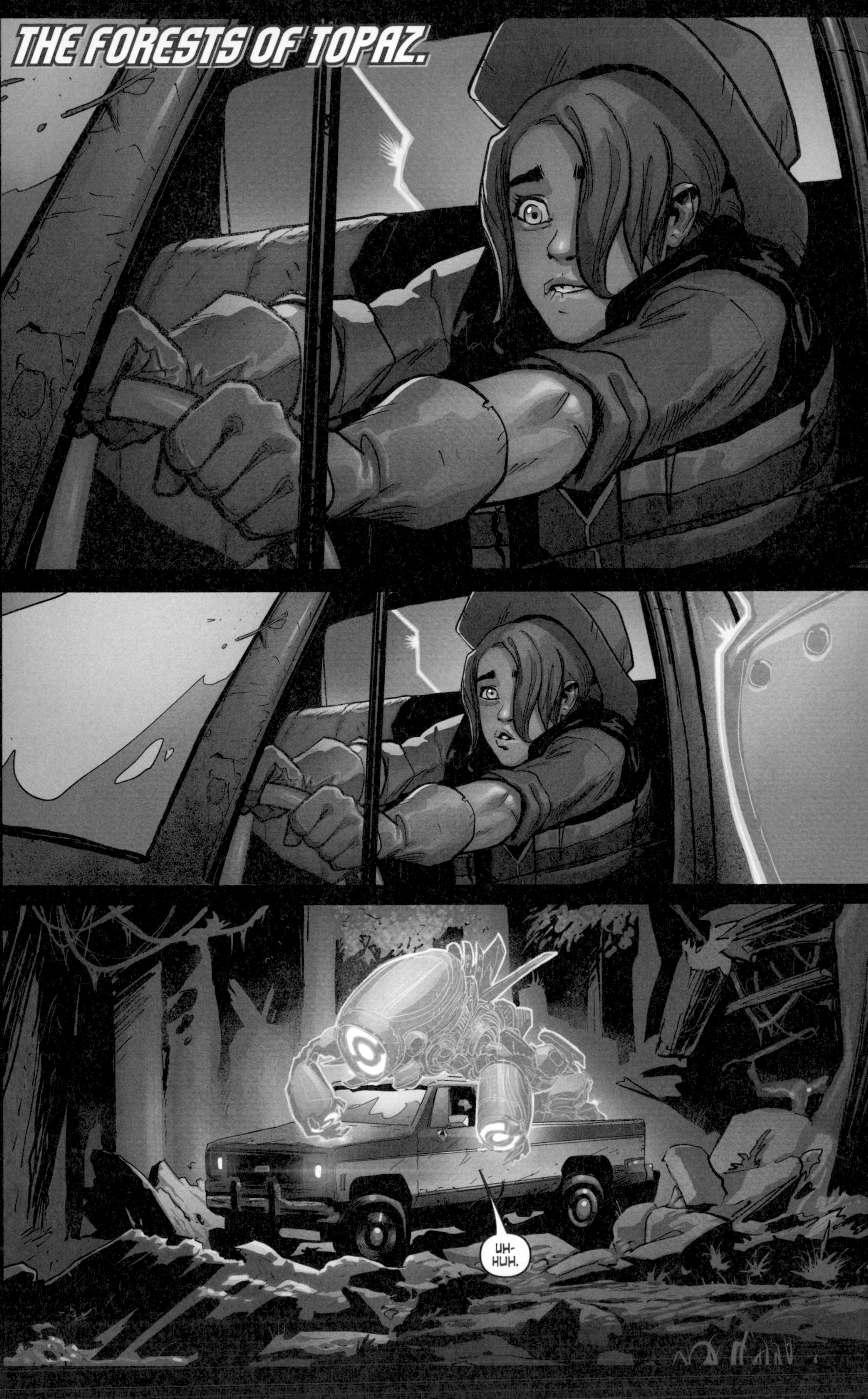
THE FORESTS OF TOPAZ.
UH-HUH.

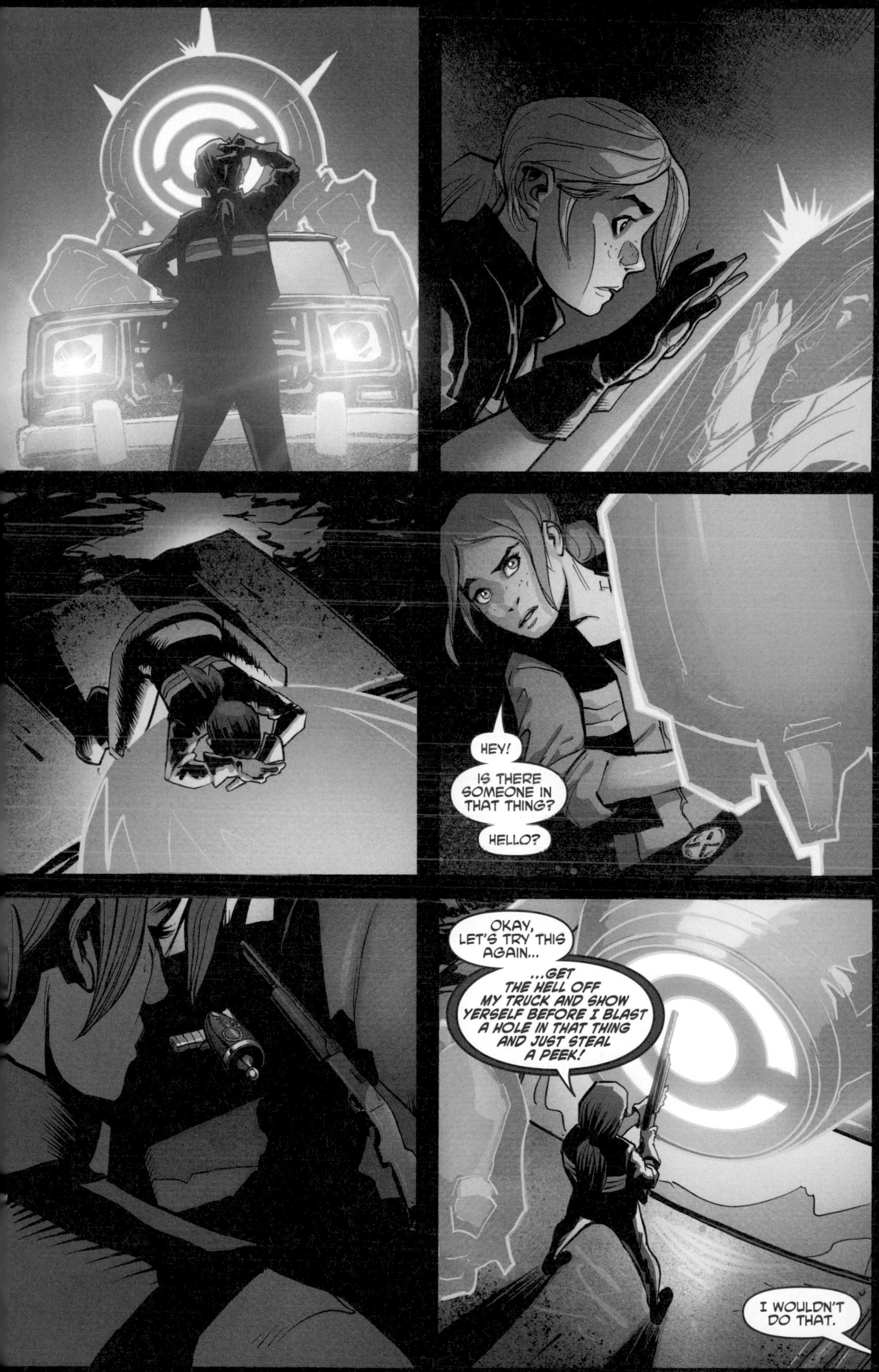
HEY!
IS THERE SOMEONE IN THAT THING?
HELLO?
OKAY, LET'S TRY THIS AGAIN...
...GET THE HELL OFF MY TRUCK AND SHOW YERSELF BEFORE I BLAST A HOLE IN THAT THING AND JUST STEAL A PEEK!
I WOULDN'T DO THAT.

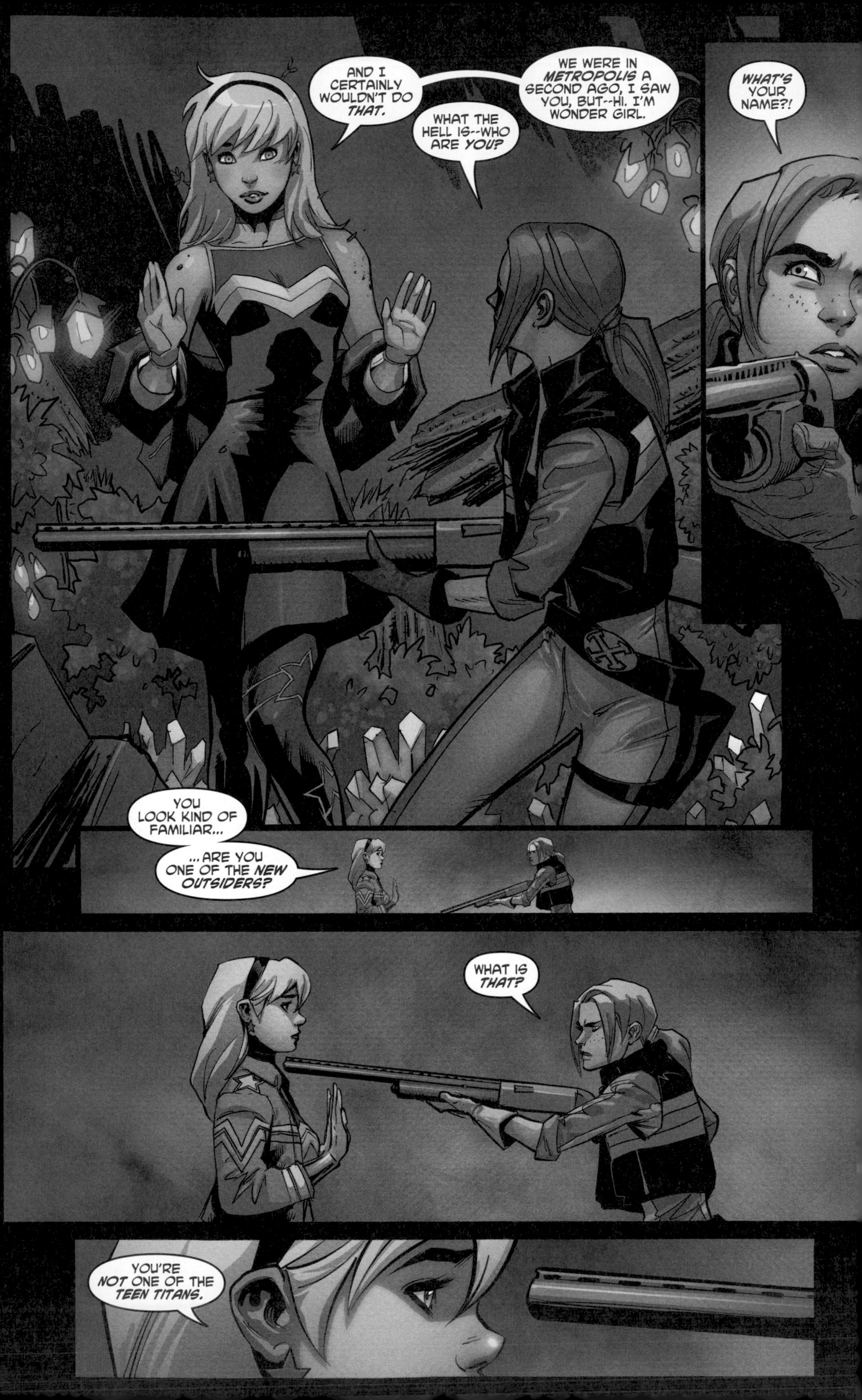

AND I CERTAINLY WOULDN'T DO THAT.
WHAT THE HELL IS--WHO ARE YOU?
WE WERE IN METROPOLIS A SECOND AGO, I SAW YOU, BUT--HI. I'M WONDER GIRL.
WHAT'S YOUR NAME?!
YOU LOOK KIND OF FAMILIAR...
...ARE YOU ONE OF THE NEW OUTSIDERS?
WHAT IS THAT?
YOU'RE NOT ONE OF THE TEEN TITANS.

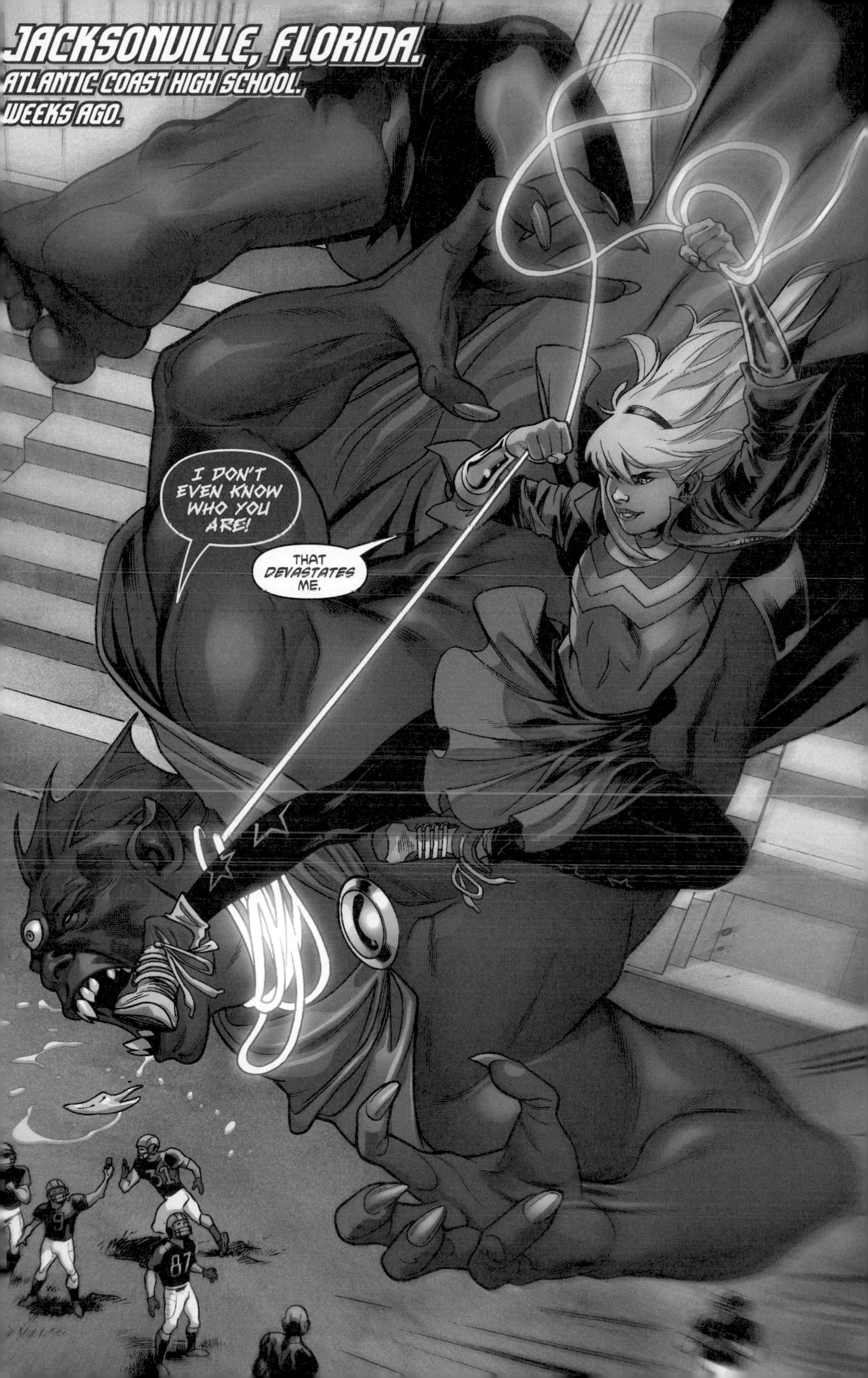
JACKSONVILLE, FLORIDA.
ATLANTIC COAST HIGH SCHOOL.
WEEKS AGO.
I DON'T EVEN KNOW WHO YOU ARE!
THAT DEVASTATES ME.

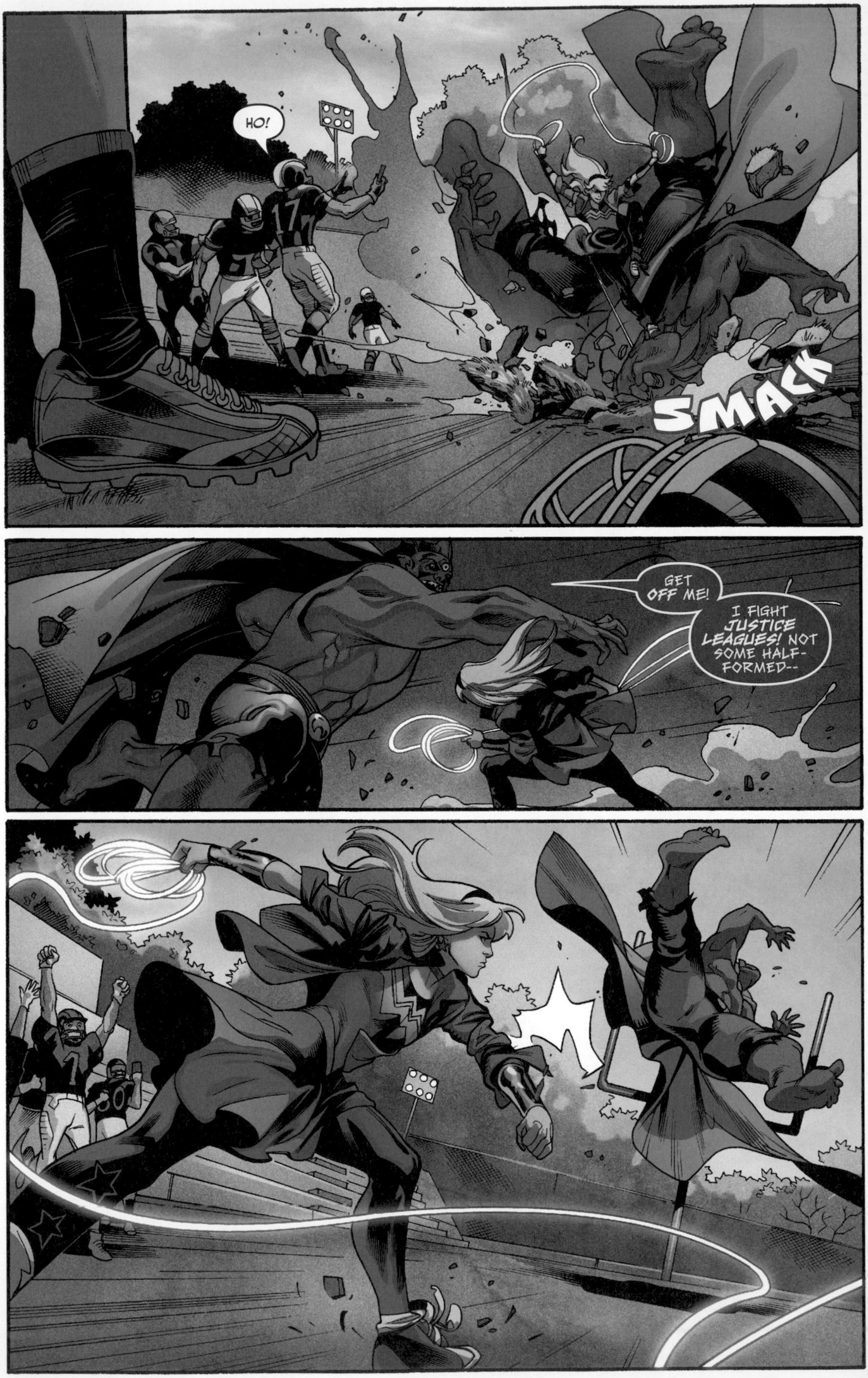
HO!
SMACK
GET OFF ME!
I FIGHT JUSTICE LEAGUES! NOT SOME HALF-FORMED--

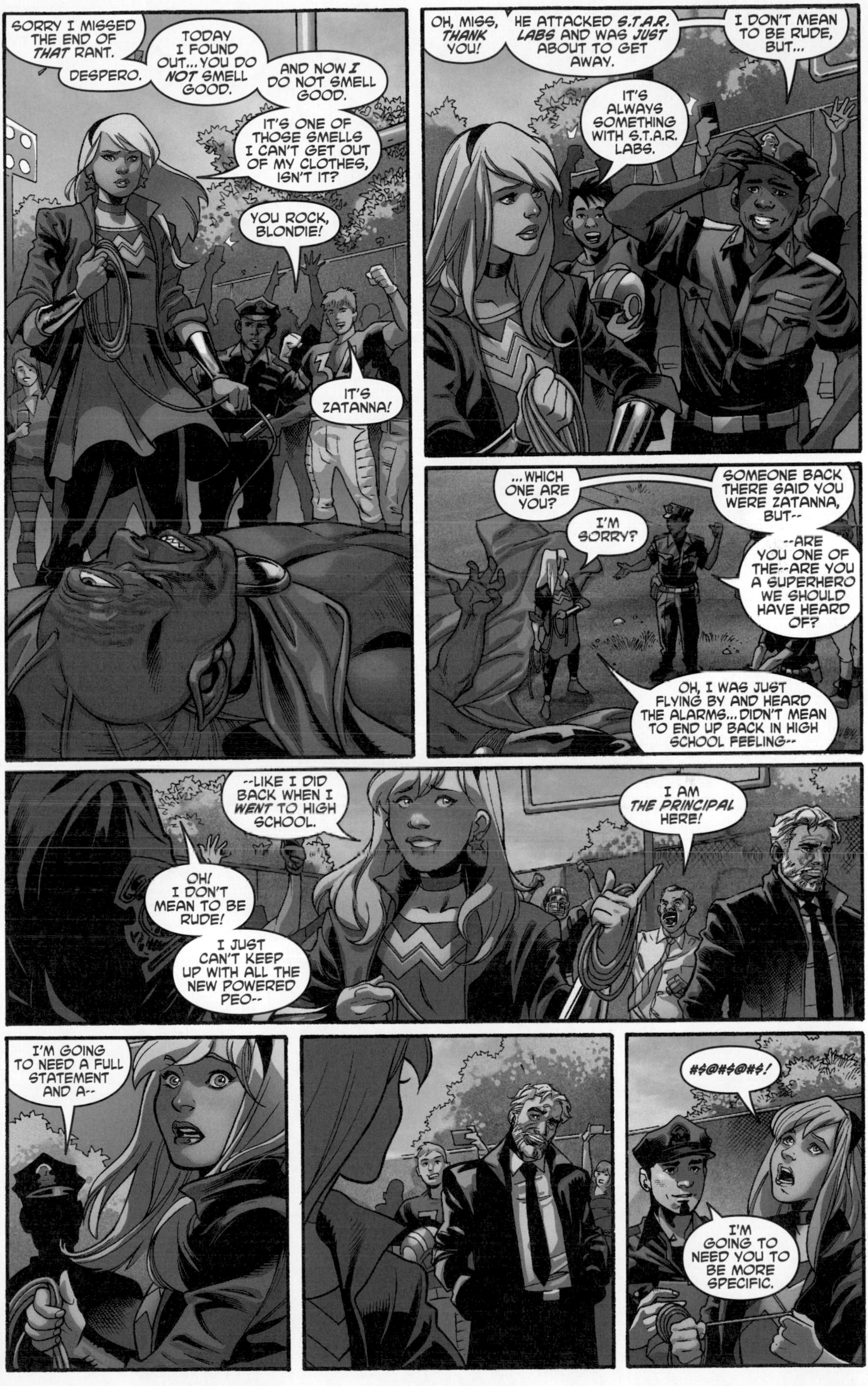

SORRY I MISSED THE END OF *THAT* RANT.
DESPERO.
TODAY I FOUND OUT...YOU DO *NOT* SMELL GOOD.
AND NOW *I* DO NOT SMELL GOOD.
IT'S ONE OF THOSE SMELLS I CAN'T GET OUT OF MY CLOTHES, ISN'T IT?
YOU ROCK, BLONDIE!
IT'S ZATANNA!
OH, MISS, *THANK* YOU!
HE ATTACKED *S.T.A.R. LABS* AND WAS *JUST* ABOUT TO GET AWAY.
I DON'T MEAN TO BE RUDE, BUT...
IT'S ALWAYS SOMETHING WITH S.T.A.R. LABS.
...WHICH ONE ARE YOU?
SOMEONE BACK THERE SAID YOU WERE ZATANNA, BUT--
I'M SORRY?
--ARE YOU ONE OF THE--ARE YOU A SUPERHERO WE SHOULD HAVE HEARD OF?
OH, I WAS JUST FLYING BY AND HEARD THE ALARMS... DIDN'T MEAN TO END UP BACK IN HIGH SCHOOL FEELING--
--LIKE I DID BACK WHEN I *WENT* TO HIGH SCHOOL.
OH! I DON'T MEAN TO BE RUDE!
I JUST CAN'T KEEP UP WITH ALL THE NEW POWERED PEO--
I AM *THE PRINCIPAL* HERE!
I'M GOING TO NEED A FULL STATEMENT AND A--
#$@#$@#$!
I'M GOING TO NEED YOU TO BE MORE SPECIFIC.

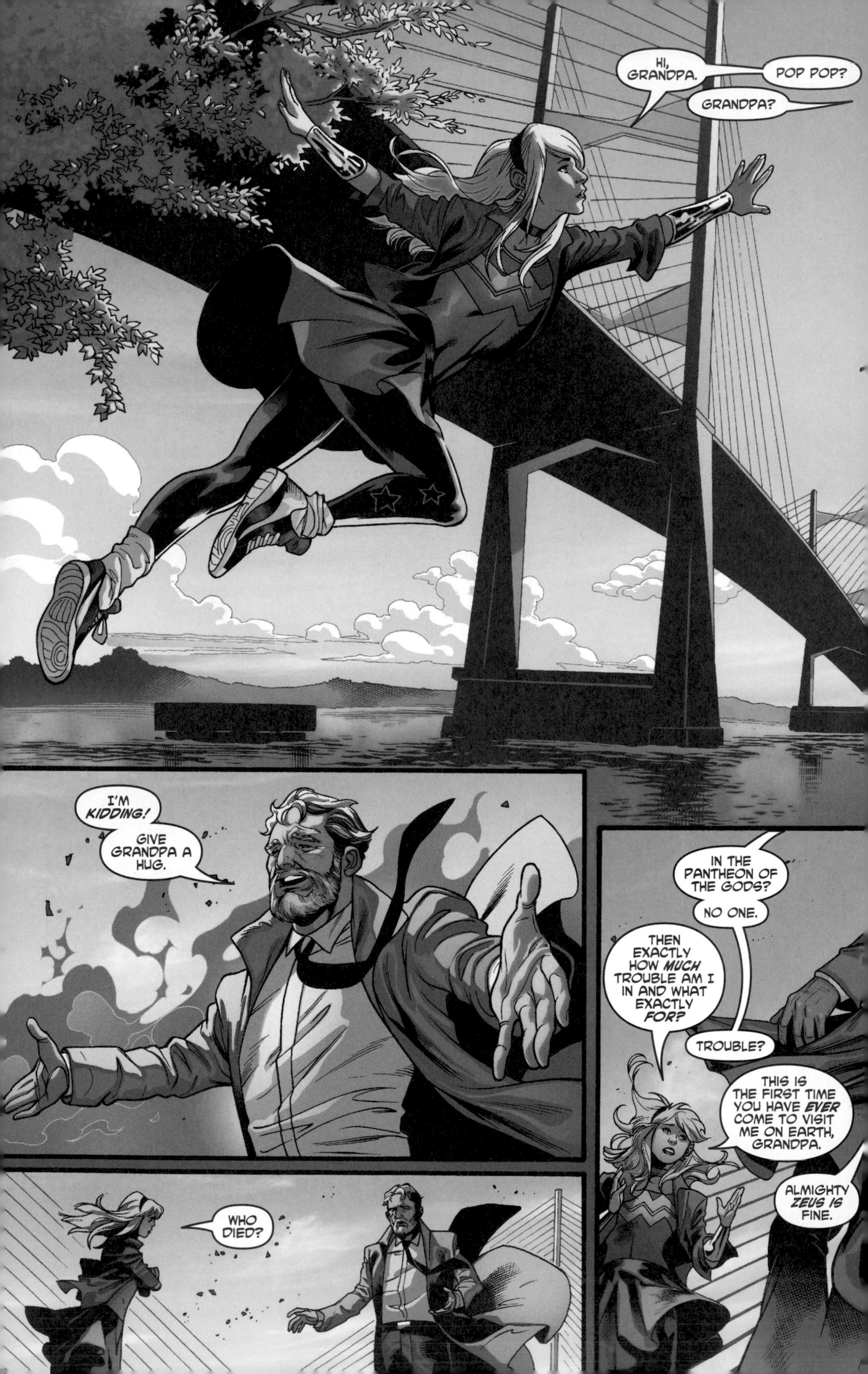
HI, GRANDPA.
POP POP?
GRANDPA?
I'M *KIDDING!*
GIVE GRANDPA A HUG.
WHO DIED?
IN THE PANTHEON OF THE GODS?
NO ONE.
THEN EXACTLY HOW *MUCH* TROUBLE AM I IN AND WHAT EXACTLY *FOR?*
TROUBLE?
THIS IS THE FIRST TIME YOU HAVE *EVER* COME TO VISIT ME ON EARTH, GRANDPA.
ALMIGHTY *ZEUS IS* FINE.

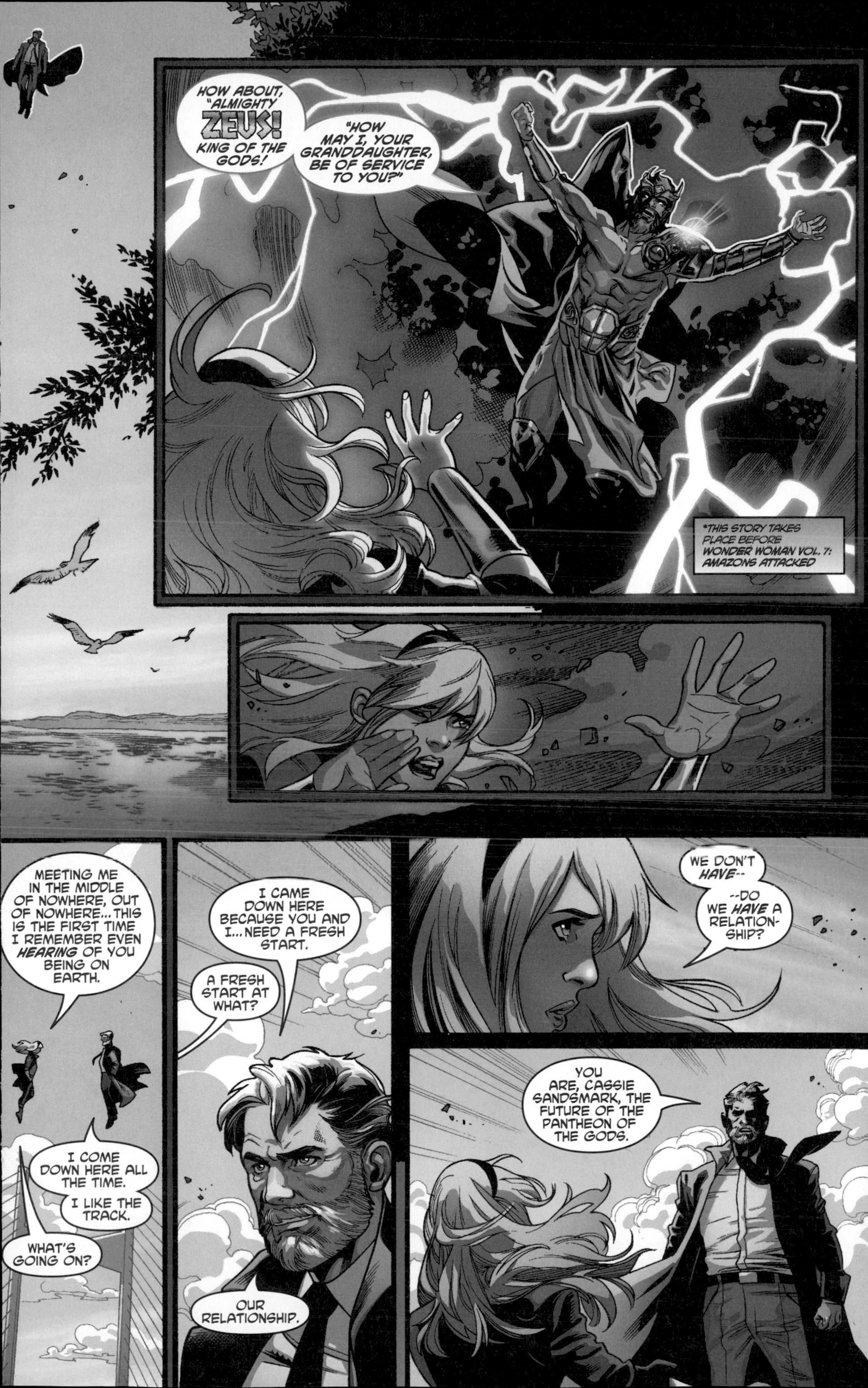
HOW ABOUT, "ALMIGHTY ZEUS! KING OF THE GODS!
"HOW MAY I, YOUR GRANDDAUGHTER, BE OF SERVICE TO YOU?"
*THIS STORY TAKES PLACE BEFORE WONDER WOMAN VOL. 7: AMAZONS ATTACKED
MEETING ME IN THE MIDDLE OF NOWHERE, OUT OF NOWHERE... THIS IS THE FIRST TIME I REMEMBER EVEN HEARING OF YOU BEING ON EARTH.
I COME DOWN HERE ALL THE TIME.
I LIKE THE TRACK.
WHAT'S GOING ON?
I CAME DOWN HERE BECAUSE YOU AND I... NEED A FRESH START.
A FRESH START AT WHAT?
OUR RELATIONSHIP.
WE DON'T HAVE--
--DO WE HAVE A RELATIONSHIP?
YOU ARE, CASSIE SANDSMARK, THE FUTURE OF THE PANTHEON OF THE GODS.

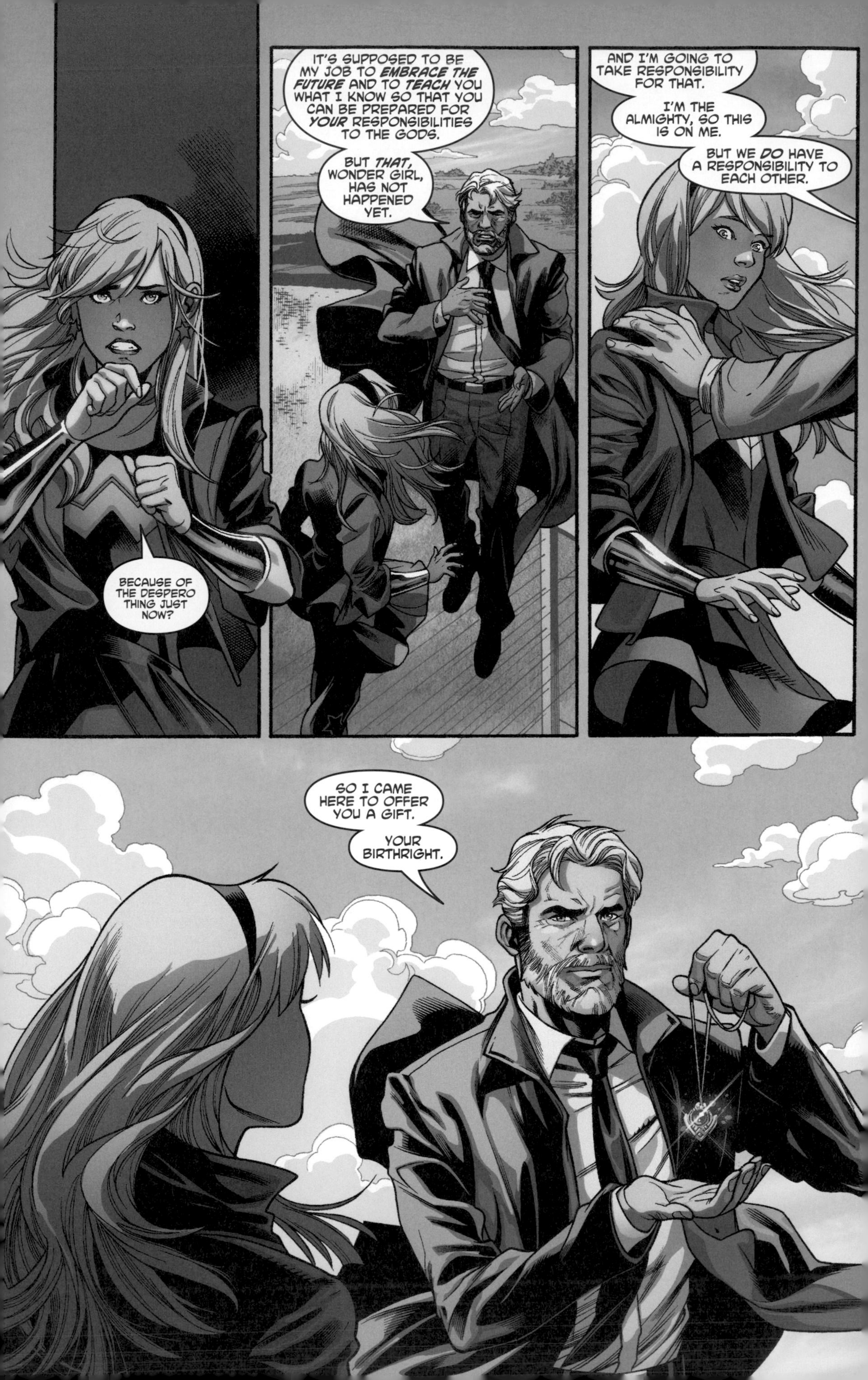

BECAUSE OF THE DESPERO THING JUST NOW?
IT'S SUPPOSED TO BE MY JOB TO EMBRACE THE FUTURE AND TO TEACH YOU WHAT I KNOW SO THAT YOU CAN BE PREPARED FOR YOUR RESPONSIBILITIES TO THE GODS.
BUT THAT, WONDER GIRL, HAS NOT HAPPENED YET.
AND I'M GOING TO TAKE RESPONSIBILITY FOR THAT.
I'M THE ALMIGHTY, SO THIS IS ON ME.
BUT WE DO HAVE A RESPONSIBILITY TO EACH OTHER.
SO I CAME HERE TO OFFER YOU A GIFT.
YOUR BIRTHRIGHT.

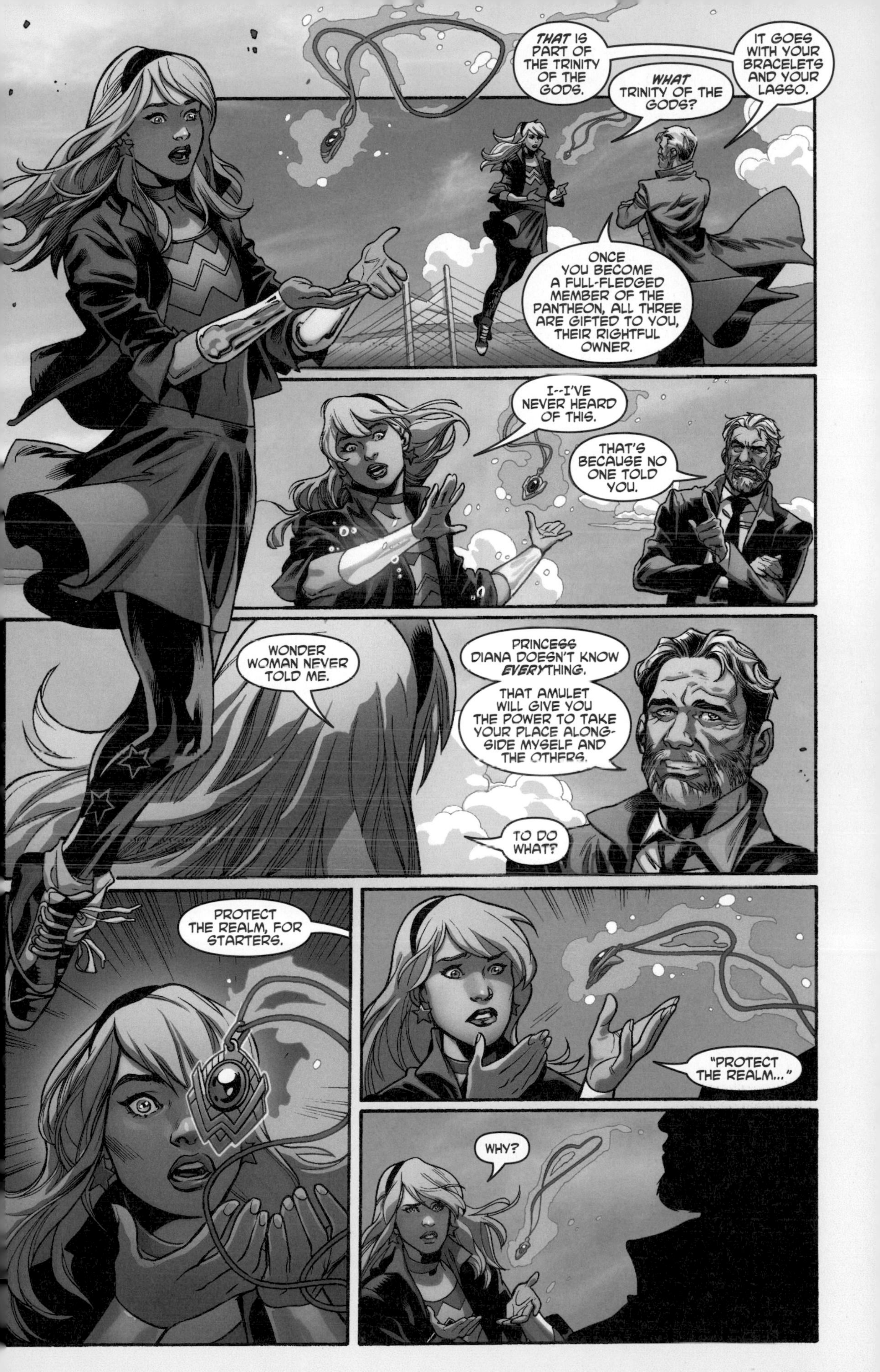
THAT IS PART OF THE TRINITY OF THE GODS.
IT GOES WITH YOUR BRACELETS AND YOUR LASSO.
WHAT TRINITY OF THE GODS?
ONCE YOU BECOME A FULL-FLEDGED MEMBER OF THE PANTHEON, ALL THREE ARE GIFTED TO YOU, THEIR RIGHTFUL OWNER.
I--I'VE NEVER HEARD OF THIS.
THAT'S BECAUSE NO ONE TOLD YOU.
WONDER WOMAN NEVER TOLD ME.
PRINCESS DIANA DOESN'T KNOW EVERYTHING.
THAT AMULET WILL GIVE YOU THE POWER TO TAKE YOUR PLACE ALONG-SIDE MYSELF AND THE OTHERS.
TO DO WHAT?
PROTECT THE REALM, FOR STARTERS.
"PROTECT THE REALM..."
WHY?

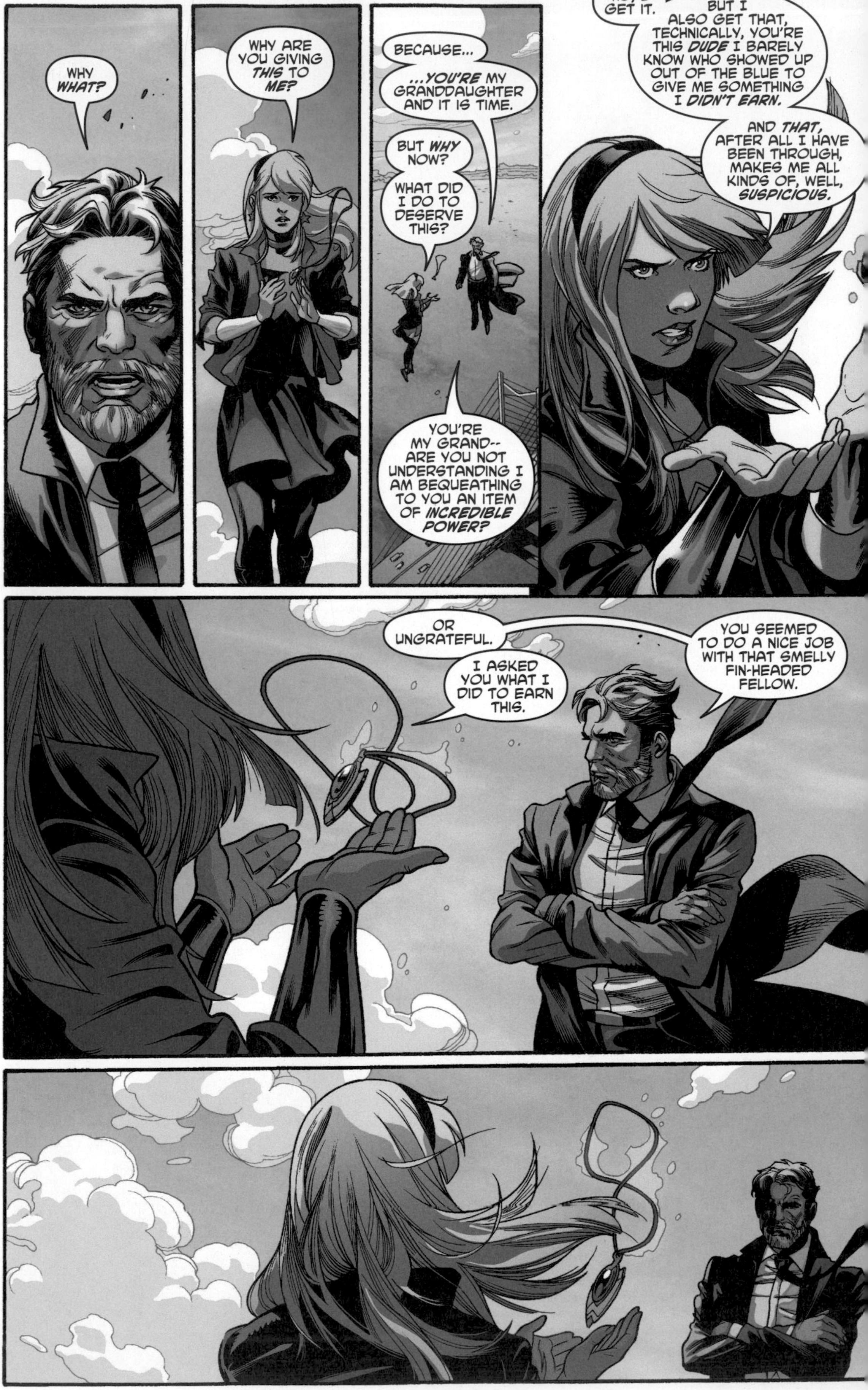
WHY WHAT?
WHY ARE YOU GIVING THIS TO ME?
BECAUSE...
...YOU'RE MY GRANDDAUGHTER AND IT IS TIME.
BUT WHY NOW?
WHAT DID I DO TO DESERVE THIS?
YOU'RE MY GRAND-- ARE YOU NOT UNDERSTANDING I AM BEQUEATHING TO YOU AN ITEM OF INCREDIBLE POWER?
NO, I GET IT.
BUT I ALSO GET THAT, TECHNICALLY, YOU'RE THIS DUDE I BARELY KNOW WHO SHOWED UP OUT OF THE BLUE TO GIVE ME SOMETHING I DIDN'T EARN.
AND THAT, AFTER ALL I HAVE BEEN THROUGH, MAKES ME ALL KINDS OF, WELL, SUSPICIOUS.
OR UNGRATEFUL.
I ASKED YOU WHAT I DID TO EARN THIS.
YOU SEEMED TO DO A NICE JOB WITH THAT SMELLY FIN-HEADED FELLOW.

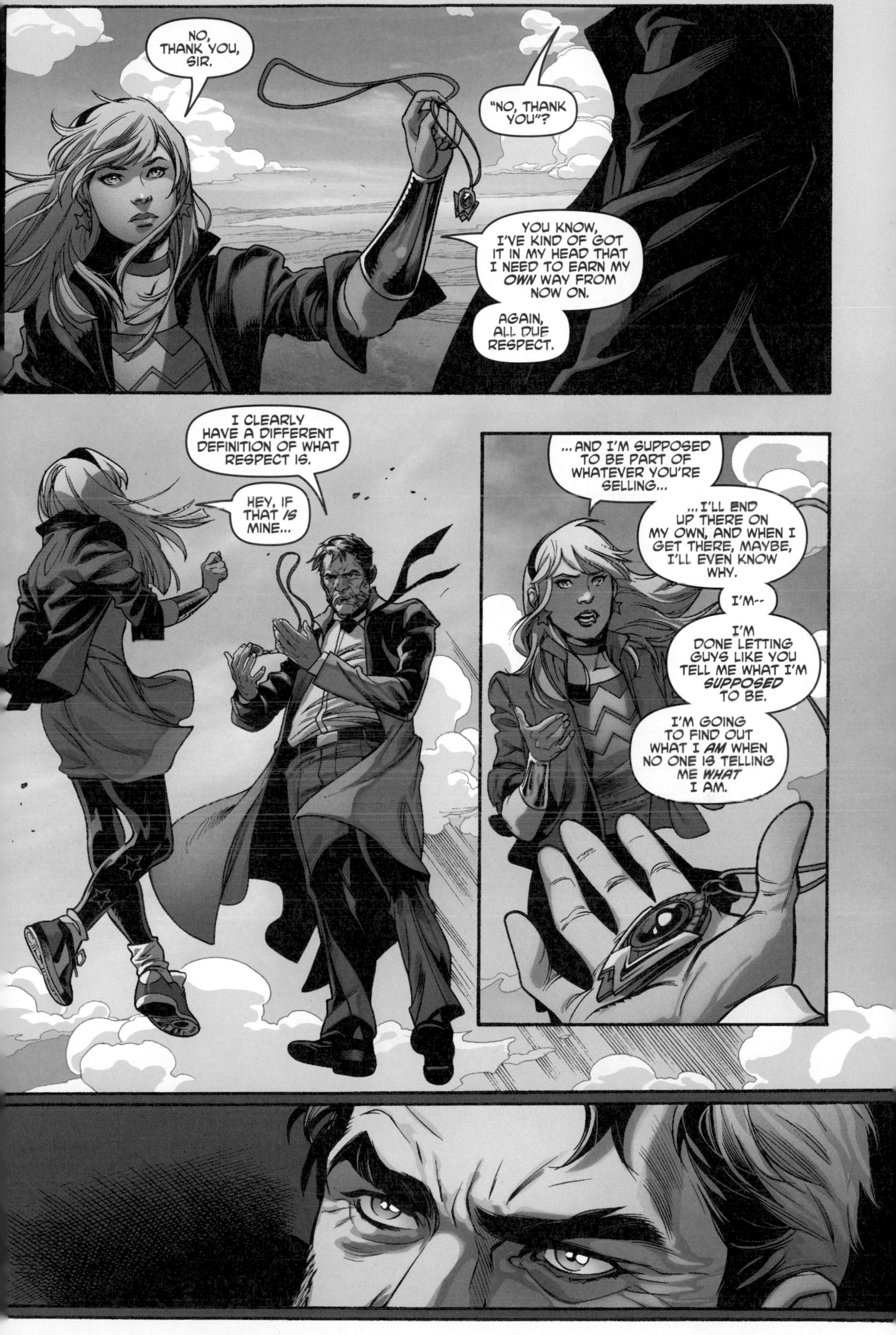
NO, THANK YOU, SIR.
"NO, THANK YOU"?
YOU KNOW, I'VE KIND OF GOT IT IN MY HEAD THAT I NEED TO EARN MY *OWN* WAY FROM NOW ON.
AGAIN, ALL DUE RESPECT.
I CLEARLY HAVE A DIFFERENT DEFINITION OF WHAT RESPECT IS.
HEY, IF THAT *IS* MINE...
...AND I'M SUPPOSED TO BE PART OF WHATEVER YOU'RE SELLING...
...I'LL END UP THERE ON MY OWN, AND WHEN I GET THERE, MAYBE, I'LL EVEN KNOW WHY.
I'M--
I'M DONE LETTING GUYS LIKE YOU TELL ME WHAT I'M *SUPPOSED* TO BE.
I'M GOING TO FIND OUT WHAT I *AM* WHEN NO ONE IS TELLING ME *WHAT* I AM.

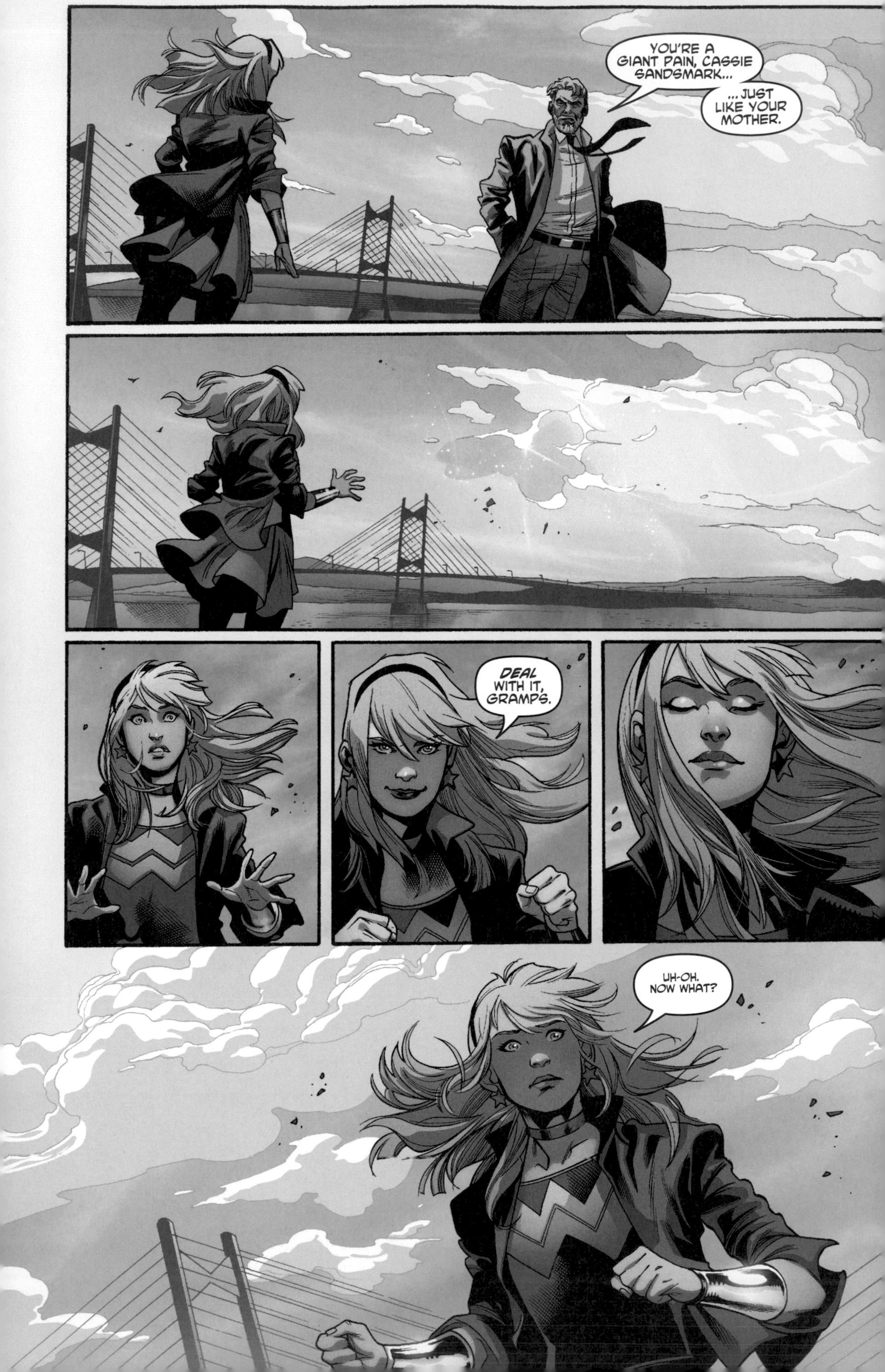
YOU'RE A GIANT PAIN, CASSIE SANDSMARK...
...JUST LIKE YOUR MOTHER.
DEAL WITH IT, GRAMPS.
UH-OH. NOW WHAT?

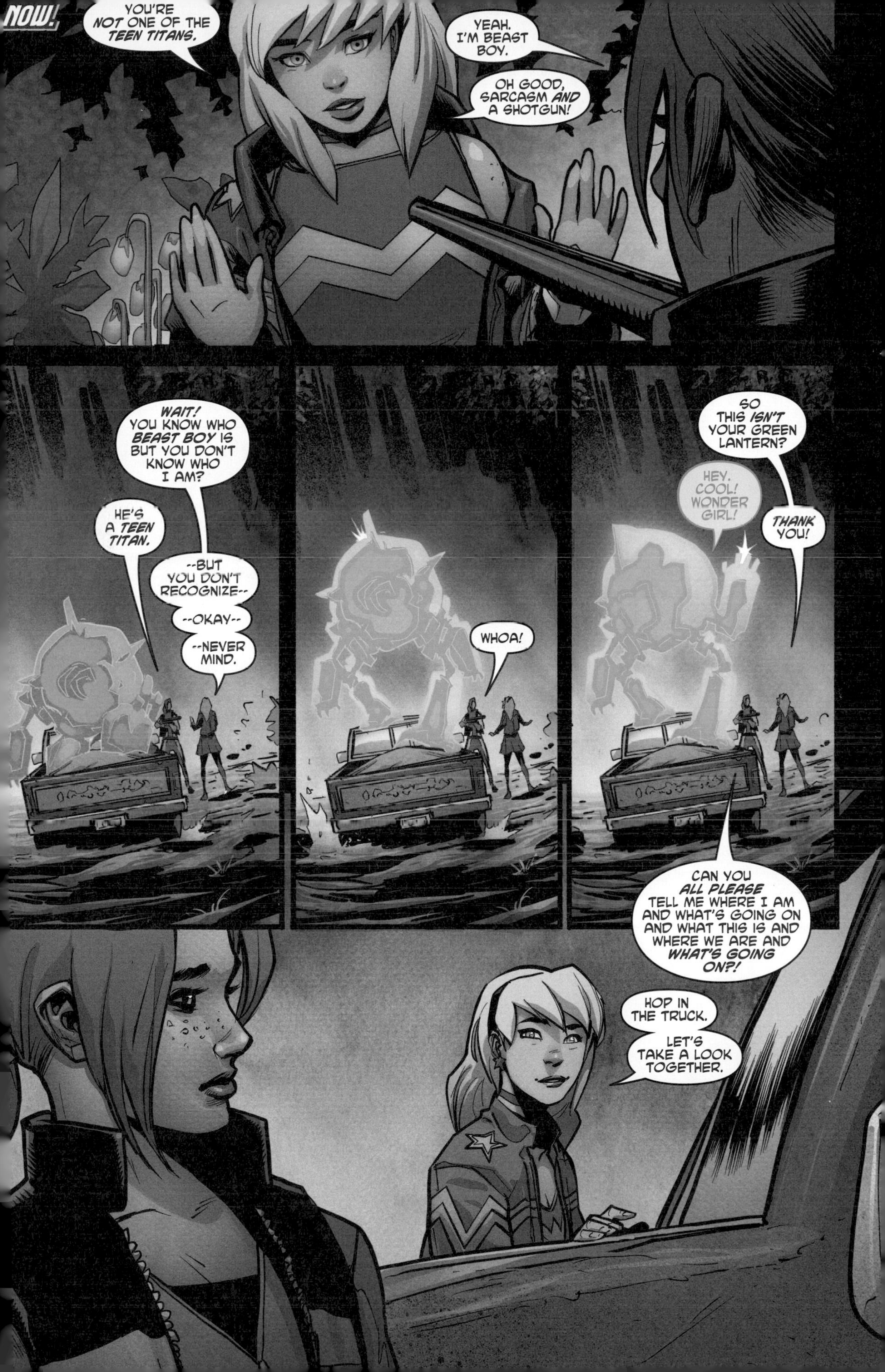
NOW!
YOU'RE NOT ONE OF THE TEEN TITANS.
YEAH. I'M BEAST BOY.
OH GOOD, SARCASM AND A SHOTGUN!
WAIT! YOU KNOW WHO BEAST BOY IS BUT YOU DON'T KNOW WHO I AM?
HE'S A TEEN TITAN.
--BUT YOU DON'T RECOGNIZE--
--OKAY--
--NEVER MIND.
WHOA!
SO THIS ISN'T YOUR GREEN LANTERN?
HEY. COOL! WONDER GIRL!
THANK YOU!
CAN YOU ALL PLEASE TELL ME WHERE I AM AND WHAT'S GOING ON AND WHAT THIS IS AND WHERE WE ARE AND WHAT'S GOING ON?!
HOP IN THE TRUCK.
LET'S TAKE A LOOK TOGETHER.

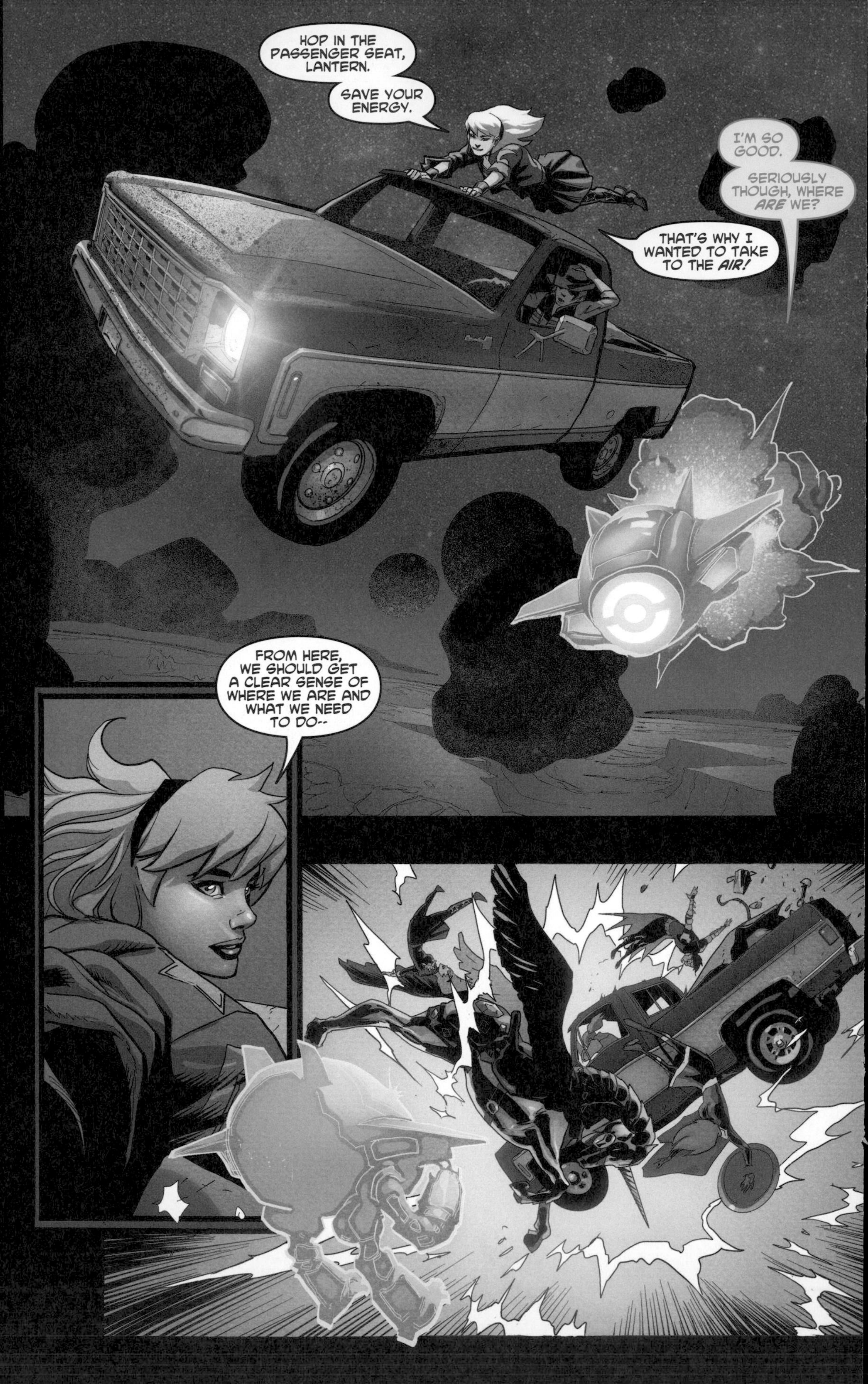
HOP IN THE PASSENGER SEAT, LANTERN.
SAVE YOUR ENERGY.
I'M SO GOOD.
SERIOUSLY THOUGH, WHERE ARE WE?
THAT'S WHY I WANTED TO TAKE TO THE AIR!
FROM HERE, WE SHOULD GET A CLEAR SENSE OF WHERE WE ARE AND WHAT WE NEED TO DO--

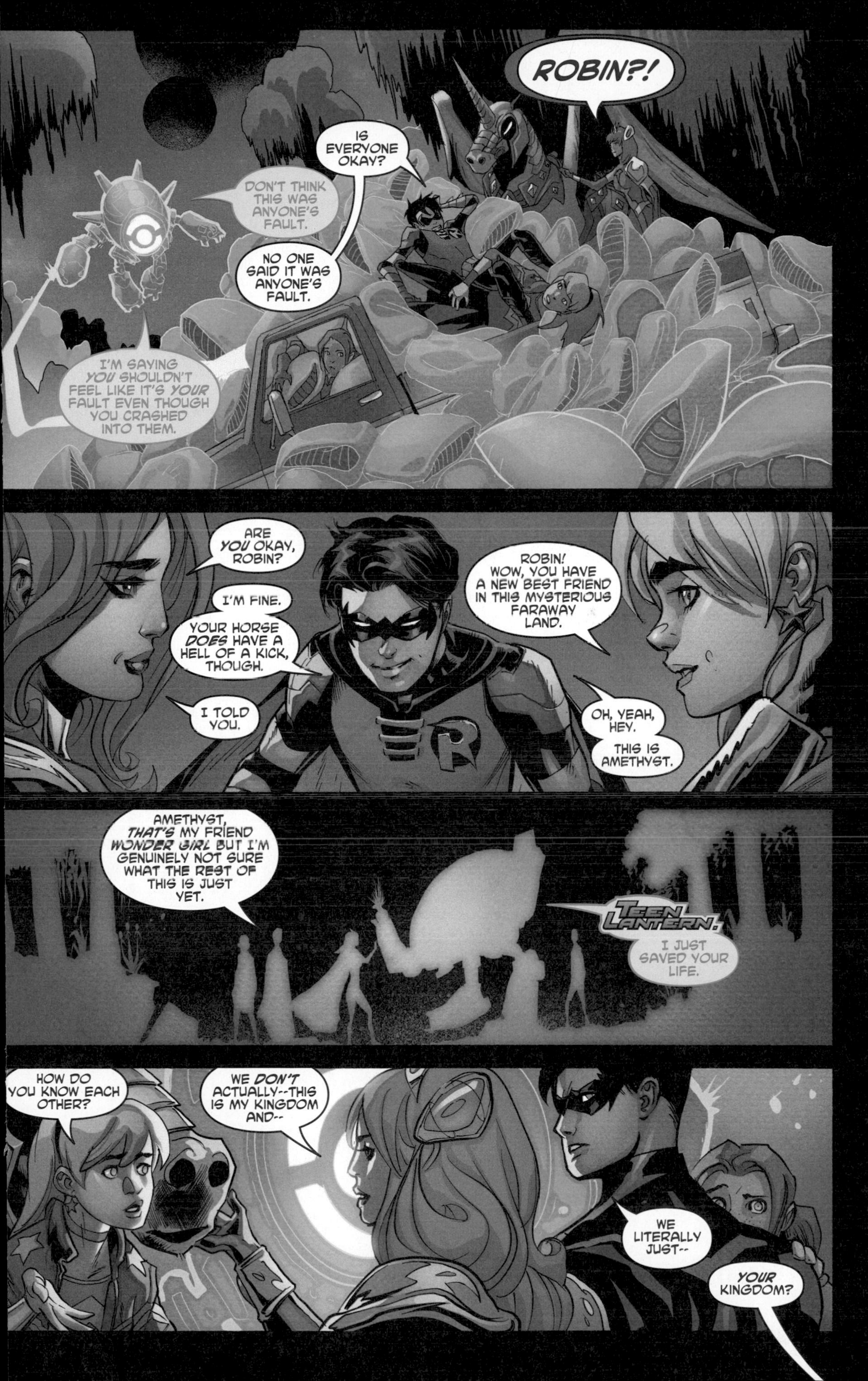
ROBIN?!
IS EVERYONE OKAY?
DON'T THINK THIS WAS ANYONE'S FAULT.
NO ONE SAID IT WAS ANYONE'S FAULT.
I'M SAYING *YOU* SHOULDN'T FEEL LIKE IT'S *YOUR* FAULT EVEN THOUGH YOU CRASHED INTO THEM.
ARE *YOU* OKAY, ROBIN?
I'M FINE.
YOUR HORSE *DOES* HAVE A HELL OF A KICK, THOUGH.
I TOLD YOU.
ROBIN! WOW, YOU HAVE A NEW BEST FRIEND IN THIS MYSTERIOUS FARAWAY LAND.
OH, YEAH, HEY.
THIS IS AMETHYST.
AMETHYST, *THAT'S* MY FRIEND *WONDER GIRL* BUT I'M GENUINELY NOT SURE WHAT THE REST OF THIS IS JUST YET.
TEEN LANTERN.
I JUST SAVED YOUR LIFE.
HOW DO YOU KNOW EACH OTHER?
WE *DON'T* ACTUALLY--THIS IS MY KINGDOM AND--
WE LITERALLY JUST--
YOUR KINGDOM?

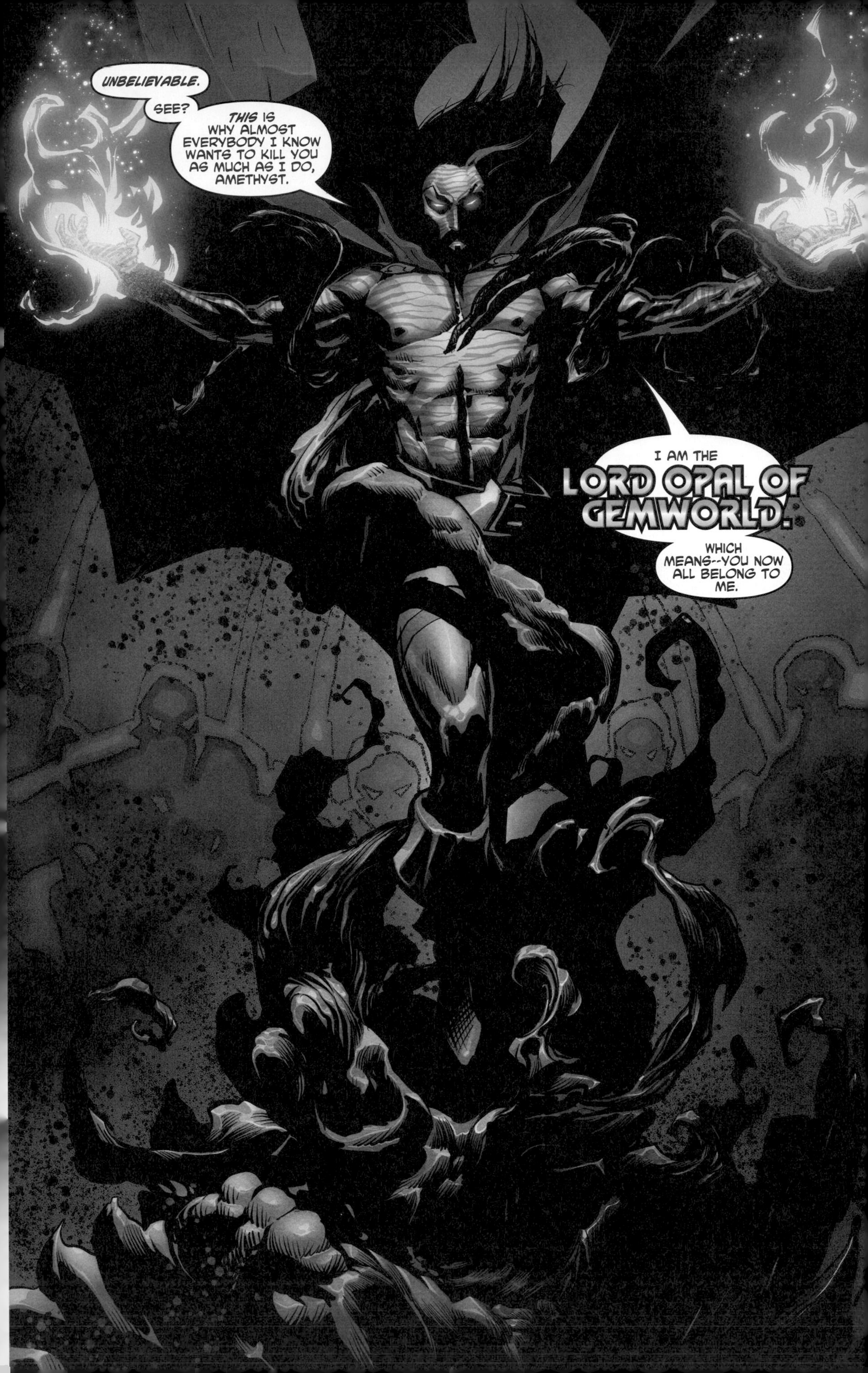
UNBELIEVABLE.
SEE?
THIS IS WHY ALMOST EVERYBODY I KNOW WANTS TO KILL YOU AS MUCH AS I DO, AMETHYST.
I AM THE LORD OPAL OF GEMWORLD.
WHICH MEANS--YOU NOW ALL BELONG TO ME.

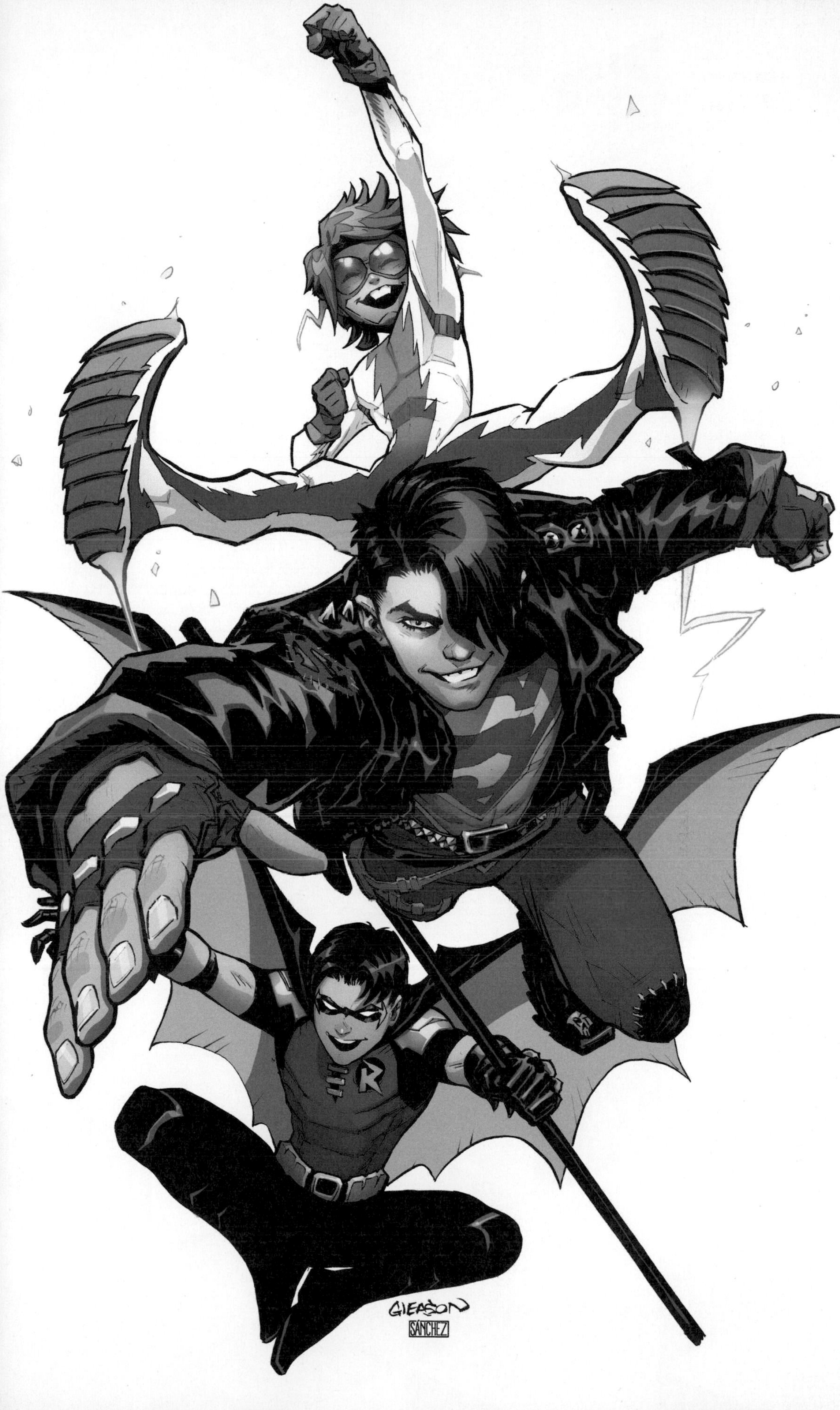
GLEASON
SÁNCHEZ

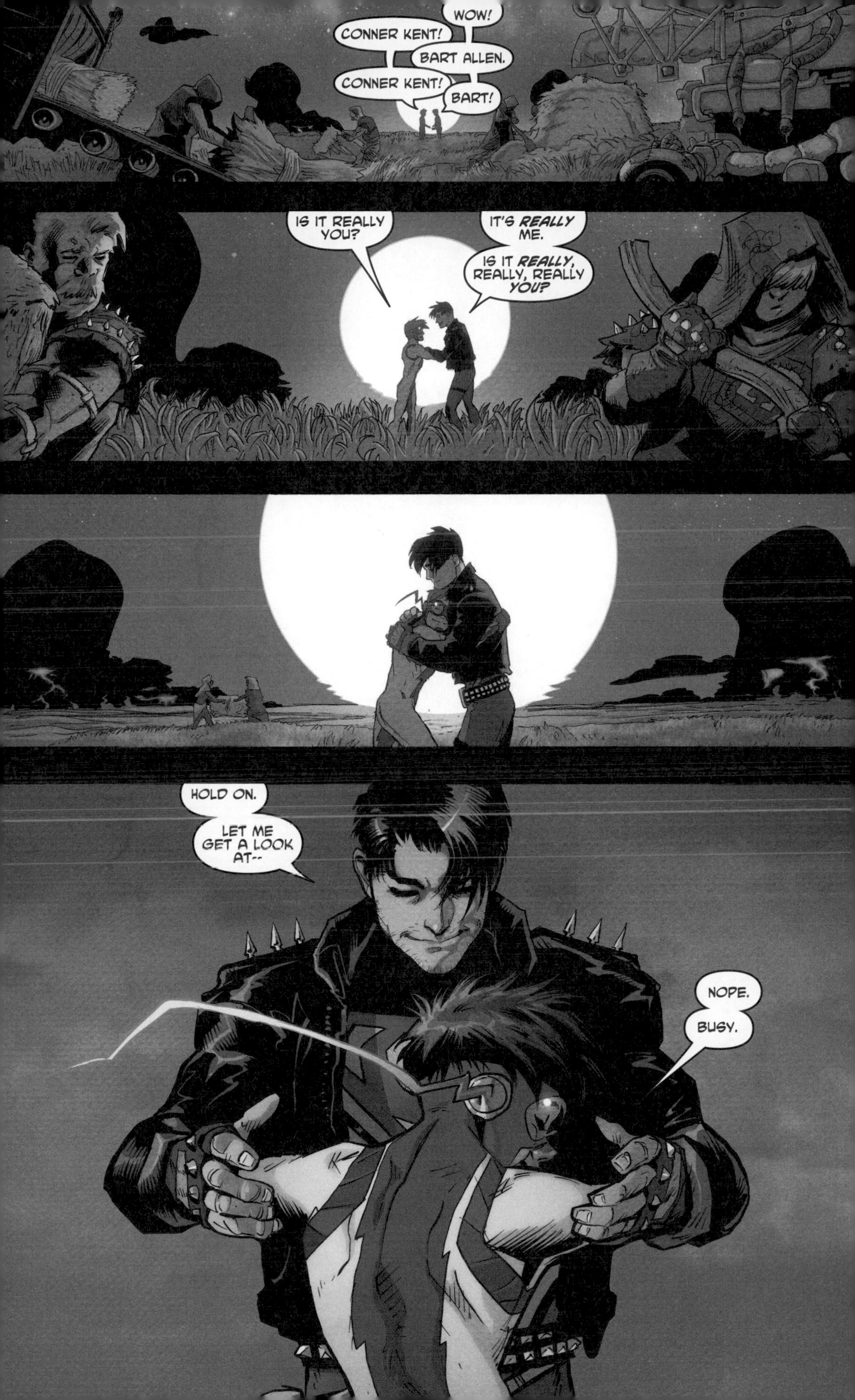
WOW!
CONNER KENT!
BART ALLEN.
CONNER KENT!
BART!
IS IT REALLY YOU?
IT'S *REALLY* ME.
IS IT *REALLY*, REALLY, REALLY *YOU?*
HOLD ON.
LET ME GET A LOOK AT--
NOPE.
BUSY.

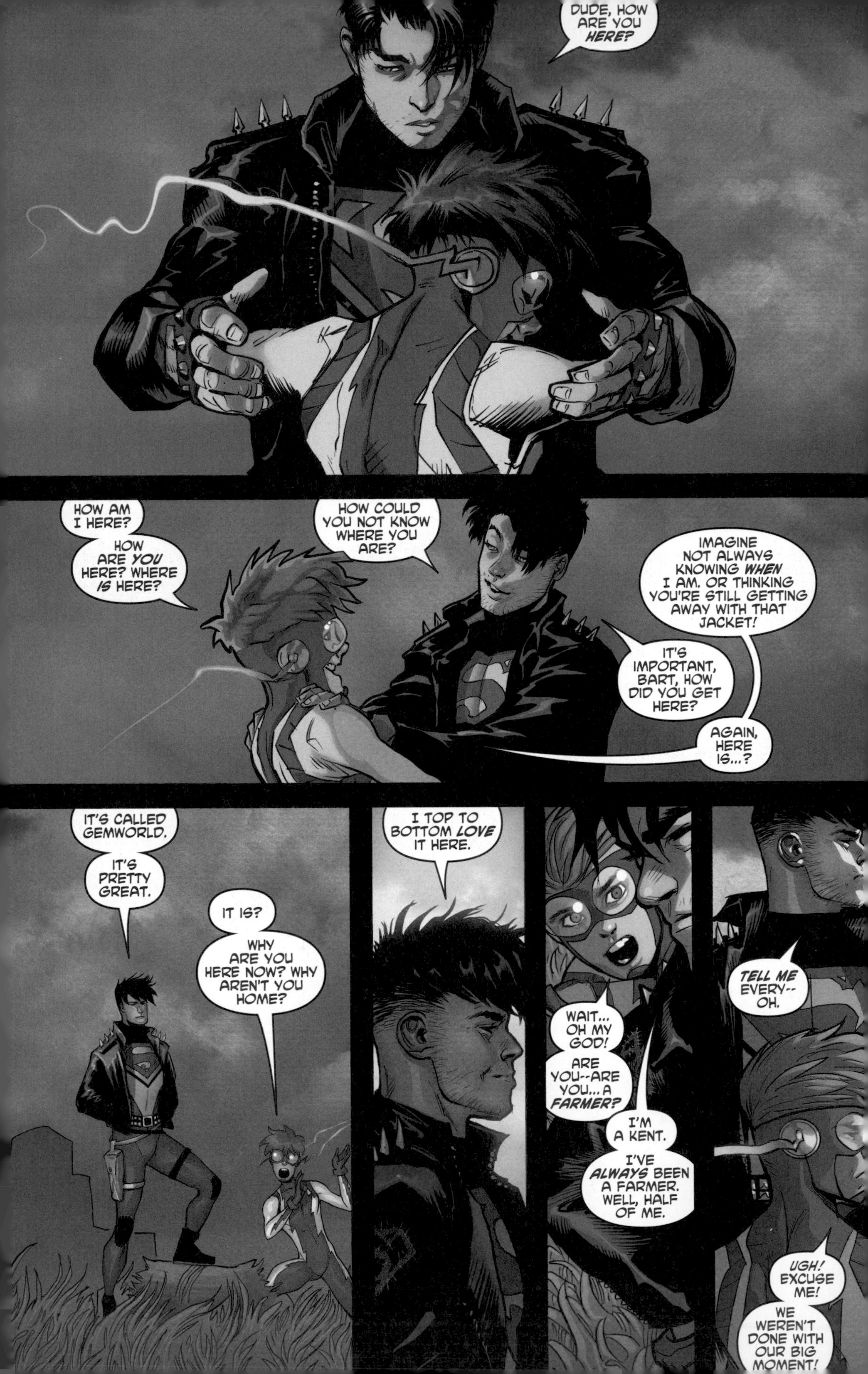
DUDE, HOW ARE YOU *HERE?*
HOW AM I HERE?
HOW ARE *YOU* HERE? WHERE *IS* HERE?
HOW COULD YOU NOT KNOW WHERE YOU ARE?
IMAGINE NOT ALWAYS KNOWING *WHEN* I AM. OR THINKING YOU'RE STILL GETTING AWAY WITH THAT JACKET!
IT'S IMPORTANT, BART, HOW DID YOU GET HERE?
AGAIN, HERE IS...?
IT'S CALLED GEMWORLD.
IT'S PRETTY GREAT.
IT IS?
WHY ARE YOU HERE NOW? WHY AREN'T YOU HOME?
I TOP TO BOTTOM *LOVE* IT HERE.
WAIT... OH MY GOD!
ARE YOU--ARE YOU... A *FARMER?*
I'M A KENT.
I'VE *ALWAYS* BEEN A FARMER. WELL, HALF OF ME.
TELL ME EVERY-- OH.
UGH! EXCUSE ME!
WE WEREN'T DONE WITH OUR BIG MOMENT!

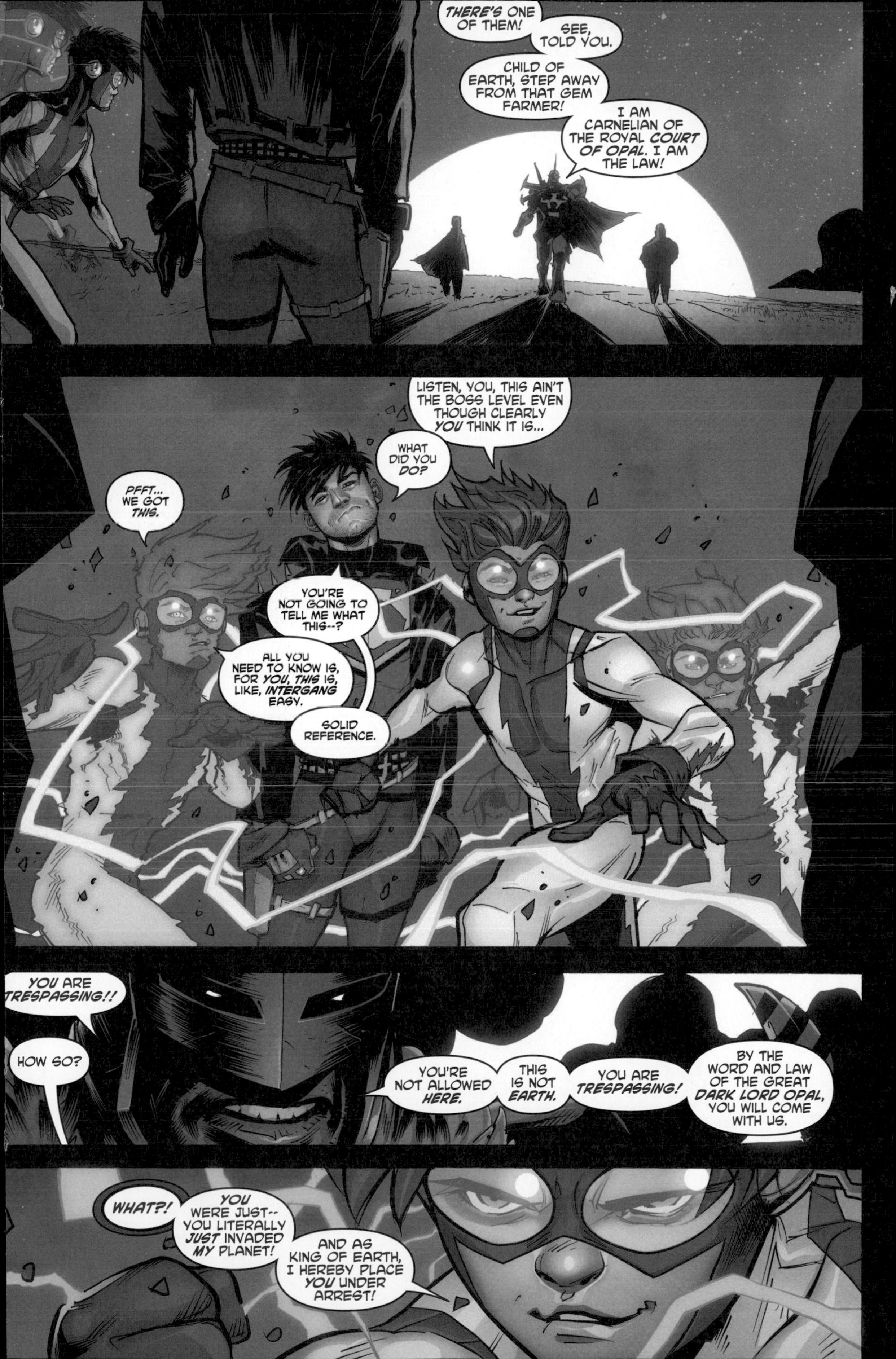
THERE'S ONE OF THEM!
SEE, TOLD YOU.
CHILD OF EARTH, STEP AWAY FROM THAT GEM FARMER!
I AM CARNELIAN OF THE ROYAL COURT OF OPAL. I AM THE LAW!
LISTEN, YOU, THIS AIN'T THE BOSS LEVEL EVEN THOUGH CLEARLY YOU THINK IT IS...
WHAT DID YOU DO?
PFFT... WE GOT THIS.
YOU'RE NOT GOING TO TELL ME WHAT THIS--?
ALL YOU NEED TO KNOW IS, FOR YOU, THIS IS, LIKE, INTERGANG EASY.
SOLID REFERENCE.
YOU ARE TRESPASSING!!
HOW SO?
YOU'RE NOT ALLOWED HERE.
THIS IS NOT EARTH.
YOU ARE TRESPASSING!
BY THE WORD AND LAW OF THE GREAT DARK LORD OPAL, YOU WILL COME WITH US.
WHAT?!
YOU WERE JUST-- YOU LITERALLY JUST INVADED MY PLANET!
AND AS KING OF EARTH, I HEREBY PLACE YOU UNDER ARREST!

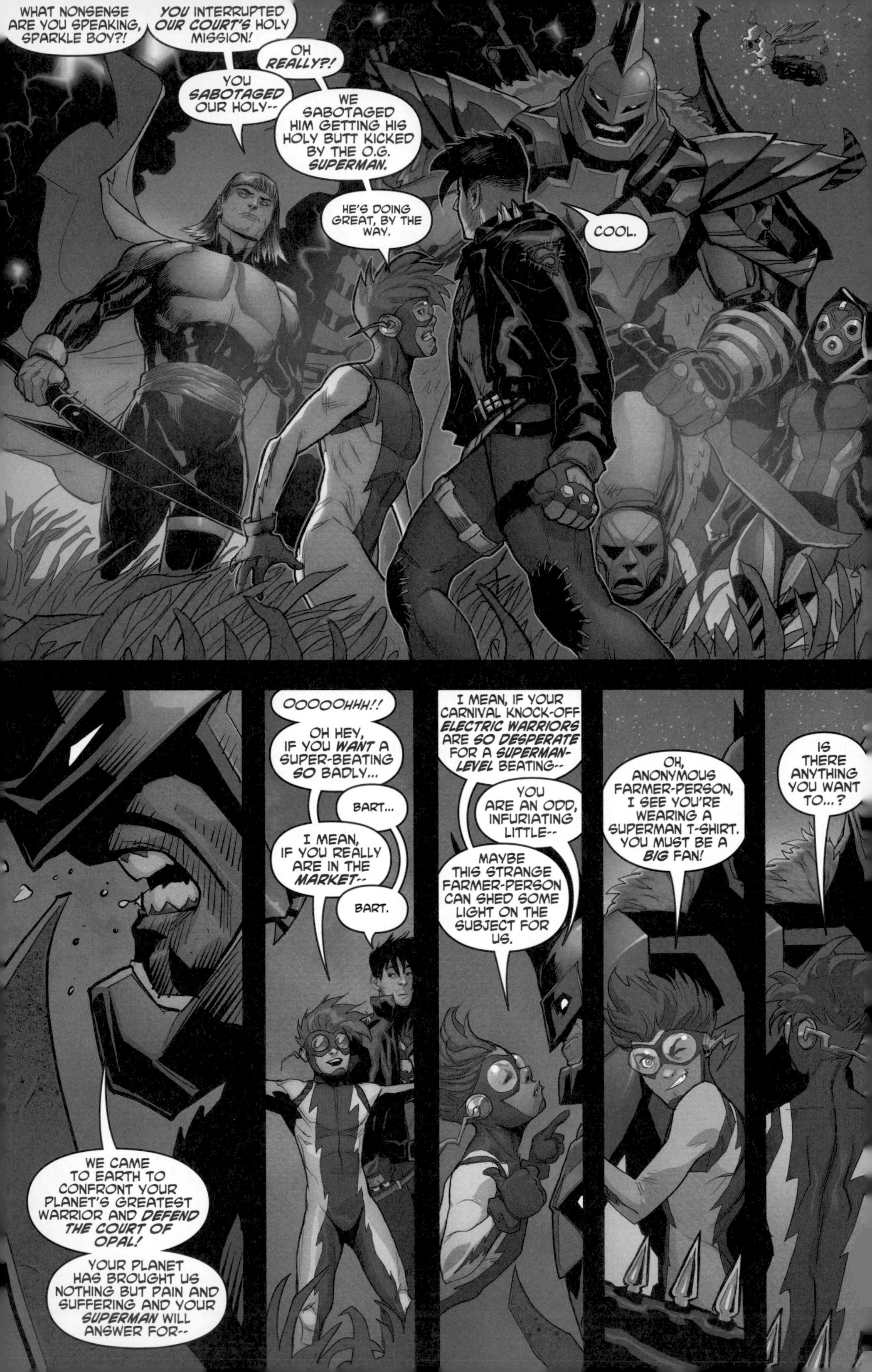
WHAT NONSENSE ARE YOU SPEAKING, SPARKLE BOY?!
YOU INTERRUPTED OUR COURT'S HOLY MISSION!
YOU SABOTAGED OUR HOLY--
OH REALLY?!
WE SABOTAGED HIM GETTING HIS HOLY BUTT KICKED BY THE O.G. SUPERMAN.
HE'S DOING GREAT, BY THE WAY.
COOL.
WE CAME TO EARTH TO CONFRONT YOUR PLANET'S GREATEST WARRIOR AND DEFEND THE COURT OF OPAL!
YOUR PLANET HAS BROUGHT US NOTHING BUT PAIN AND SUFFERING AND YOUR SUPERMAN WILL ANSWER FOR--
OOOOOHHH!!
OH HEY, IF YOU WANT A SUPER-BEATING SO BADLY...
BART...
I MEAN, IF YOU REALLY ARE IN THE MARKET--
BART.
I MEAN, IF YOUR CARNIVAL KNOCK-OFF ELECTRIC WARRIORS ARE SO DESPERATE FOR A SUPERMAN-LEVEL BEATING--
YOU ARE AN ODD, INFURIATING LITTLE--
MAYBE THIS STRANGE FARMER-PERSON CAN SHED SOME LIGHT ON THE SUBJECT FOR US.
OH, ANONYMOUS FARMER-PERSON, I SEE YOU'RE WEARING A SUPERMAN T-SHIRT. YOU MUST BE A BIG FAN!
IS THERE ANYTHING YOU WANT TO...?

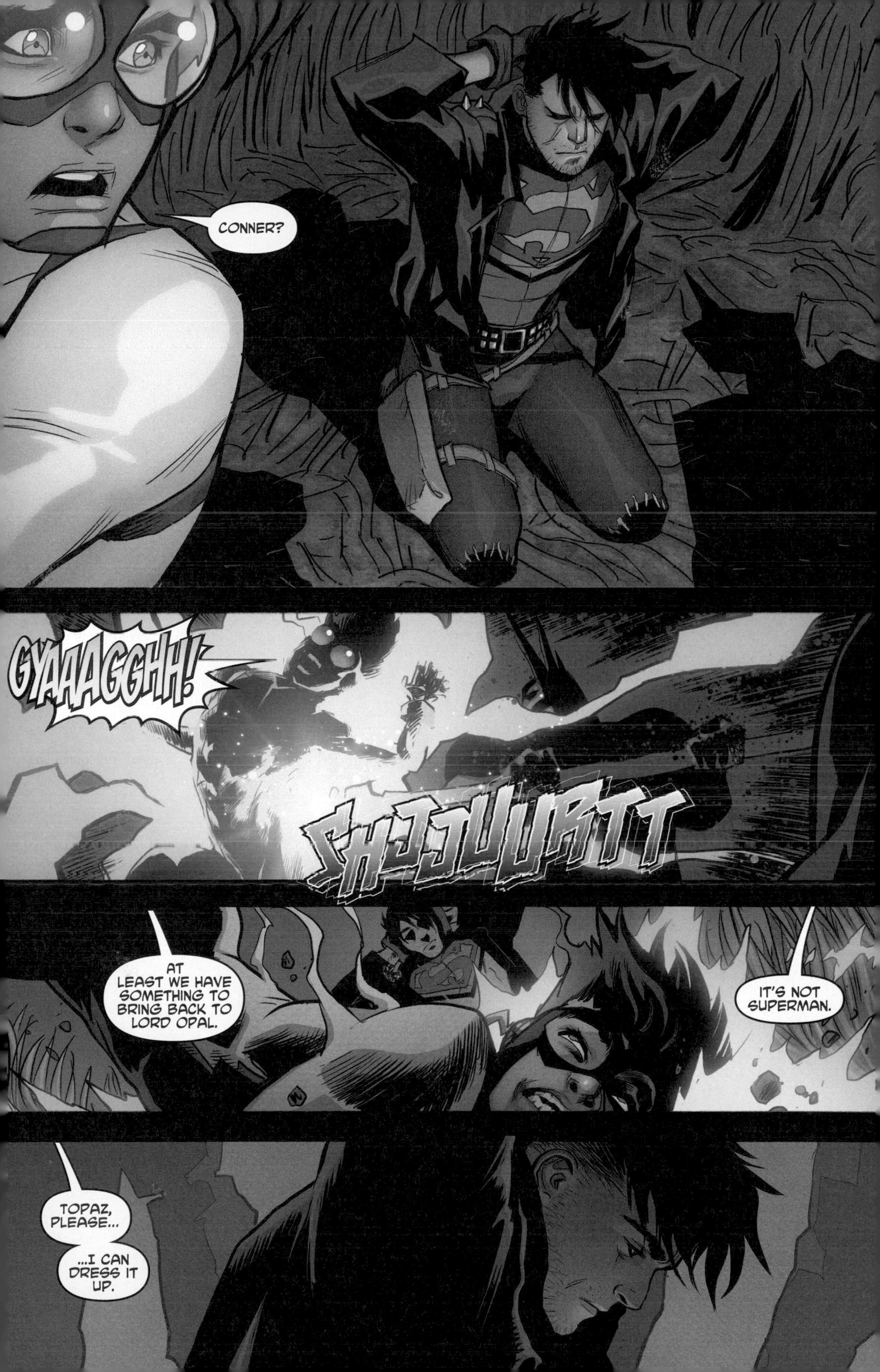
CONNER?
GYAAAGGHH!
SHJJUURTT
AT LEAST WE HAVE SOMETHING TO BRING BACK TO LORD OPAL.
IT'S NOT SUPERMAN.
TOPAZ, PLEASE...
...I CAN DRESS IT UP.

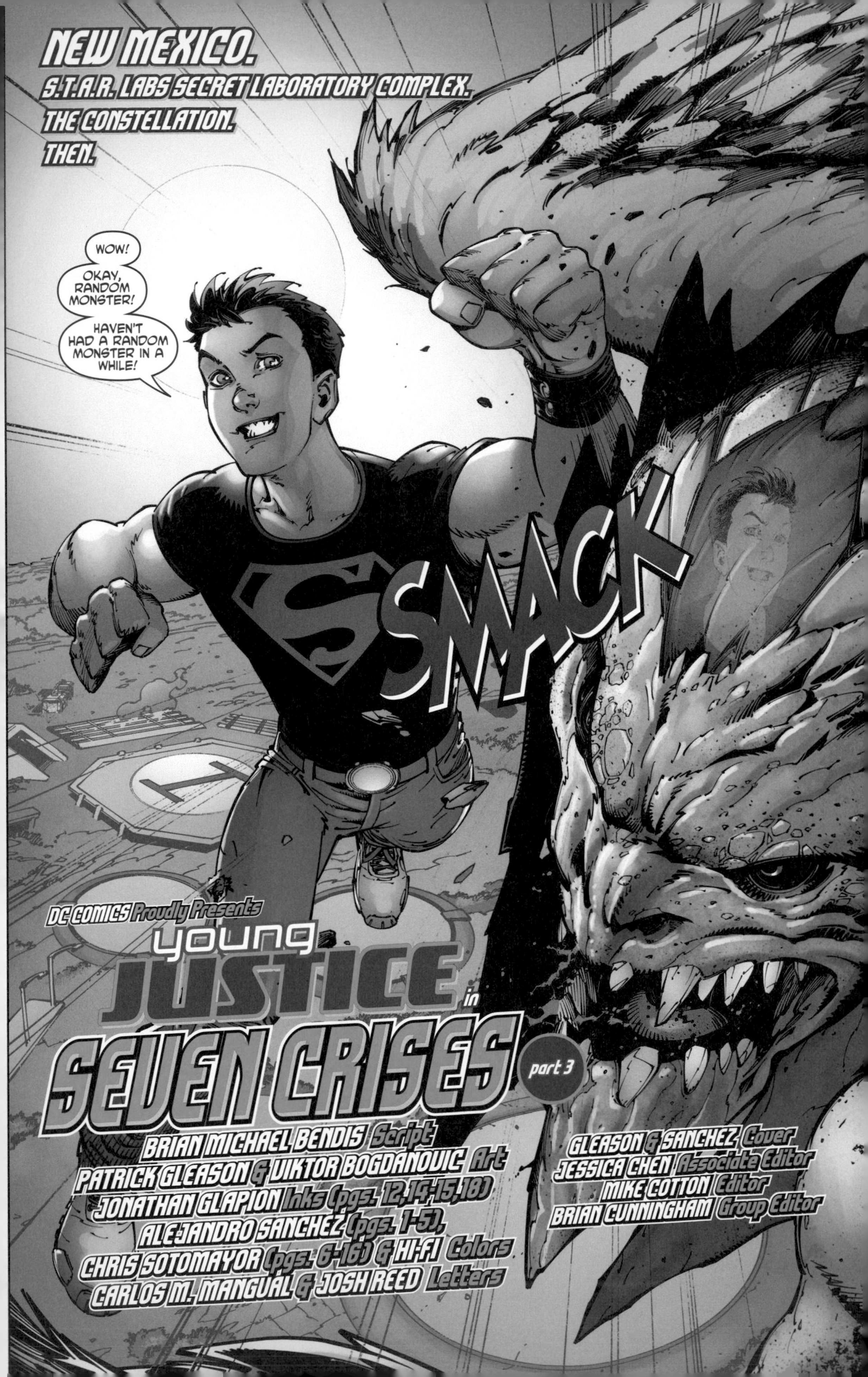
NEW MEXICO.
S.T.A.R. LABS SECRET LABORATORY COMPLEX.
THE CONSTELLATION.
THEN.
WOW!
OKAY, RANDOM MONSTER!
HAVEN'T HAD A RANDOM MONSTER IN A WHILE!
SMACK
DC COMICS Proudly Presents
YOUNG JUSTICE in
SEVEN CRISES part 3
BRIAN MICHAEL BENDIS Script
PATRICK GLEASON & VIKTOR BOGDANOVIC Art
JONATHAN GLAPION Inks (pgs. 12,14-15,18)
ALEJANDRO SANCHEZ (pgs. 1-5),
CHRIS SOTOMAYOR (pgs. 6-16) & HI-FI Colors
CARLOS M. MANGUAL & JOSH REED Letters
GLEASON & SANCHEZ Cover
JESSICA CHEN Associate Editor
MIKE COTTON Editor
BRIAN CUNNINGHAM Group Editor

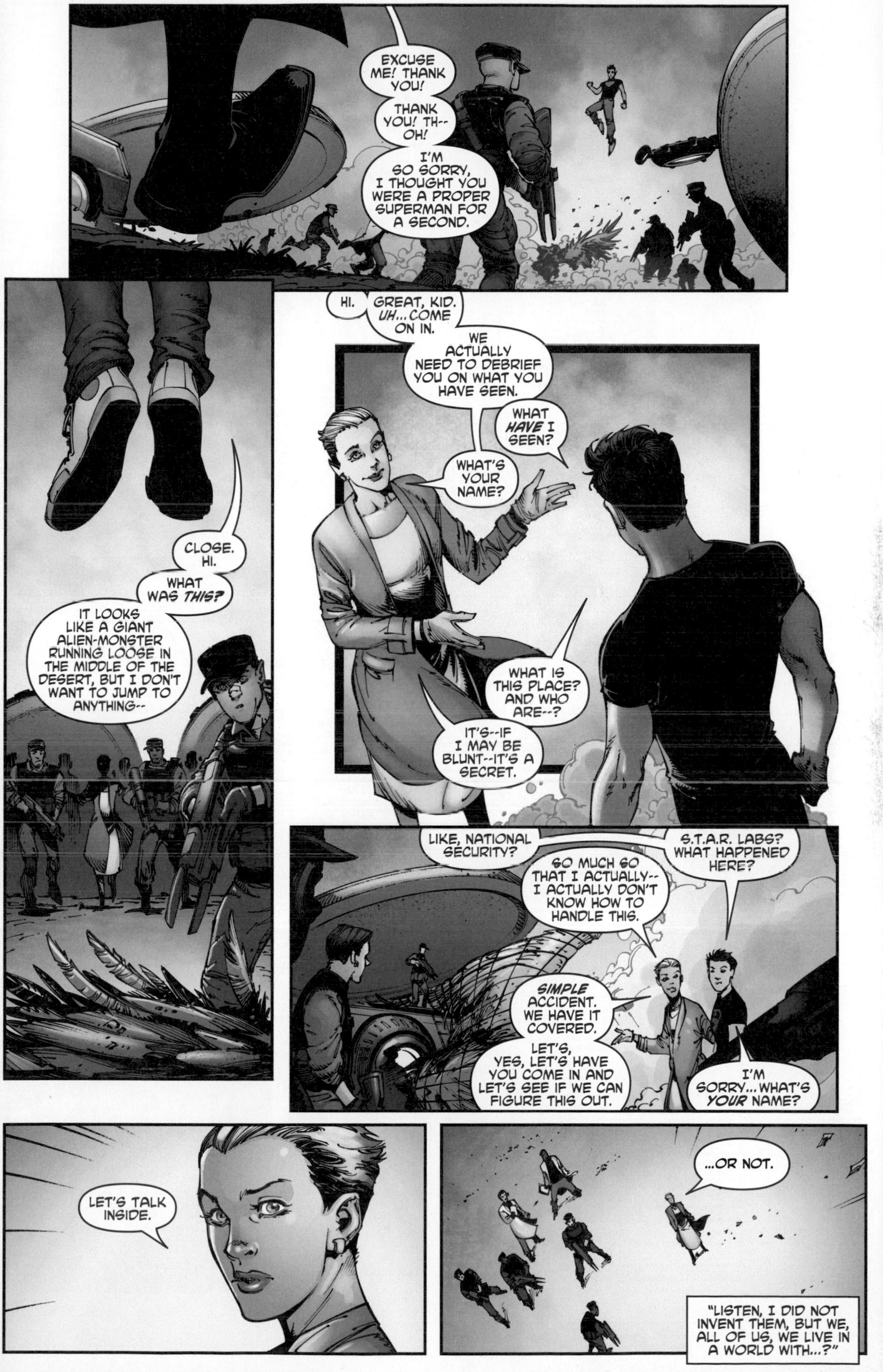
EXCUSE ME! THANK YOU!
THANK YOU! TH-- OH!
I'M SO SORRY, I THOUGHT YOU WERE A PROPER SUPERMAN FOR A SECOND.
CLOSE. HI.
WHAT WAS *THIS?*
IT LOOKS LIKE A GIANT ALIEN-MONSTER RUNNING LOOSE IN THE MIDDLE OF THE DESERT, BUT I DON'T WANT TO JUMP TO ANYTHING--
HI.
GREAT, KID. *UH*... COME ON IN.
WE ACTUALLY NEED TO DEBRIEF YOU ON WHAT YOU HAVE SEEN.
WHAT *HAVE* I SEEN?
WHAT'S YOUR NAME?
WHAT IS THIS PLACE? AND WHO ARE--?
IT'S--IF I MAY BE BLUNT--IT'S A SECRET.
LIKE, NATIONAL SECURITY?
SO MUCH SO THAT I ACTUALLY-- I ACTUALLY DON'T KNOW HOW TO HANDLE THIS.
S.T.A.R. LABS? WHAT HAPPENED HERE?
SIMPLE ACCIDENT. WE HAVE IT COVERED.
LET'S, YES, LET'S HAVE YOU COME IN AND LET'S SEE IF WE CAN FIGURE THIS OUT.
I'M SORRY... WHAT'S *YOUR* NAME?
LET'S TALK INSIDE.
...OR NOT.
"LISTEN, I DID NOT INVENT THEM, BUT WE, ALL OF US, WE LIVE IN A WORLD WITH...?"

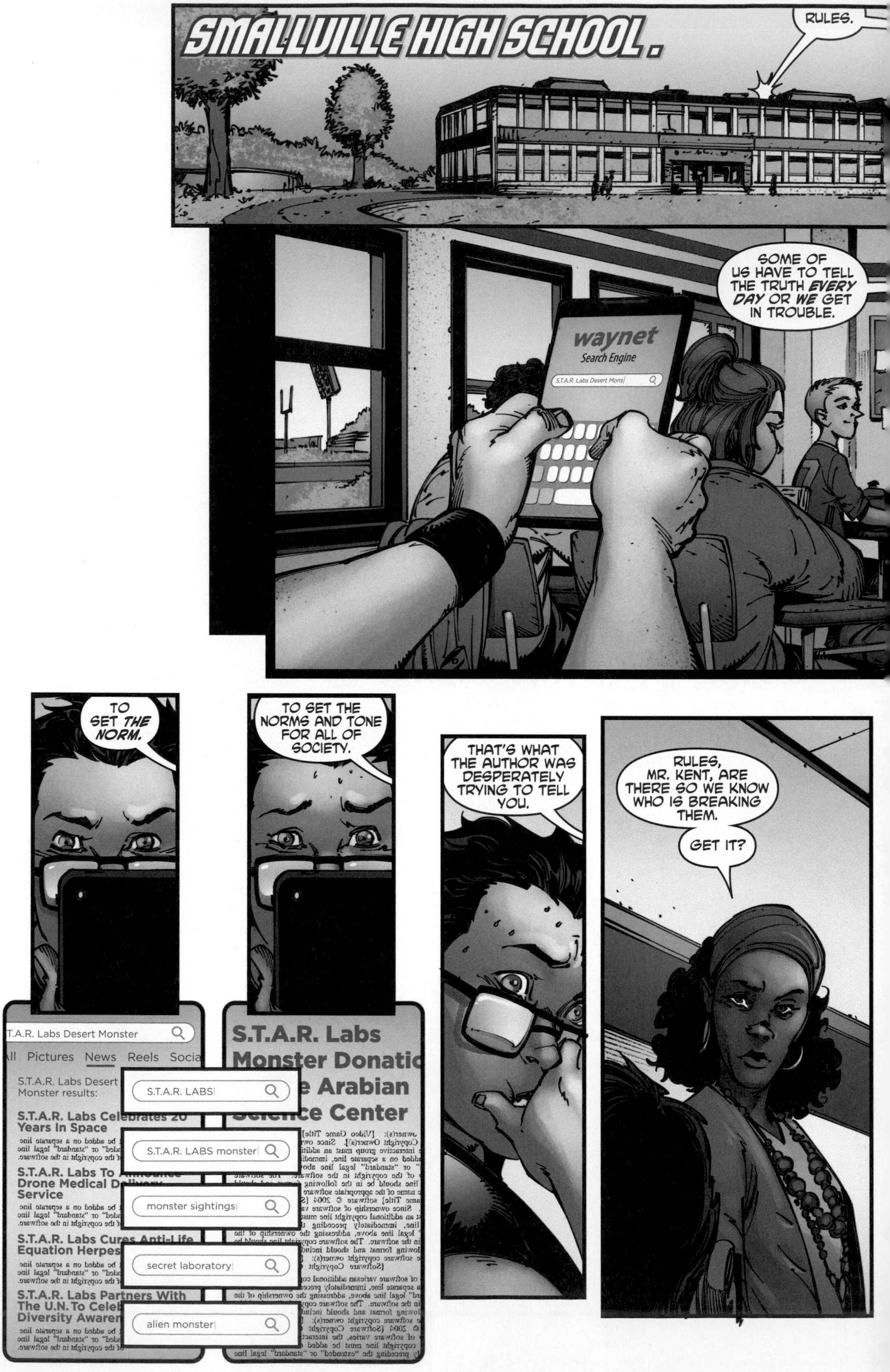
SMALLVILLE HIGH SCHOOL.
RULES.
SOME OF US HAVE TO TELL THE TRUTH EVERY DAY OR WE GET IN TROUBLE.
waynet
Search Engine
S.T.A.R. Labs Desert Mons
TO SET THE NORM.
TO SET THE NORMS AND TONE FOR ALL OF SOCIETY.
THAT'S WHAT THE AUTHOR WAS DESPERATELY TRYING TO TELL YOU.
RULES, MR. KENT, ARE THERE SO WE KNOW WHO IS BREAKING THEM.
GET IT?
S.T.A.R. Labs Desert Monster
Pictures News Reels
S.T.A.R. Labs Desert Monster results:
S.T.A.R. Labs
S.T.A.R. LABS
S.T.A.R. LABS monster
monster sightings
secret laboratory
alien monster

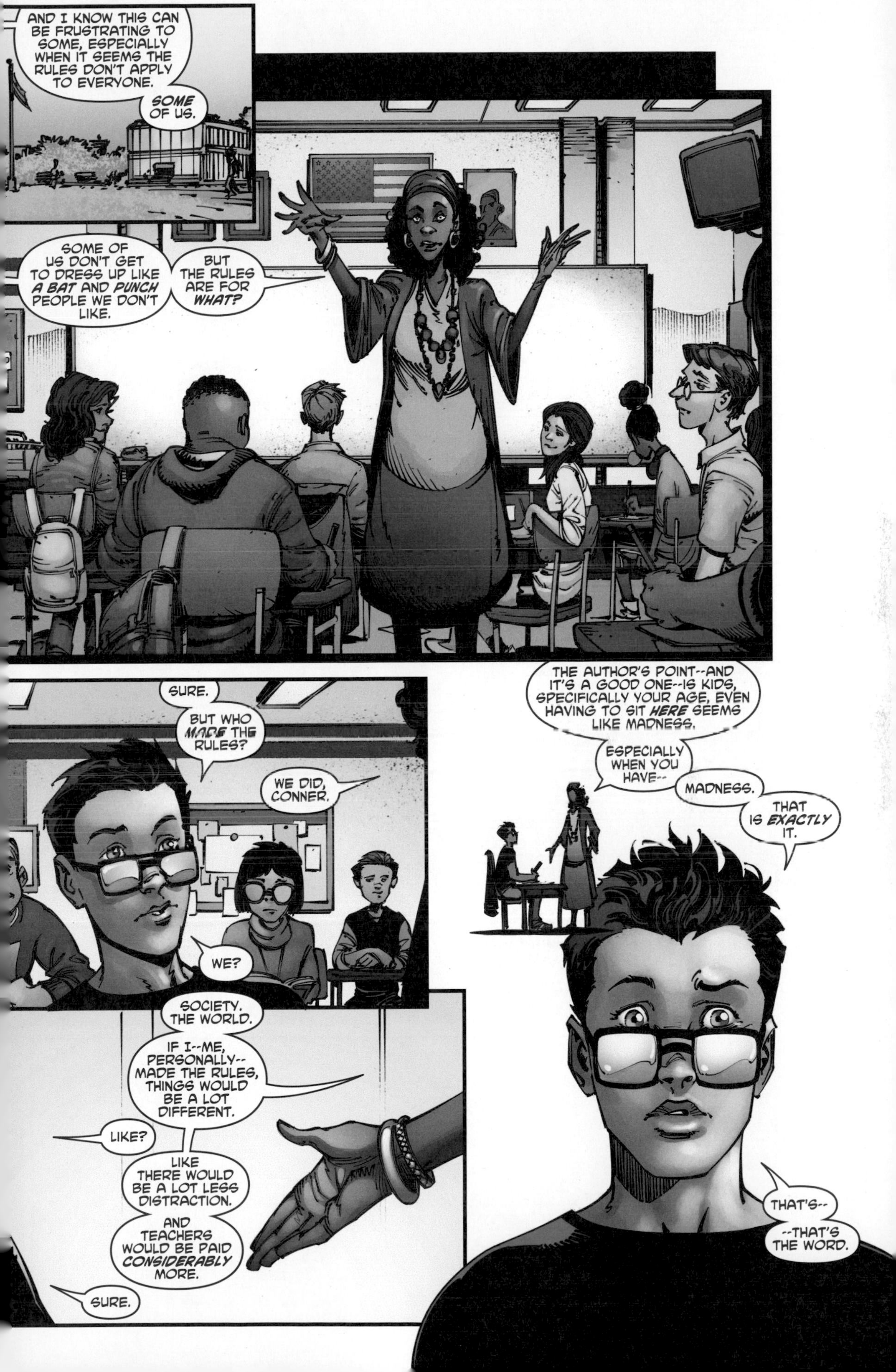
AND I KNOW THIS CAN BE FRUSTRATING TO SOME, ESPECIALLY WHEN IT SEEMS THE RULES DON'T APPLY TO EVERYONE.
SOME OF US.
SOME OF US DON'T GET TO DRESS UP LIKE A BAT AND PUNCH PEOPLE WE DON'T LIKE.
BUT THE RULES ARE FOR WHAT?
SURE.
BUT WHO MADE THE RULES?
WE DID, CONNER.
WE?
SOCIETY. THE WORLD.
IF I--ME, PERSONALLY--MADE THE RULES, THINGS WOULD BE A LOT DIFFERENT.
LIKE?
LIKE THERE WOULD BE A LOT LESS DISTRACTION.
AND TEACHERS WOULD BE PAID CONSIDERABLY MORE.
SURE.
THE AUTHOR'S POINT--AND IT'S A GOOD ONE--IS KIDS, SPECIFICALLY YOUR AGE, EVEN HAVING TO SIT HERE SEEMS LIKE MADNESS.
ESPECIALLY WHEN YOU HAVE--
MADNESS.
THAT IS EXACTLY IT.
THAT'S--
--THAT'S THE WORD.

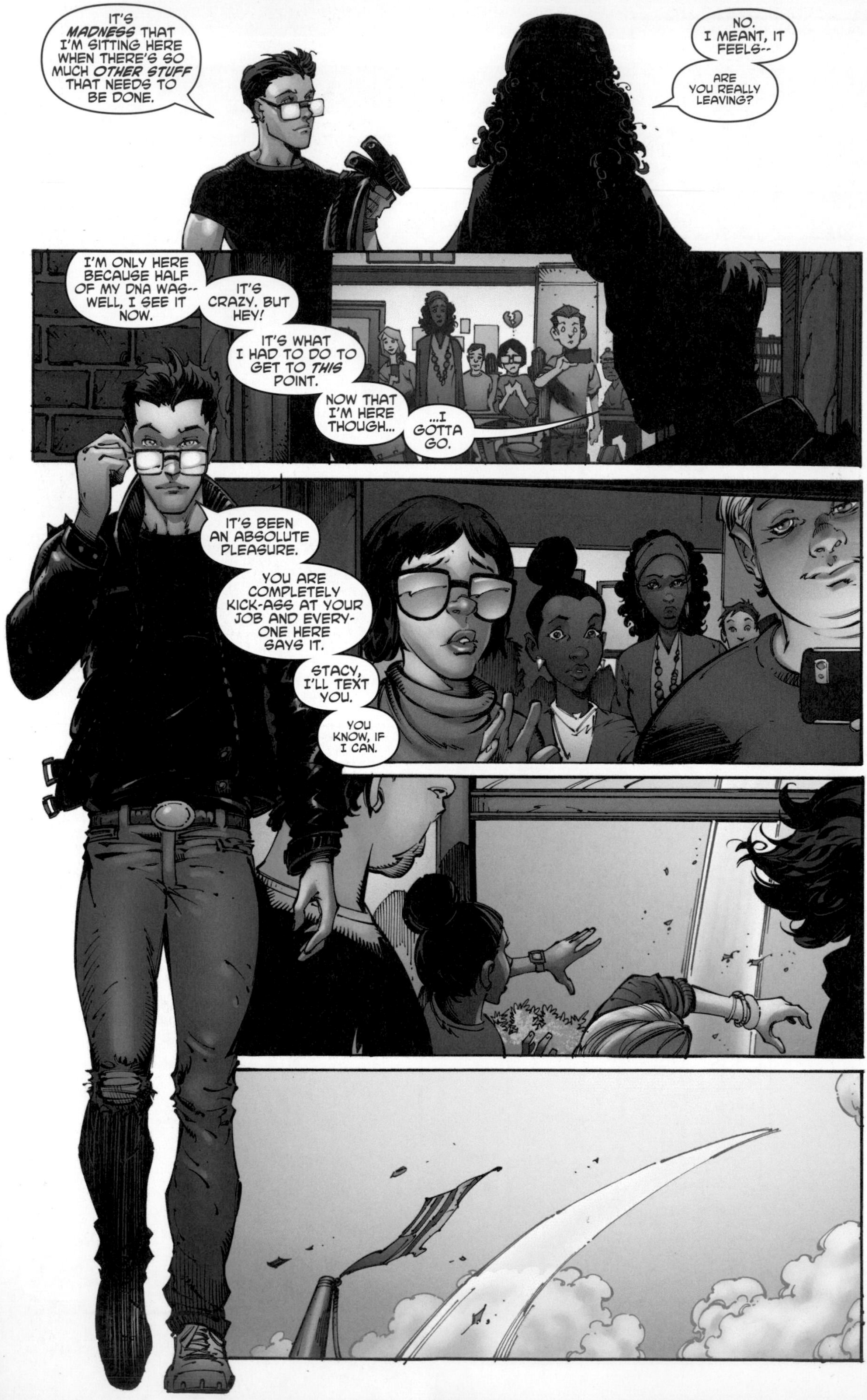
IT'S MADNESS THAT I'M SITTING HERE WHEN THERE'S SO MUCH OTHER STUFF THAT NEEDS TO BE DONE.
NO. I MEANT, IT FEELS--
ARE YOU REALLY LEAVING?
I'M ONLY HERE BECAUSE HALF OF MY DNA WAS-- WELL, I SEE IT NOW.
IT'S CRAZY. BUT HEY!
IT'S WHAT I HAD TO DO TO GET TO THIS POINT.
NOW THAT I'M HERE THOUGH...
...I GOTTA GO.
IT'S BEEN AN ABSOLUTE PLEASURE.
YOU ARE COMPLETELY KICK-ASS AT YOUR JOB AND EVERY-ONE HERE SAYS IT.
STACY, I'LL TEXT YOU.
YOU KNOW, IF I CAN.

I'M SORRY, DR. GLORY.

NOBODY WANTS TO TOUCH THE CREATURE WITH THEIR BARE HANDS *OR* WITH THE GLOVES!

THAT SUPERBOY PERSON TOUCHED IT WITH *HIS* BARE HANDS!

WELL, DR. GLORY, THAT WAS A SUPER-PERSON. WE ARE NOT--

YOU'RE BACK. LOVELY.

SO, YEAH, I WAS SITTING IN CLASS--

HIGH SCHOOL OR COLLEGE?

OH, HIGH SCHOOL.

HUH.

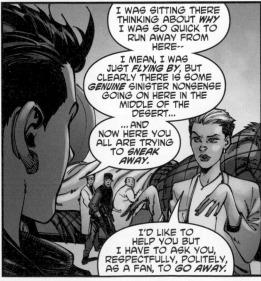

I WAS SITTING THERE THINKING ABOUT *WHY* I WAS SO QUICK TO RUN AWAY FROM HERE--

I MEAN, I WAS JUST *FLYING BY*, BUT CLEARLY THERE IS SOME *GENUINE* SINISTER NONSENSE GOING ON HERE IN THE MIDDLE OF THE DESERT...

...AND NOW HERE YOU ALL ARE TRYING TO *SNEAK AWAY.*

I'D LIKE TO HELP YOU BUT I HAVE TO ASK YOU, RESPECTFULLY, POLITELY, AS A FAN, TO *GO AWAY.*

THIS IS PRIVATE PROPERTY, *SUPERBOY.*

YOU NEED TO RESPECT THE LAWS OF THE LAND AND MOVE ALONG.

OH! WOW.

YOU HIT ME WITH *THAT ONE* ON THE WRONG DAY.

WHAT COULD THAT POSSIBLY MEAN?

IT *JUST* SO HAPPENS THAT *TODAY* WAS THE DAY I DECIDED I DON'T CARE ABOUT ALL THE RULES.

LET ME DEMONSTRATE...

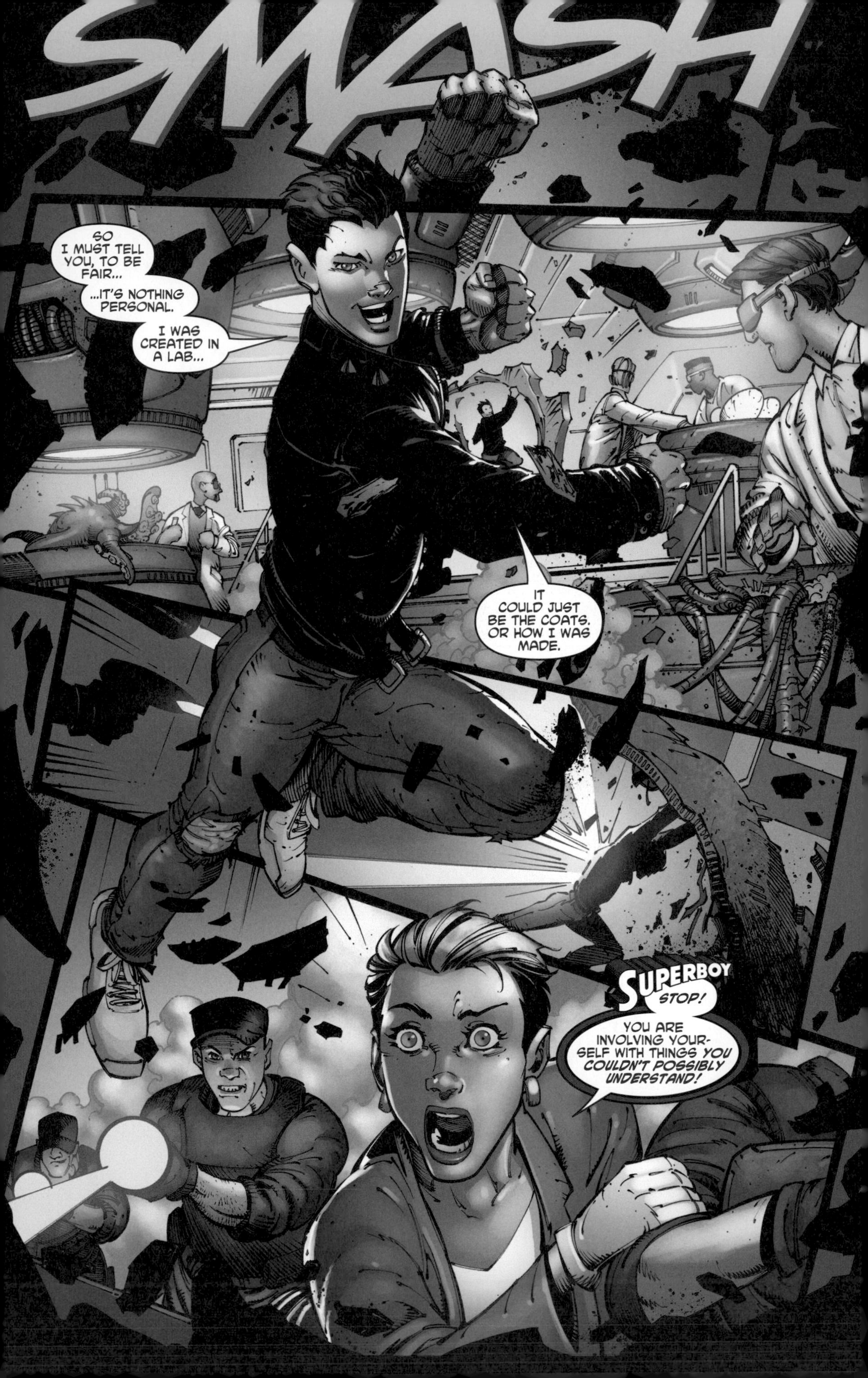
SMASH
SO I MUST TELL YOU, TO BE FAIR...
...IT'S NOTHING PERSONAL.
I WAS CREATED IN A LAB...
IT COULD JUST BE THE COATS. OR HOW I WAS MADE.
SUPERBOY STOP!
YOU ARE INVOLVING YOURSELF WITH THINGS YOU COULDN'T POSSIBLY UNDERSTAND!

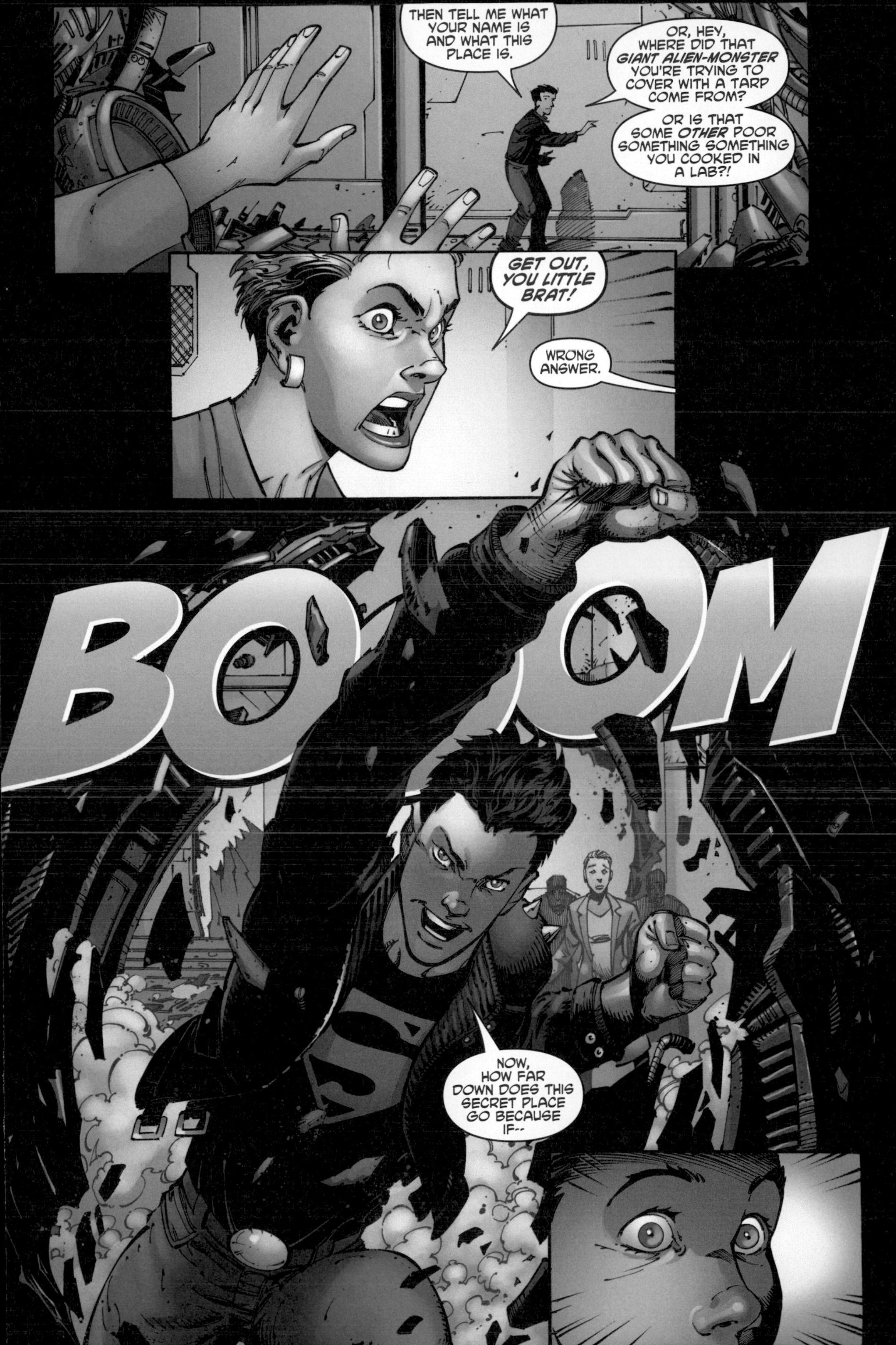
THEN TELL ME WHAT YOUR NAME IS AND WHAT THIS PLACE IS.
OR, HEY, WHERE DID THAT GIANT ALIEN-MONSTER YOU'RE TRYING TO COVER WITH A TARP COME FROM?
OR IS THAT SOME OTHER POOR SOMETHING SOMETHING YOU COOKED IN A LAB?!
GET OUT, YOU LITTLE BRAT!
WRONG ANSWER.
BOOOM
NOW, HOW FAR DOWN DOES THIS SECRET PLACE GO BECAUSE IF--

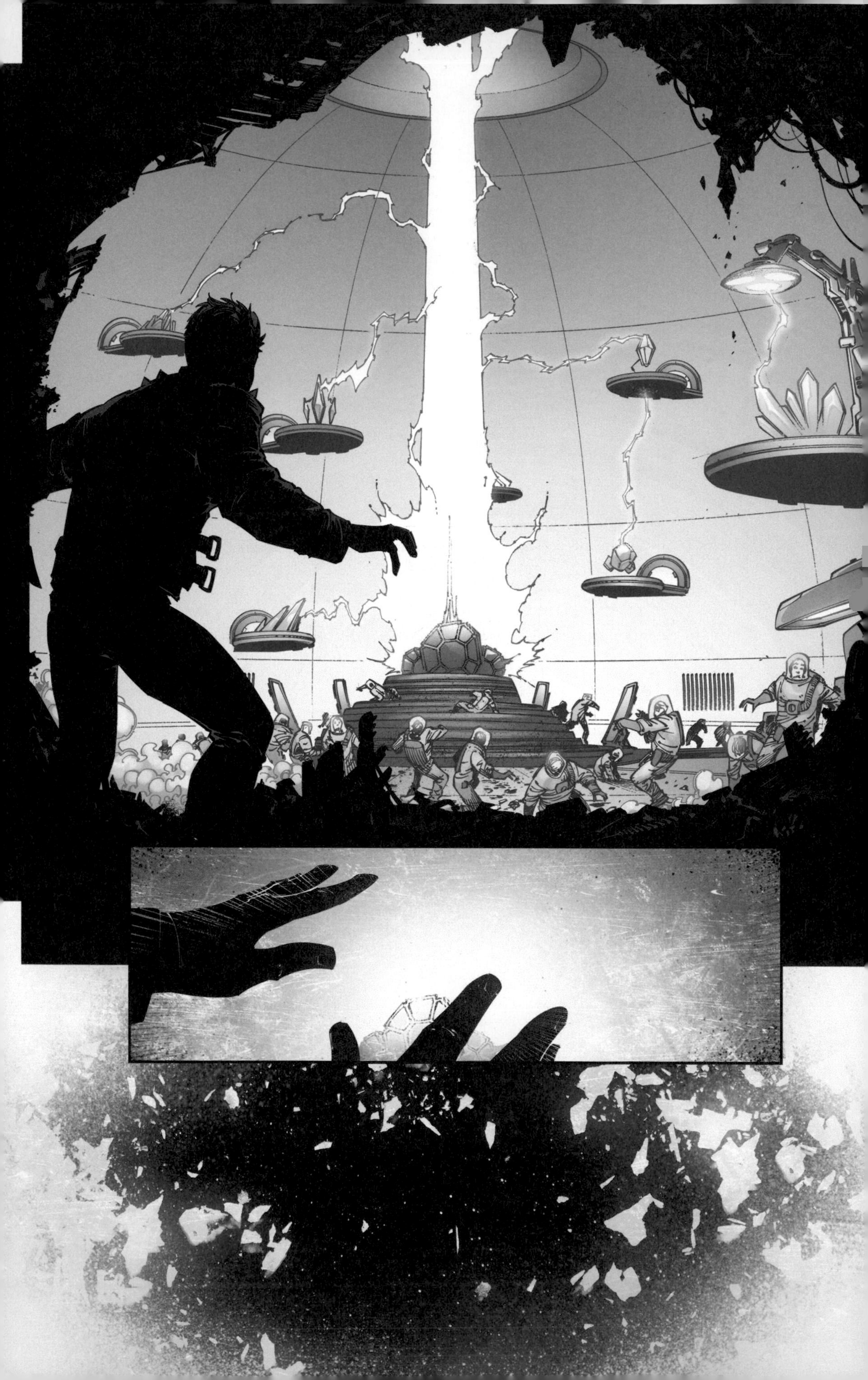

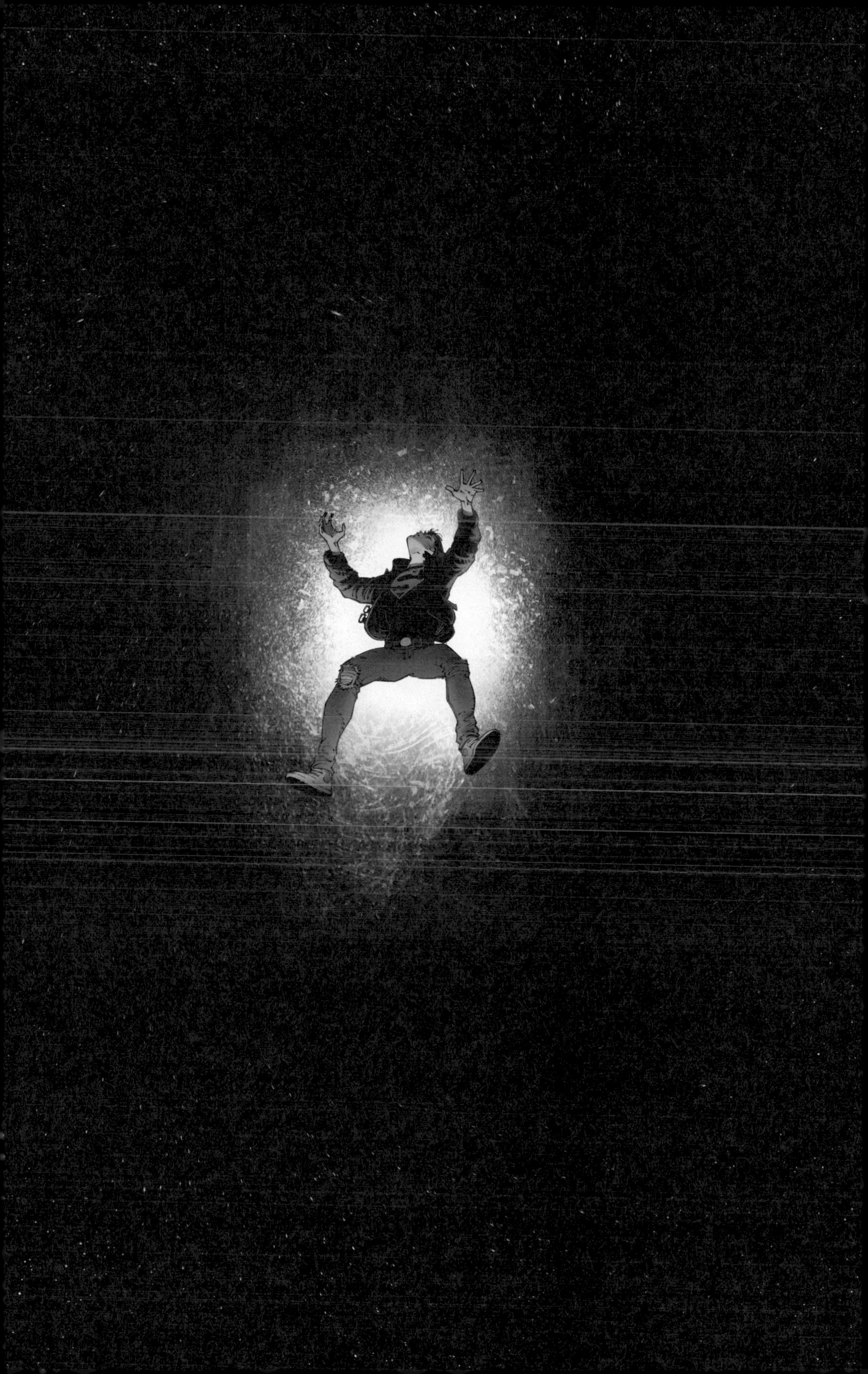

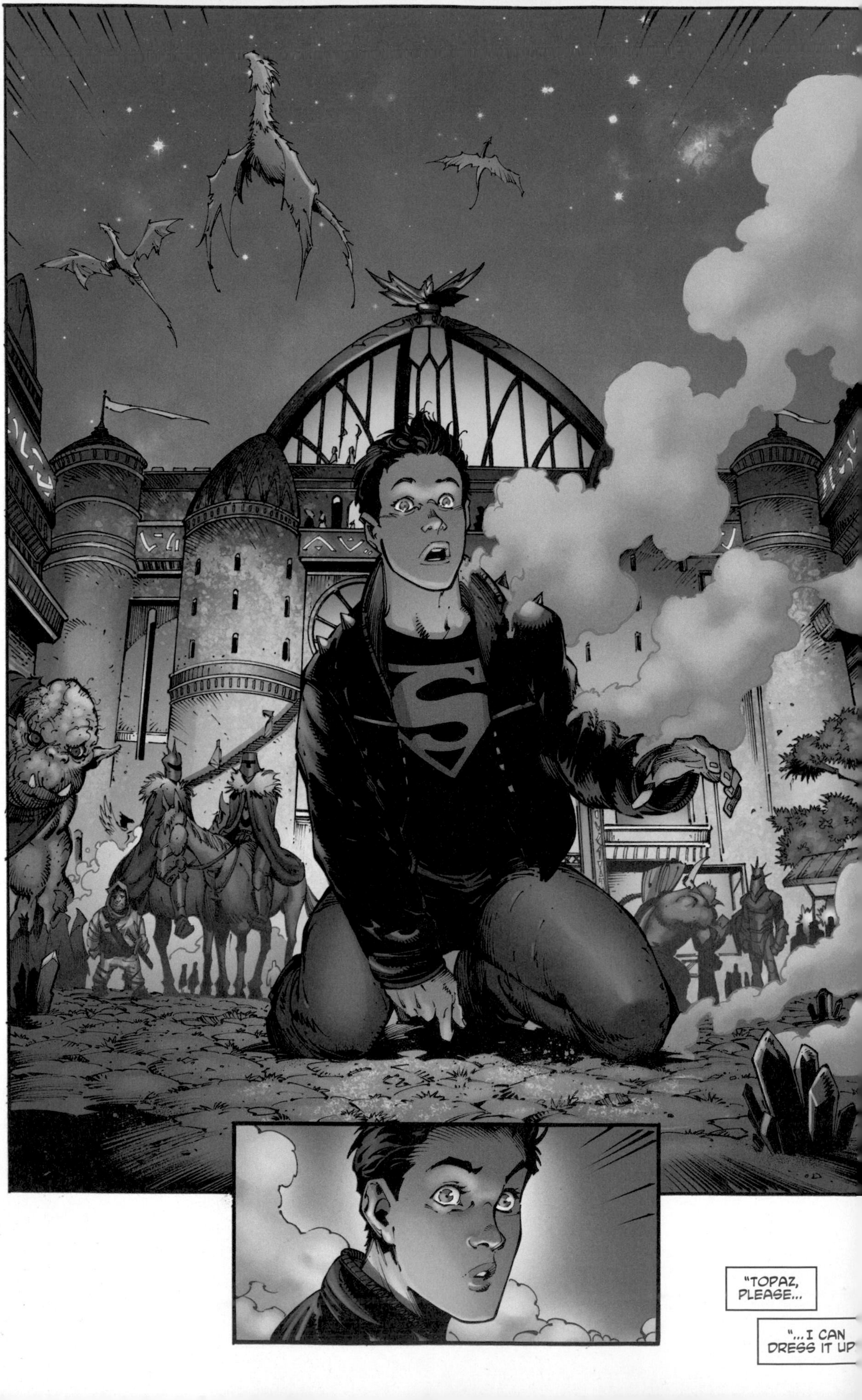
"TOPAZ, PLEASE...
"...I CAN DRESS IT UP

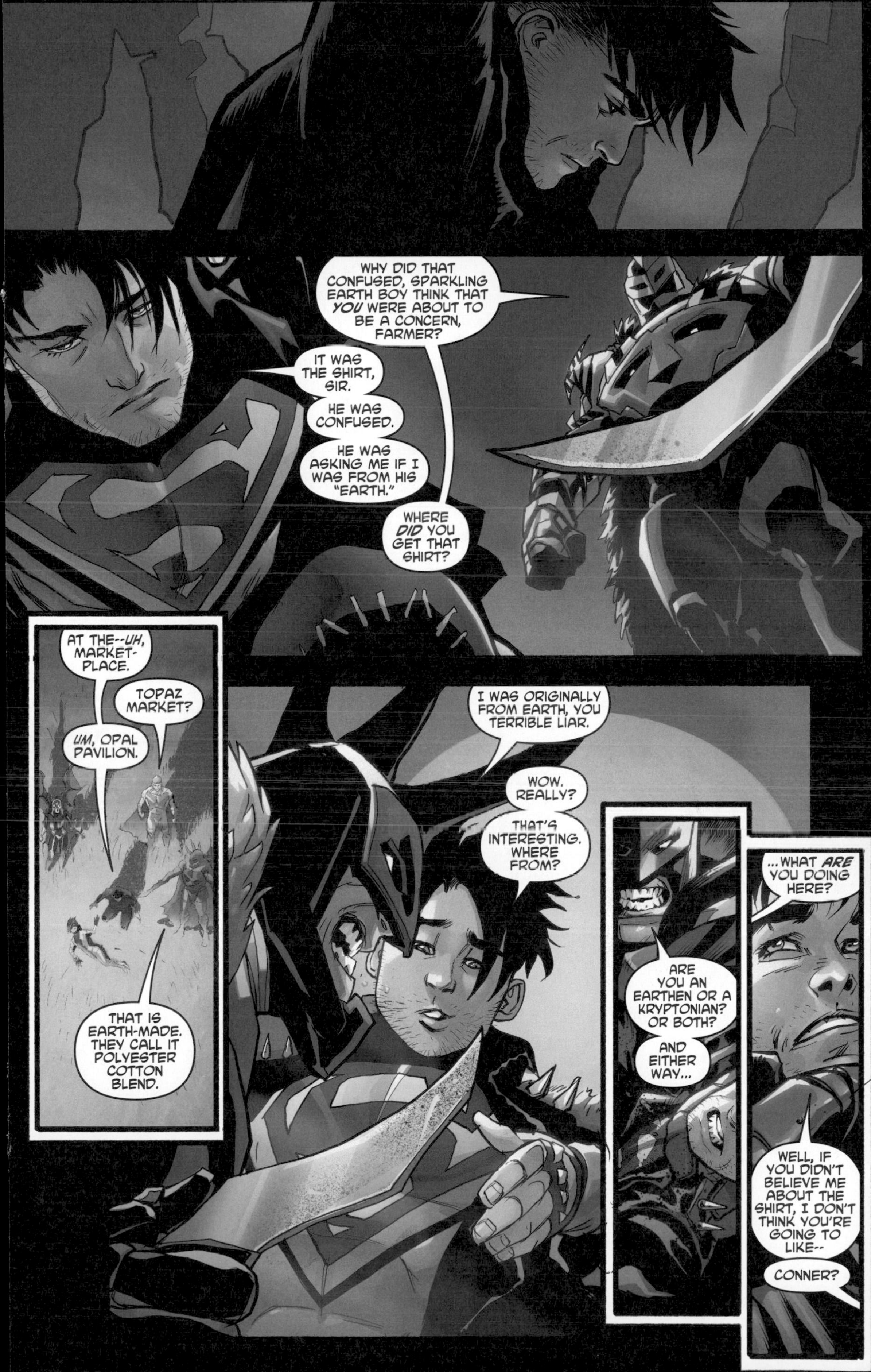
WHY DID THAT CONFUSED, SPARKLING EARTH BOY THINK THAT *YOU* WERE ABOUT TO BE A CONCERN, FARMER?
IT WAS THE SHIRT, SIR.
HE WAS CONFUSED.
HE WAS ASKING ME IF I WAS FROM HIS "EARTH."
WHERE *DID* YOU GET THAT SHIRT?
AT THE--*UH*, MARKET-PLACE.
TOPAZ MARKET?
UM, OPAL PAVILION.
THAT IS EARTH-MADE. THEY CALL IT POLYESTER COTTON BLEND.
I WAS ORIGINALLY FROM EARTH, YOU TERRIBLE LIAR.
WOW. REALLY?
THAT'S INTERESTING. WHERE FROM?
ARE YOU AN EARTHEN OR A KRYPTONIAN? OR BOTH?
AND EITHER WAY...
...WHAT *ARE* YOU DOING HERE?
WELL, IF YOU DIDN'T BELIEVE ME ABOUT THE SHIRT, I DON'T THINK YOU'RE GOING TO LIKE--
CONNER?

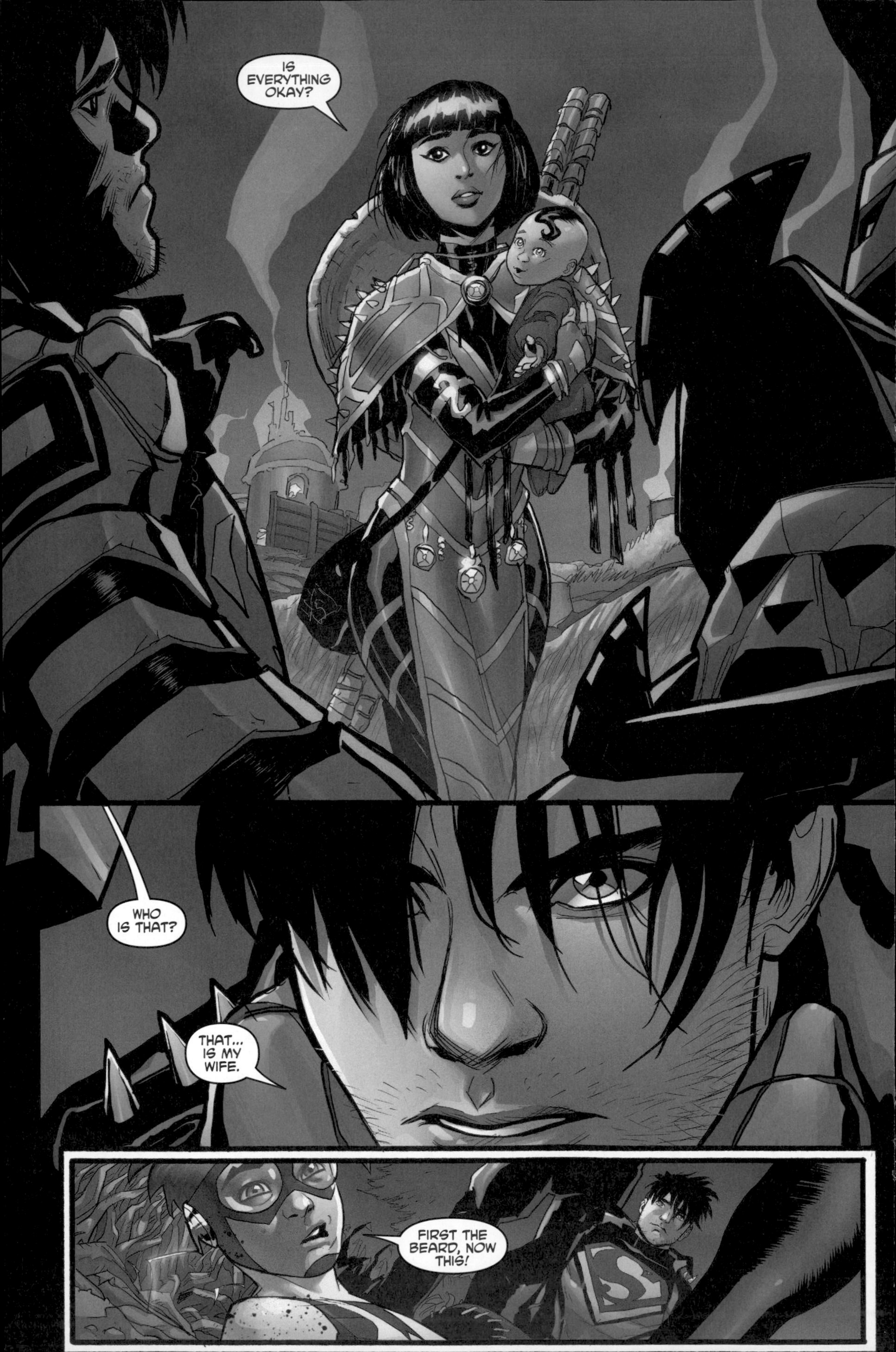
IS EVERYTHING OKAY?
WHO IS THAT?
THAT... IS MY WIFE.
FIRST THE BEARD, NOW THIS!

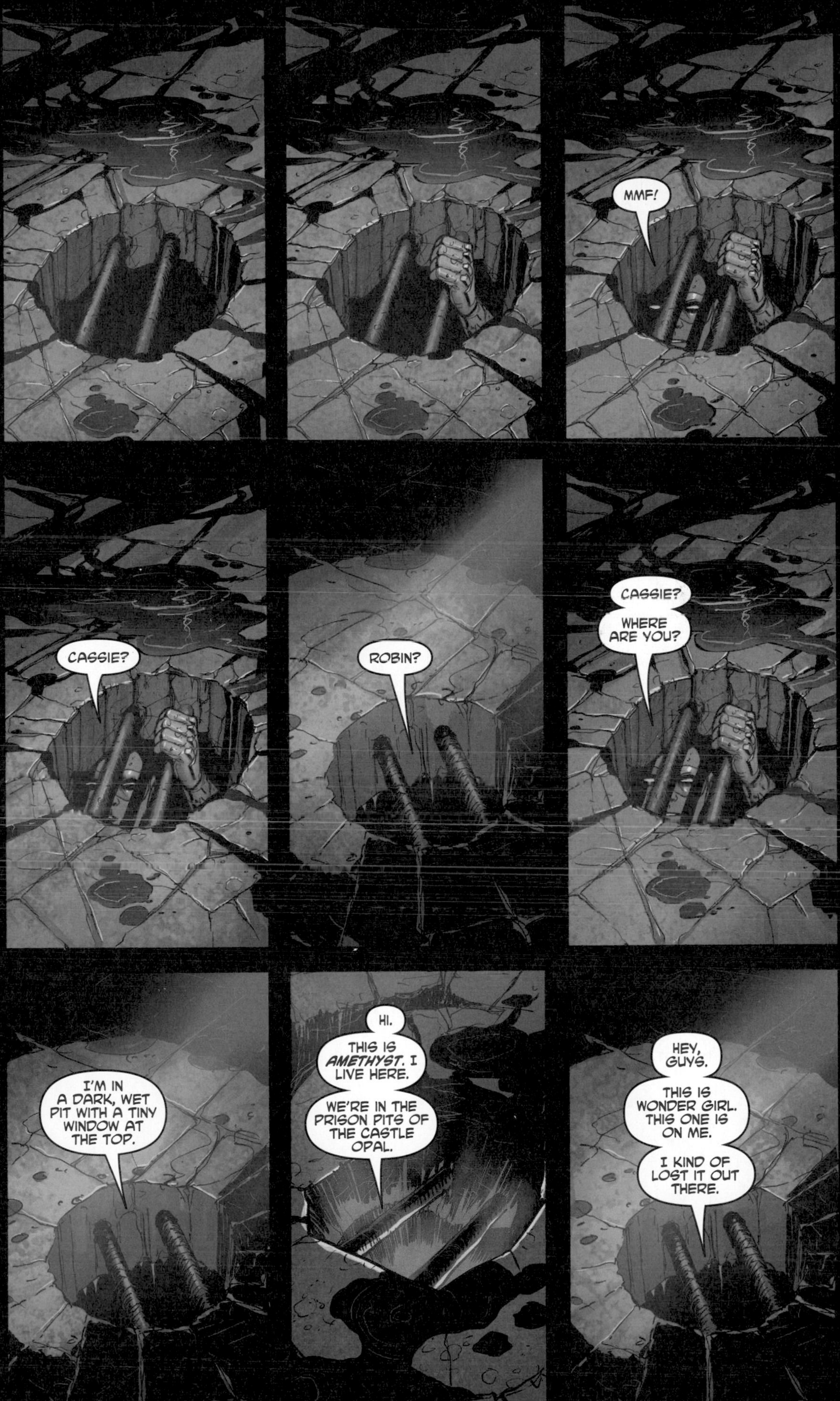
MMF!
CASSIE?
ROBIN?
CASSIE?
WHERE ARE YOU?
I'M IN A DARK, WET PIT WITH A TINY WINDOW AT THE TOP.
HI.
THIS IS *AMETHYST*. I LIVE HERE.
WE'RE IN THE PRISON PITS OF THE CASTLE OPAL.
HEY, GUYS.
THIS IS WONDER GIRL. THIS ONE IS ON ME.
I KIND OF LOST IT OUT THERE.

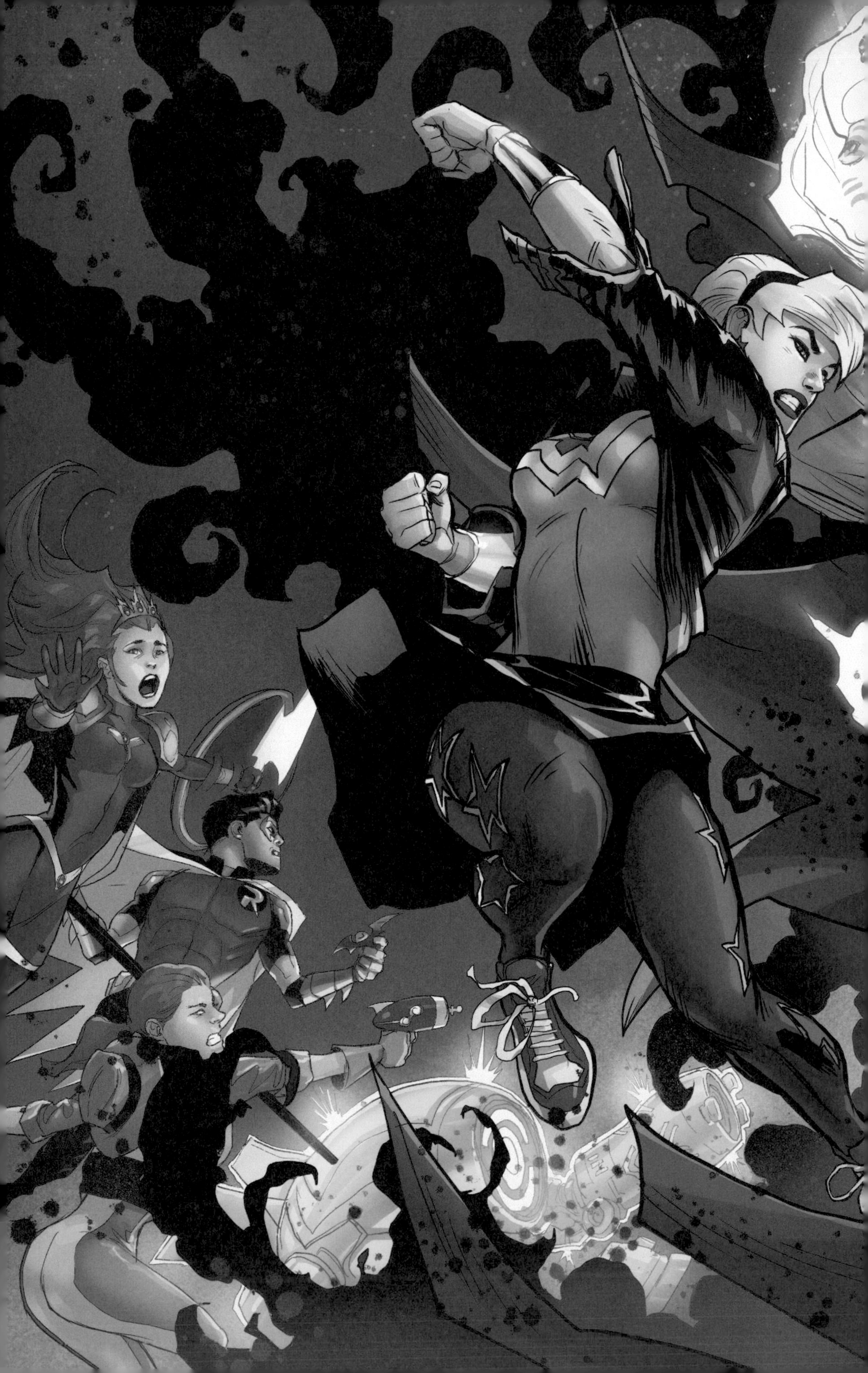

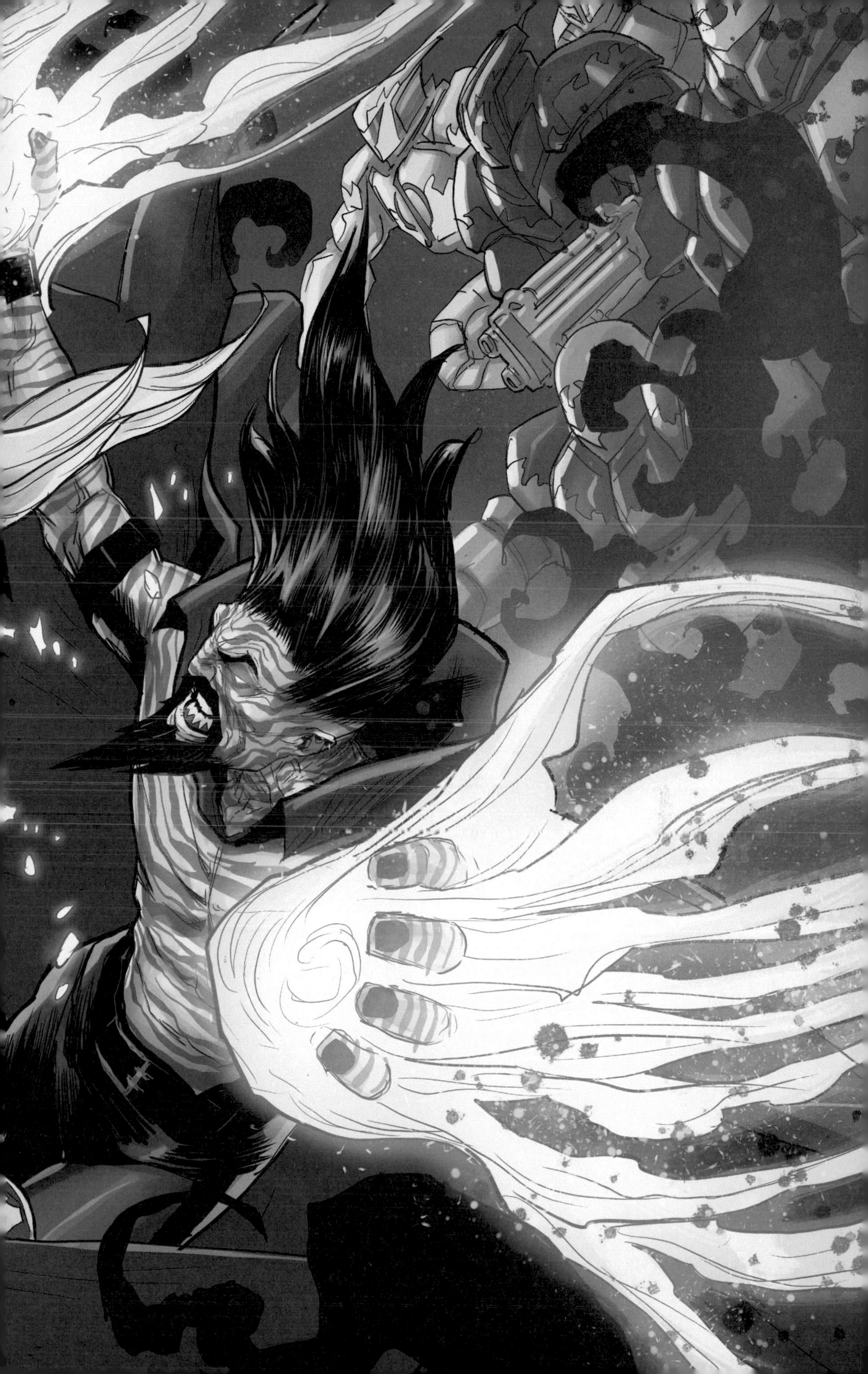

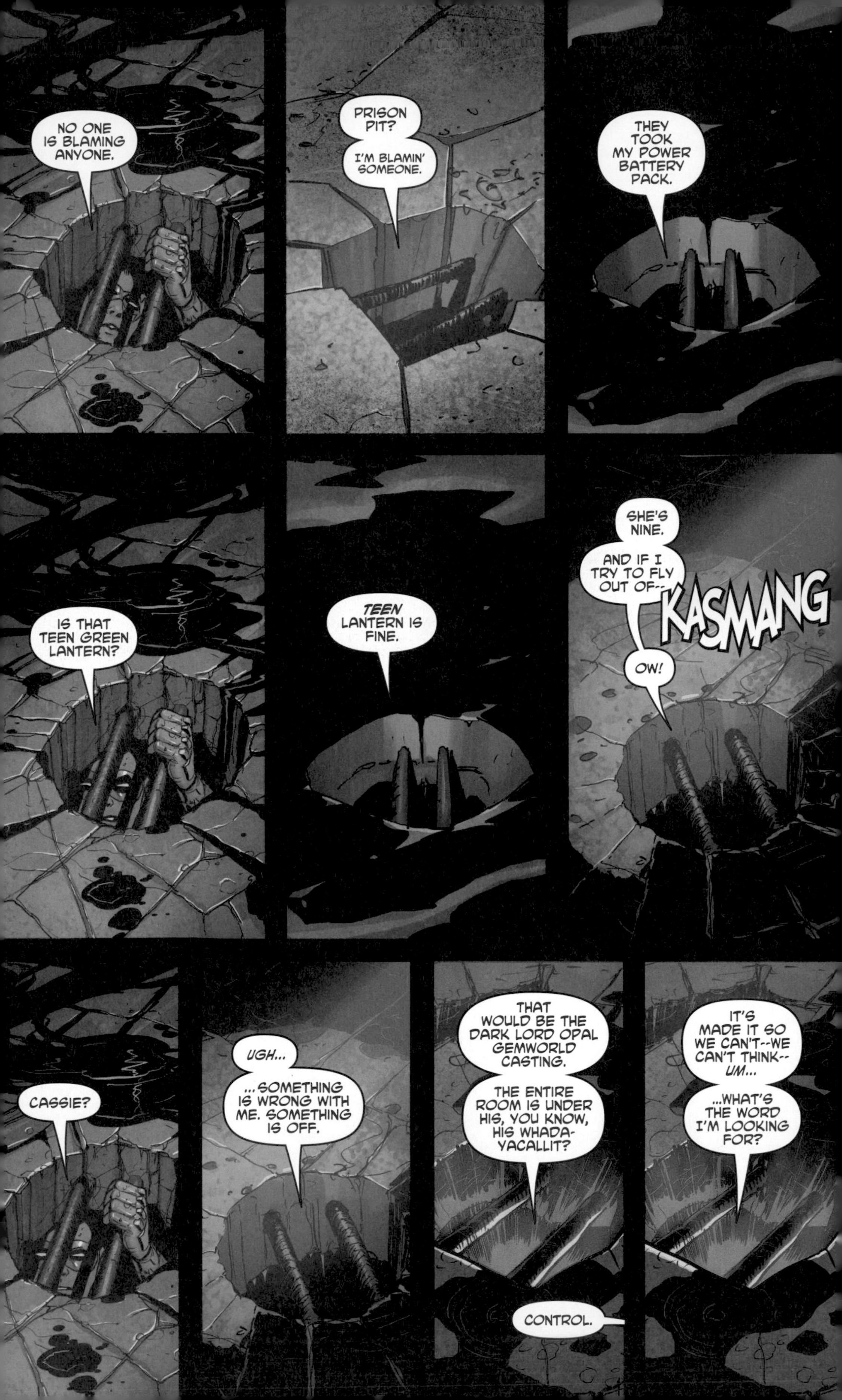
NO ONE IS BLAMING ANYONE.
PRISON PIT?
I'M BLAMIN' SOMEONE.
THEY TOOK MY POWER BATTERY PACK.
IS THAT TEEN GREEN LANTERN?
TEEN LANTERN IS FINE.
SHE'S NINE.
AND IF I TRY TO FLY OUT OF--
KASMANG
OW!
CASSIE?
UGH...
...SOMETHING IS WRONG WITH ME. SOMETHING IS OFF.
THAT WOULD BE THE DARK LORD OPAL GEMWORLD CASTING.
THE ENTIRE ROOM IS UNDER HIS, YOU KNOW, HIS WHADA-YACALLIT?
CONTROL.
IT'S MADE IT SO WE CAN'T--WE CAN'T THINK--UM...
...WHAT'S THE WORD I'M LOOKING FOR?

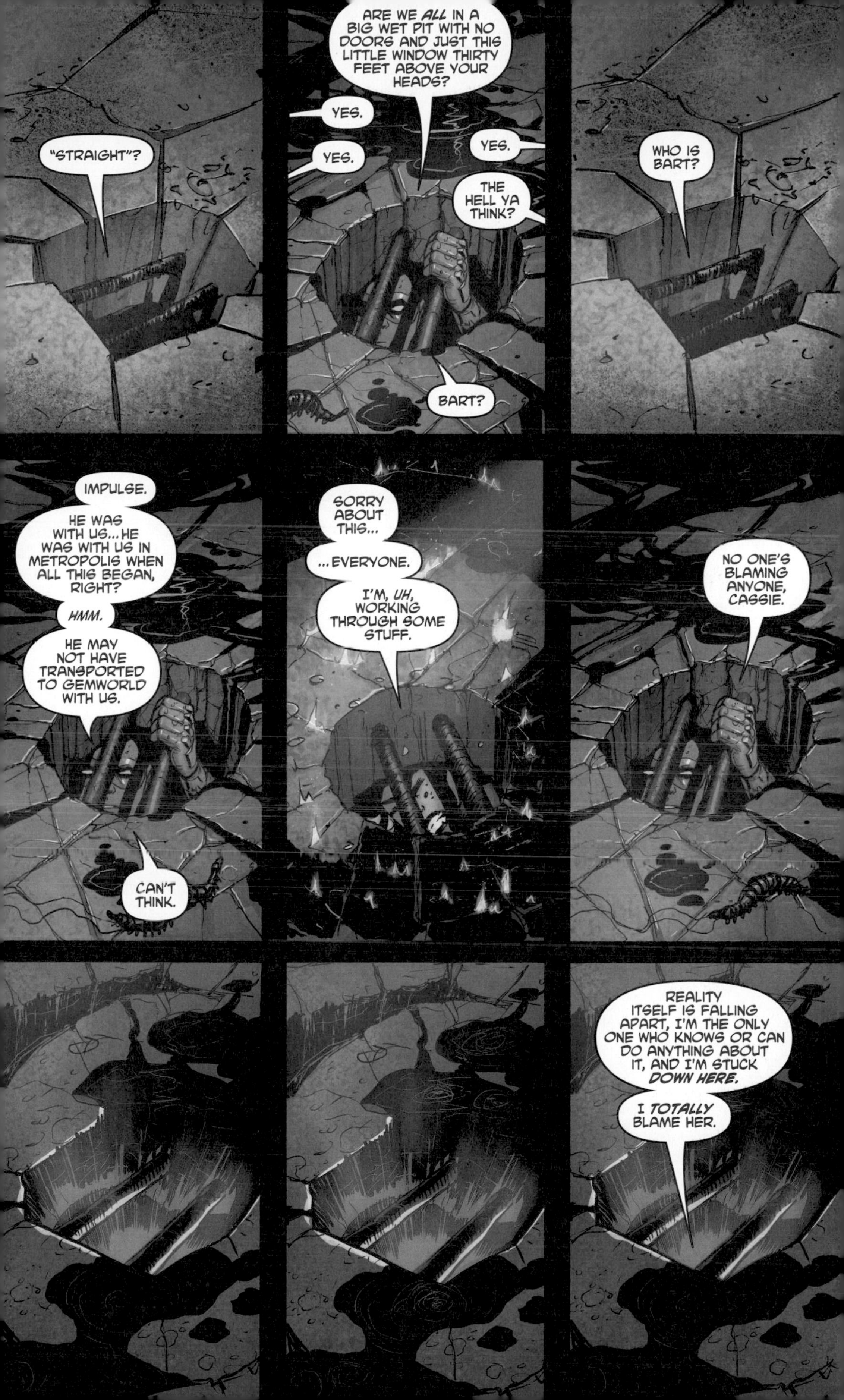
"STRAIGHT"?
ARE WE ALL IN A BIG WET PIT WITH NO DOORS AND JUST THIS LITTLE WINDOW THIRTY FEET ABOVE YOUR HEADS?
YES.
YES.
YES.
THE HELL YA THINK?
BART?
WHO IS BART?
IMPULSE.
HE WAS WITH US...HE WAS WITH US IN METROPOLIS WHEN ALL THIS BEGAN, RIGHT?
HMM.
HE MAY NOT HAVE TRANSPORTED TO GEMWORLD WITH US.
CAN'T THINK.
SORRY ABOUT THIS...
...EVERYONE.
I'M, UH, WORKING THROUGH SOME STUFF.
NO ONE'S BLAMING ANYONE, CASSIE.
REALITY ITSELF IS FALLING APART, I'M THE ONLY ONE WHO KNOWS OR CAN DO ANYTHING ABOUT IT, AND I'M STUCK DOWN HERE.
I TOTALLY BLAME HER.

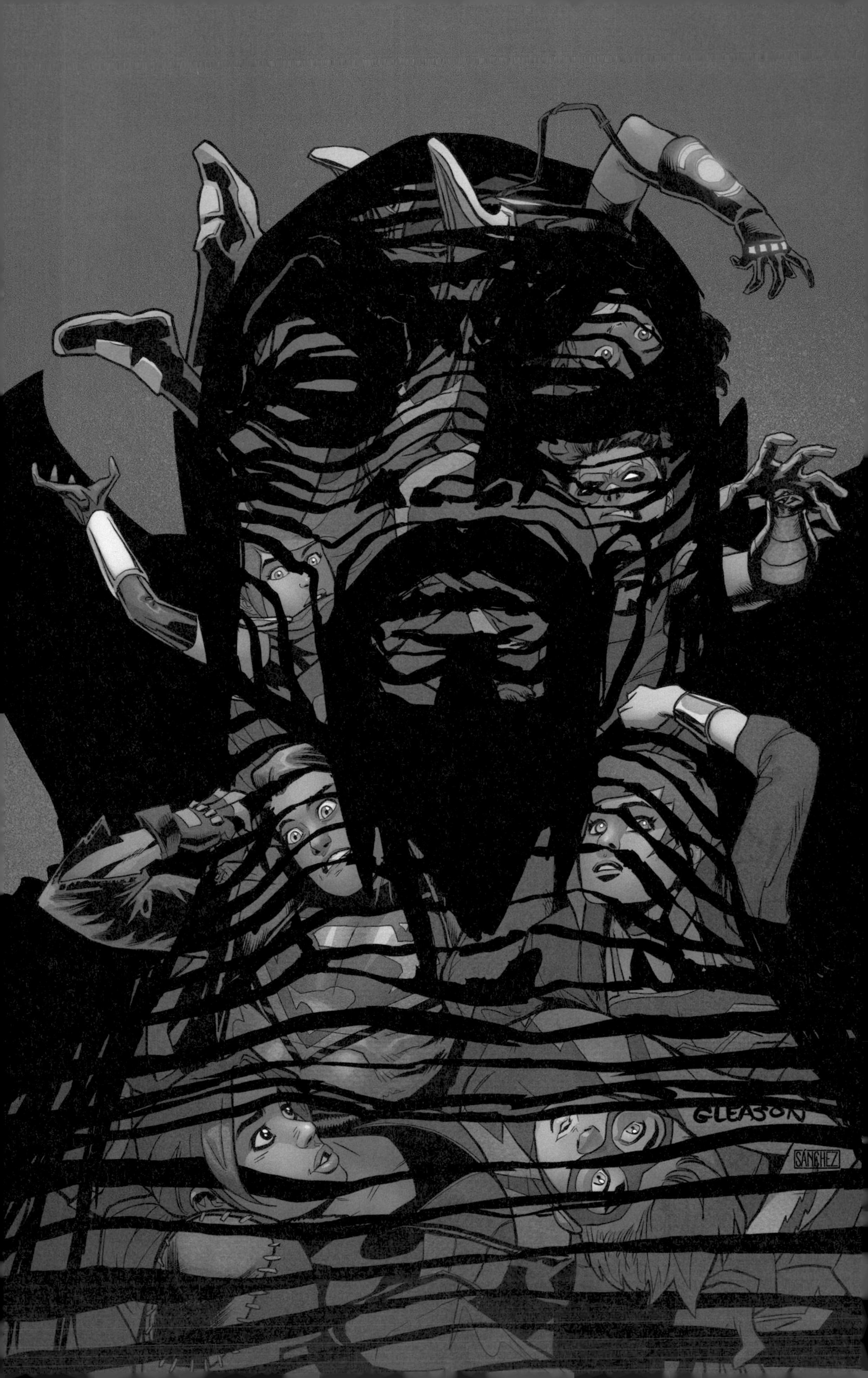
GLEASON
SÁNCHEZ

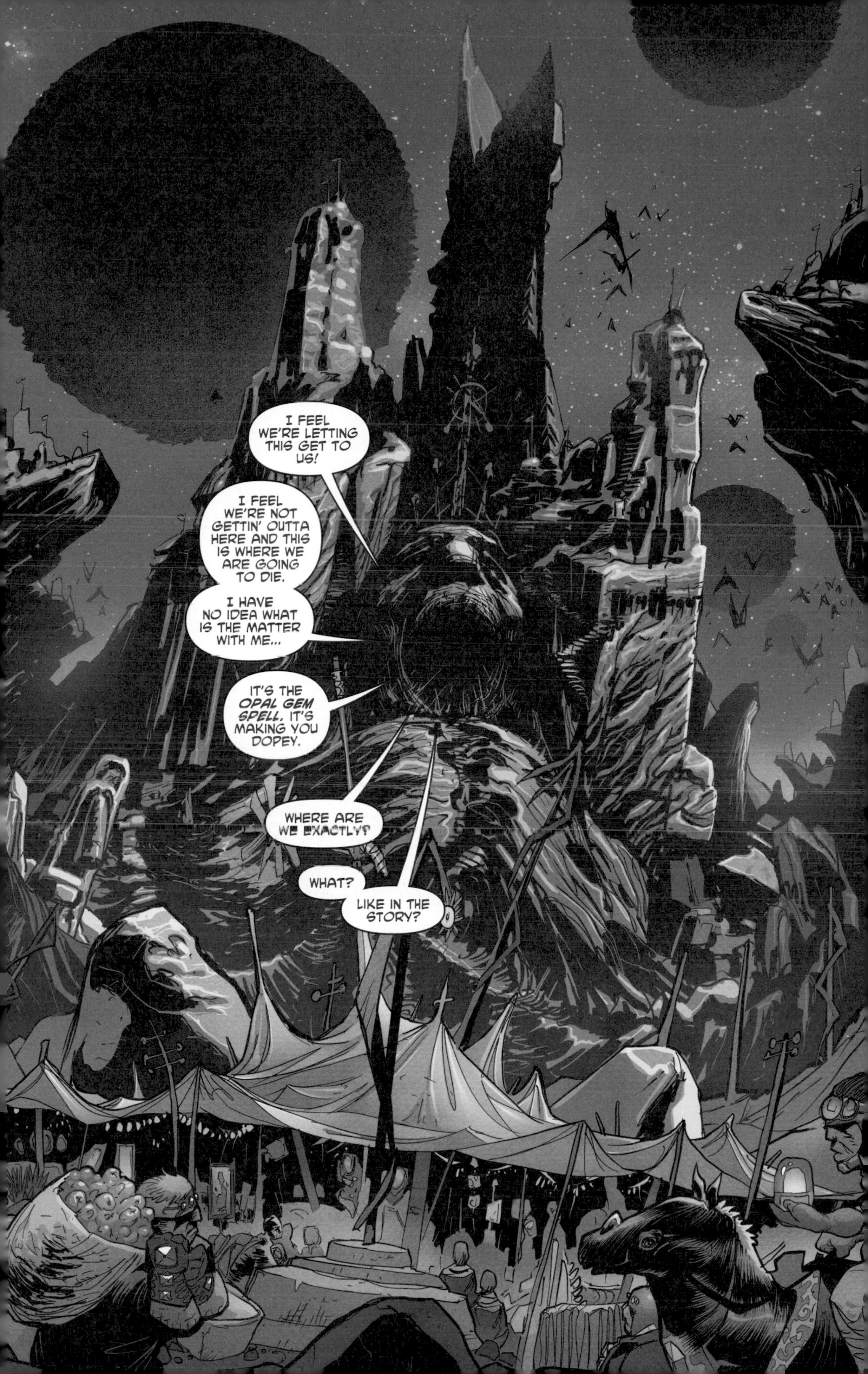
I FEEL WE'RE LETTING THIS GET TO US!
I FEEL WE'RE NOT GETTIN' OUTTA HERE AND THIS IS WHERE WE ARE GOING TO DIE.
I HAVE NO IDEA WHAT IS THE MATTER WITH ME...
IT'S THE *OPAL GEM SPELL*. IT'S MAKING YOU DOPEY.
WHERE ARE WE EXACTLY?
WHAT?
LIKE IN THE STORY?

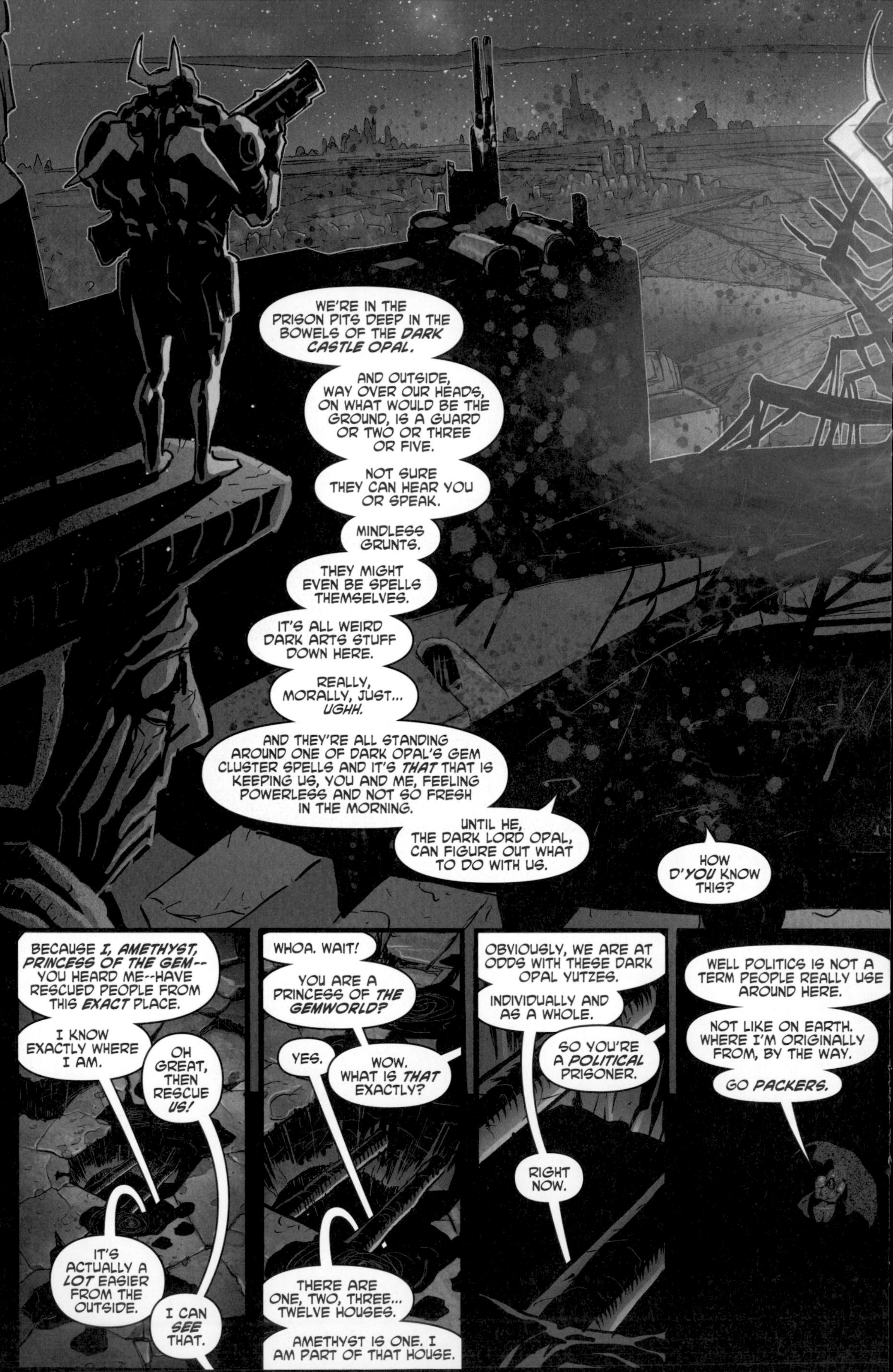
WE'RE IN THE PRISON PITS DEEP IN THE BOWELS OF THE DARK CASTLE OPAL.
AND OUTSIDE, WAY OVER OUR HEADS, ON WHAT WOULD BE THE GROUND, IS A GUARD OR TWO OR THREE OR FIVE.
NOT SURE THEY CAN HEAR YOU OR SPEAK.
MINDLESS GRUNTS.
THEY MIGHT EVEN BE SPELLS THEMSELVES.
IT'S ALL WEIRD DARK ARTS STUFF DOWN HERE.
REALLY, MORALLY, JUST... UGHH.
AND THEY'RE ALL STANDING AROUND ONE OF DARK OPAL'S GEM CLUSTER SPELLS AND IT'S THAT THAT IS KEEPING US, YOU AND ME, FEELING POWERLESS AND NOT SO FRESH IN THE MORNING.
UNTIL HE, THE DARK LORD OPAL, CAN FIGURE OUT WHAT TO DO WITH US.
HOW D'YOU KNOW THIS?
BECAUSE I, AMETHYST, PRINCESS OF THE GEM-- YOU HEARD ME--HAVE RESCUED PEOPLE FROM THIS EXACT PLACE.
I KNOW EXACTLY WHERE I AM.
OH GREAT, THEN RESCUE US!
IT'S ACTUALLY A LOT EASIER FROM THE OUTSIDE.
I CAN SEE THAT.
WHOA. WAIT!
YOU ARE A PRINCESS OF THE GEMWORLD?
YES.
WOW. WHAT IS THAT EXACTLY?
THERE ARE ONE, TWO, THREE... TWELVE HOUSES.
AMETHYST IS ONE. I AM PART OF THAT HOUSE.
OBVIOUSLY, WE ARE AT ODDS WITH THESE DARK OPAL YUTZES.
INDIVIDUALLY AND AS A WHOLE.
SO YOU'RE A POLITICAL PRISONER.
RIGHT NOW.
WELL POLITICS IS NOT A TERM PEOPLE REALLY USE AROUND HERE.
NOT LIKE ON EARTH. WHERE I'M ORIGINALLY FROM, BY THE WAY.
GO PACKERS.

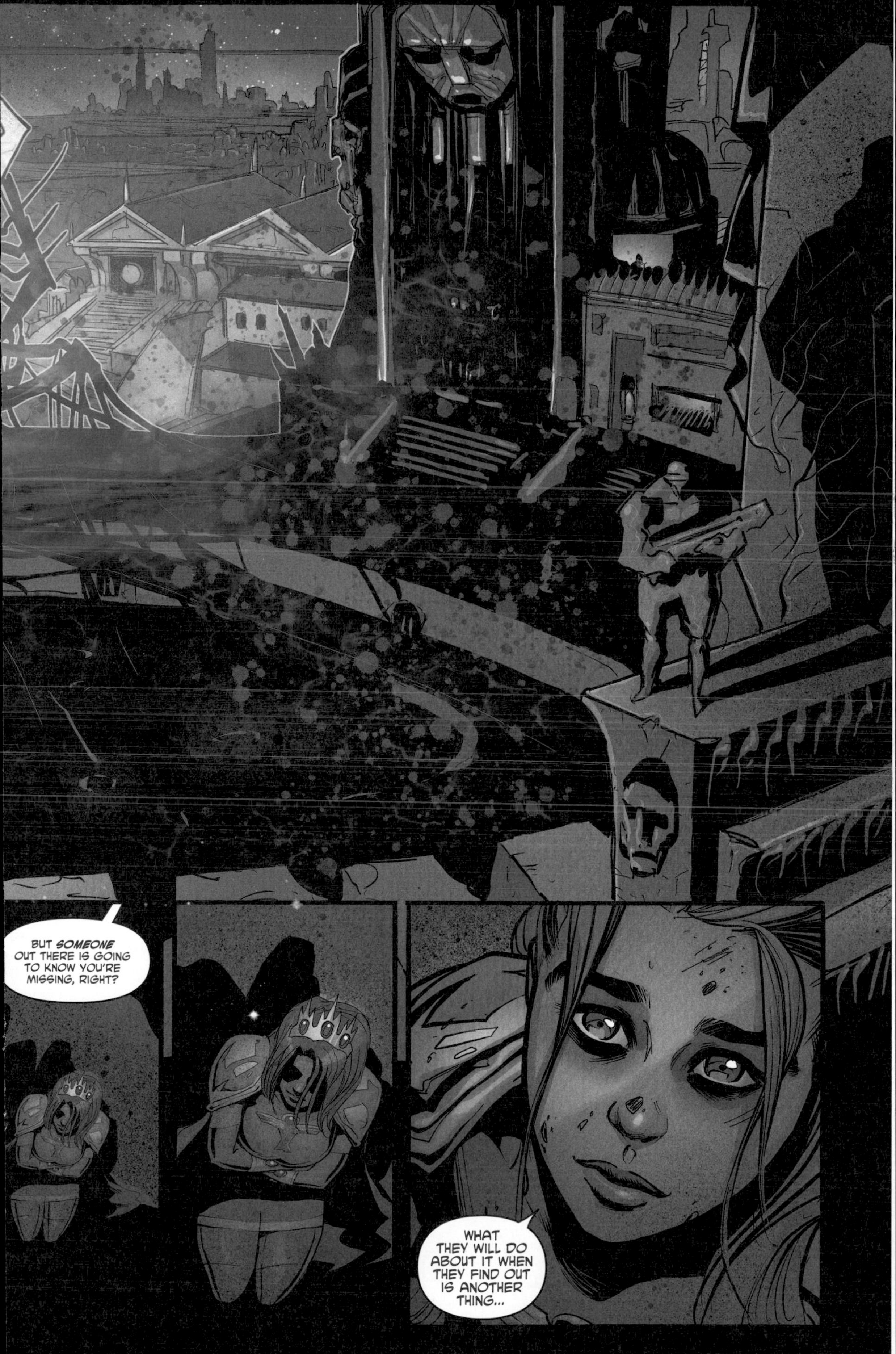
BUT SOMEONE OUT THERE IS GOING TO KNOW YOU'RE MISSING, RIGHT?
WHAT THEY WILL DO ABOUT IT WHEN THEY FIND OUT IS ANOTHER THING...

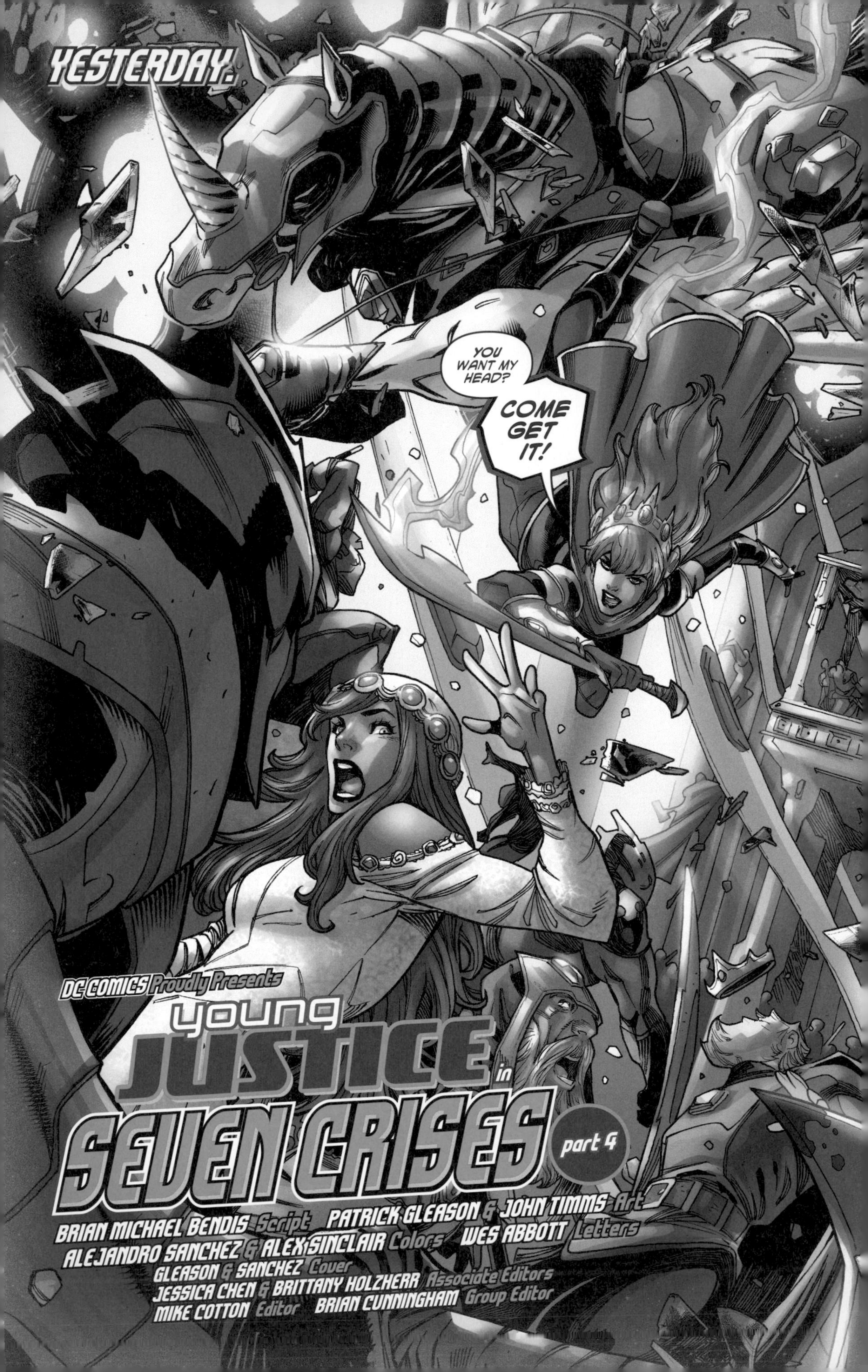
YESTERDAY.
YOU WANT MY HEAD?
COME GET IT!
DC COMICS Proudly Presents
YOUNG JUSTICE in
SEVEN CRISES
part 4
BRIAN MICHAEL BENDIS Script PATRICK GLEASON & JOHN TIMMS Art
ALEJANDRO SANCHEZ & ALEX SINCLAIR Colors WES ABBOTT Letters
GLEASON & SANCHEZ Cover
JESSICA CHEN & BRITTANY HOLZHERR Associate Editors
MIKE COTTON Editor BRIAN CUNNINGHAM Group Editor

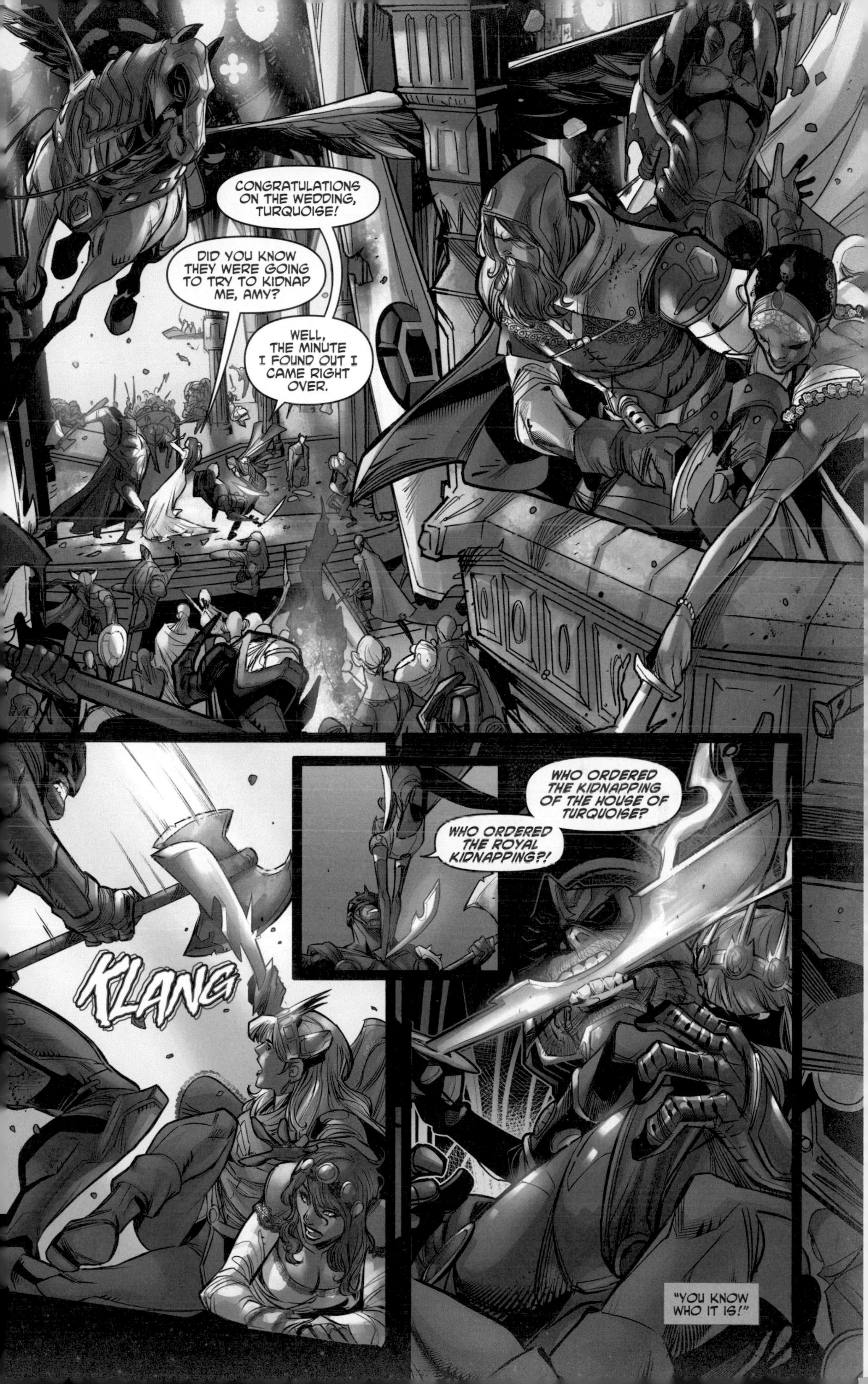
CONGRATULATIONS ON THE WEDDING, TURQUOISE!
DID YOU KNOW THEY WERE GOING TO TRY TO KIDNAP ME, AMY?
WELL, THE MINUTE I FOUND OUT I CAME RIGHT OVER.
KLANG
WHO ORDERED THE KIDNAPPING OF THE HOUSE OF TURQUOISE?
WHO ORDERED THE ROYAL KIDNAPPING?!
"YOU KNOW WHO IT IS!"

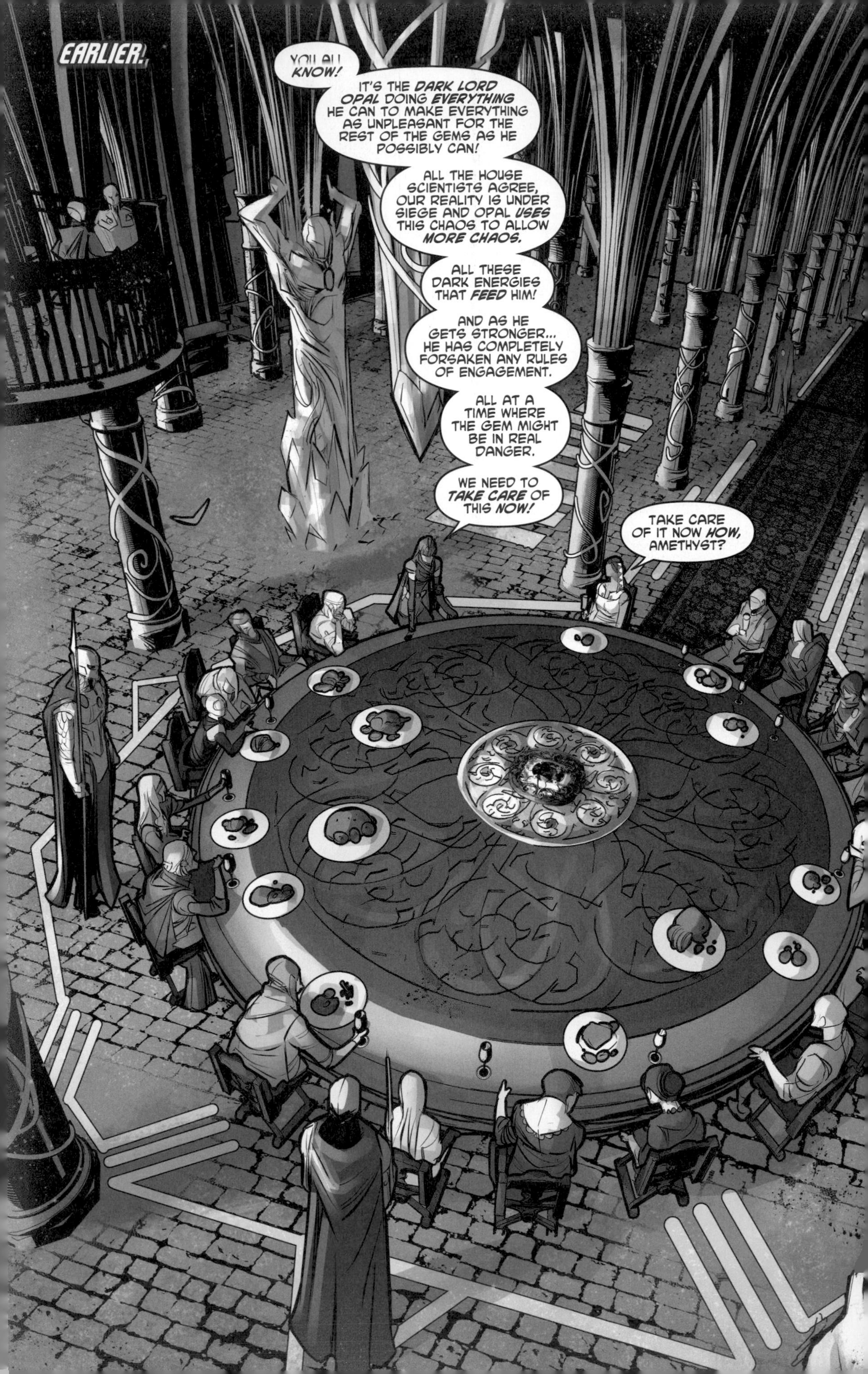
EARLIER:
YOU ALL KNOW!
IT'S THE DARK LORD OPAL DOING EVERYTHING HE CAN TO MAKE EVERYTHING AS UNPLEASANT FOR THE REST OF THE GEMS AS HE POSSIBLY CAN!
ALL THE HOUSE SCIENTISTS AGREE, OUR REALITY IS UNDER SIEGE AND OPAL USES THIS CHAOS TO ALLOW MORE CHAOS.
ALL THESE DARK ENERGIES THAT FEED HIM!
AND AS HE GETS STRONGER... HE HAS COMPLETELY FORSAKEN ANY RULES OF ENGAGEMENT.
ALL AT A TIME WHERE THE GEM MIGHT BE IN REAL DANGER.
WE NEED TO TAKE CARE OF THIS NOW!
TAKE CARE OF IT NOW HOW, AMETHYST?

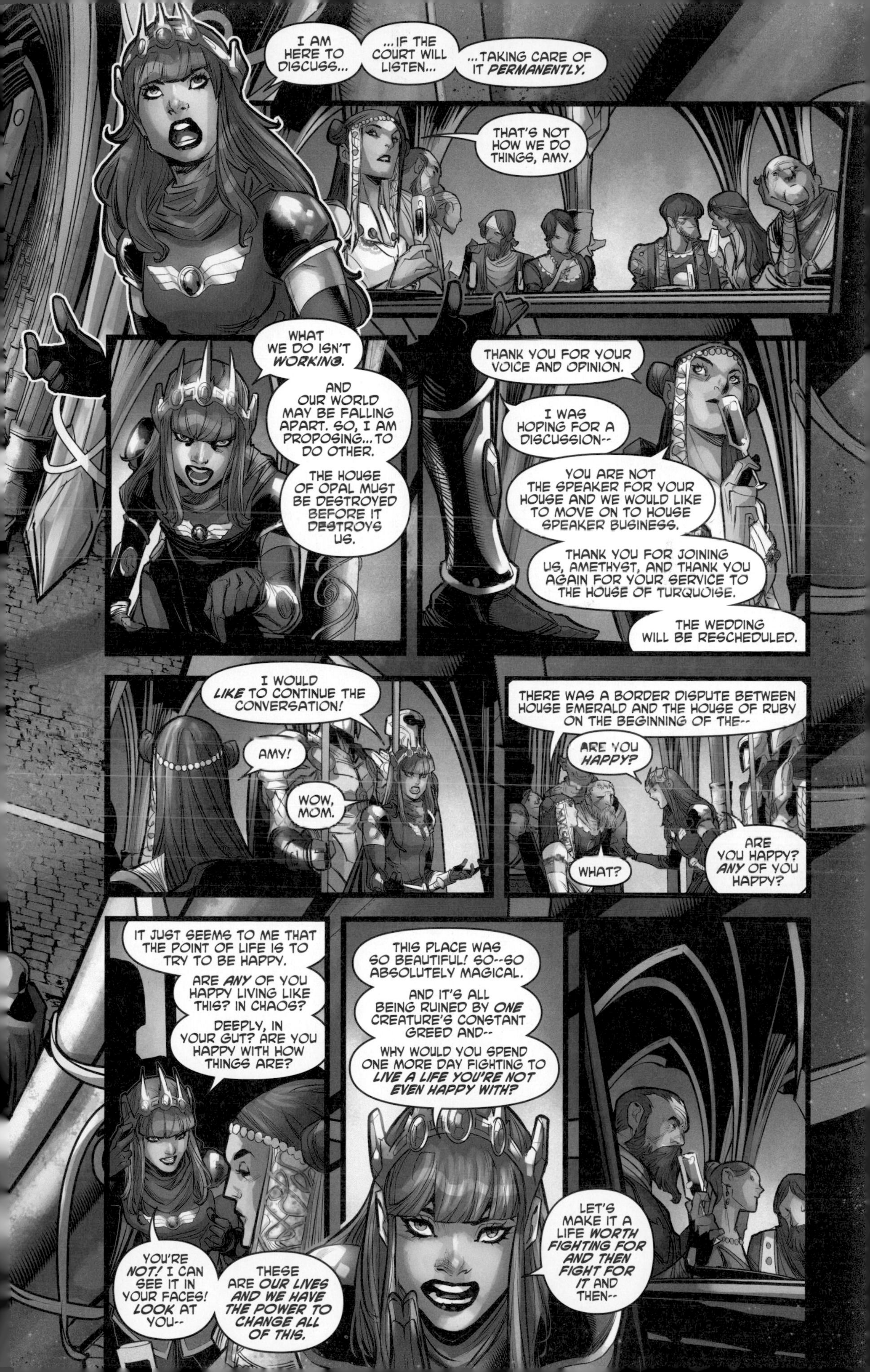

I AM HERE TO DISCUSS...
...IF THE COURT WILL LISTEN...
...TAKING CARE OF IT PERMANENTLY.
THAT'S NOT HOW WE DO THINGS, AMY.
WHAT WE DO ISN'T WORKING.
AND OUR WORLD MAY BE FALLING APART. SO, I AM PROPOSING...TO DO OTHER.
THE HOUSE OF OPAL MUST BE DESTROYED BEFORE IT DESTROYS US.
THANK YOU FOR YOUR VOICE AND OPINION.
I WAS HOPING FOR A DISCUSSION--
YOU ARE NOT THE SPEAKER FOR YOUR HOUSE AND WE WOULD LIKE TO MOVE ON TO HOUSE SPEAKER BUSINESS.
THANK YOU FOR JOINING US, AMETHYST, AND THANK YOU AGAIN FOR YOUR SERVICE TO THE HOUSE OF TURQUOISE.
THE WEDDING WILL BE RESCHEDULED.
I WOULD LIKE TO CONTINUE THE CONVERSATION!
AMY!
WOW, MOM.
THERE WAS A BORDER DISPUTE BETWEEN HOUSE EMERALD AND THE HOUSE OF RUBY ON THE BEGINNING OF THE--
ARE YOU HAPPY?
WHAT?
ARE YOU HAPPY? ANY OF YOU HAPPY?
IT JUST SEEMS TO ME THAT THE POINT OF LIFE IS TO TRY TO BE HAPPY.
ARE ANY OF YOU HAPPY LIVING LIKE THIS? IN CHAOS?
DEEPLY, IN YOUR GUT? ARE YOU HAPPY WITH HOW THINGS ARE?
YOU'RE NOT! I CAN SEE IT IN YOUR FACES! LOOK AT YOU--
THIS PLACE WAS SO BEAUTIFUL! SO--SO ABSOLUTELY MAGICAL.
AND IT'S ALL BEING RUINED BY ONE CREATURE'S CONSTANT GREED AND--
WHY WOULD YOU SPEND ONE MORE DAY FIGHTING TO LIVE A LIFE YOU'RE NOT EVEN HAPPY WITH?
THESE ARE OUR LIVES AND WE HAVE THE POWER TO CHANGE ALL OF THIS.
LET'S MAKE IT A LIFE WORTH FIGHTING FOR AND THEN FIGHT FOR IT AND THEN--

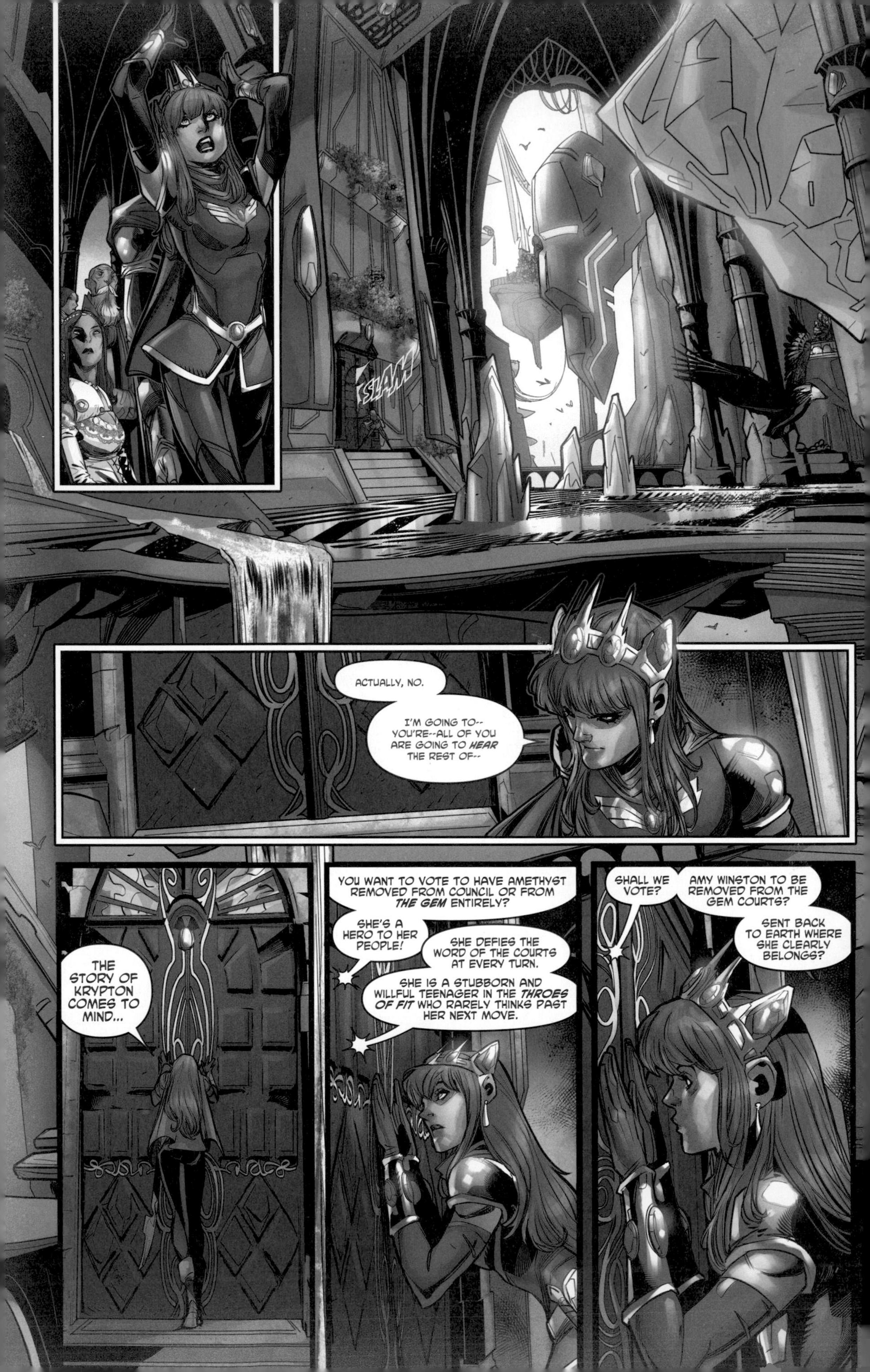
SLAM
ACTUALLY, NO.
I'M GOING TO-- YOU'RE--ALL OF YOU ARE GOING TO HEAR THE REST OF--
THE STORY OF KRYPTON COMES TO MIND...
YOU WANT TO VOTE TO HAVE AMETHYST REMOVED FROM COUNCIL OR FROM THE GEM ENTIRELY?
SHE'S A HERO TO HER PEOPLE!
SHE DEFIES THE WORD OF THE COURTS AT EVERY TURN.
SHE IS A STUBBORN AND WILLFUL TEENAGER IN THE THROES OF FIT WHO RARELY THINKS PAST HER NEXT MOVE.
SHALL WE VOTE?
AMY WINSTON TO BE REMOVED FROM THE GEM COURTS?
SENT BACK TO EARTH WHERE SHE CLEARLY BELONGS?

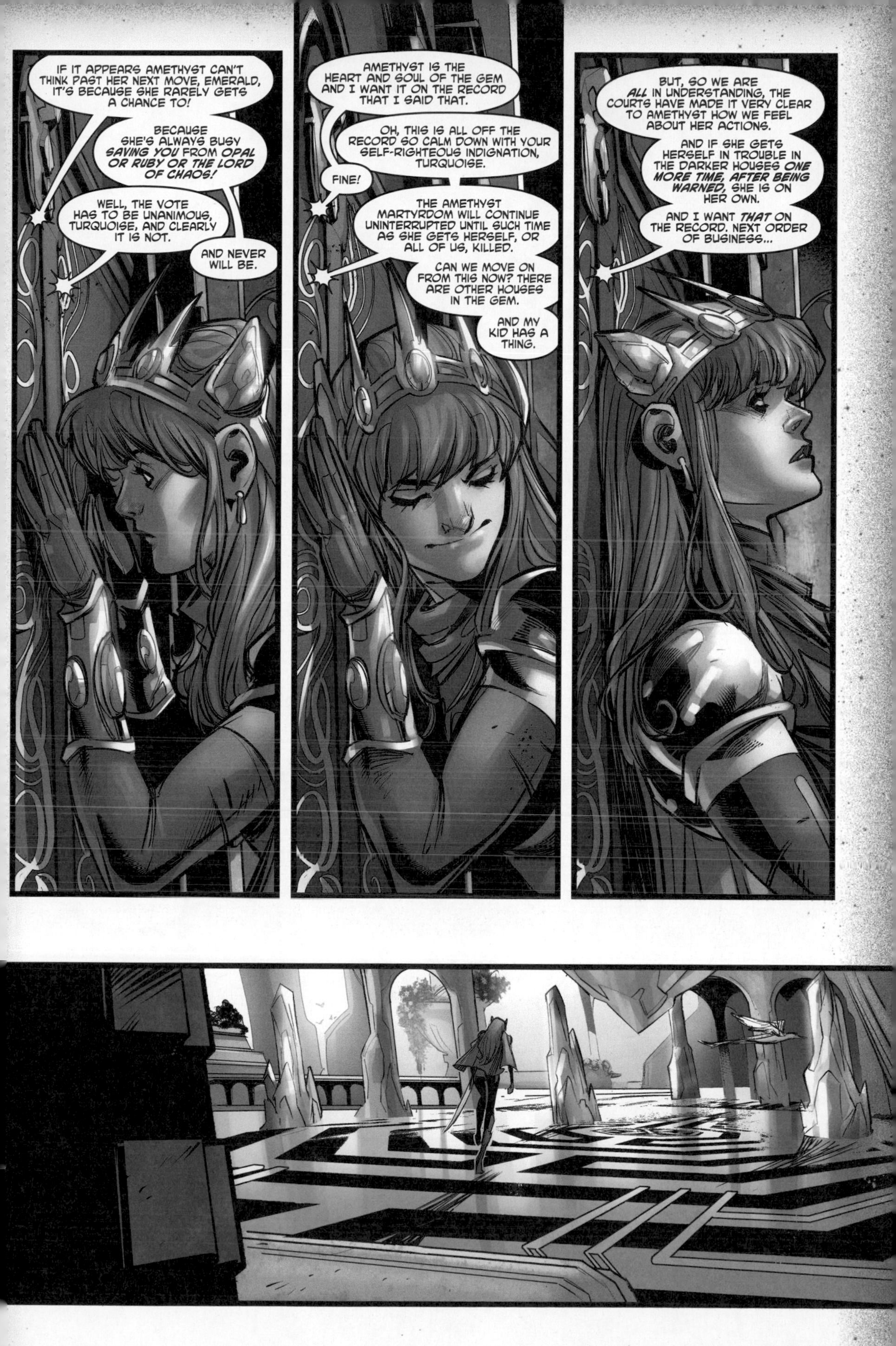
IF IT APPEARS AMETHYST CAN'T THINK PAST HER NEXT MOVE, EMERALD, IT'S BECAUSE SHE RARELY GETS A CHANCE TO!
BECAUSE SHE'S ALWAYS BUSY SAVING YOU FROM OPAL OR RUBY OR THE LORD OF CHAOS!
WELL, THE VOTE HAS TO BE UNANIMOUS, TURQUOISE, AND CLEARLY IT IS NOT.
AND NEVER WILL BE.
AMETHYST IS THE HEART AND SOUL OF THE GEM AND I WANT IT ON THE RECORD THAT I SAID THAT.
OH, THIS IS ALL OFF THE RECORD SO CALM DOWN WITH YOUR SELF-RIGHTEOUS INDIGNATION, TURQUOISE.
FINE!
THE AMETHYST MARTYRDOM WILL CONTINUE UNINTERRUPTED UNTIL SUCH TIME AS SHE GETS HERSELF, OR ALL OF US, KILLED.
CAN WE MOVE ON FROM THIS NOW? THERE ARE OTHER HOUSES IN THE GEM.
AND MY KID HAS A THING.
BUT, SO WE ARE ALL IN UNDERSTANDING, THE COURTS HAVE MADE IT VERY CLEAR TO AMETHYST HOW WE FEEL ABOUT HER ACTIONS.
AND IF SHE GETS HERSELF IN TROUBLE IN THE DARKER HOUSES ONE MORE TIME, AFTER BEING WARNED, SHE IS ON HER OWN.
AND I WANT THAT ON THE RECORD. NEXT ORDER OF BUSINESS...

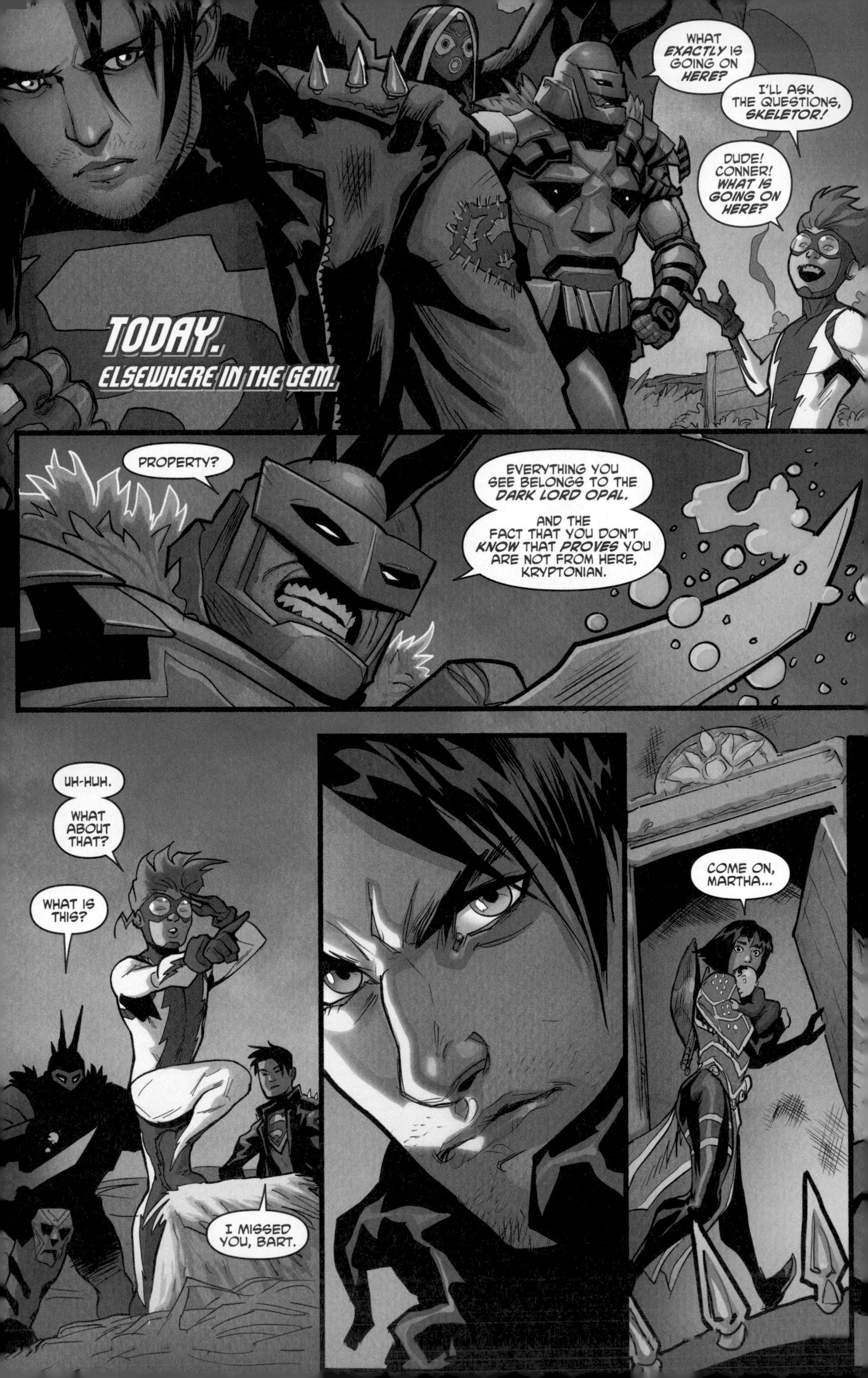

TODAY.
ELSEWHERE IN THE GEM!
WHAT EXACTLY IS GOING ON HERE?
I'LL ASK THE QUESTIONS, SKELETOR!
DUDE! CONNER! WHAT IS GOING ON HERE?
PROPERTY?
EVERYTHING YOU SEE BELONGS TO THE DARK LORD OPAL.
AND THE FACT THAT YOU DON'T KNOW THAT PROVES YOU ARE NOT FROM HERE, KRYPTONIAN.
UH-HUH.
WHAT ABOUT THAT?
WHAT IS THIS?
I MISSED YOU, BART.
COME ON, MARTHA...

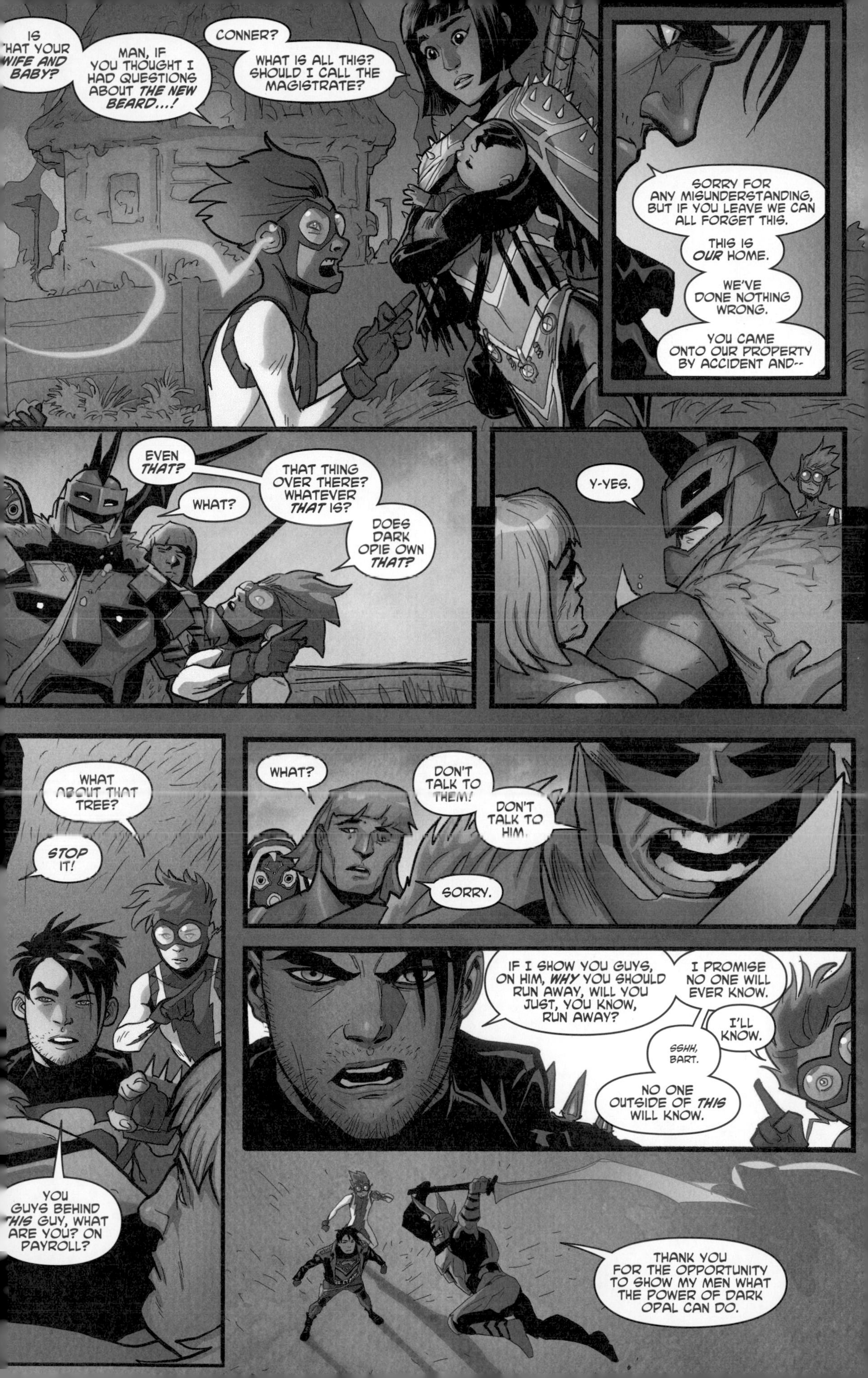

IS THAT YOUR WIFE AND BABY?
MAN, IF YOU THOUGHT I HAD QUESTIONS ABOUT THE NEW BEARD...!
CONNER?
WHAT IS ALL THIS? SHOULD I CALL THE MAGISTRATE?
SORRY FOR ANY MISUNDERSTANDING, BUT IF YOU LEAVE WE CAN ALL FORGET THIS.
THIS IS OUR HOME.
WE'VE DONE NOTHING WRONG.
YOU CAME ONTO OUR PROPERTY BY ACCIDENT AND--
EVEN THAT?
THAT THING OVER THERE? WHATEVER THAT IS?
WHAT?
DOES DARK OPIE OWN THAT?
Y-YES.
WHAT ABOUT THAT TREE?
STOP IT!
YOU GUYS BEHIND THIS GUY, WHAT ARE YOU? ON PAYROLL?
WHAT?
DON'T TALK TO THEM!
DON'T TALK TO HIM.
SORRY.
IF I SHOW YOU GUYS, ON HIM, WHY YOU SHOULD RUN AWAY, WILL YOU JUST, YOU KNOW, RUN AWAY?
I PROMISE NO ONE WILL EVER KNOW.
I'LL KNOW.
SSHH, BART.
NO ONE OUTSIDE OF THIS WILL KNOW.
THANK YOU FOR THE OPPORTUNITY TO SHOW MY MEN WHAT THE POWER OF DARK OPAL CAN DO.

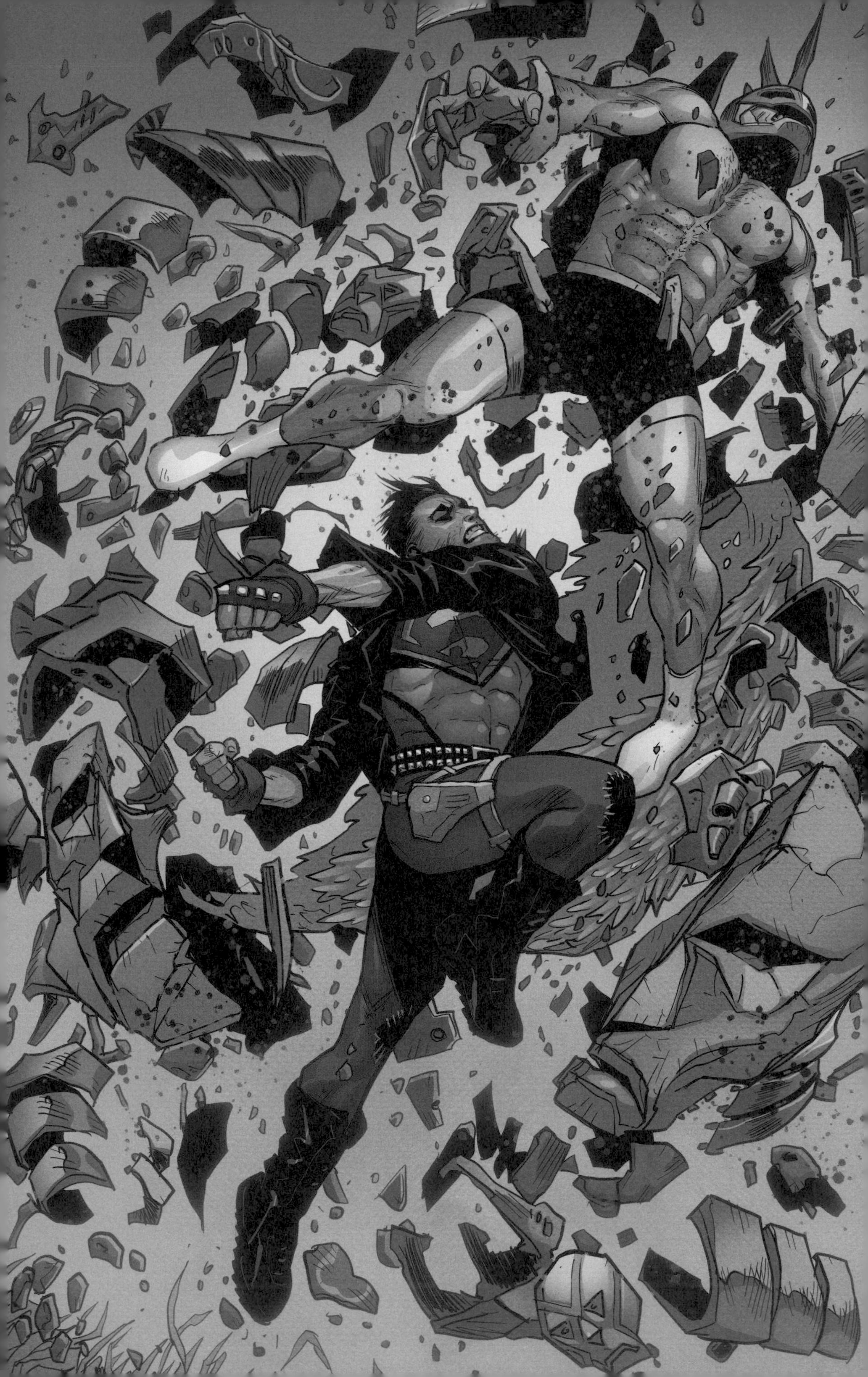

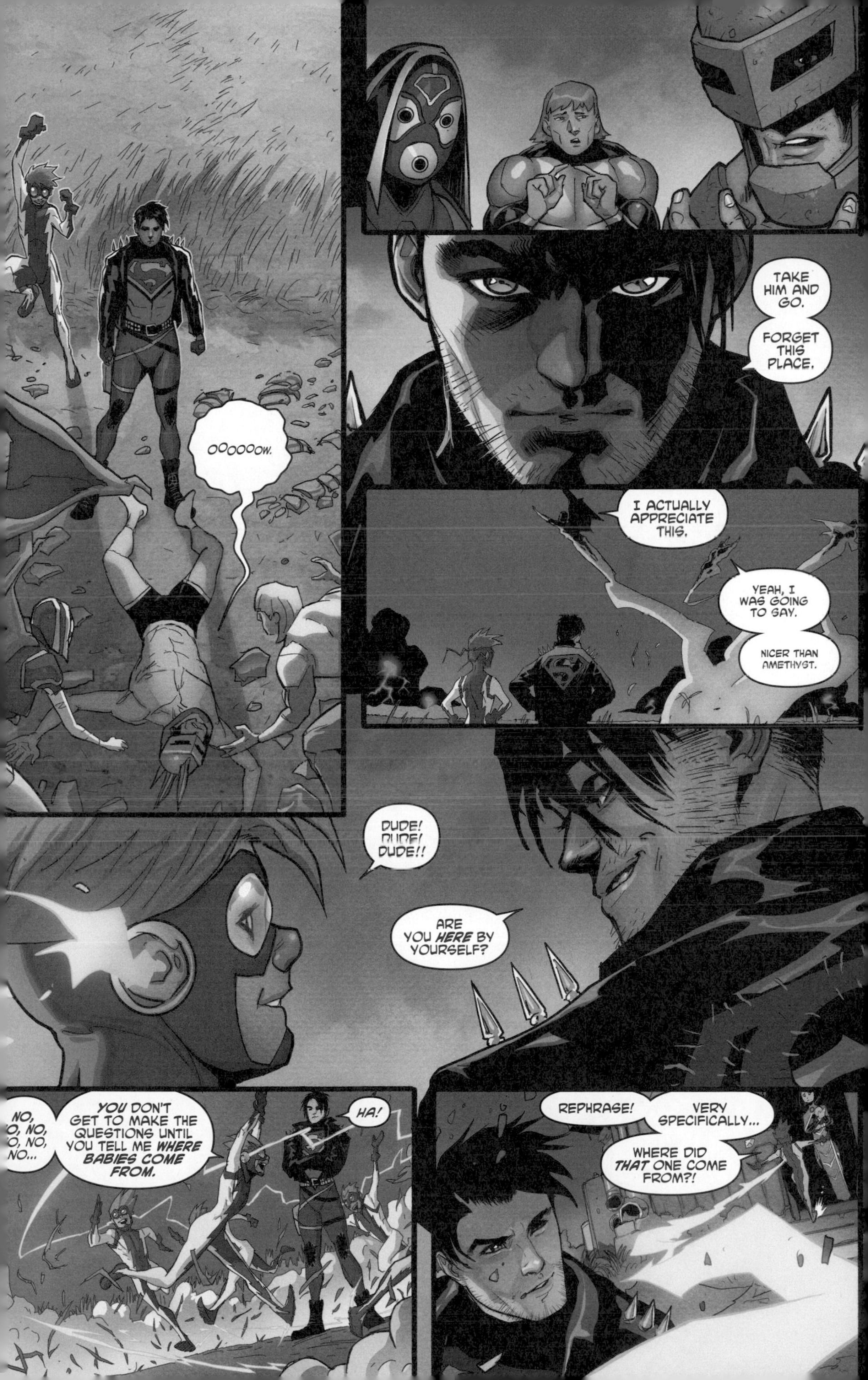

OOOOOOW.
TAKE HIM AND GO.
FORGET THIS PLACE.
I ACTUALLY APPRECIATE THIS.
YEAH, I WAS GOING TO SAY.
NICER THAN AMETHYST.
DUDE! DUDE! DUDE!!
ARE YOU *HERE* BY YOURSELF?
NO, NO, NO, NO, NO, NO...
YOU DON'T GET TO MAKE THE QUESTIONS UNTIL YOU TELL ME *WHERE BABIES COME FROM.*
HA!
REPHRASE!
VERY SPECIFICALLY...
WHERE DID *THAT* ONE COME FROM?!

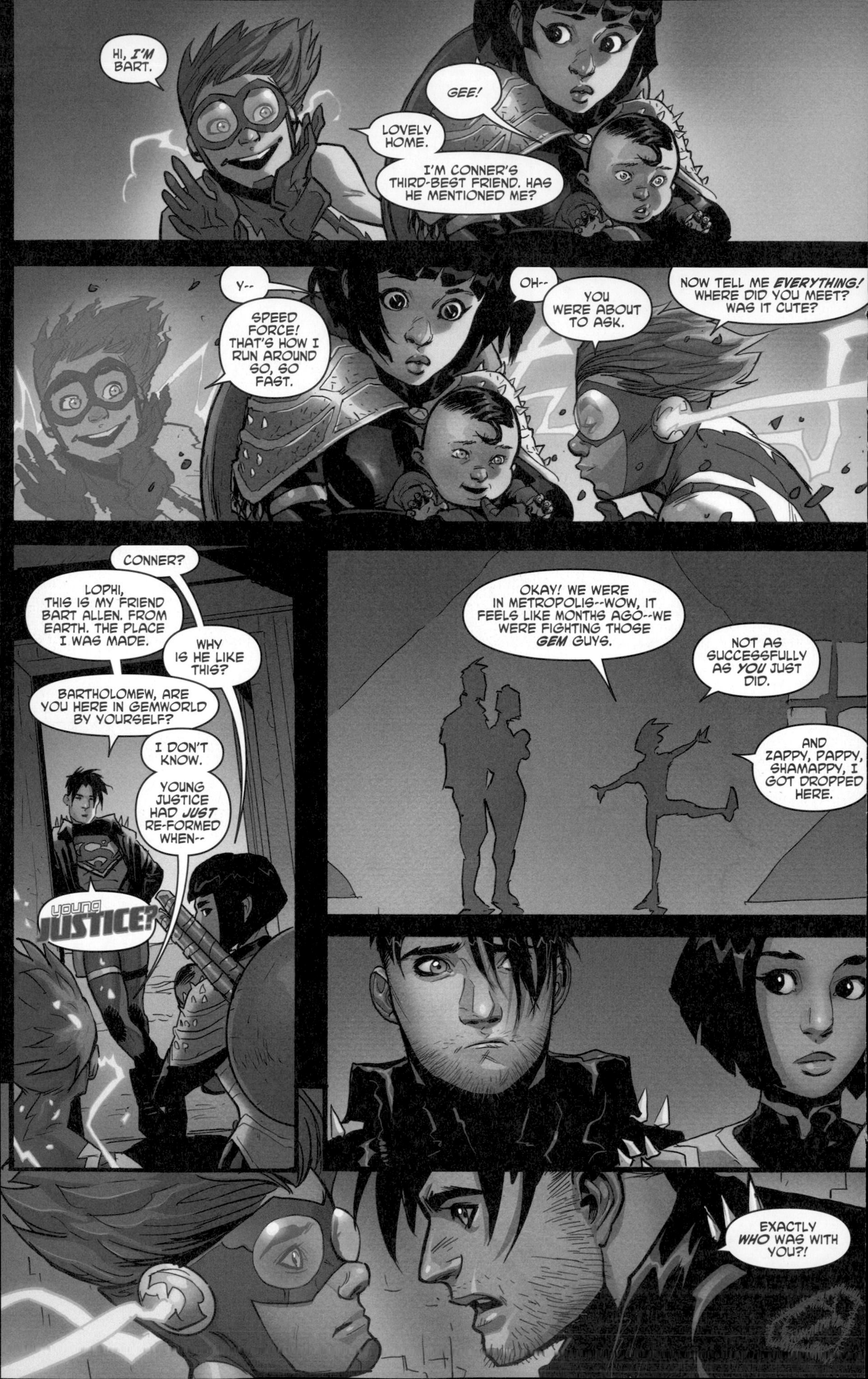

HI, *I'M* BART.
GEE!
LOVELY HOME.
I'M CONNER'S THIRD-BEST FRIEND. HAS HE MENTIONED ME?
Y--
SPEED FORCE! THAT'S HOW I RUN AROUND SO, SO FAST.
OH--
YOU WERE ABOUT TO ASK.
NOW TELL ME *EVERYTHING!* WHERE DID YOU MEET? WAS IT CUTE?
CONNER?
LOPHI, THIS IS MY FRIEND BART ALLEN. FROM EARTH. THE PLACE I WAS MADE.
WHY IS HE LIKE THIS?
BARTHOLOMEW, ARE YOU HERE IN GEMWORLD BY YOURSELF?
I DON'T KNOW.
YOUNG JUSTICE HAD *JUST* RE-FORMED WHEN--
YOUNG JUSTICE?
OKAY! WE WERE IN METROPOLIS--WOW, IT FEELS LIKE MONTHS AGO--WE WERE FIGHTING THOSE *GEM* GUYS.
NOT AS SUCCESSFULLY AS *YOU* JUST DID.
AND ZAPPY, PAPPY, SHAMAPPY, I GOT DROPPED HERE.
EXACTLY *WHO* WAS WITH YOU?!

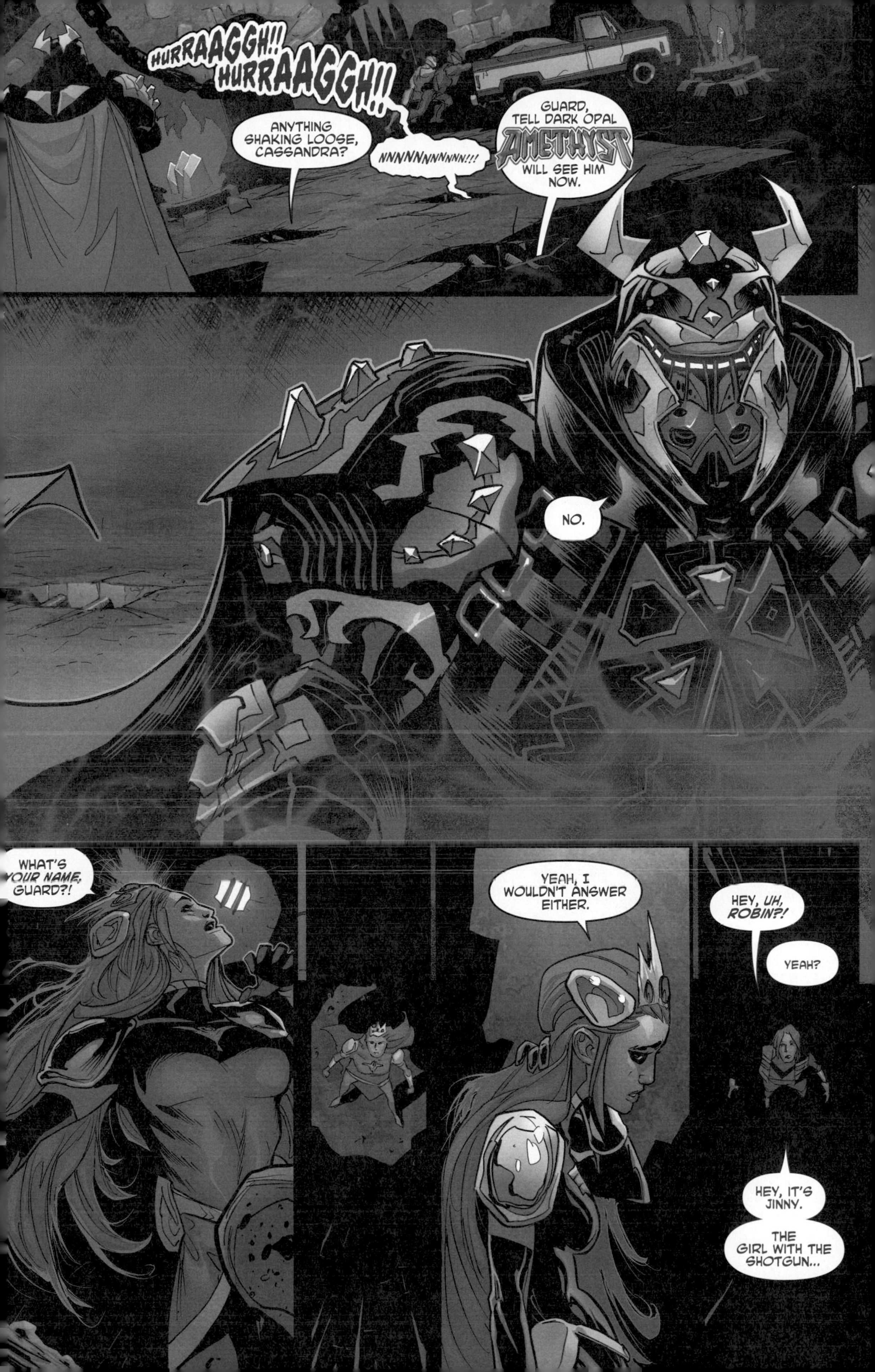
HURRAAGGH!! HURRAAGGH!!
ANYTHING SHAKING LOOSE, CASSANDRA?
NNNNNNNNNNN!!!
GUARD, TELL DARK OPAL AMETHYST WILL SEE HIM NOW.
NO.
WHAT'S YOUR NAME, GUARD?!
YEAH, I WOULDN'T ANSWER EITHER.
HEY, UH, ROBIN?!
YEAH?
HEY, IT'S JINNY.
THE GIRL WITH THE SHOTGUN...

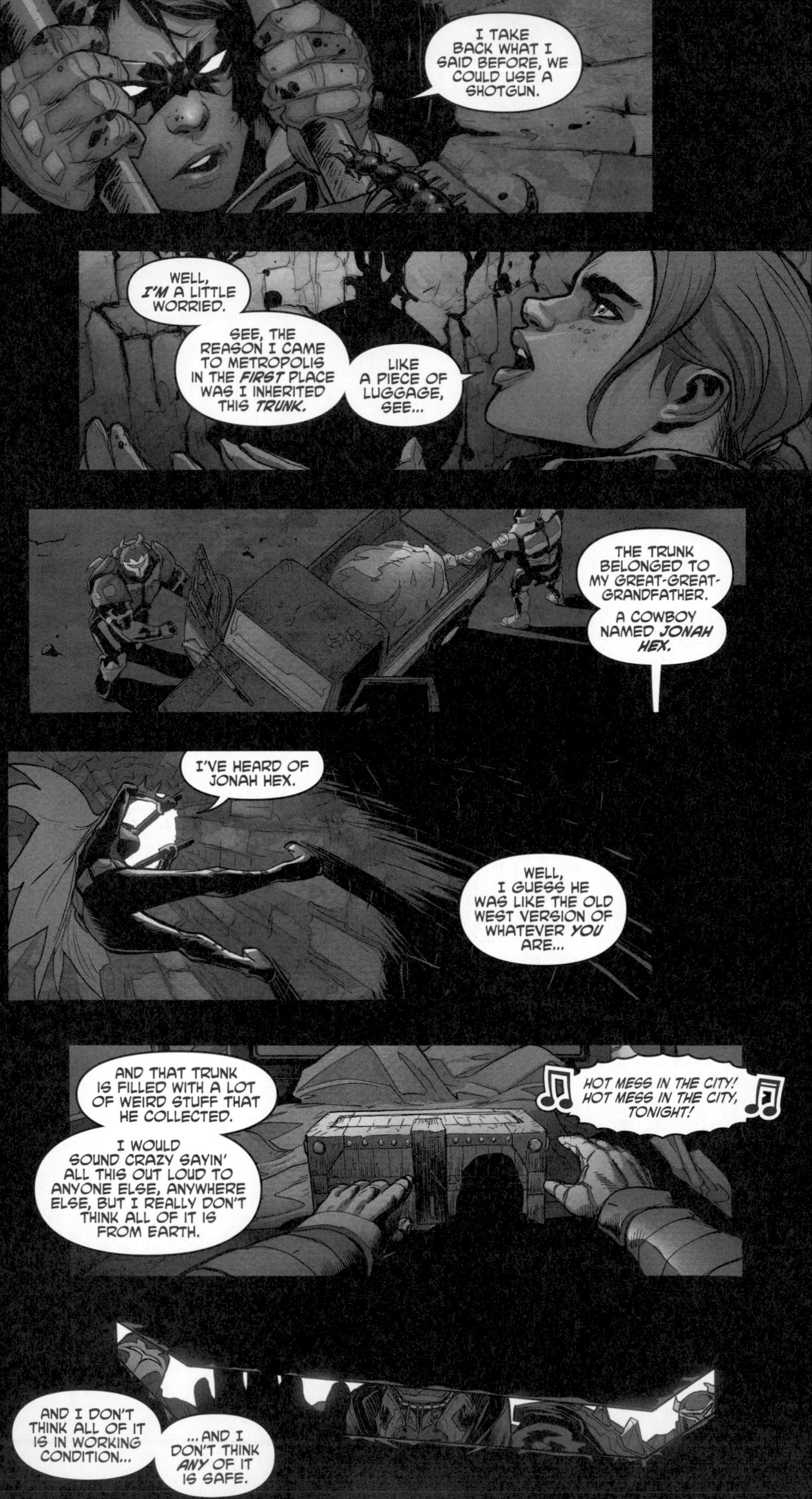
I TAKE BACK WHAT I SAID BEFORE, WE COULD USE A SHOTGUN.
WELL, *I'M* A LITTLE WORRIED.
SEE, THE REASON I CAME TO METROPOLIS IN THE *FIRST* PLACE WAS I INHERITED THIS *TRUNK.*
LIKE A PIECE OF LUGGAGE, SEE...
THE TRUNK BELONGED TO MY GREAT-GREAT-GRANDFATHER.
A COWBOY NAMED *JONAH HEX.*
I'VE HEARD OF JONAH HEX.
WELL, I GUESS HE WAS LIKE THE OLD WEST VERSION OF WHATEVER *YOU* ARE...
AND THAT TRUNK IS FILLED WITH A LOT OF WEIRD STUFF THAT HE COLLECTED.
HOT MESS IN THE CITY! HOT MESS IN THE CITY, TONIGHT!
I WOULD SOUND CRAZY SAYIN' ALL THIS OUT LOUD TO ANYONE ELSE, ANYWHERE ELSE, BUT I REALLY DON'T THINK ALL OF IT IS FROM EARTH.
AND I DON'T THINK ALL OF IT IS IN WORKING CONDITION...
...AND I DON'T THINK *ANY* OF IT IS SAFE.

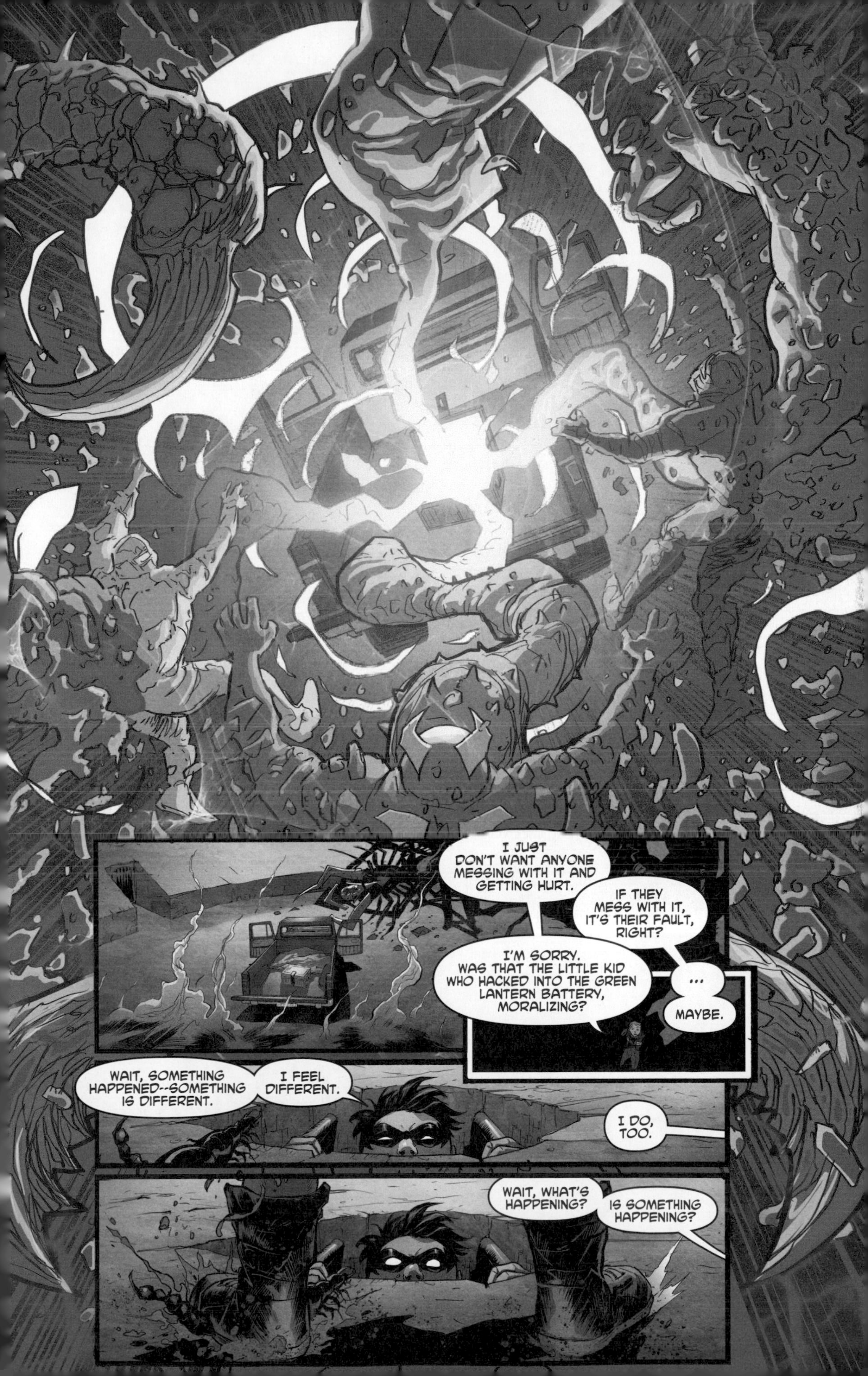

I JUST DON'T WANT ANYONE MESSING WITH IT AND GETTING HURT.
IF THEY MESS WITH IT, IT'S THEIR FAULT, RIGHT?
I'M SORRY. WAS THAT THE LITTLE KID WHO HACKED INTO THE GREEN LANTERN BATTERY, MORALIZING?
...
MAYBE.
WAIT, SOMETHING HAPPENED--SOMETHING IS DIFFERENT.
I FEEL DIFFERENT.
I DO, TOO.
WAIT, WHAT'S HAPPENING?
IS SOMETHING HAPPENING?

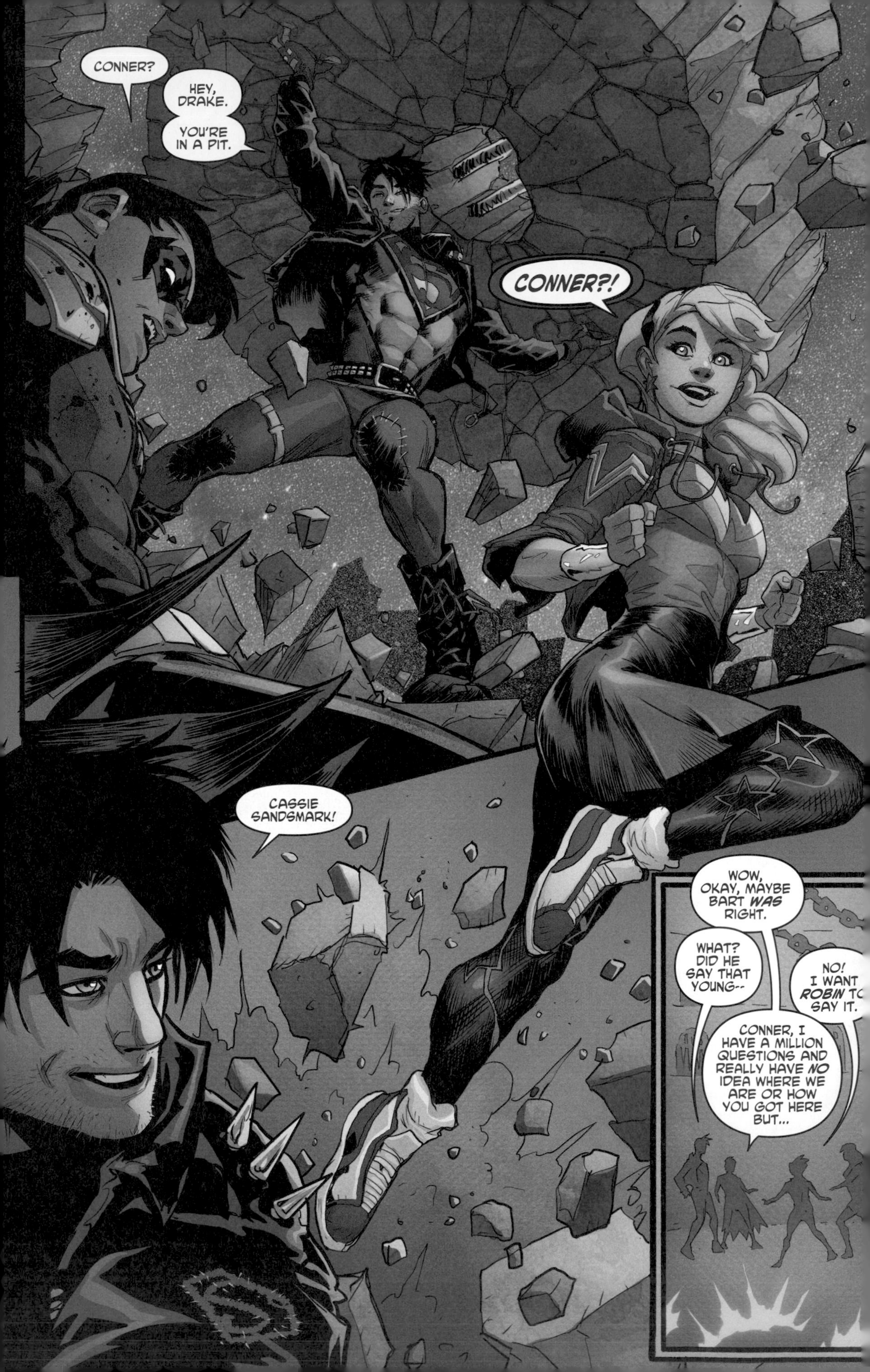
CONNER?
HEY, DRAKE.
YOU'RE IN A PIT.
CONNER?!
CASSIE SANDSMARK!
WOW, OKAY, MAYBE BART WAS RIGHT.
WHAT? DID HE SAY THAT YOUNG--
NO! I WANT ROBIN TO SAY IT.
CONNER, I HAVE A MILLION QUESTIONS AND REALLY HAVE NO IDEA WHERE WE ARE OR HOW YOU GOT HERE BUT...

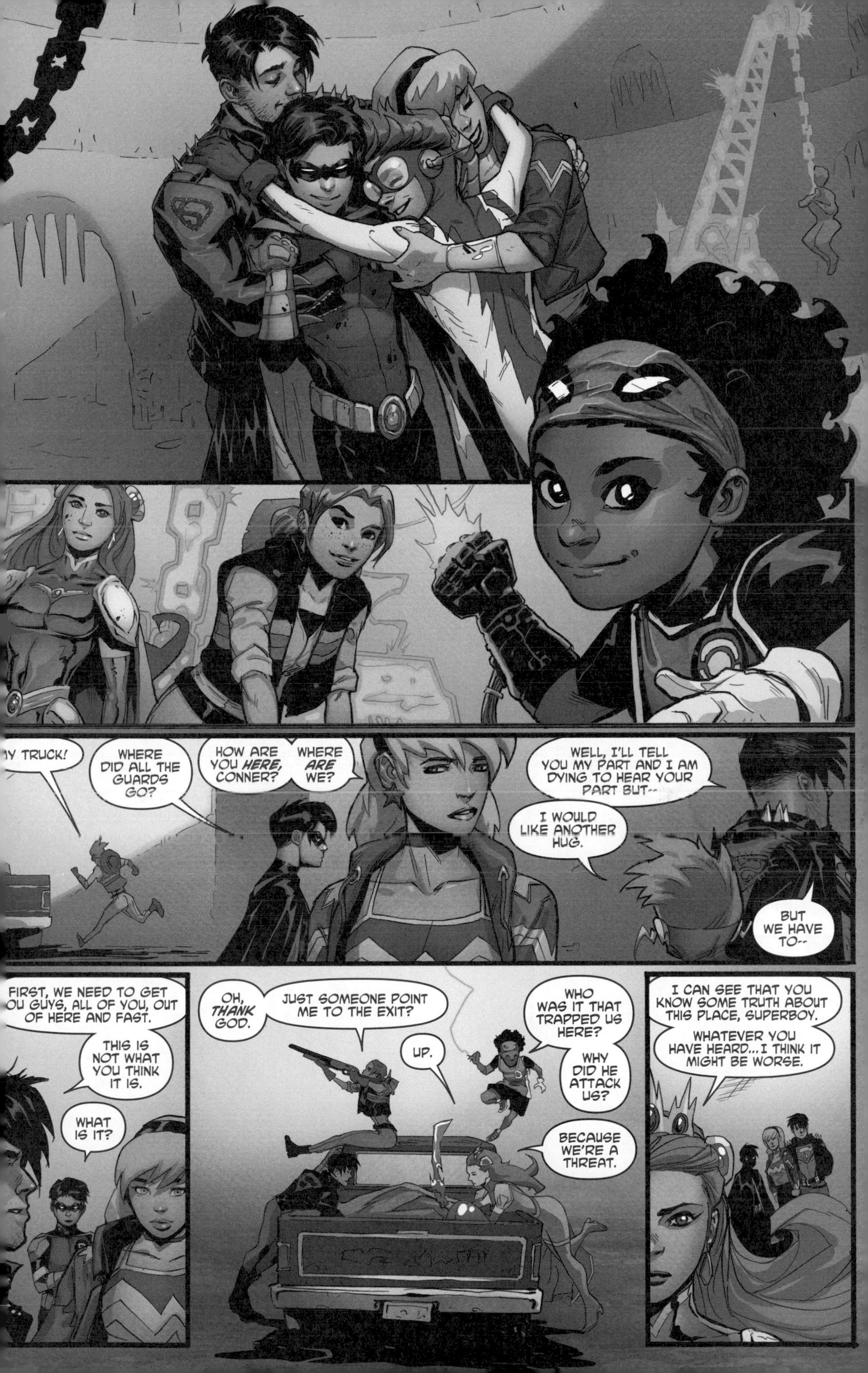

MY TRUCK!
WHERE DID ALL THE GUARDS GO?
HOW ARE YOU *HERE,* CONNER?
WHERE *ARE* WE?
WELL, I'LL TELL YOU MY PART AND I AM DYING TO HEAR YOUR PART BUT--
I WOULD LIKE ANOTHER HUG.
BUT WE HAVE TO--
FIRST, WE NEED TO GET YOU GUYS, ALL OF YOU, OUT OF HERE AND FAST.
THIS IS NOT WHAT YOU THINK IT IS.
WHAT IS IT?
OH, *THANK* GOD.
JUST SOMEONE POINT ME TO THE EXIT?
UP.
WHO WAS IT THAT TRAPPED US HERE?
WHY DID HE ATTACK US?
BECAUSE WE'RE A THREAT.
I CAN SEE THAT YOU KNOW SOME TRUTH ABOUT THIS PLACE, SUPERBOY.
WHATEVER YOU HAVE HEARD... I THINK IT MIGHT BE WORSE.

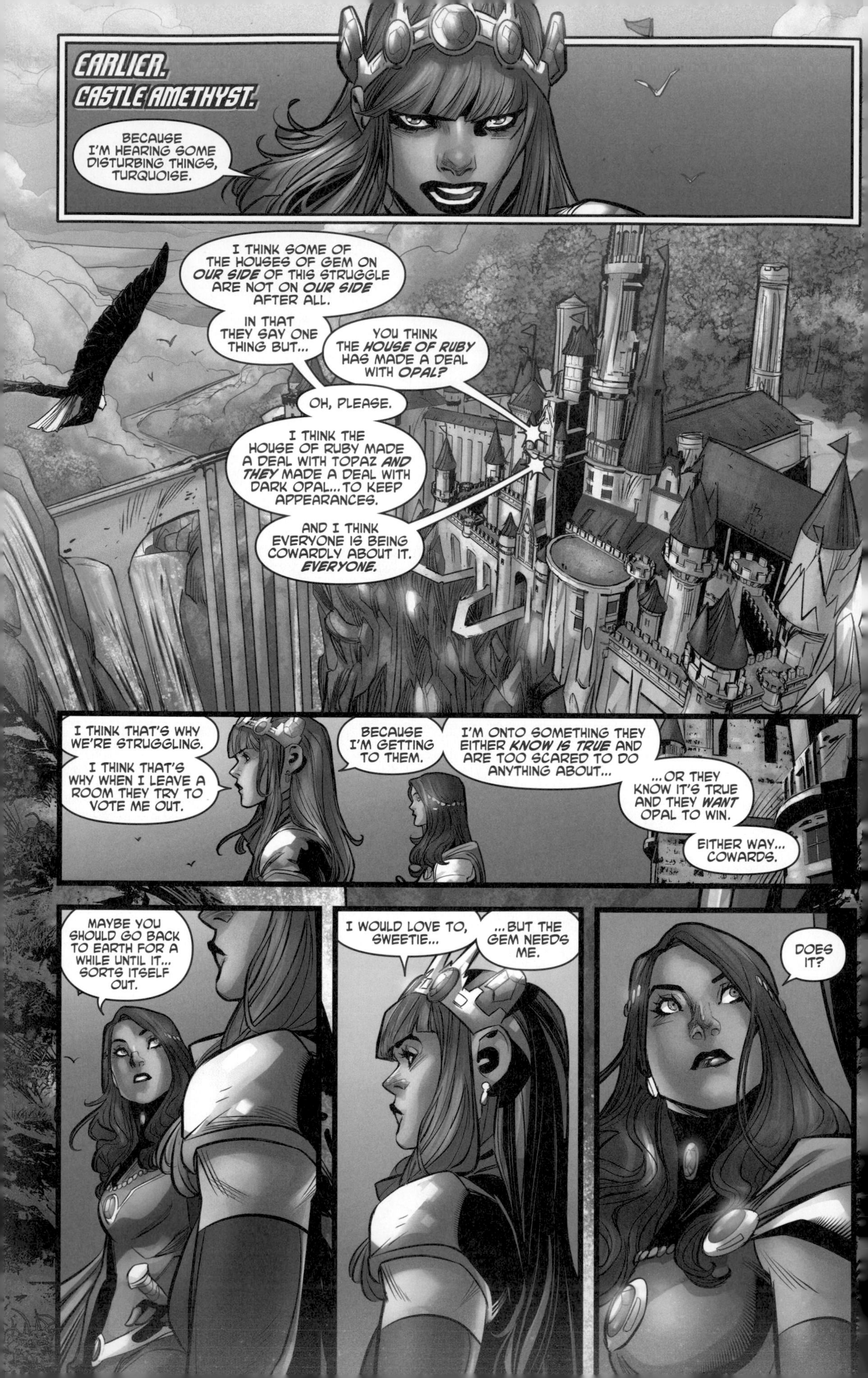

EARLIER.
CASTLE AMETHYST.
BECAUSE I'M HEARING SOME DISTURBING THINGS, TURQUOISE.
I THINK SOME OF THE HOUSES OF GEM ON OUR SIDE OF THIS STRUGGLE ARE NOT ON OUR SIDE AFTER ALL.
IN THAT THEY SAY ONE THING BUT...
YOU THINK THE HOUSE OF RUBY HAS MADE A DEAL WITH OPAL?
OH, PLEASE.
I THINK THE HOUSE OF RUBY MADE A DEAL WITH TOPAZ AND THEY MADE A DEAL WITH DARK OPAL...TO KEEP APPEARANCES.
AND I THINK EVERYONE IS BEING COWARDLY ABOUT IT. EVERYONE.
I THINK THAT'S WHY WE'RE STRUGGLING.
I THINK THAT'S WHY WHEN I LEAVE A ROOM THEY TRY TO VOTE ME OUT.
BECAUSE I'M GETTING TO THEM.
I'M ONTO SOMETHING THEY EITHER KNOW IS TRUE AND ARE TOO SCARED TO DO ANYTHING ABOUT...
...OR THEY KNOW IT'S TRUE AND THEY WANT OPAL TO WIN.
EITHER WAY... COWARDS.
MAYBE YOU SHOULD GO BACK TO EARTH FOR A WHILE UNTIL IT... SORTS ITSELF OUT.
I WOULD LOVE TO, SWEETIE...
...BUT THE GEM NEEDS ME.
DOES IT?

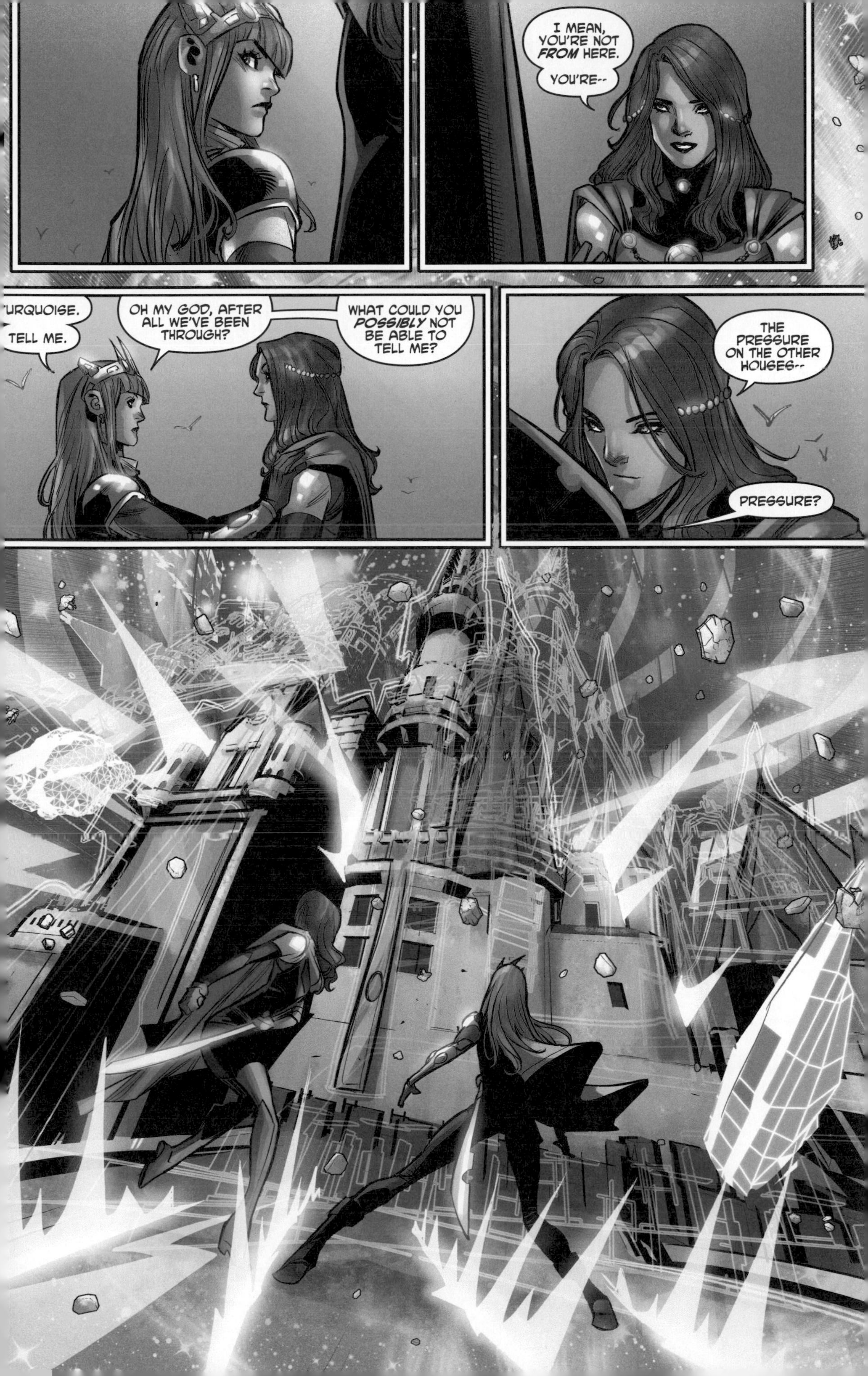
I MEAN, YOU'RE NOT FROM HERE.
YOU'RE--
TURQUOISE.
TELL ME.
OH MY GOD, AFTER ALL WE'VE BEEN THROUGH?
WHAT COULD YOU POSSIBLY NOT BE ABLE TO TELL ME?
THE PRESSURE ON THE OTHER HOUSES--
PRESSURE?

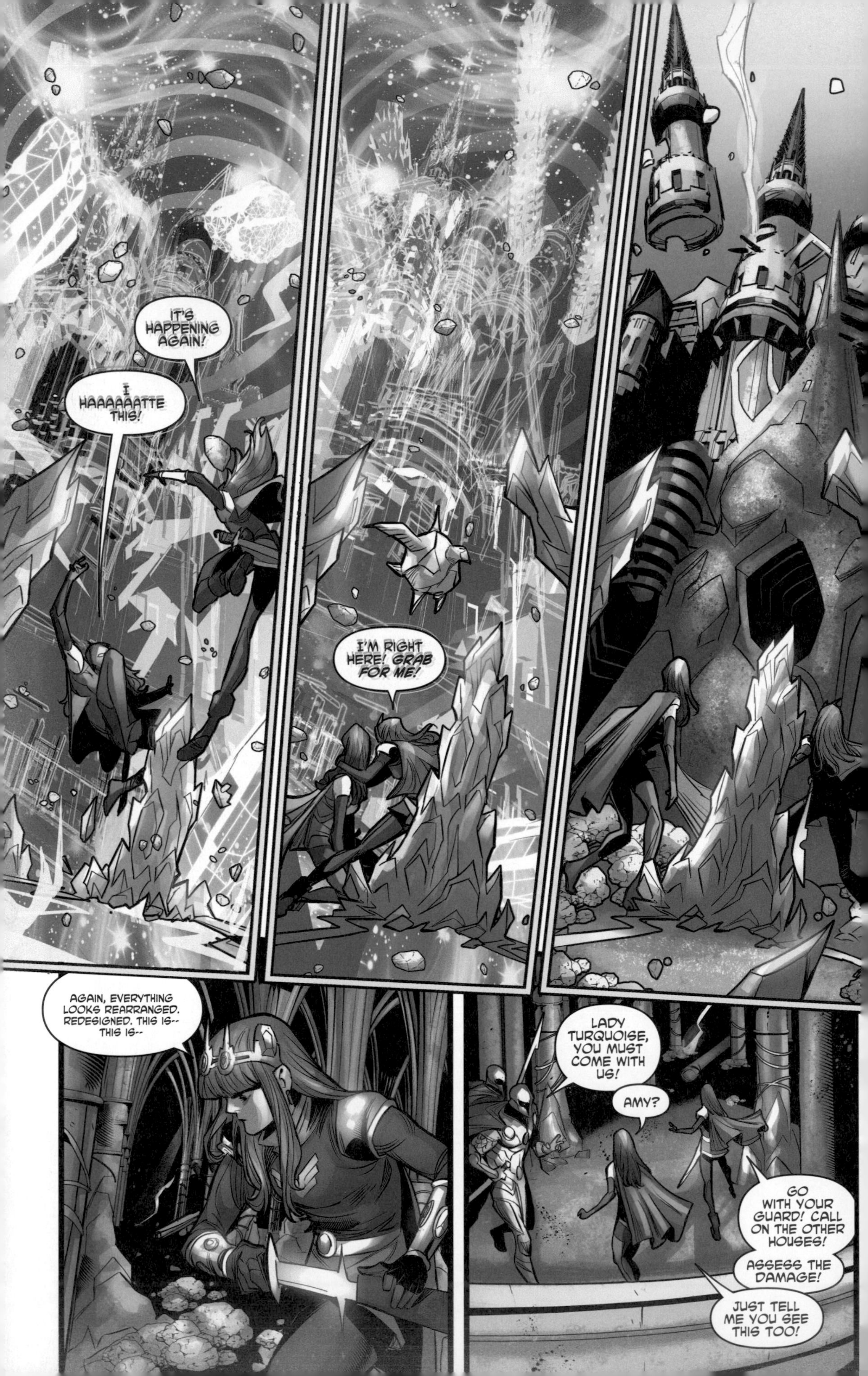
IT'S HAPPENING AGAIN!
I HAAAAAATTE THIS!
I'M RIGHT HERE! GRAB FOR ME!
AGAIN, EVERYTHING LOOKS REARRANGED. REDESIGNED. THIS IS-- THIS IS--
LADY TURQUOISE, YOU MUST COME WITH US!
AMY?
GO WITH YOUR GUARD! CALL ON THE OTHER HOUSES!
ASSESS THE DAMAGE!
JUST TELL ME YOU SEE THIS TOO!

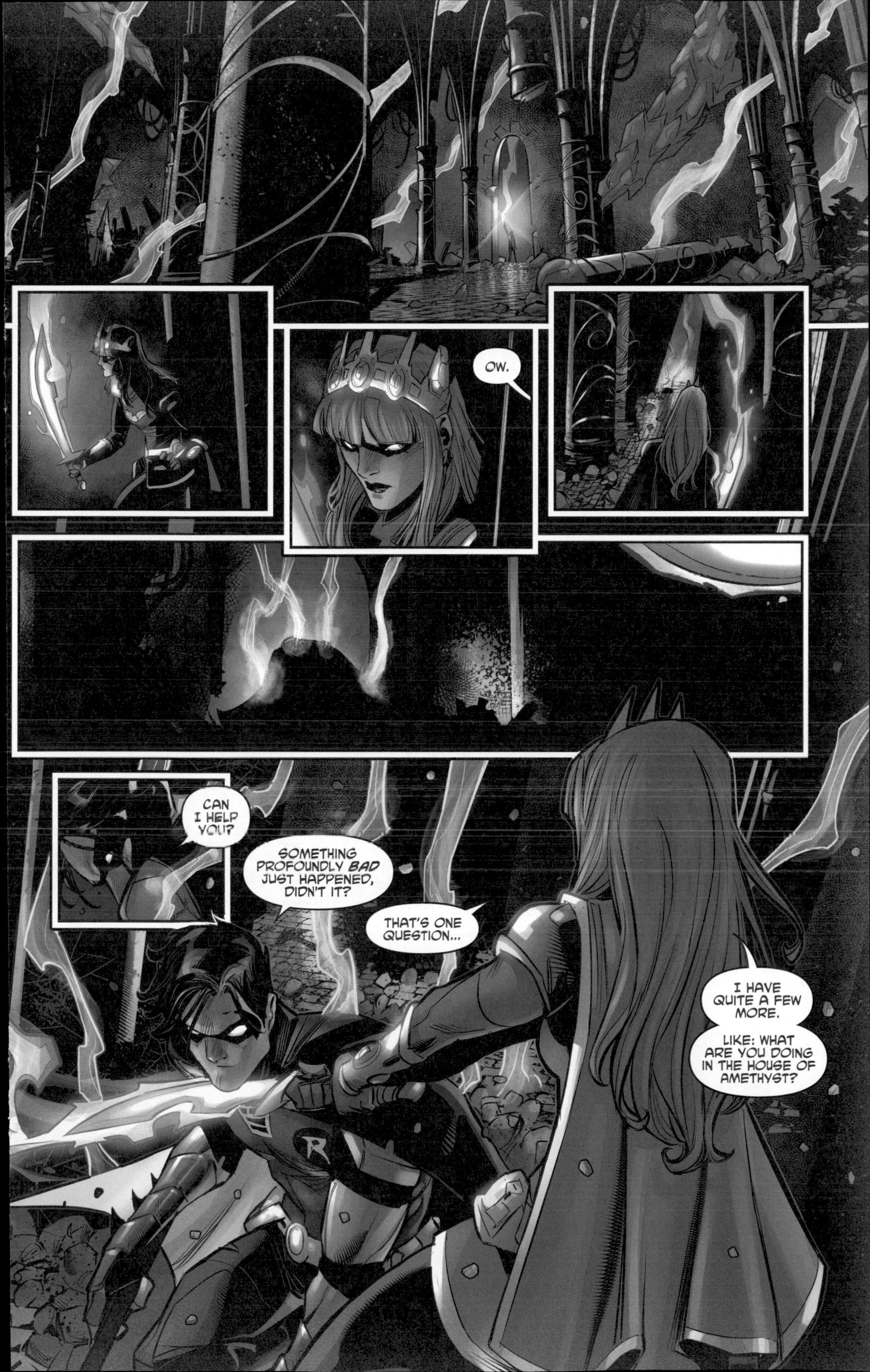
OW.
CAN I HELP YOU?
SOMETHING PROFOUNDLY *BAD* JUST HAPPENED, DIDN'T IT?
THAT'S ONE QUESTION...
I HAVE QUITE A FEW MORE.
LIKE: WHAT ARE YOU DOING IN THE HOUSE OF AMETHYST?

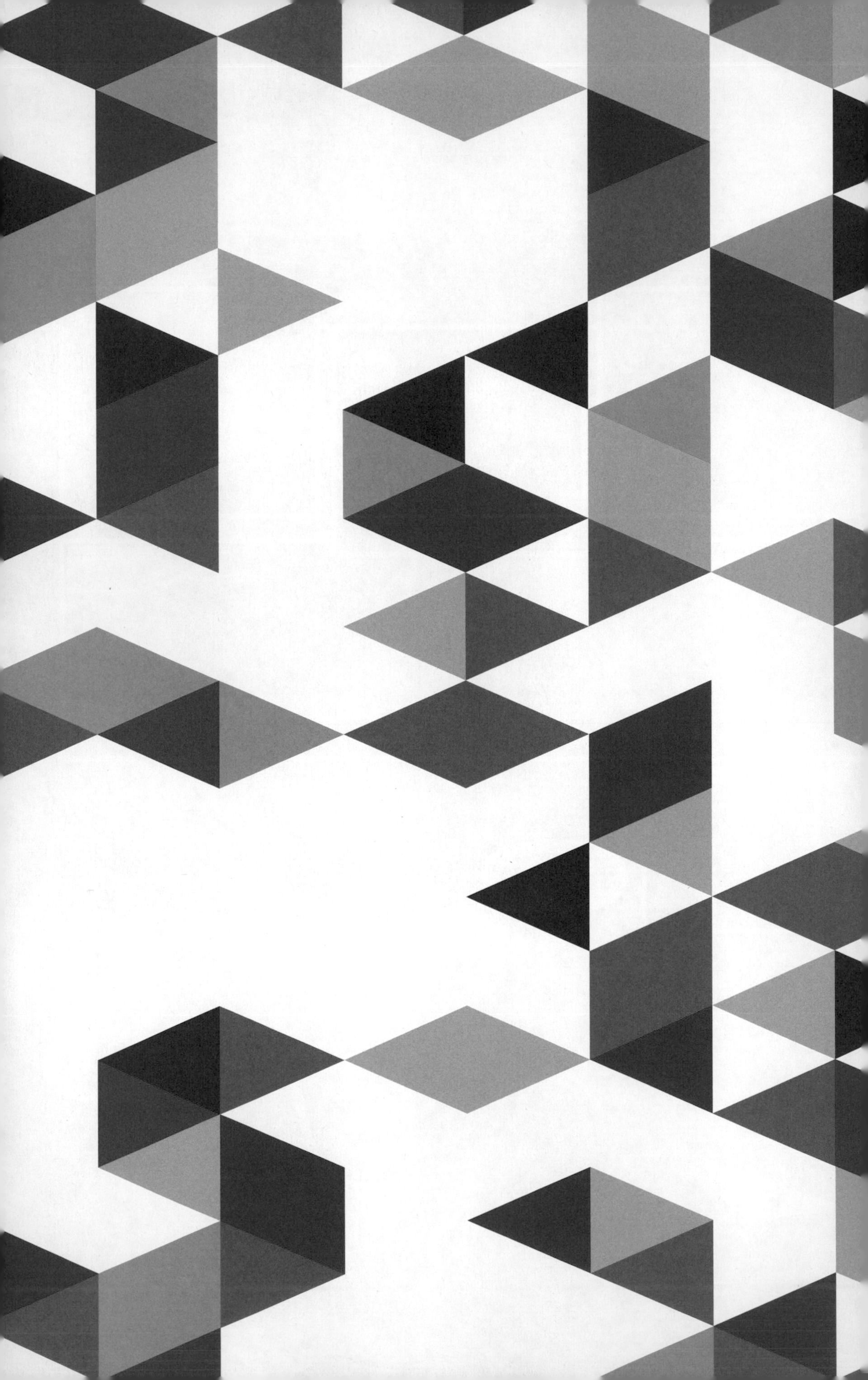

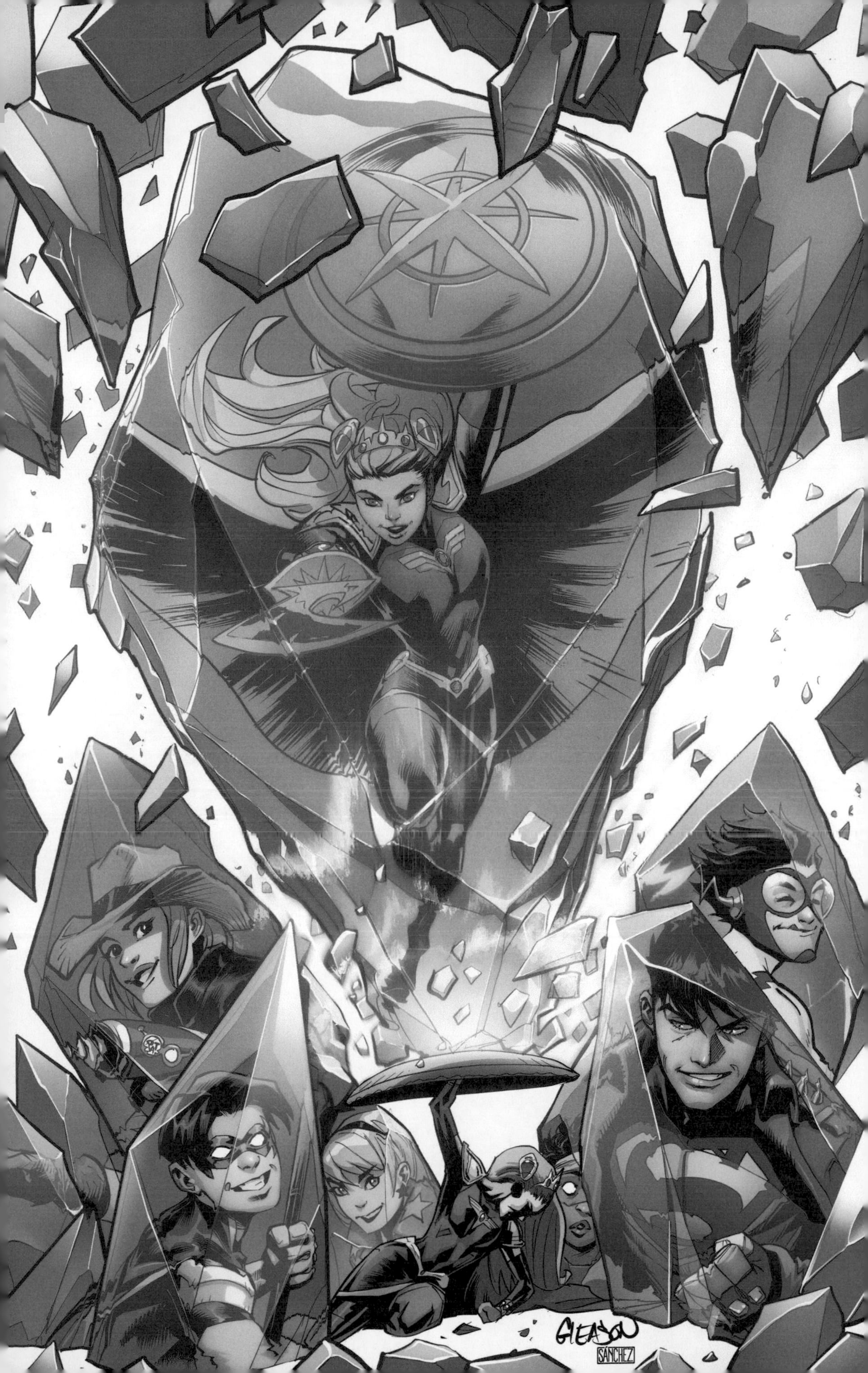
GLEASON
SÁNCHEZ

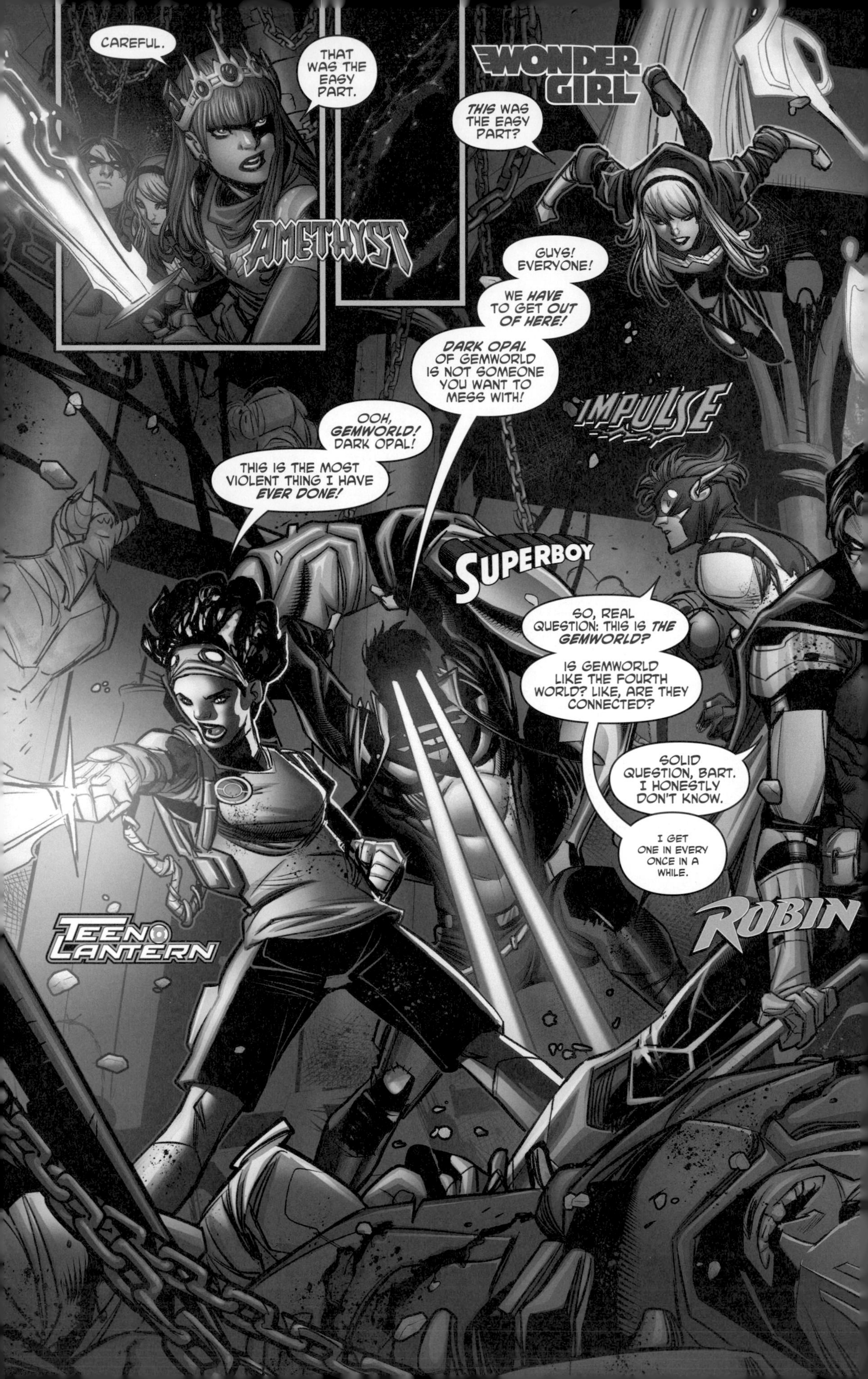
CAREFUL.
THAT WAS THE EASY PART.
AMETHYST
WONDER GIRL
THIS WAS THE EASY PART?
GUYS! EVERYONE!
WE HAVE TO GET OUT OF HERE!
DARK OPAL OF GEMWORLD IS NOT SOMEONE YOU WANT TO MESS WITH!
IMPULSE
OOH, GEMWORLD! DARK OPAL!
THIS IS THE MOST VIOLENT THING I HAVE EVER DONE!
SUPERBOY
SO, REAL QUESTION: THIS IS THE GEMWORLD?
IS GEMWORLD LIKE THE FOURTH WORLD? LIKE, ARE THEY CONNECTED?
SOLID QUESTION, BART. I HONESTLY DON'T KNOW.
I GET ONE IN EVERY ONCE IN A WHILE.
ROBIN
TEEN LANTERN

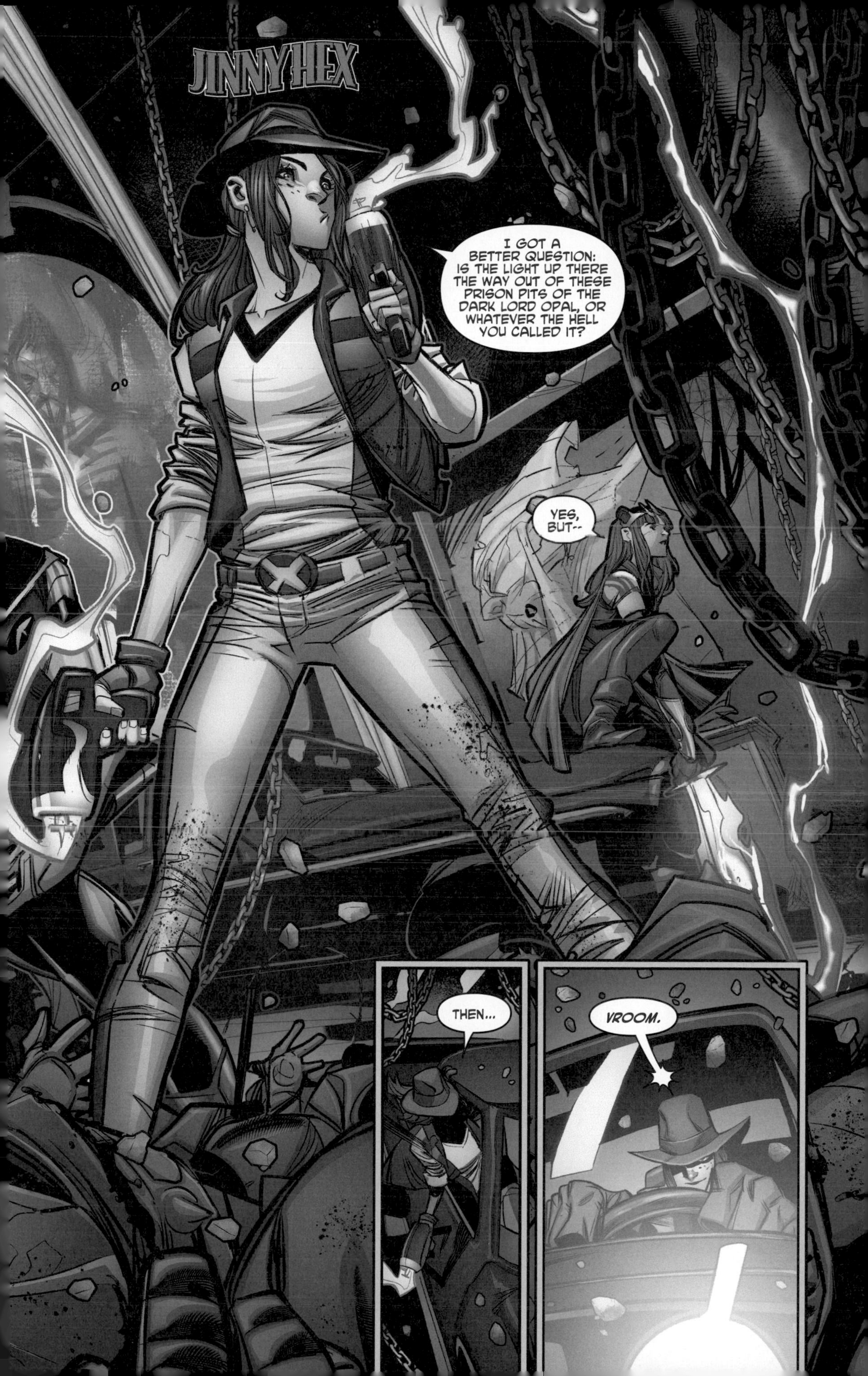
JINNY HEX
I GOT A BETTER QUESTION: IS THE LIGHT UP THERE THE WAY OUT OF THESE PRISON PITS OF THE DARK LORD OPAL, OR WHATEVER THE HELL YOU CALLED IT?
YES, BUT--
THEN...
VROOM.

DC COMICS Proudly Presents
YOUNG JUSTICE
HEY, PRINCESS LADY!
WHAT'S THAT PURPLE FLASH OF LIGHT FOR?
YOU EVER MEET BATMAN?! YOU DRIVE JUST LIKE HIM!
I HAVE, ACTUALLY.
OH, I WAS KIDDING.
IS IT OKAY THAT JINNY HEX'S MY NEW FAVORITE?
WAS I YOUR OLD FAVORITE?
YOU WERE IN THE TOP TEN.
AWWW!
JHX
I JUST WANT TO SAY: THOUGH I AM HAVING THE BEST TIME, I HAVE NEVER BEEN LESS SURE OF WHERE I PHYSICALLY AM IN MY ENTIRE LIFE!
AND I HAVE BEEN TO SOME WEEEEEIRD-ASS PLACES.
LIKE BURBANK.
SEVEN CRISES part 5
BRIAN MICHAEL BENDIS Script JOHN TIMMS, KRIS ANKA & EVAN "DOC" SHANER Art
GABE ELTAEB Colors WES ABBOTT Letters
PATRICK GLEASON & ALEJANDRO SANCHEZ Cover
BRITTANY HOLZHERR Associate Editor MIKE COTTON Editor BRIAN CUNNINGHAM Group Editor

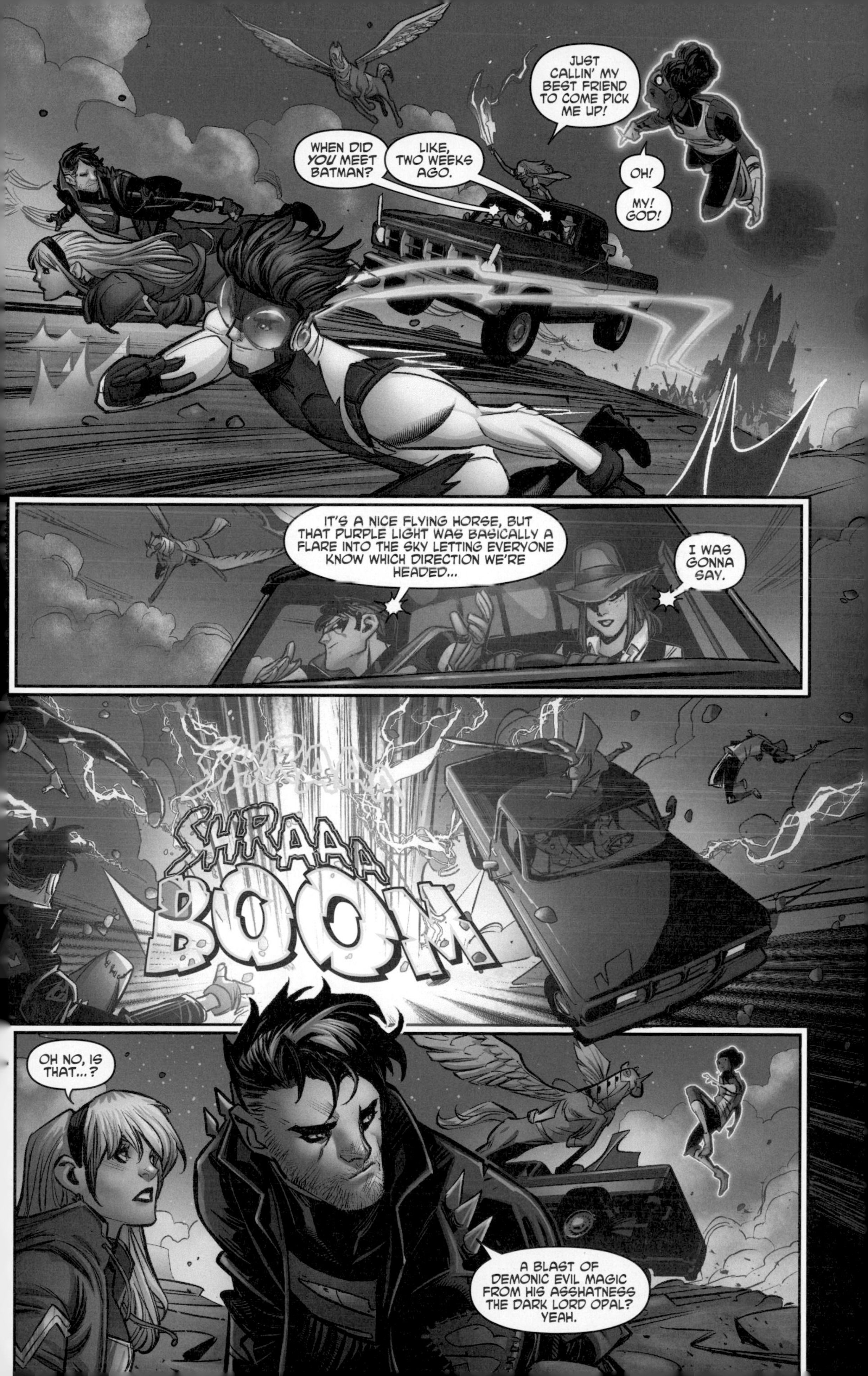
JUST CALLIN' MY BEST FRIEND TO COME PICK ME UP!
WHEN DID *YOU* MEET BATMAN?
LIKE, TWO WEEKS AGO.
OH!
MY! GOD!
IT'S A NICE FLYING HORSE, BUT THAT PURPLE LIGHT WAS BASICALLY A FLARE INTO THE SKY LETTING EVERYONE KNOW WHICH DIRECTION WE'RE HEADED...
I WAS GONNA SAY.
SHRAAAA
BOOM
OH NO, IS THAT...?
A BLAST OF DEMONIC EVIL MAGIC FROM HIS ASSHATNESS THE DARK LORD OPAL? YEAH.

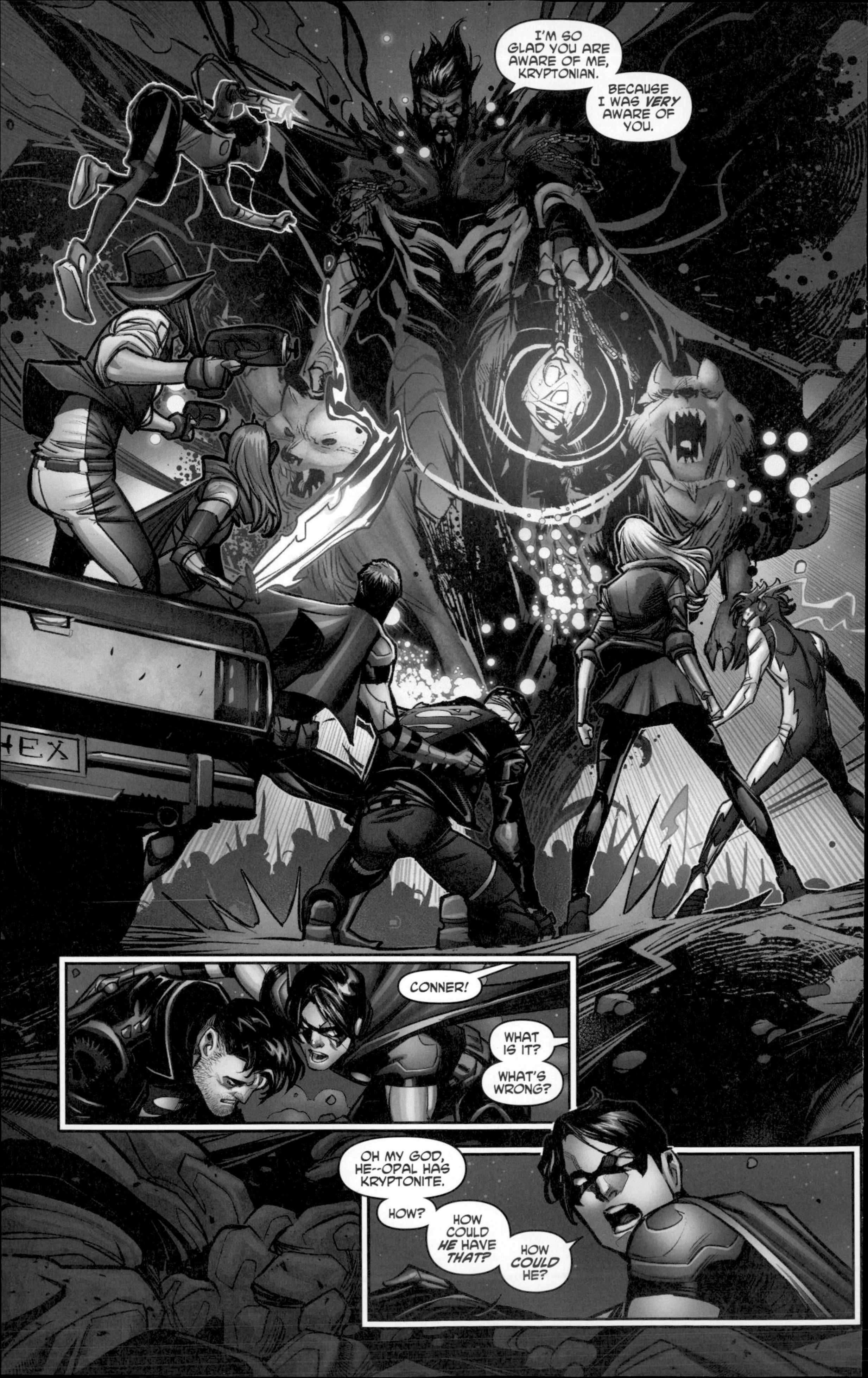

I'M SO GLAD YOU ARE AWARE OF ME, KRYPTONIAN.
BECAUSE I WAS VERY AWARE OF YOU.
HEX
CONNER!
WHAT IS IT?
WHAT'S WRONG?
OH MY GOD, HE--OPAL HAS KRYPTONITE.
HOW?
HOW COULD HE HAVE THAT?
HOW COULD HE?

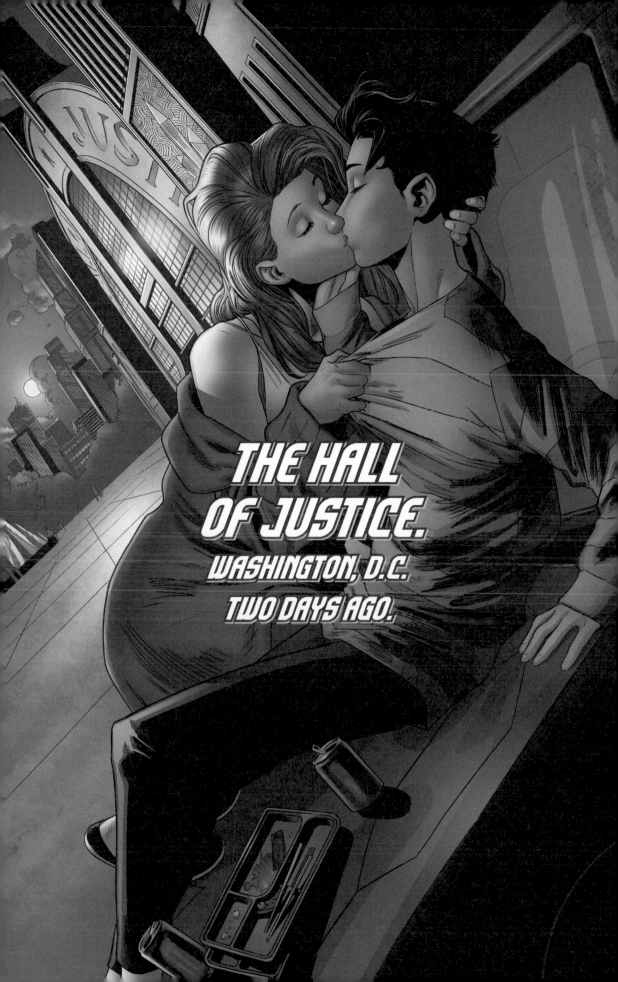

THE HALL
OF JUSTICE.
WASHINGTON, D.C.
TWO DAYS AGO.

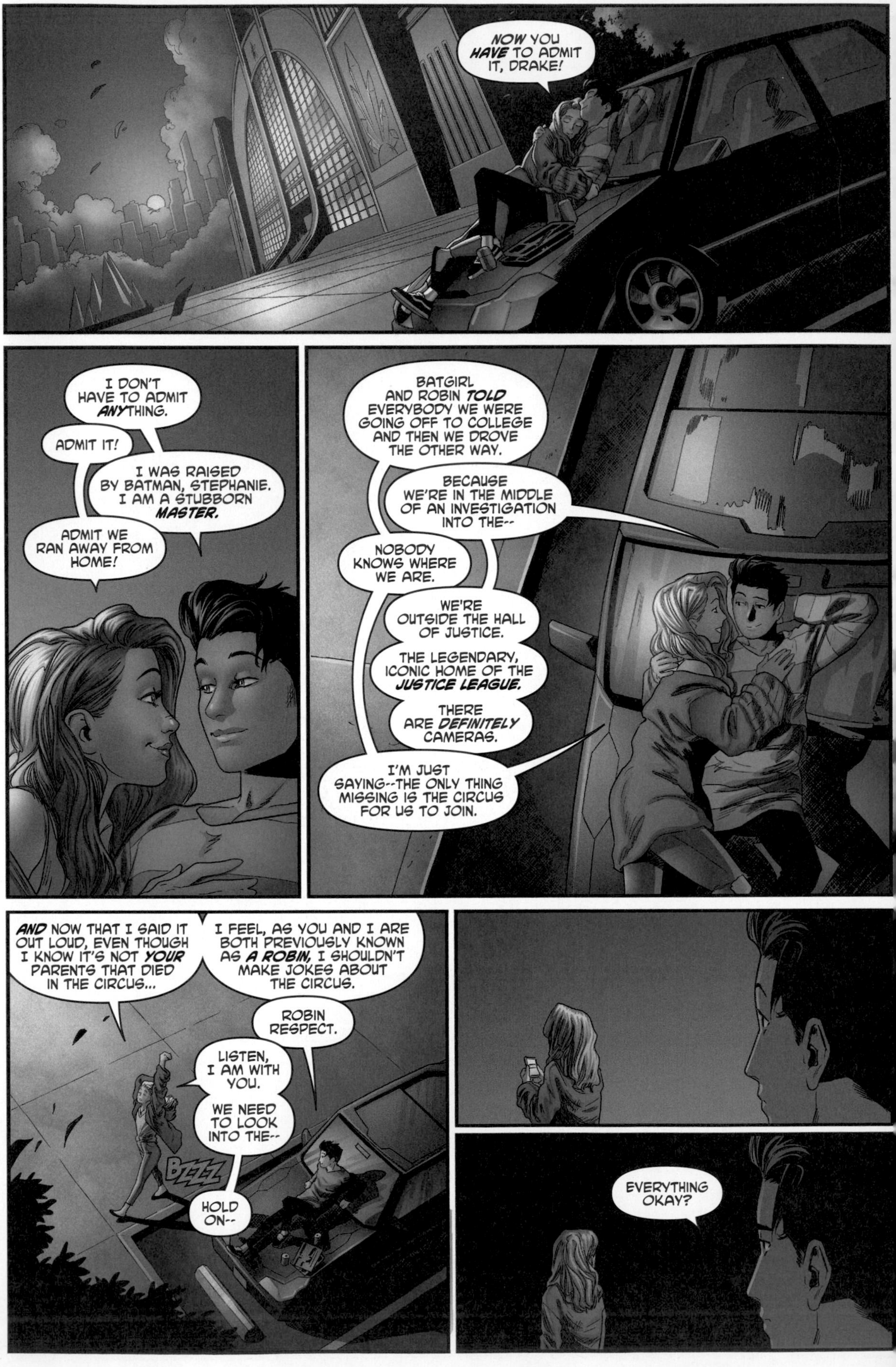
NOW YOU HAVE TO ADMIT IT, DRAKE!
I DON'T HAVE TO ADMIT ANYTHING.
ADMIT IT!
I WAS RAISED BY BATMAN, STEPHANIE. I AM A STUBBORN MASTER.
ADMIT WE RAN AWAY FROM HOME!
BATGIRL AND ROBIN TOLD EVERYBODY WE WERE GOING OFF TO COLLEGE AND THEN WE DROVE THE OTHER WAY.
BECAUSE WE'RE IN THE MIDDLE OF AN INVESTIGATION INTO THE--
NOBODY KNOWS WHERE WE ARE.
WE'RE OUTSIDE THE HALL OF JUSTICE.
THE LEGENDARY, ICONIC HOME OF THE JUSTICE LEAGUE.
THERE ARE DEFINITELY CAMERAS.
I'M JUST SAYING--THE ONLY THING MISSING IS THE CIRCUS FOR US TO JOIN.
AND NOW THAT I SAID IT OUT LOUD, EVEN THOUGH I KNOW IT'S NOT YOUR PARENTS THAT DIED IN THE CIRCUS...
I FEEL, AS YOU AND I ARE BOTH PREVIOUSLY KNOWN AS A ROBIN, I SHOULDN'T MAKE JOKES ABOUT THE CIRCUS.
ROBIN RESPECT.
LISTEN, I AM WITH YOU.
WE NEED TO LOOK INTO THE--
BZZZ
HOLD ON--
EVERYTHING OKAY?

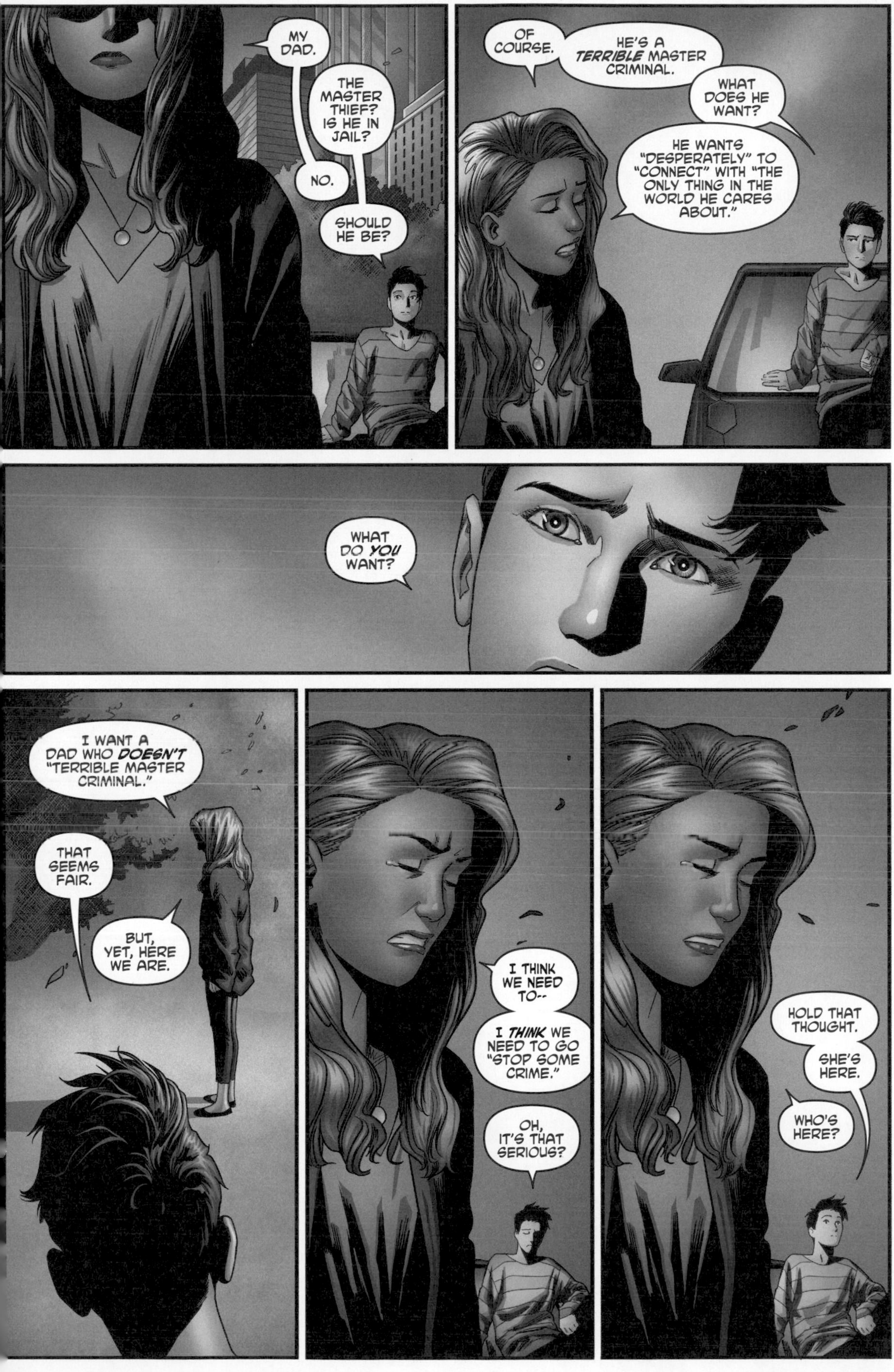
MY DAD.
THE MASTER THIEF? IS HE IN JAIL?
NO.
SHOULD HE BE?
OF COURSE.
HE'S A *TERRIBLE* MASTER CRIMINAL.
WHAT DOES HE WANT?
HE WANTS "DESPERATELY" TO "CONNECT" WITH "THE ONLY THING IN THE WORLD HE CARES ABOUT."
WHAT DO *YOU* WANT?
I WANT A DAD WHO *DOESN'T* "TERRIBLE MASTER CRIMINAL."
THAT SEEMS FAIR.
BUT, YET, HERE WE ARE.
I THINK WE NEED TO--
I *THINK* WE NEED TO GO "STOP SOME CRIME."
OH, IT'S THAT SERIOUS?
HOLD THAT THOUGHT.
SHE'S HERE.
WHO'S HERE?

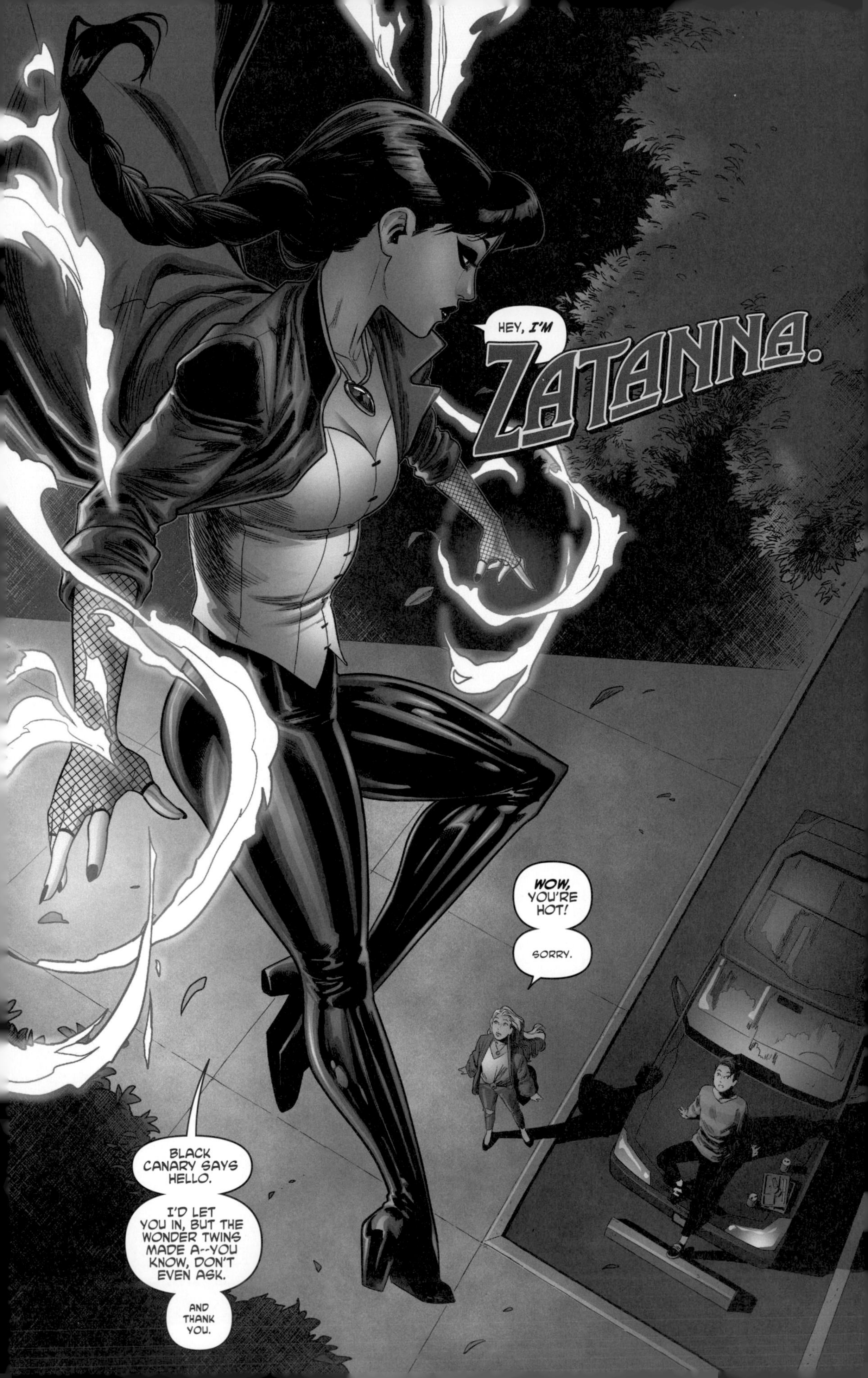
HEY, I'M
ZATANNA.
WOW, YOU'RE HOT!
SORRY.
BLACK CANARY SAYS HELLO.
I'D LET YOU IN, BUT THE WONDER TWINS MADE A--YOU KNOW, DON'T EVEN ASK.
AND THANK YOU.

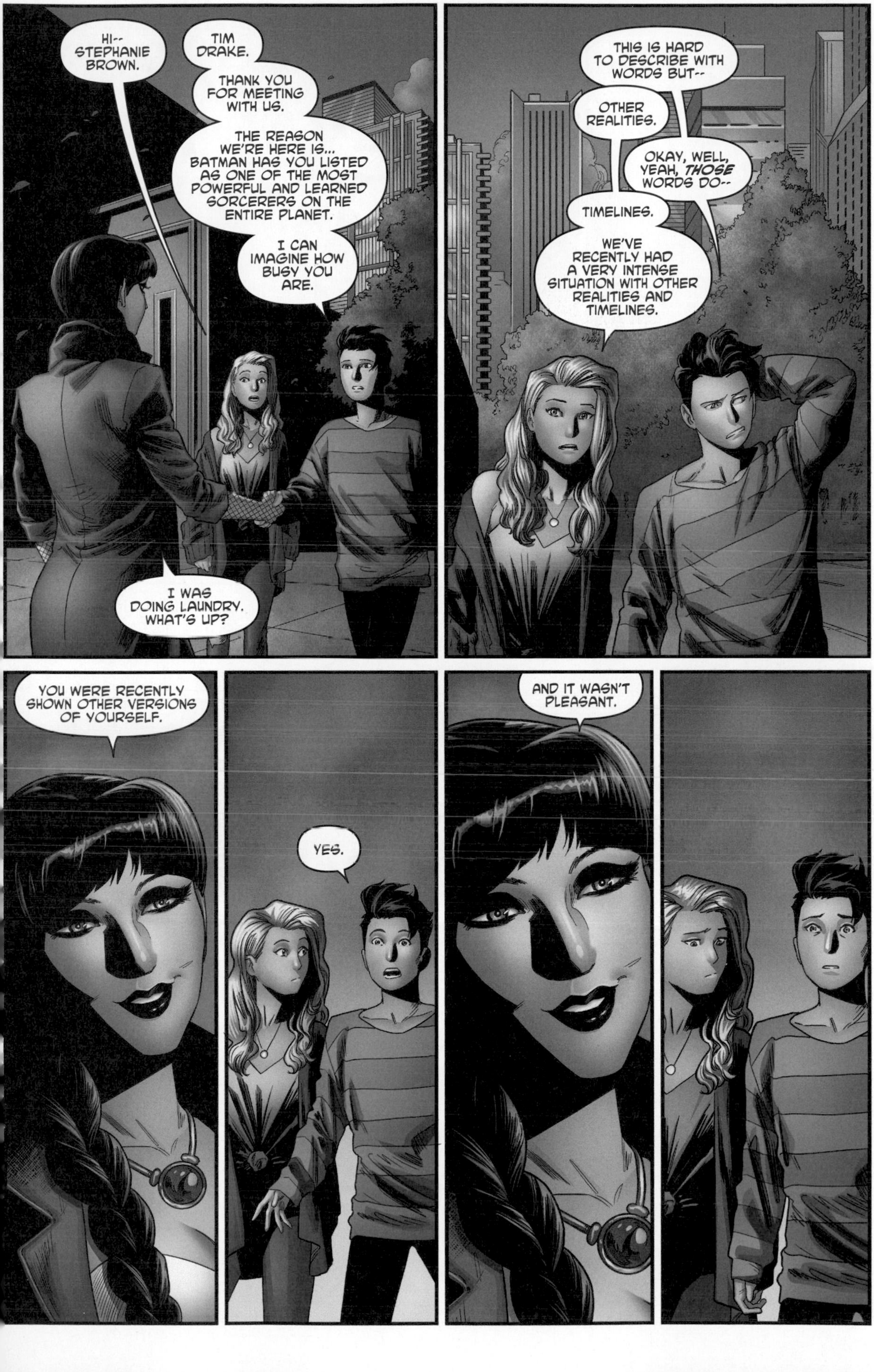
HI-- STEPHANIE BROWN.
TIM DRAKE.
THANK YOU FOR MEETING WITH US.
THE REASON WE'RE HERE IS... BATMAN HAS YOU LISTED AS ONE OF THE MOST POWERFUL AND LEARNED SORCERERS ON THE ENTIRE PLANET.
I CAN IMAGINE HOW BUSY YOU ARE.
I WAS DOING LAUNDRY. WHAT'S UP?
THIS IS HARD TO DESCRIBE WITH WORDS BUT--
OTHER REALITIES.
OKAY, WELL, YEAH, *THOSE* WORDS DO--
TIMELINES.
WE'VE RECENTLY HAD A VERY INTENSE SITUATION WITH OTHER REALITIES AND TIMELINES.
YOU WERE RECENTLY SHOWN OTHER VERSIONS OF YOURSELF.
YES.
AND IT WASN'T PLEASANT.

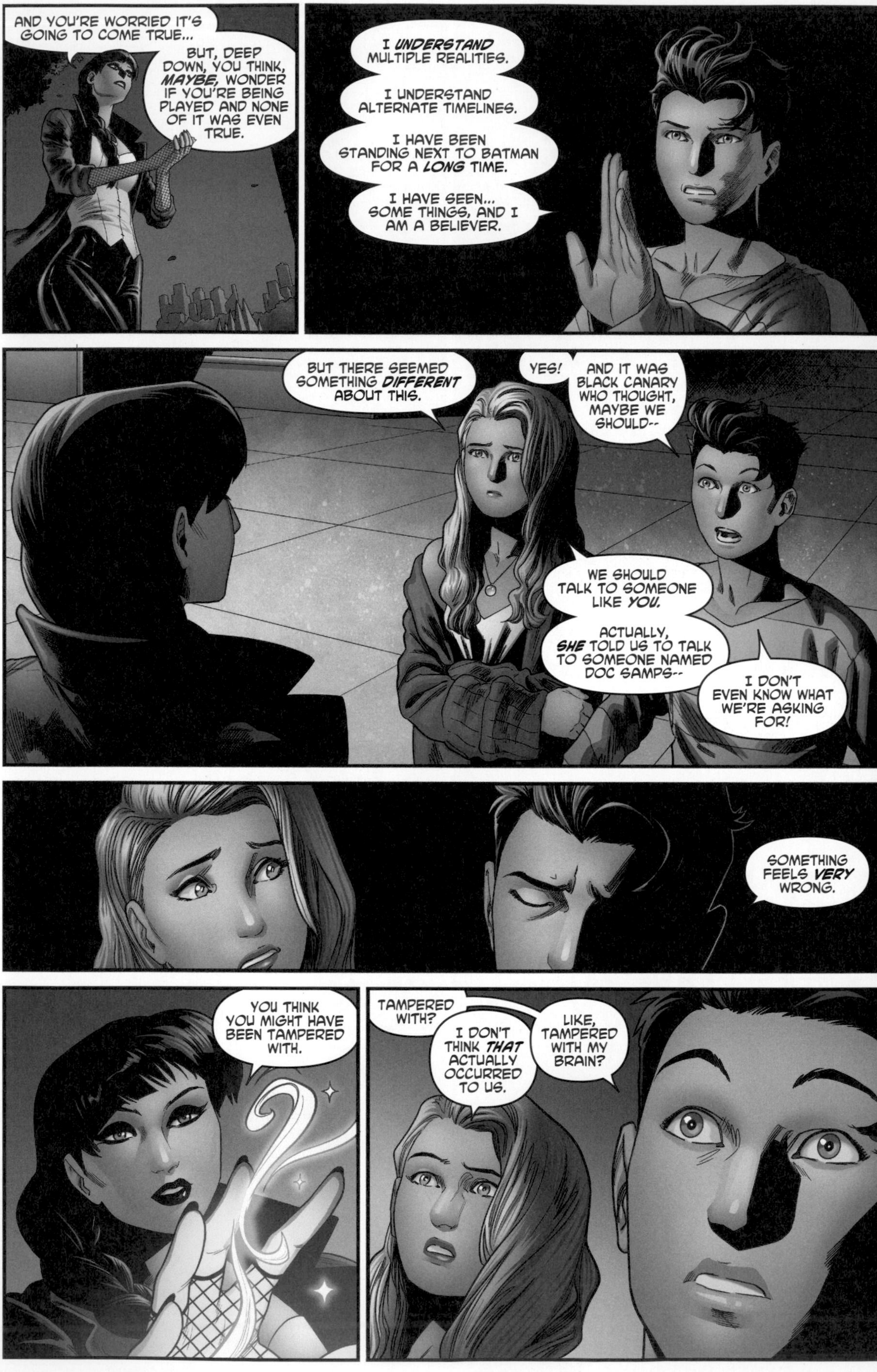

AND YOU'RE WORRIED IT'S GOING TO COME TRUE...
BUT, DEEP DOWN, YOU THINK, MAYBE, WONDER IF YOU'RE BEING PLAYED AND NONE OF IT WAS EVEN TRUE.
I UNDERSTAND MULTIPLE REALITIES.
I UNDERSTAND ALTERNATE TIMELINES.
I HAVE BEEN STANDING NEXT TO BATMAN FOR A LONG TIME.
I HAVE SEEN... SOME THINGS, AND I AM A BELIEVER.
BUT THERE SEEMED SOMETHING DIFFERENT ABOUT THIS.
YES!
AND IT WAS BLACK CANARY WHO THOUGHT, MAYBE WE SHOULD--
WE SHOULD TALK TO SOMEONE LIKE YOU.
ACTUALLY, SHE TOLD US TO TALK TO SOMEONE NAMED DOC SAMPS--
I DON'T EVEN KNOW WHAT WE'RE ASKING FOR!
SOMETHING FEELS VERY WRONG.
YOU THINK YOU MIGHT HAVE BEEN TAMPERED WITH.
TAMPERED WITH?
LIKE, TAMPERED WITH MY BRAIN?
I DON'T THINK THAT ACTUALLY OCCURRED TO US.

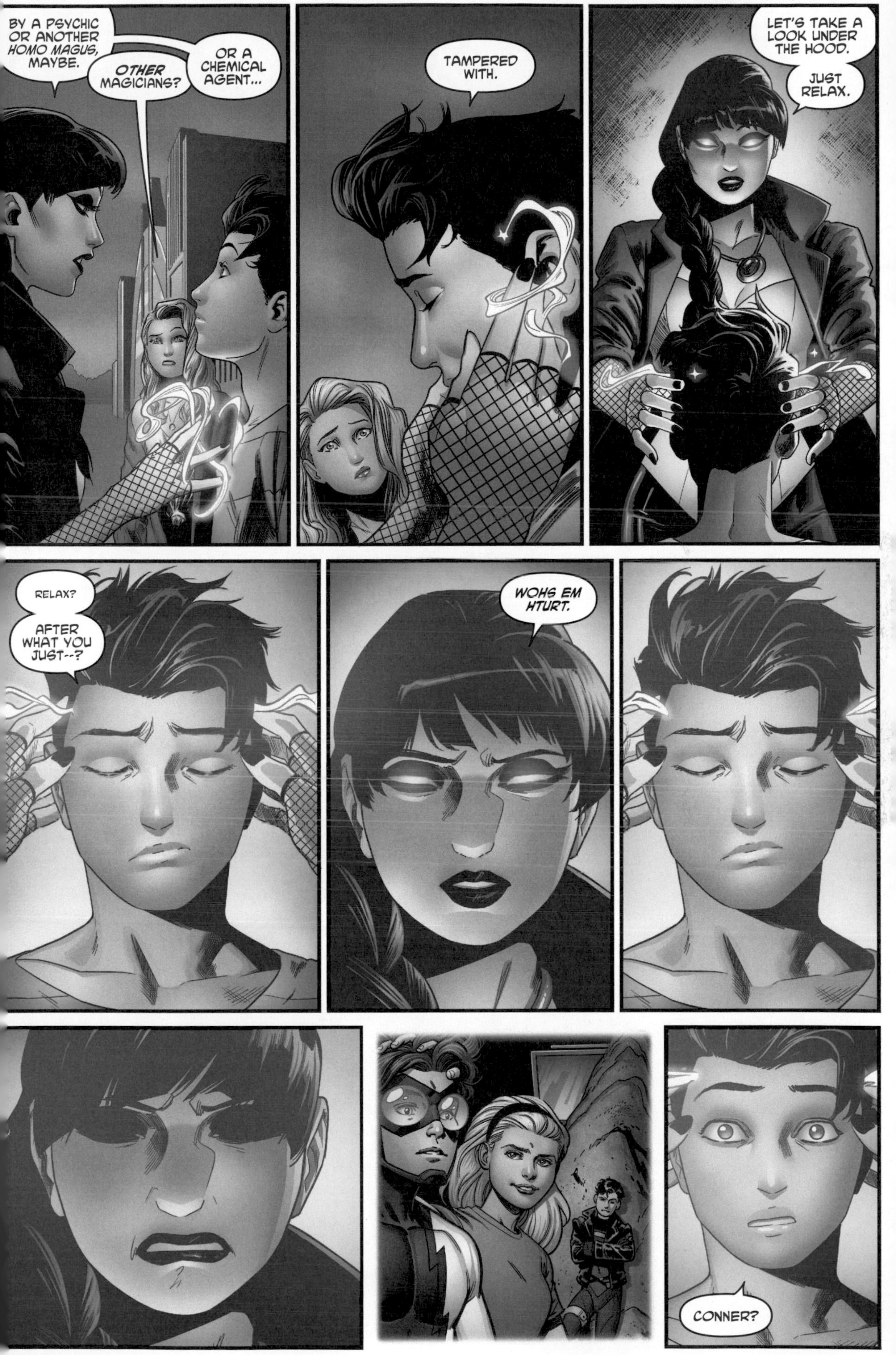
BY A PSYCHIC OR ANOTHER HOMO MAGUS, MAYBE.
OTHER MAGICIANS?
OR A CHEMICAL AGENT...
TAMPERED WITH.
LET'S TAKE A LOOK UNDER THE HOOD.
JUST RELAX.
RELAX?
AFTER WHAT YOU JUST--?
WOHS EM HTURT.
CONNER?

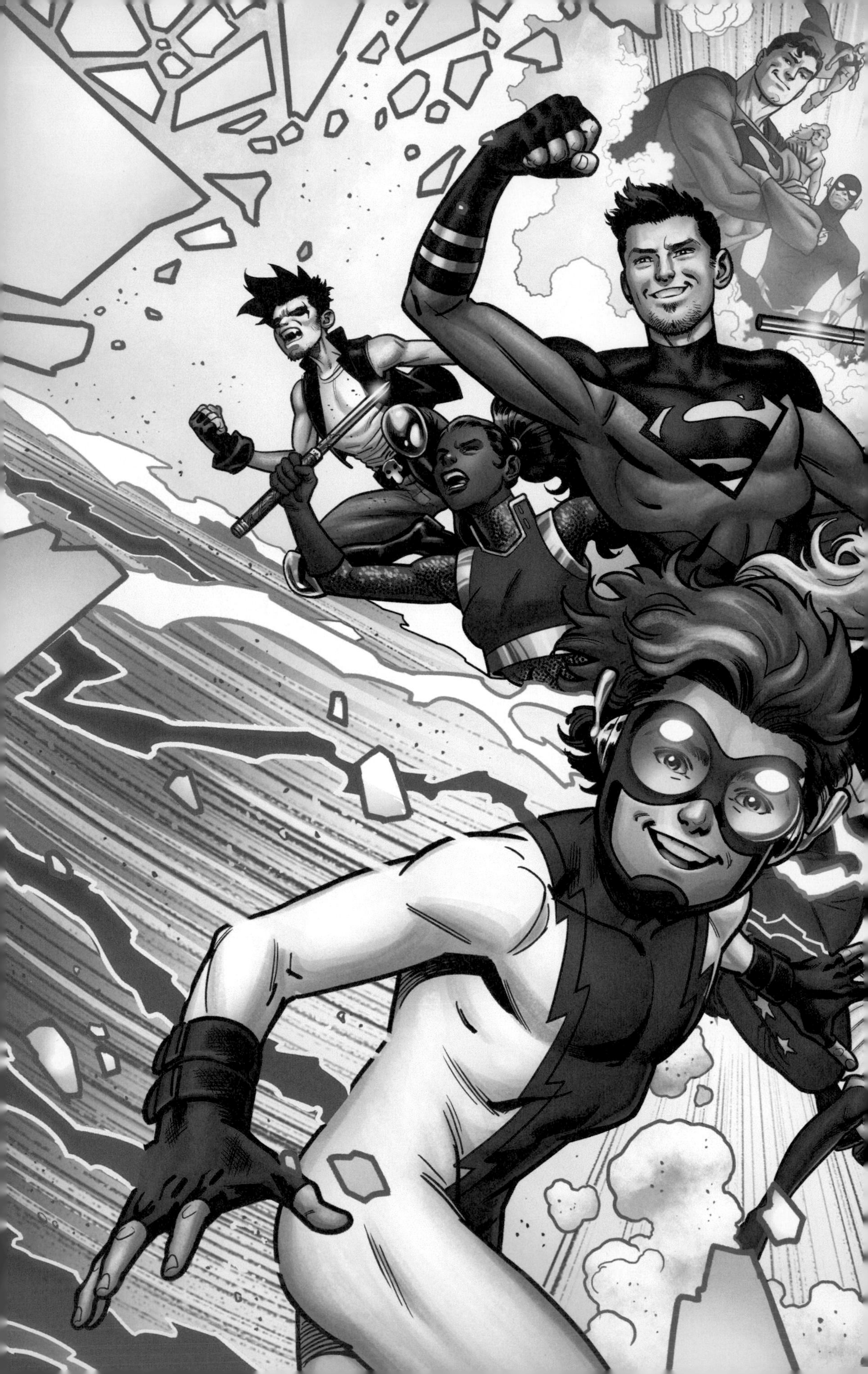

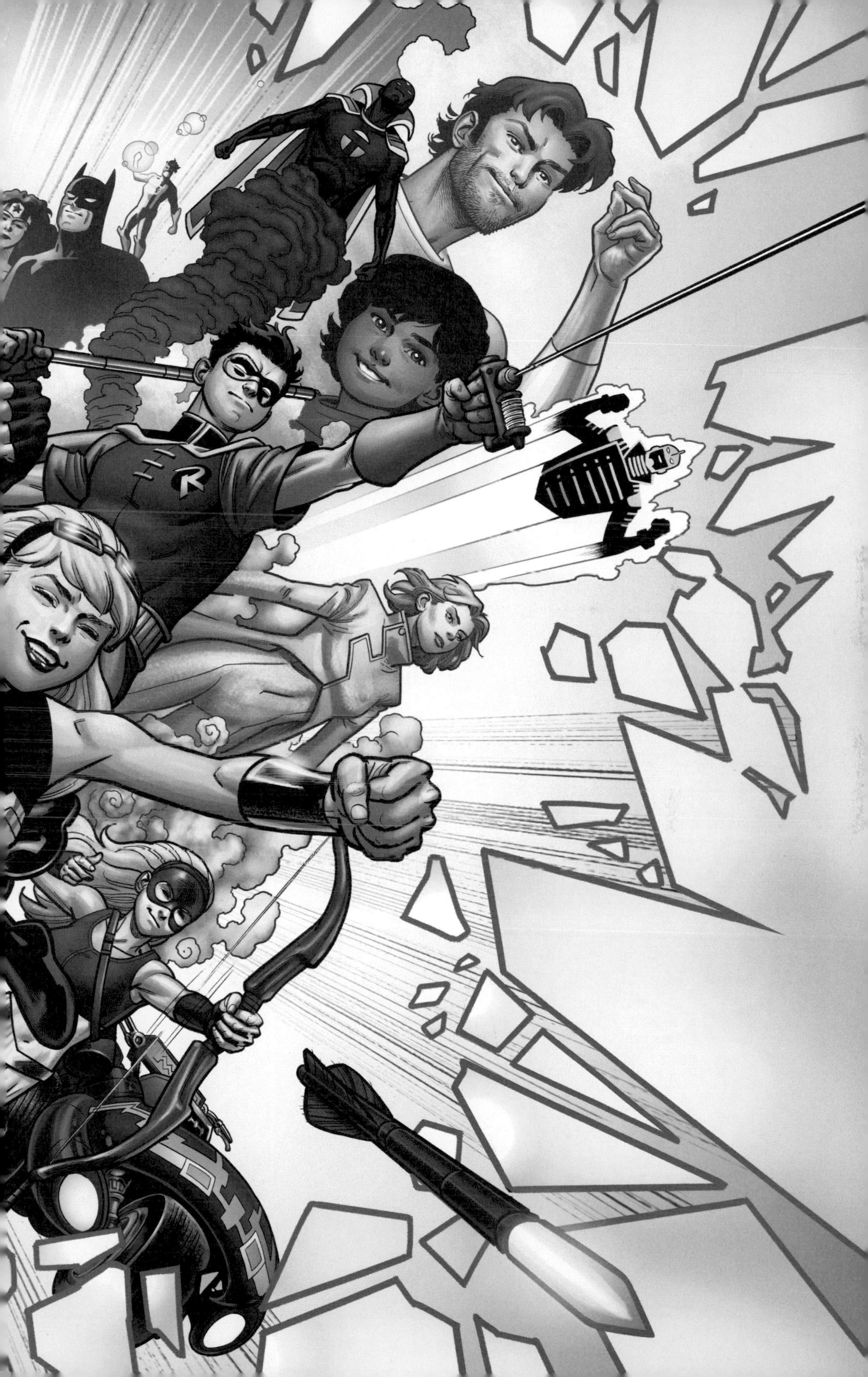

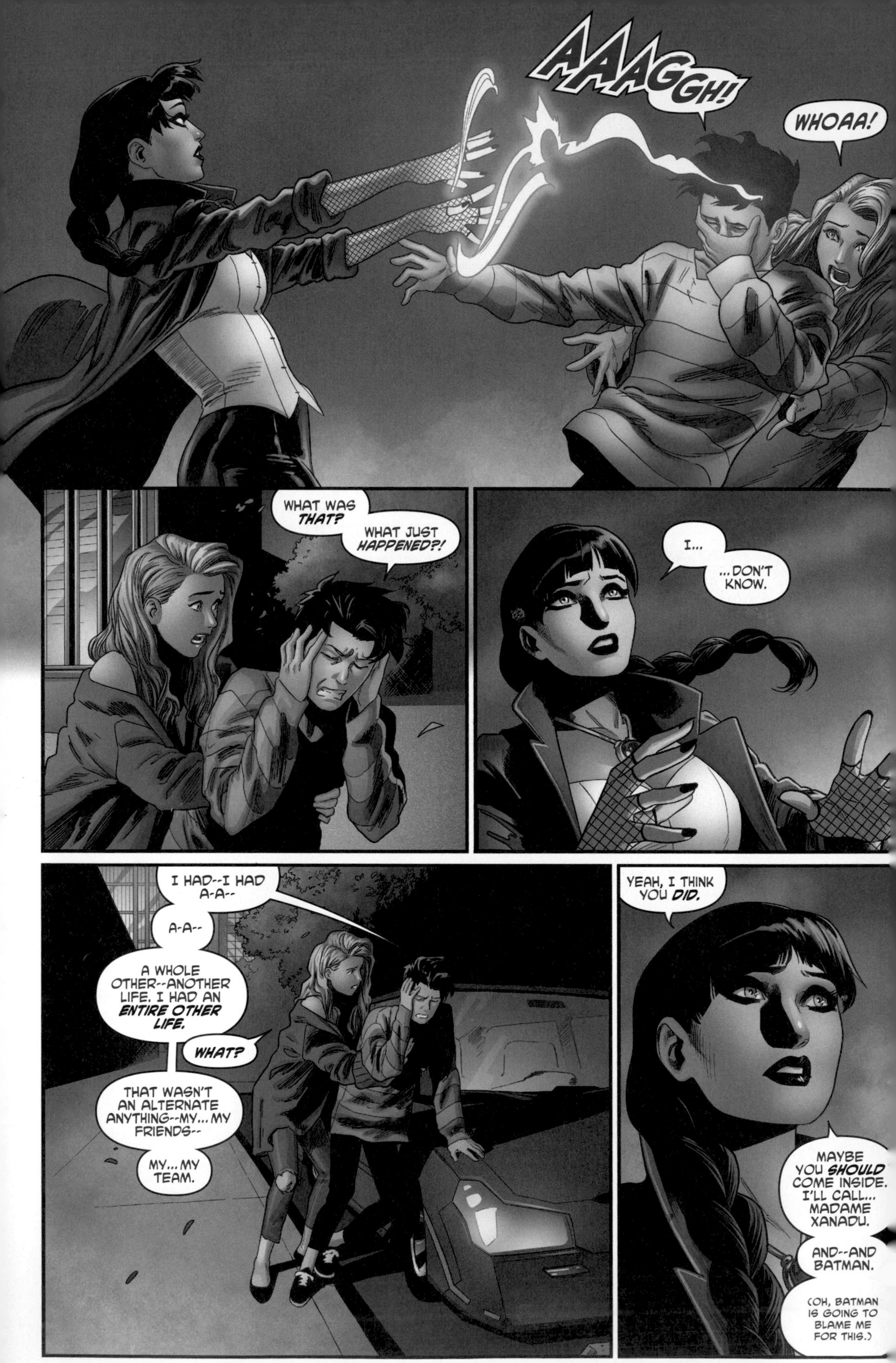
AAAAGGH!
WHOAA!
WHAT WAS THAT?
WHAT JUST HAPPENED?!
I...
...DON'T KNOW.
I HAD--I HAD A-A--
A-A--
A WHOLE OTHER--ANOTHER LIFE. I HAD AN ENTIRE OTHER LIFE.
WHAT?
THAT WASN'T AN ALTERNATE ANYTHING--MY... MY FRIENDS--
MY... MY TEAM.
YEAH, I THINK YOU DID.
MAYBE YOU SHOULD COME INSIDE. I'LL CALL... MADAME XANADU.
AND--AND BATMAN.
(OH, BATMAN IS GOING TO BLAME ME FOR THIS.)

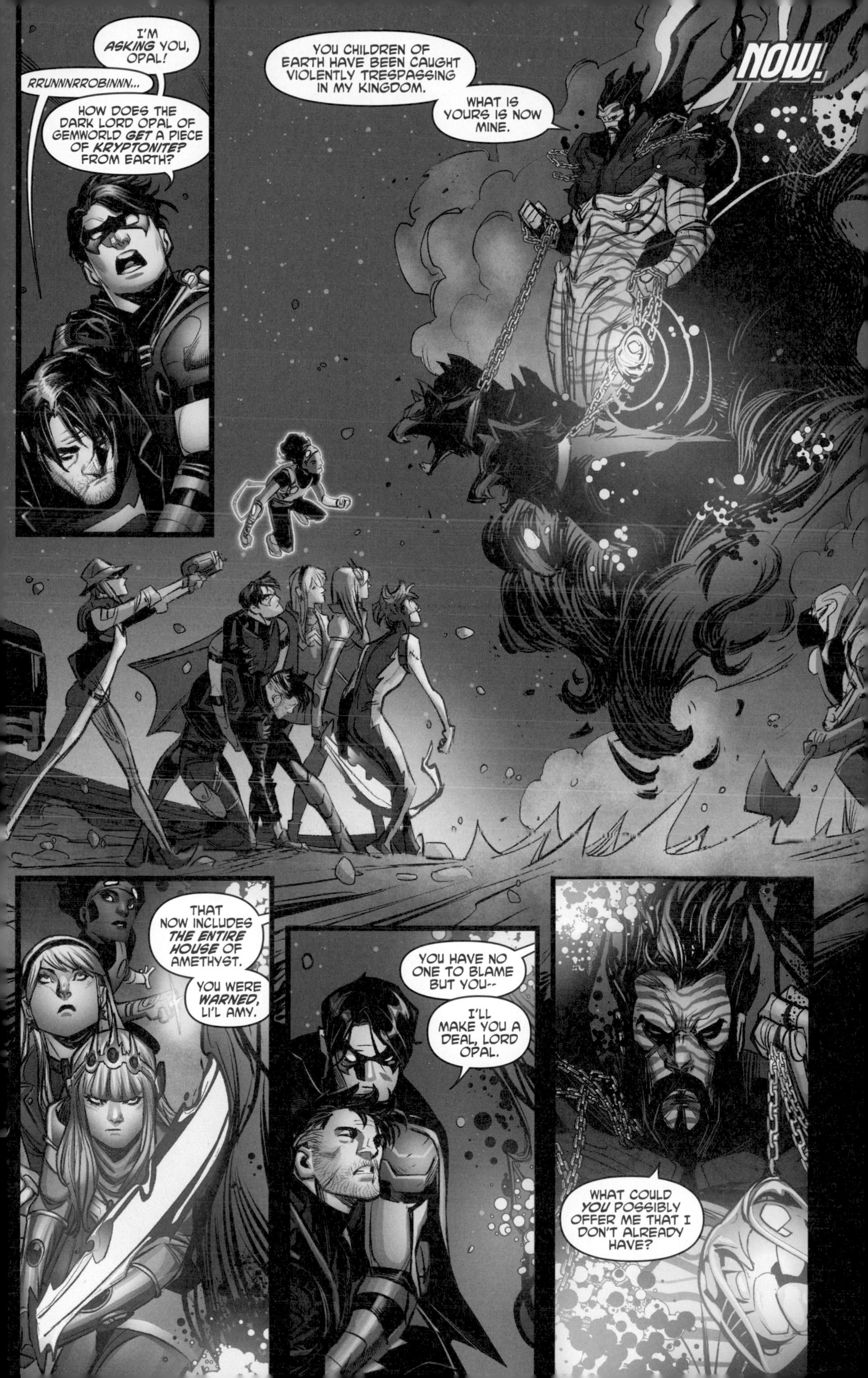
I'M *ASKING* YOU, OPAL!
RRUNNNRROBINNN...
HOW DOES THE DARK LORD OPAL OF GEMWORLD *GET* A PIECE OF *KRYPTONITE?* FROM EARTH?
YOU CHILDREN OF EARTH HAVE BEEN CAUGHT VIOLENTLY TRESPASSING IN MY KINGDOM.
WHAT IS YOURS IS NOW MINE.
NOW.
THAT NOW INCLUDES *THE ENTIRE HOUSE* OF AMETHYST.
YOU WERE *WARNED,* LI'L AMY.
YOU HAVE NO ONE TO BLAME BUT YOU--
I'LL MAKE YOU A DEAL, LORD OPAL.
WHAT COULD *YOU* POSSIBLY OFFER ME THAT I DON'T ALREADY HAVE?

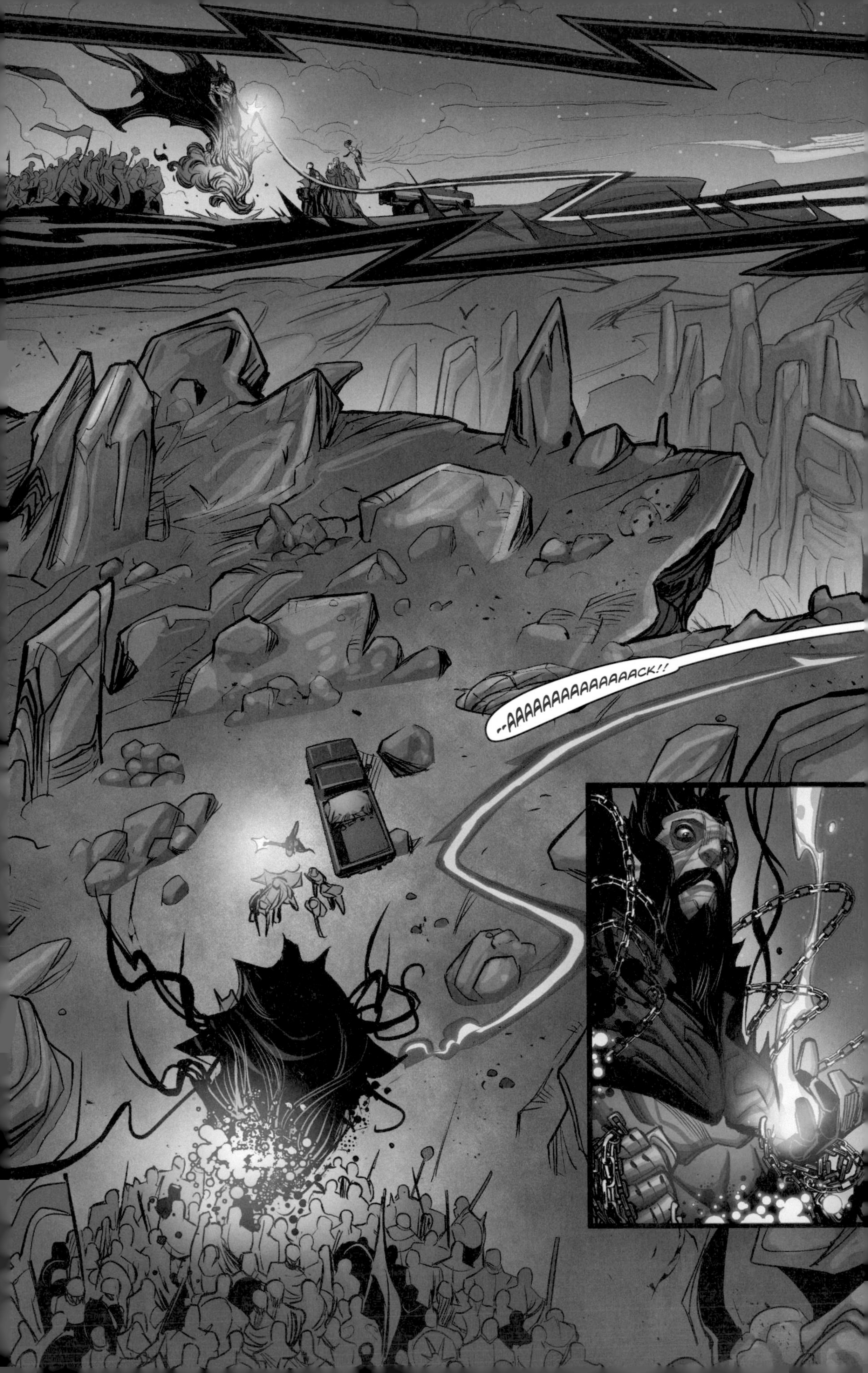
--AAAAAAAAAAAAAAACK!!

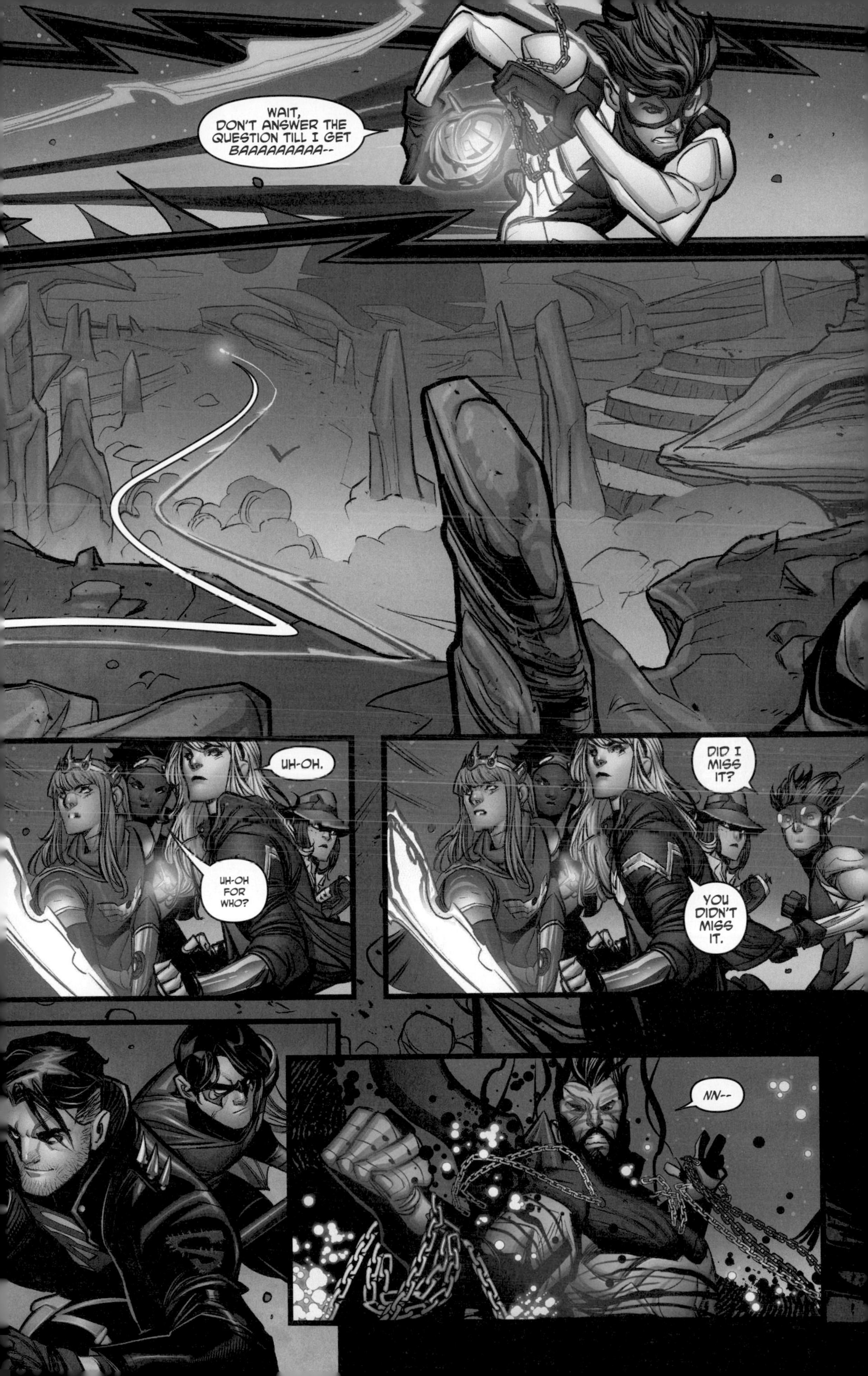
WAIT, DON'T ANSWER THE QUESTION TILL I GET BAAAAAAAAA--
UH-OH.
UH-OH FOR WHO?
DID I MISS IT?
YOU DIDN'T MISS IT.
NN--

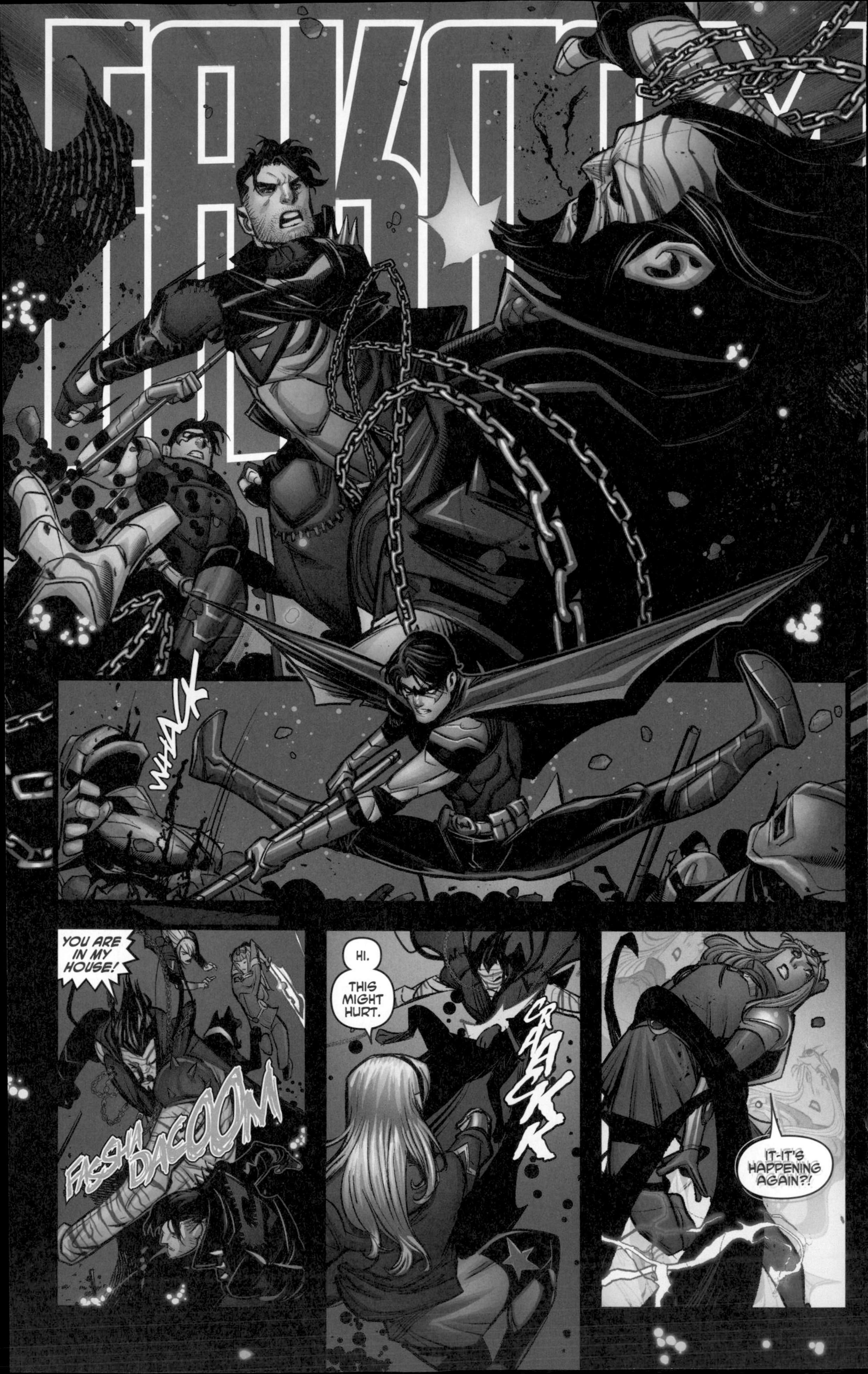
WHAK
YOU ARE IN MY HOUSE!
FASHA DACOOM
HI.
THIS MIGHT HURT.
CRAACK
IT-IT'S HAPPENING AGAIN?!

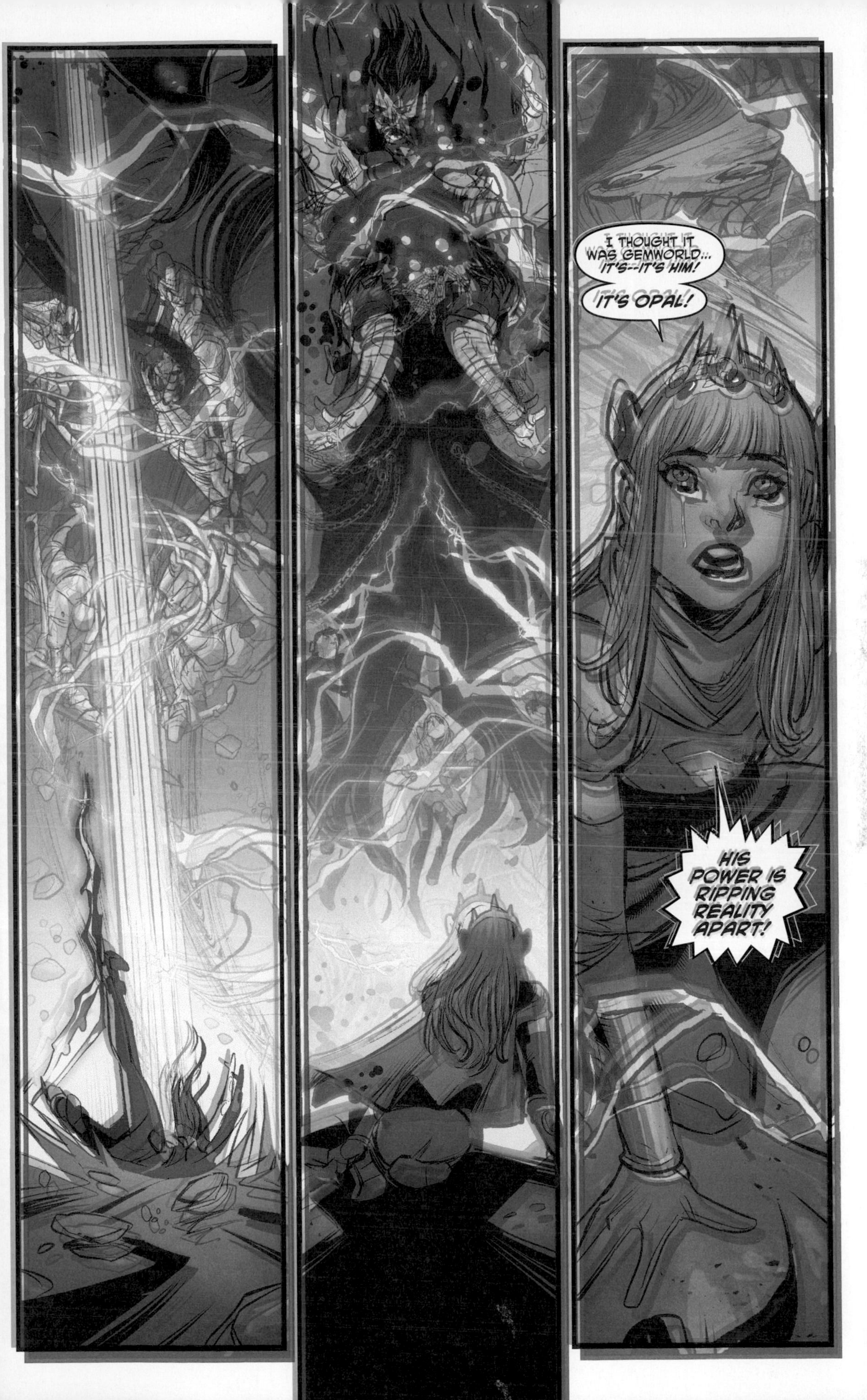
I THOUGHT IT WAS GEMWORLD... IT'S--IT'S HIM!
IT'S OPAL!
HIS POWER IS RIPPING REALITY APART!

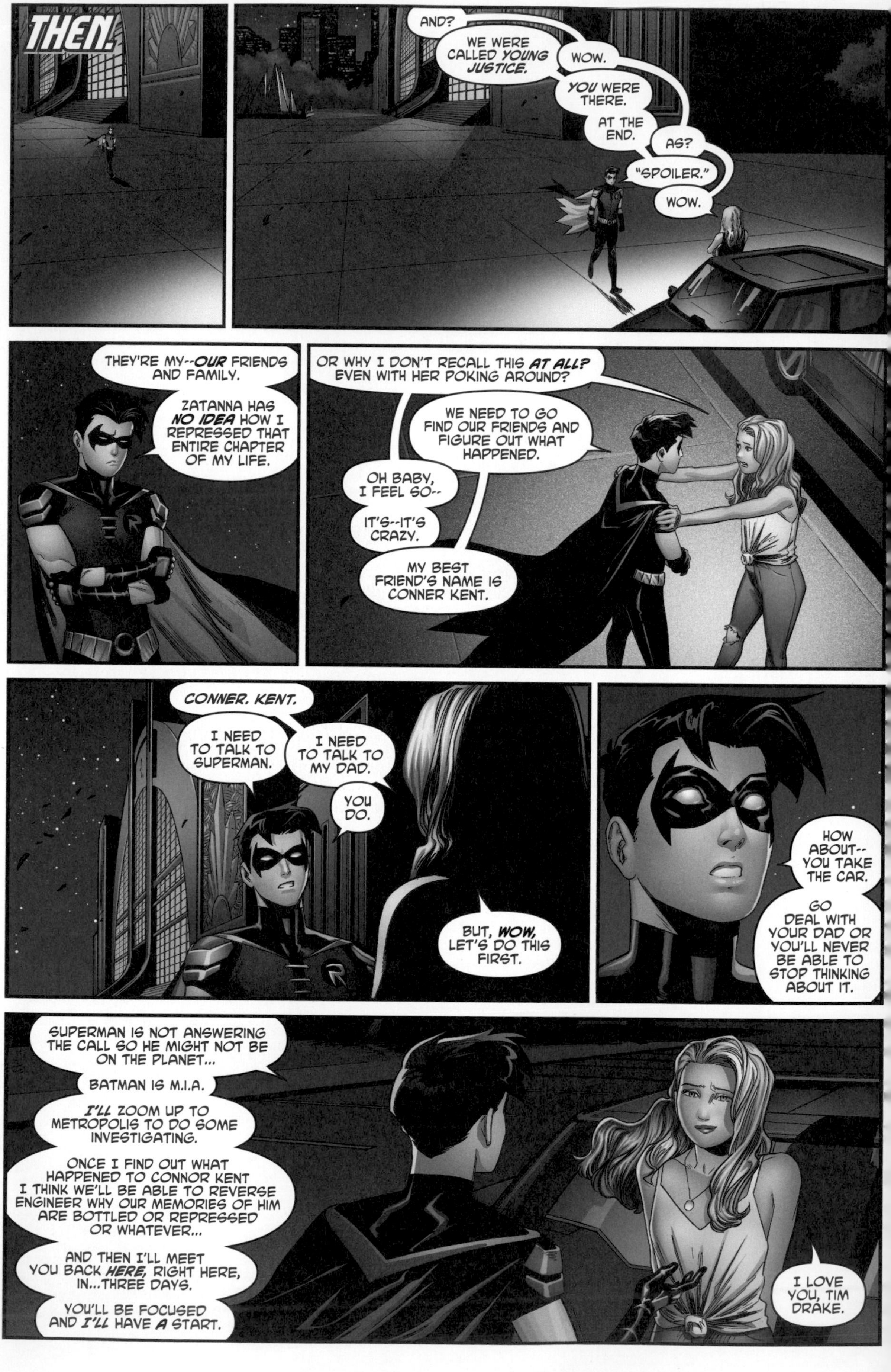
THEN.
AND?
WE WERE CALLED YOUNG JUSTICE.
WOW.
YOU WERE THERE.
AT THE END.
AS?
"SPOILER."
WOW.
THEY'RE MY--OUR FRIENDS AND FAMILY.
ZATANNA HAS NO IDEA HOW I REPRESSED THAT ENTIRE CHAPTER OF MY LIFE.
OR WHY I DON'T RECALL THIS AT ALL? EVEN WITH HER POKING AROUND?
WE NEED TO GO FIND OUR FRIENDS AND FIGURE OUT WHAT HAPPENED.
OH BABY, I FEEL SO--
IT'S--IT'S CRAZY.
MY BEST FRIEND'S NAME IS CONNER KENT.
CONNER. KENT.
I NEED TO TALK TO SUPERMAN.
I NEED TO TALK TO MY DAD.
YOU DO.
BUT, WOW, LET'S DO THIS FIRST.
HOW ABOUT-- YOU TAKE THE CAR.
GO DEAL WITH YOUR DAD OR YOU'LL NEVER BE ABLE TO STOP THINKING ABOUT IT.
SUPERMAN IS NOT ANSWERING THE CALL SO HE MIGHT NOT BE ON THE PLANET...
BATMAN IS M.I.A.
I'LL ZOOM UP TO METROPOLIS TO DO SOME INVESTIGATING.
ONCE I FIND OUT WHAT HAPPENED TO CONNOR KENT I THINK WE'LL BE ABLE TO REVERSE ENGINEER WHY OUR MEMORIES OF HIM ARE BOTTLED OR REPRESSED OR WHATEVER...
AND THEN I'LL MEET YOU BACK HERE, RIGHT HERE, IN...THREE DAYS.
YOU'LL BE FOCUSED AND I'LL HAVE A START.
I LOVE YOU, TIM DRAKE.

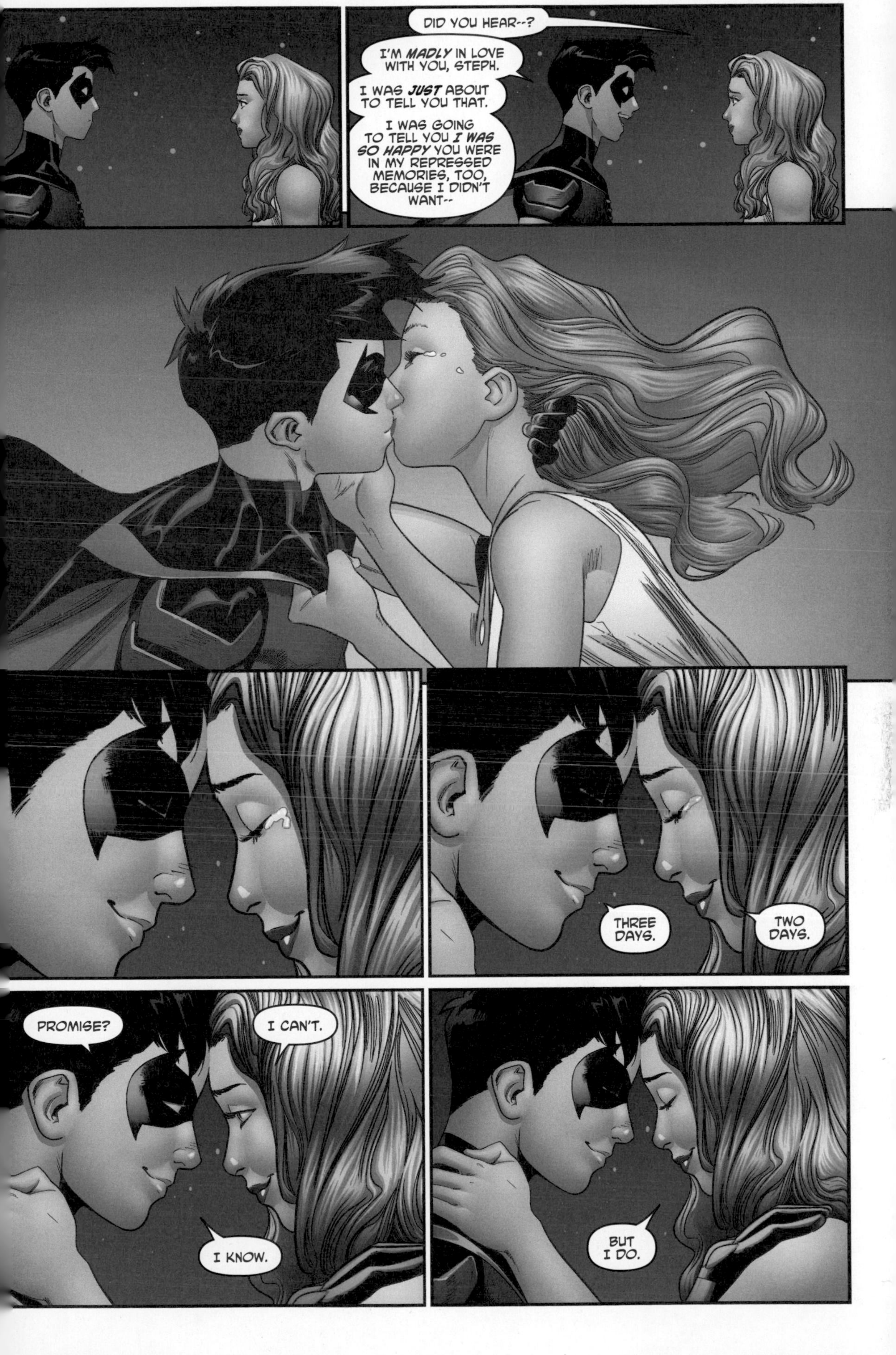
DID YOU HEAR--?
I'M MADLY IN LOVE WITH YOU, STEPH.
I WAS JUST ABOUT TO TELL YOU THAT.
I WAS GOING TO TELL YOU I WAS SO HAPPY YOU WERE IN MY REPRESSED MEMORIES, TOO, BECAUSE I DIDN'T WANT--
THREE DAYS.
TWO DAYS.
PROMISE?
I CAN'T.
I KNOW.
BUT I DO.

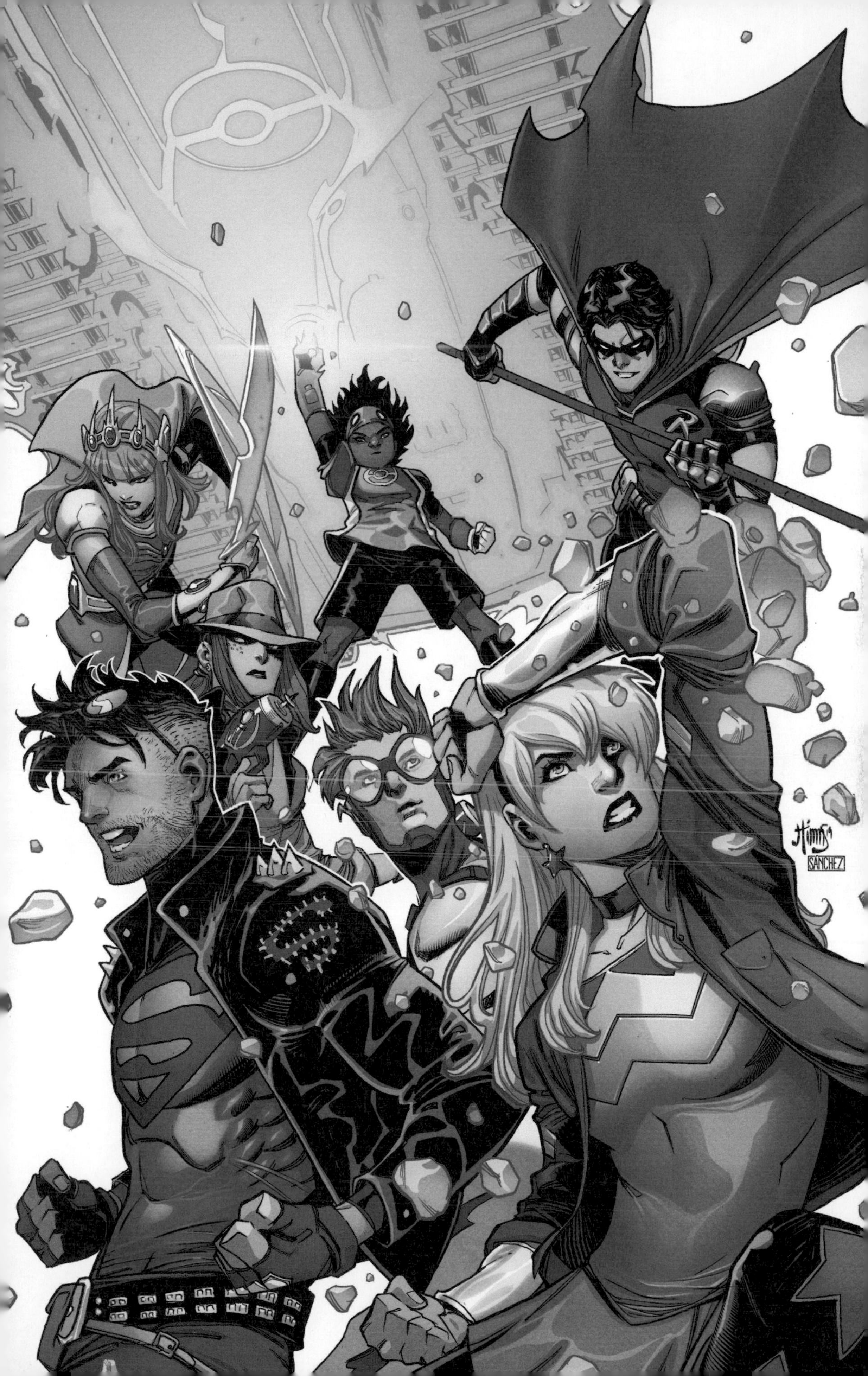
SANCHEZ

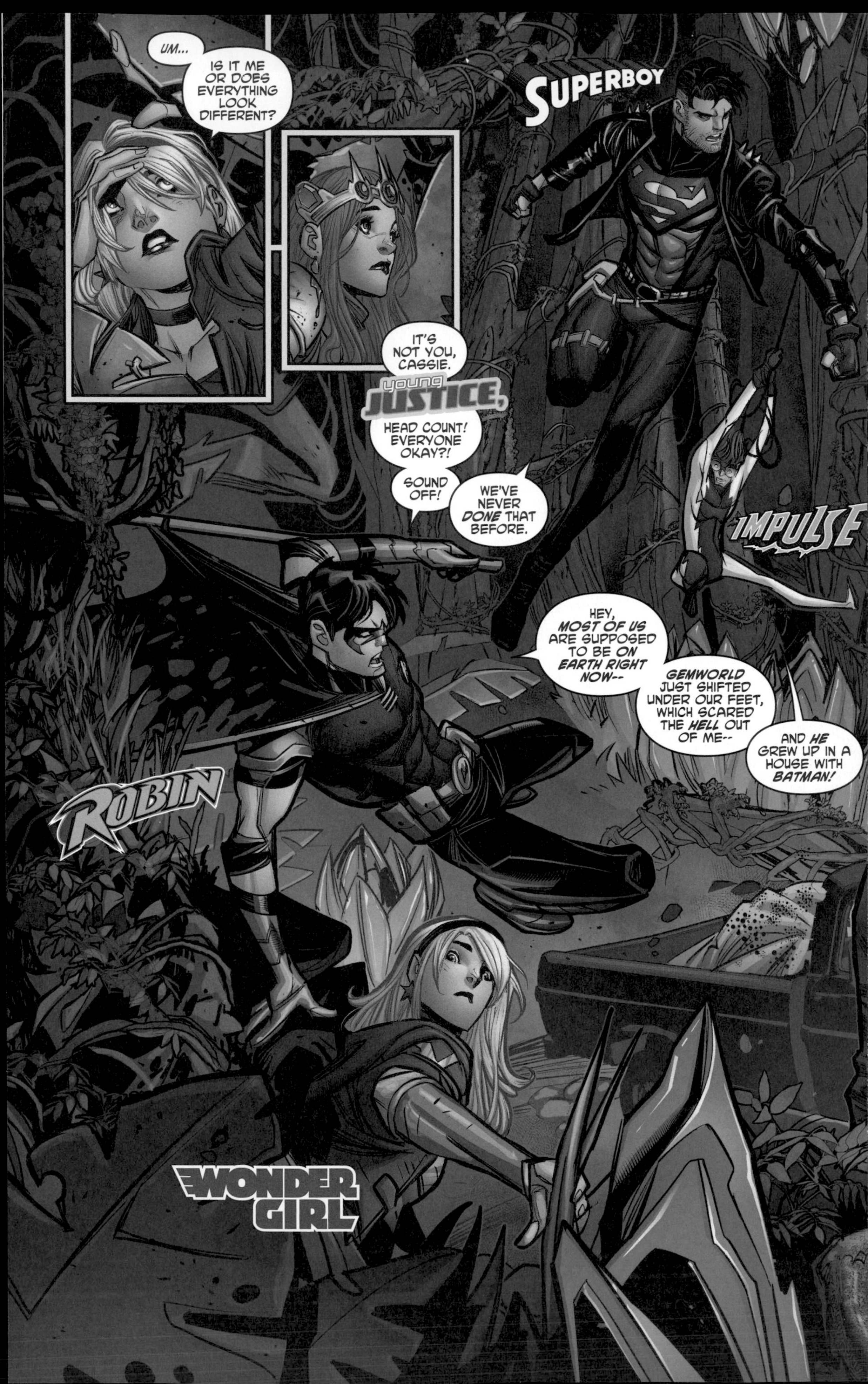
UM... IS IT ME OR DOES EVERYTHING LOOK DIFFERENT?
SUPERBOY
IT'S NOT YOU, CASSIE.
YOUNG JUSTICE,
HEAD COUNT! EVERYONE OKAY?!
SOUND OFF!
WE'VE NEVER DONE THAT BEFORE.
IMPULSE
HEY, MOST OF US ARE SUPPOSED TO BE ON EARTH RIGHT NOW--
GEMWORLD JUST SHIFTED UNDER OUR FEET, WHICH SCARED THE HELL OUT OF ME--
AND HE GREW UP IN A HOUSE WITH BATMAN!
ROBIN
WONDER GIRL

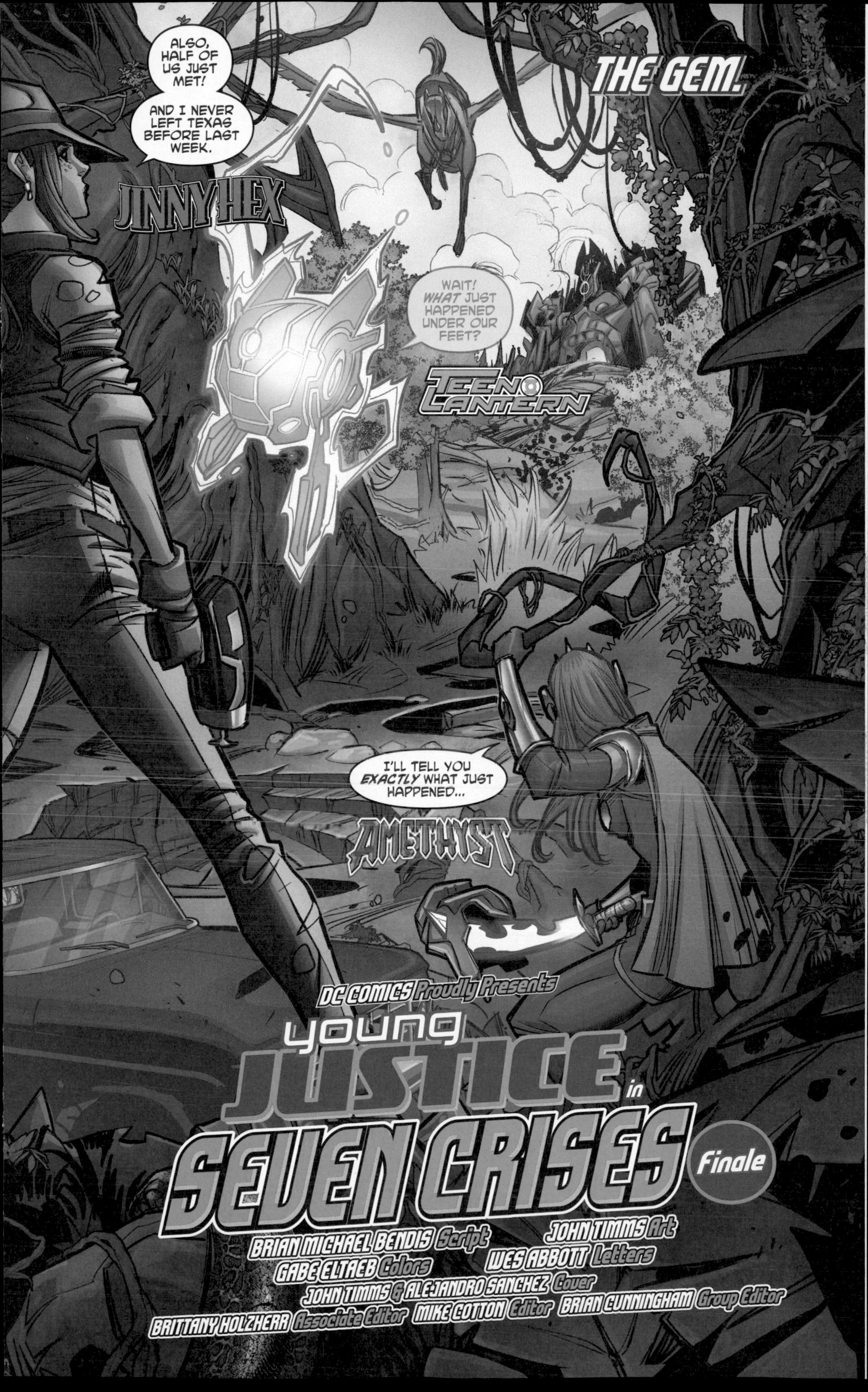
ALSO, HALF OF US JUST MET!
AND I NEVER LEFT TEXAS BEFORE LAST WEEK.
JINNY HEX
THE GEM.
WAIT! WHAT JUST HAPPENED UNDER OUR FEET?
TEEN LANTERN
I'LL TELL YOU EXACTLY WHAT JUST HAPPENED...
AMETHYST
DC COMICS Proudly Presents
young JUSTICE in
SEVEN CRISES Finale
BRIAN MICHAEL BENDIS Script
JOHN TIMMS Art
GABE ELTAEB Colors
WES ABBOTT Letters
JOHN TIMMS & ALEJANDRO SANCHEZ Cover
BRITTANY HOLZHERR Associate Editor
MIKE COTTON Editor
BRIAN CUNNINGHAM Group Editor

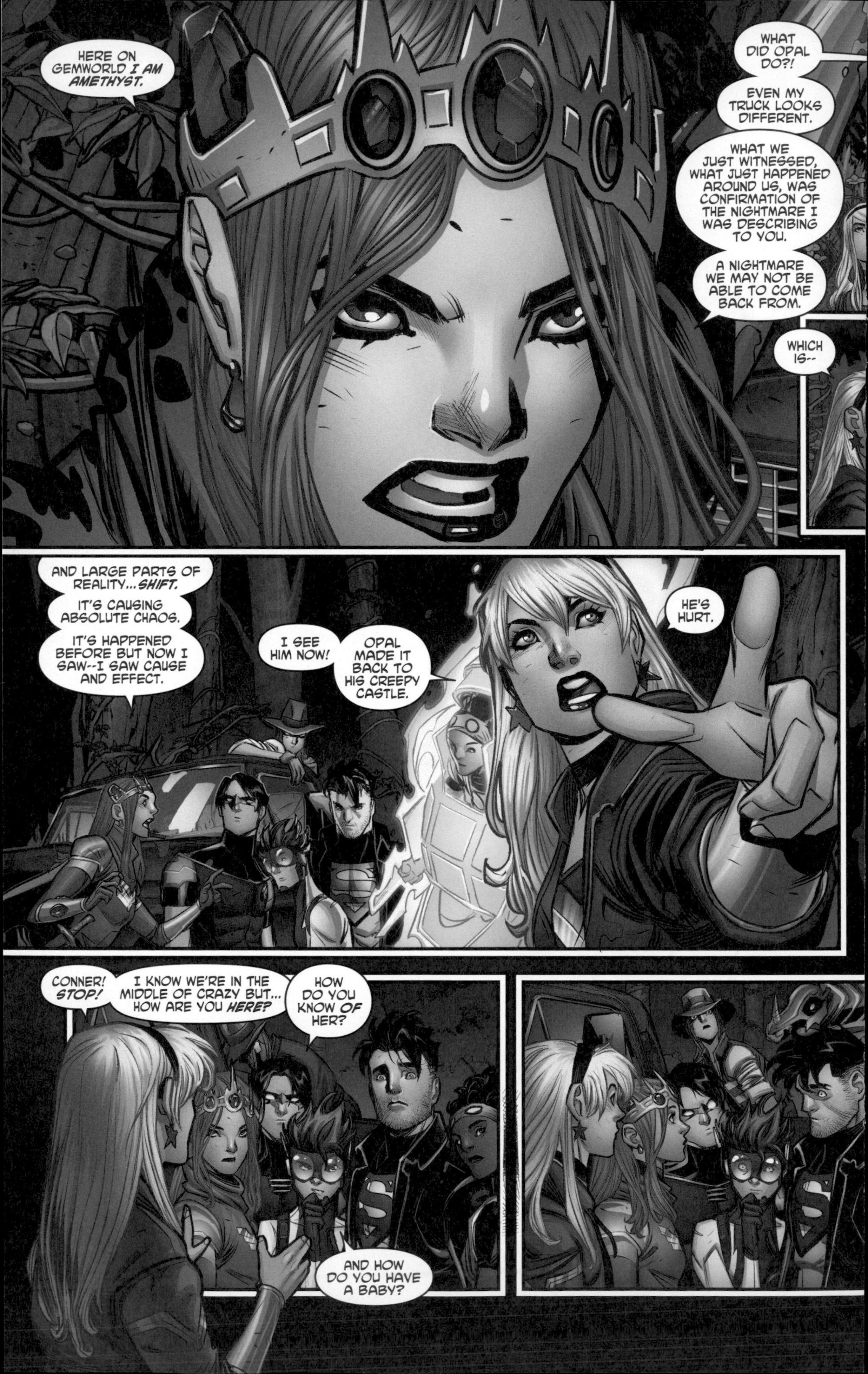
HERE ON GEMWORLD I AM AMETHYST.
WHAT DID OPAL DO?!
EVEN MY TRUCK LOOKS DIFFERENT.
WHAT WE JUST WITNESSED, WHAT JUST HAPPENED AROUND US, WAS CONFIRMATION OF THE NIGHTMARE I WAS DESCRIBING TO YOU.
A NIGHTMARE WE MAY NOT BE ABLE TO COME BACK FROM.
WHICH IS--
AND LARGE PARTS OF REALITY... SHIFT.
IT'S CAUSING ABSOLUTE CHAOS.
IT'S HAPPENED BEFORE BUT NOW I SAW--I SAW CAUSE AND EFFECT.
I SEE HIM NOW!
OPAL MADE IT BACK TO HIS CREEPY CASTLE.
HE'S HURT.
CONNER! STOP!
I KNOW WE'RE IN THE MIDDLE OF CRAZY BUT... HOW ARE YOU HERE?
HOW DO YOU KNOW OF HER?
AND HOW DO YOU HAVE A BABY?

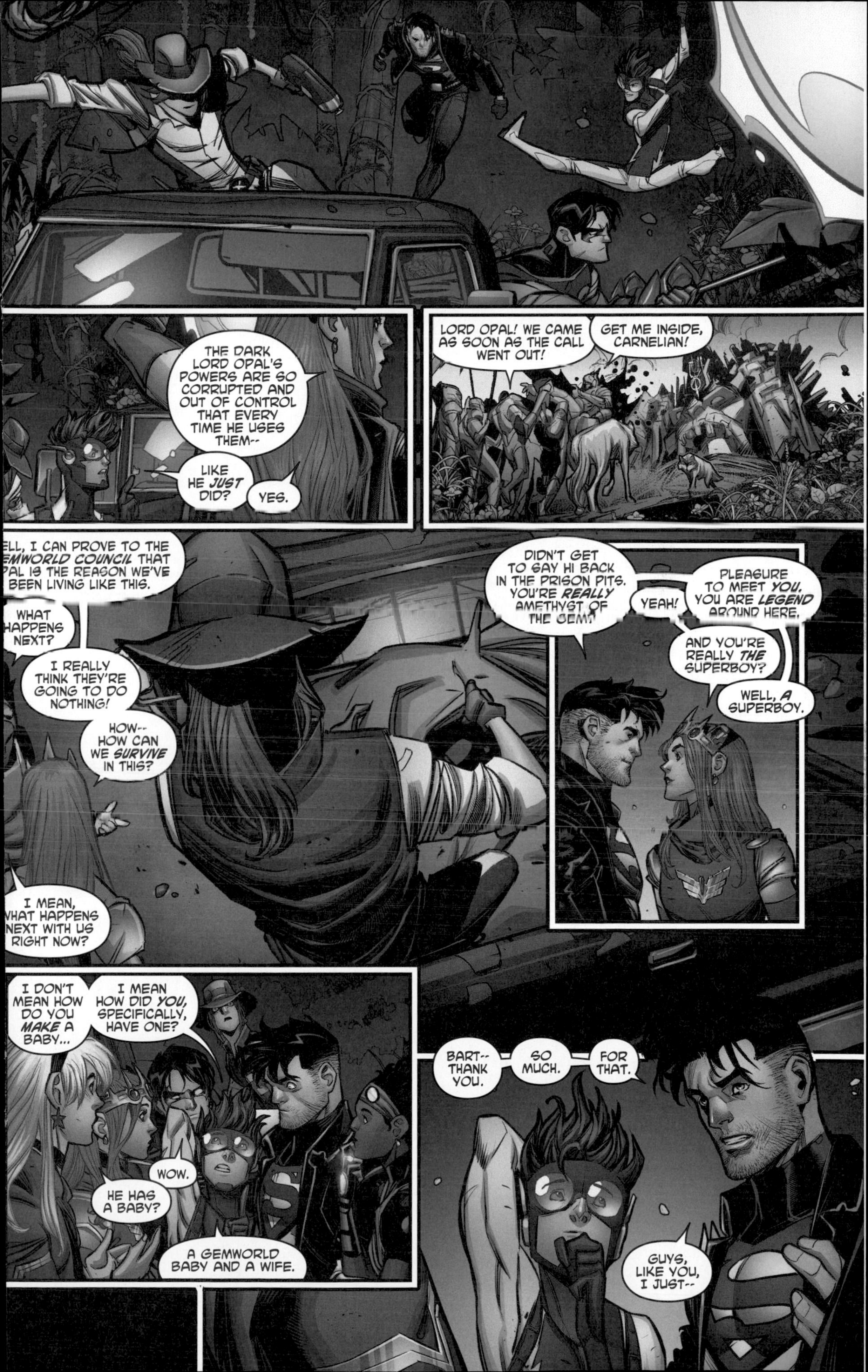

THE DARK LORD OPAL'S POWERS ARE SO CORRUPTED AND OUT OF CONTROL THAT EVERY TIME HE USES THEM--
LIKE HE JUST DID?
YES.
LORD OPAL! WE CAME AS SOON AS THE CALL WENT OUT!
GET ME INSIDE, CARNELIAN!
ELL, I CAN PROVE TO THE GEMWORLD COUNCIL THAT PAL IS THE REASON WE'VE BEEN LIVING LIKE THIS.
WHAT HAPPENS NEXT?
I REALLY THINK THEY'RE GOING TO DO NOTHING!
HOW-- HOW CAN WE SURVIVE IN THIS?
I MEAN, WHAT HAPPENS NEXT WITH US RIGHT NOW?
DIDN'T GET TO SAY HI BACK IN THE PRISON PITS. YOU'RE REALLY AMETHYST OF THE GEM!
YEAH!
PLEASURE TO MEET YOU. YOU ARE LEGEND AROUND HERE.
AND YOU'RE REALLY THE SUPERBOY?
WELL, A SUPERBOY.
I DON'T MEAN HOW DO YOU MAKE A BABY...
I MEAN HOW DID YOU, SPECIFICALLY, HAVE ONE?
WOW.
HE HAS A BABY?
A GEMWORLD BABY AND A WIFE.
BART-- THANK YOU.
SO MUCH.
FOR THAT.
GUYS, LIKE YOU, I JUST--

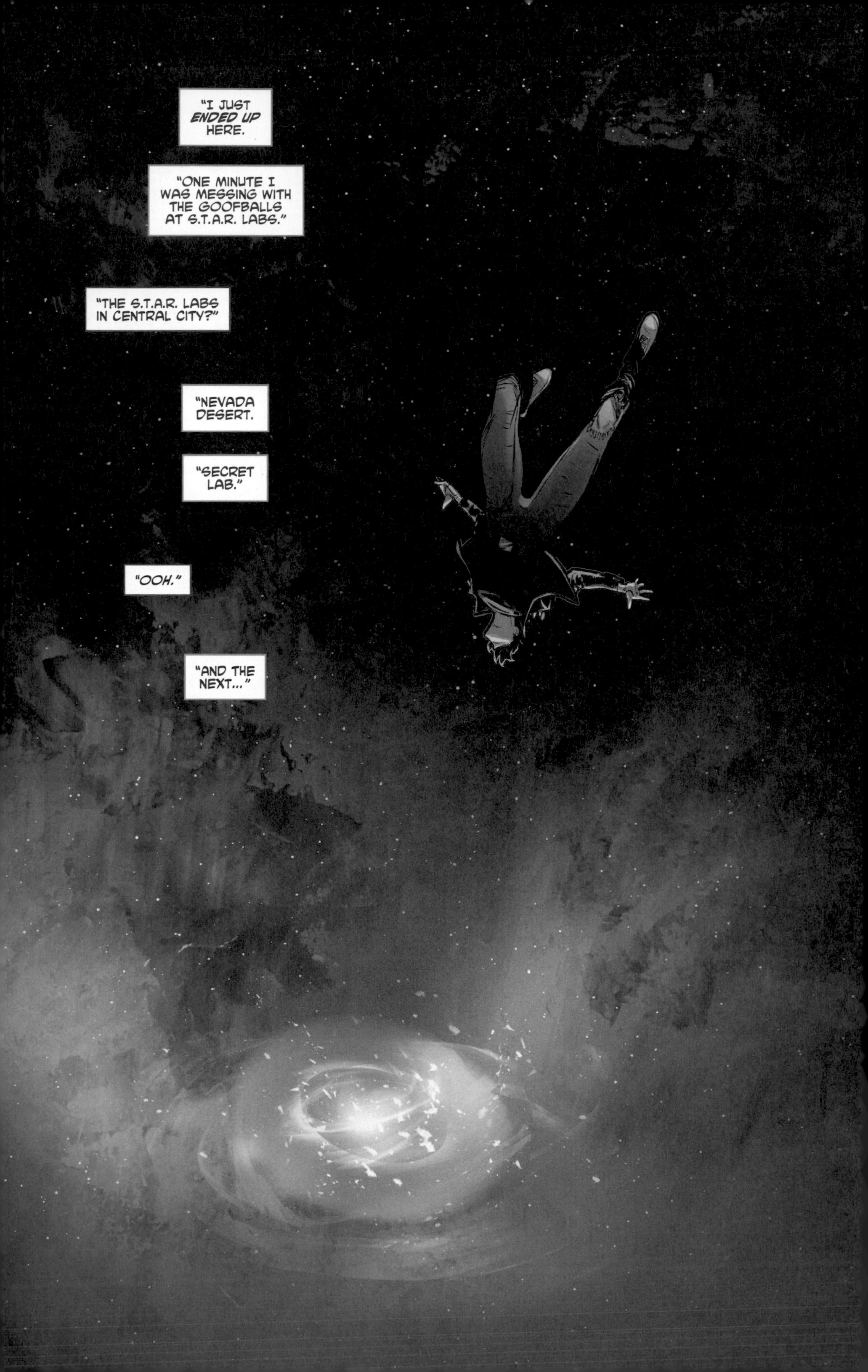
"I JUST *ENDED UP* HERE.
"ONE MINUTE I WAS MESSING WITH THE GOOFBALLS AT S.T.A.R. LABS."
"THE S.T.A.R. LABS IN CENTRAL CITY?"
"NEVADA DESERT.
"SECRET LAB."
"OOH."
"AND THE NEXT..."

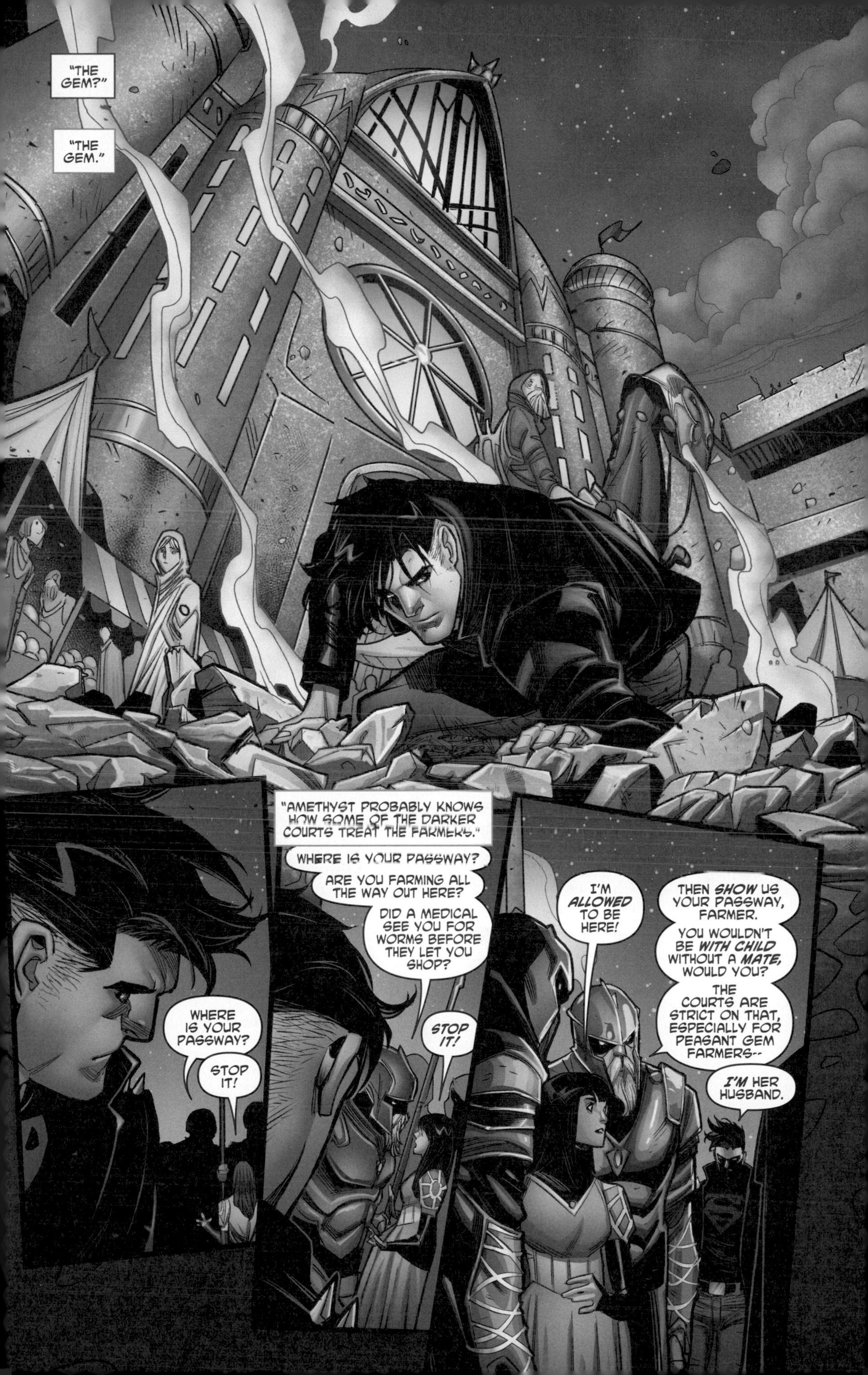
"THE GEM?"
"THE GEM."
"AMETHYST PROBABLY KNOWS HOW SOME OF THE DARKER COURTS TREAT THE FARMERS."
WHERE IS YOUR PASSWAY?
STOP IT!
WHERE IS YOUR PASSWAY?
ARE YOU FARMING ALL THE WAY OUT HERE?
DID A MEDICAL SEE YOU FOR WORMS BEFORE THEY LET YOU SHOP?
STOP IT!
I'M ALLOWED TO BE HERE!
THEN SHOW US YOUR PASSWAY, FARMER.
YOU WOULDN'T BE WITH CHILD WITHOUT A MATE, WOULD YOU?
THE COURTS ARE STRICT ON THAT, ESPECIALLY FOR PEASANT GEM FARMERS--
I'M HER HUSBAND.

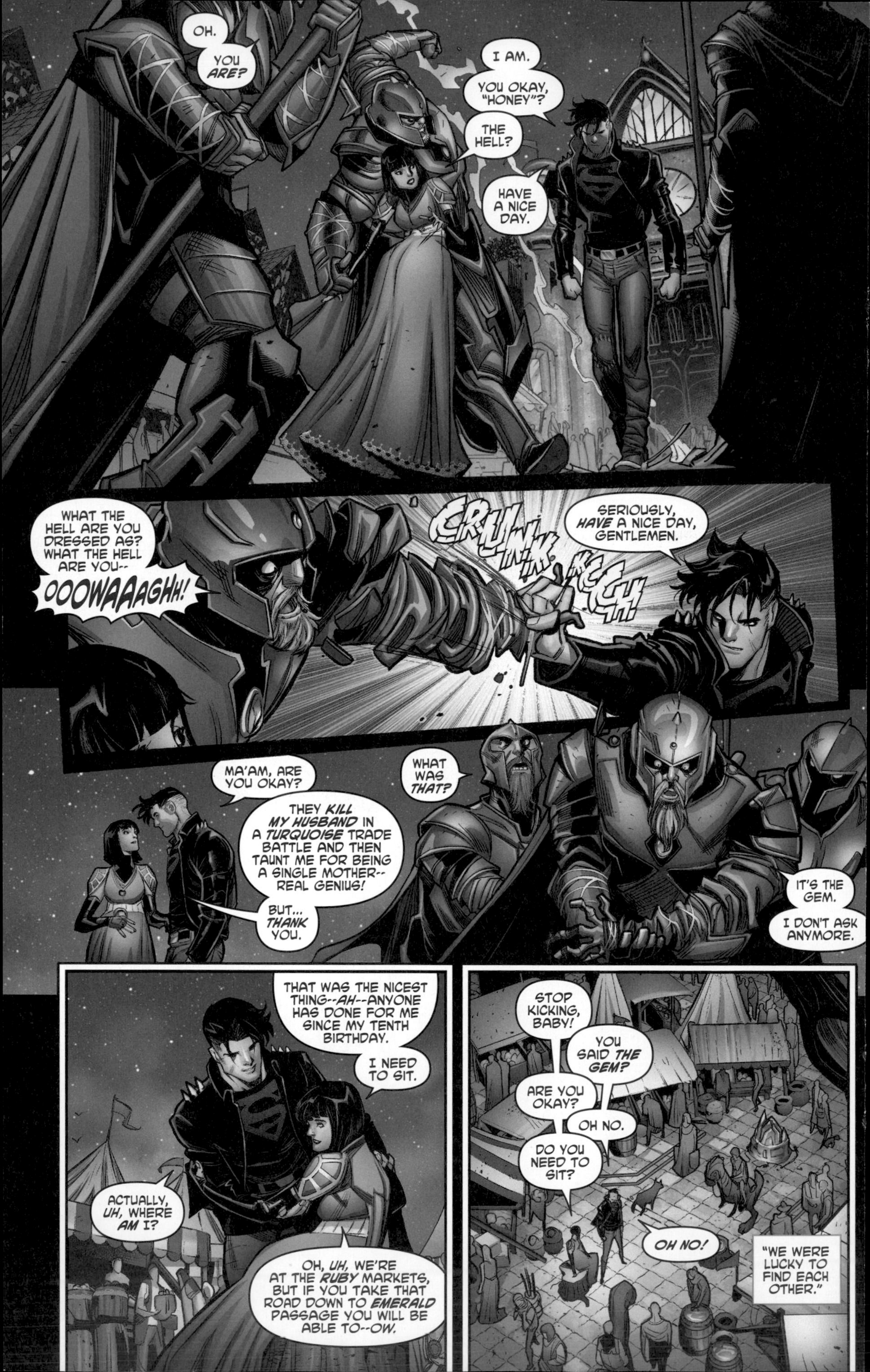
OH.
YOU ARE?
I AM.
YOU OKAY, "HONEY"?
THE HELL?
HAVE A NICE DAY.
WHAT THE HELL ARE YOU DRESSED AS? WHAT THE HELL ARE YOU--
OOOWAAAAGHH!
CRUNK
SERIOUSLY, HAVE A NICE DAY, GENTLEMEN.
MA'AM, ARE YOU OKAY?
THEY KILL MY HUSBAND IN A TURQUOISE TRADE BATTLE AND THEN TAUNT ME FOR BEING A SINGLE MOTHER--REAL GENIUS!
BUT... THANK YOU.
WHAT WAS THAT?
IT'S THE GEM.
I DON'T ASK ANYMORE.
THAT WAS THE NICEST THING--AH--ANYONE HAS DONE FOR ME SINCE MY TENTH BIRTHDAY.
I NEED TO SIT.
ACTUALLY, UH, WHERE AM I?
OH, UH, WE'RE AT THE RUBY MARKETS, BUT IF YOU TAKE THAT ROAD DOWN TO EMERALD PASSAGE YOU WILL BE ABLE TO--OW.
STOP KICKING, BABY!
YOU SAID THE GEM?
ARE YOU OKAY?
OH NO.
DO YOU NEED TO SIT?
OH NO!
"WE WERE LUCKY TO FIND EACH OTHER."

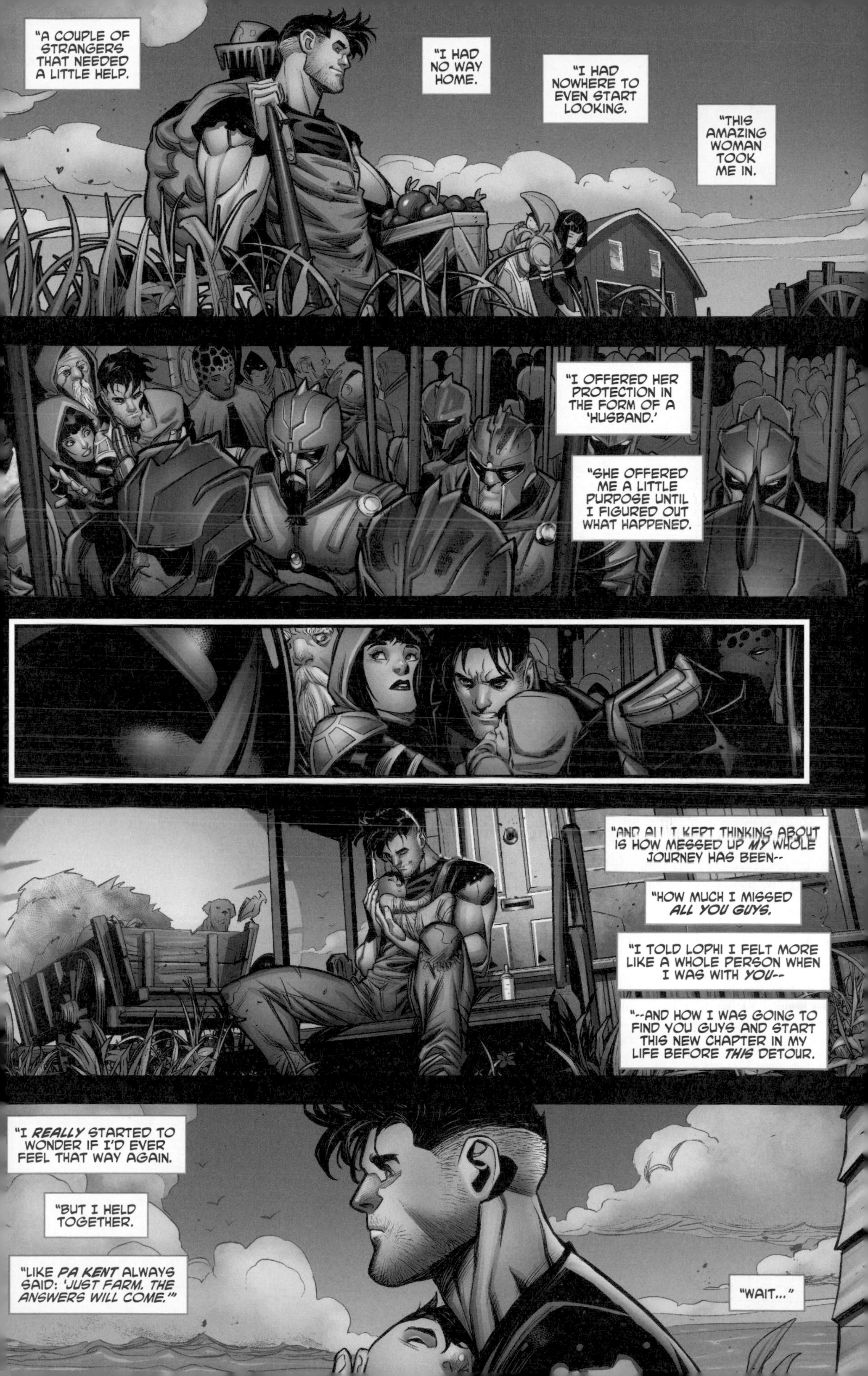
"A COUPLE OF STRANGERS THAT NEEDED A LITTLE HELP.
"I HAD NO WAY HOME.
"I HAD NOWHERE TO EVEN START LOOKING.
"THIS AMAZING WOMAN TOOK ME IN.
"I OFFERED HER PROTECTION IN THE FORM OF A 'HUSBAND.'
"SHE OFFERED ME A LITTLE PURPOSE UNTIL I FIGURED OUT WHAT HAPPENED.
"AND ALL I KEPT THINKING ABOUT IS HOW MESSED UP MY WHOLE JOURNEY HAS BEEN--
"HOW MUCH I MISSED ALL YOU GUYS.
"I TOLD LOPHI I FELT MORE LIKE A WHOLE PERSON WHEN I WAS WITH YOU--
"--AND HOW I WAS GOING TO FIND YOU GUYS AND START THIS NEW CHAPTER IN MY LIFE BEFORE THIS DETOUR.
"I REALLY STARTED TO WONDER IF I'D EVER FEEL THAT WAY AGAIN.
"BUT I HELD TOGETHER.
"LIKE PA KENT ALWAYS SAID: 'JUST FARM. THE ANSWERS WILL COME.'"
"WAIT..."

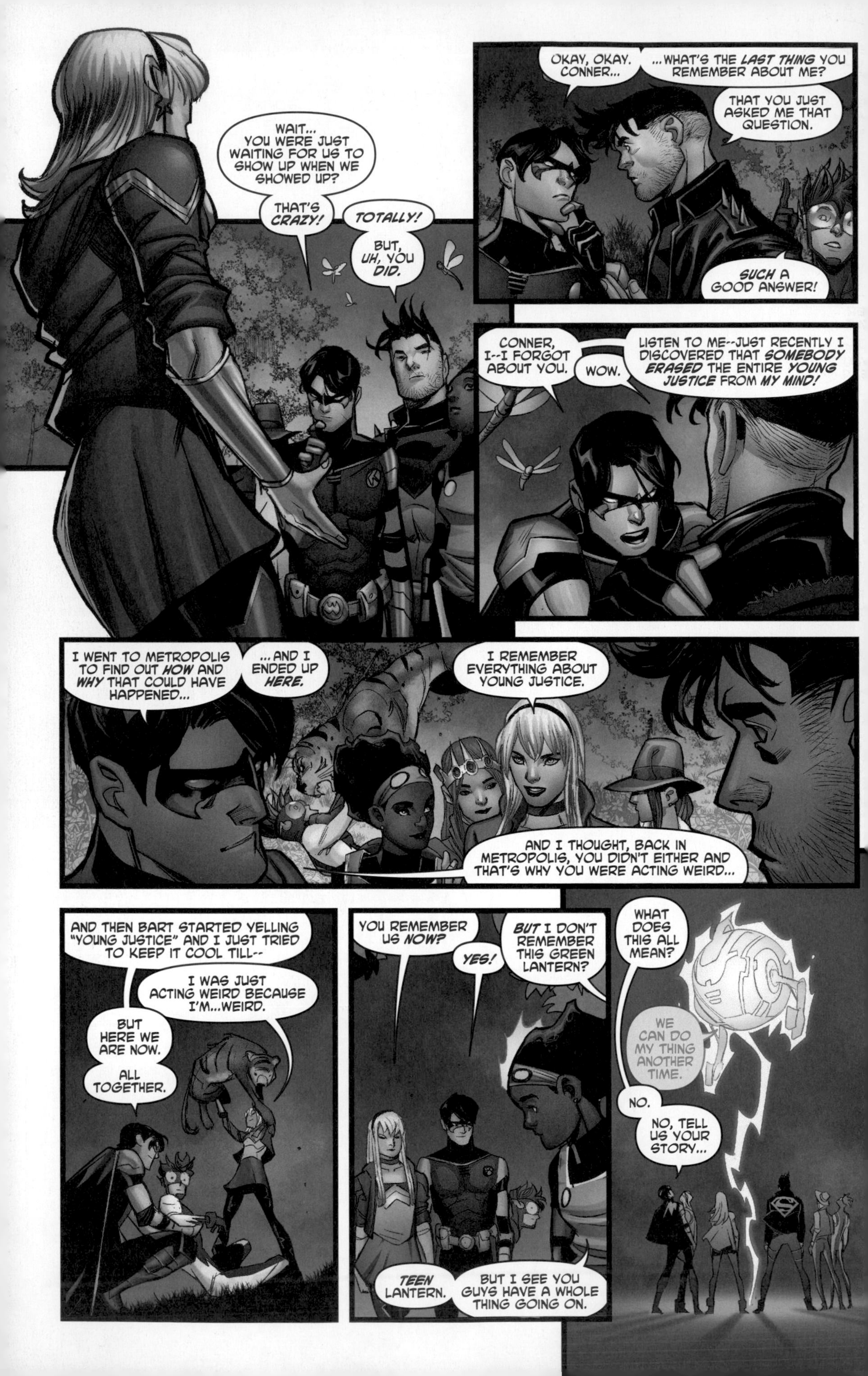
WAIT... YOU WERE JUST WAITING FOR US TO SHOW UP WHEN WE SHOWED UP?
THAT'S CRAZY!
TOTALLY!
BUT, UH, YOU DID.
OKAY, OKAY. CONNER...
...WHAT'S THE LAST THING YOU REMEMBER ABOUT ME?
THAT YOU JUST ASKED ME THAT QUESTION.
SUCH A GOOD ANSWER!
CONNER, I--I FORGOT ABOUT YOU.
WOW.
LISTEN TO ME--JUST RECENTLY I DISCOVERED THAT SOMEBODY ERASED THE ENTIRE YOUNG JUSTICE FROM MY MIND!
I WENT TO METROPOLIS TO FIND OUT HOW AND WHY THAT COULD HAVE HAPPENED...
...AND I ENDED UP HERE.
I REMEMBER EVERYTHING ABOUT YOUNG JUSTICE.
AND I THOUGHT, BACK IN METROPOLIS, YOU DIDN'T EITHER AND THAT'S WHY YOU WERE ACTING WEIRD...
AND THEN BART STARTED YELLING "YOUNG JUSTICE" AND I JUST TRIED TO KEEP IT COOL TILL--
I WAS JUST ACTING WEIRD BECAUSE I'M...WEIRD.
BUT HERE WE ARE NOW.
ALL TOGETHER.
YOU REMEMBER US NOW?
YES!
BUT I DON'T REMEMBER THIS GREEN LANTERN?
TEEN LANTERN.
BUT I SEE YOU GUYS HAVE A WHOLE THING GOING ON.
WHAT DOES THIS ALL MEAN?
WE CAN DO MY THING ANOTHER TIME.
NO.
NO, TELL US YOUR STORY...

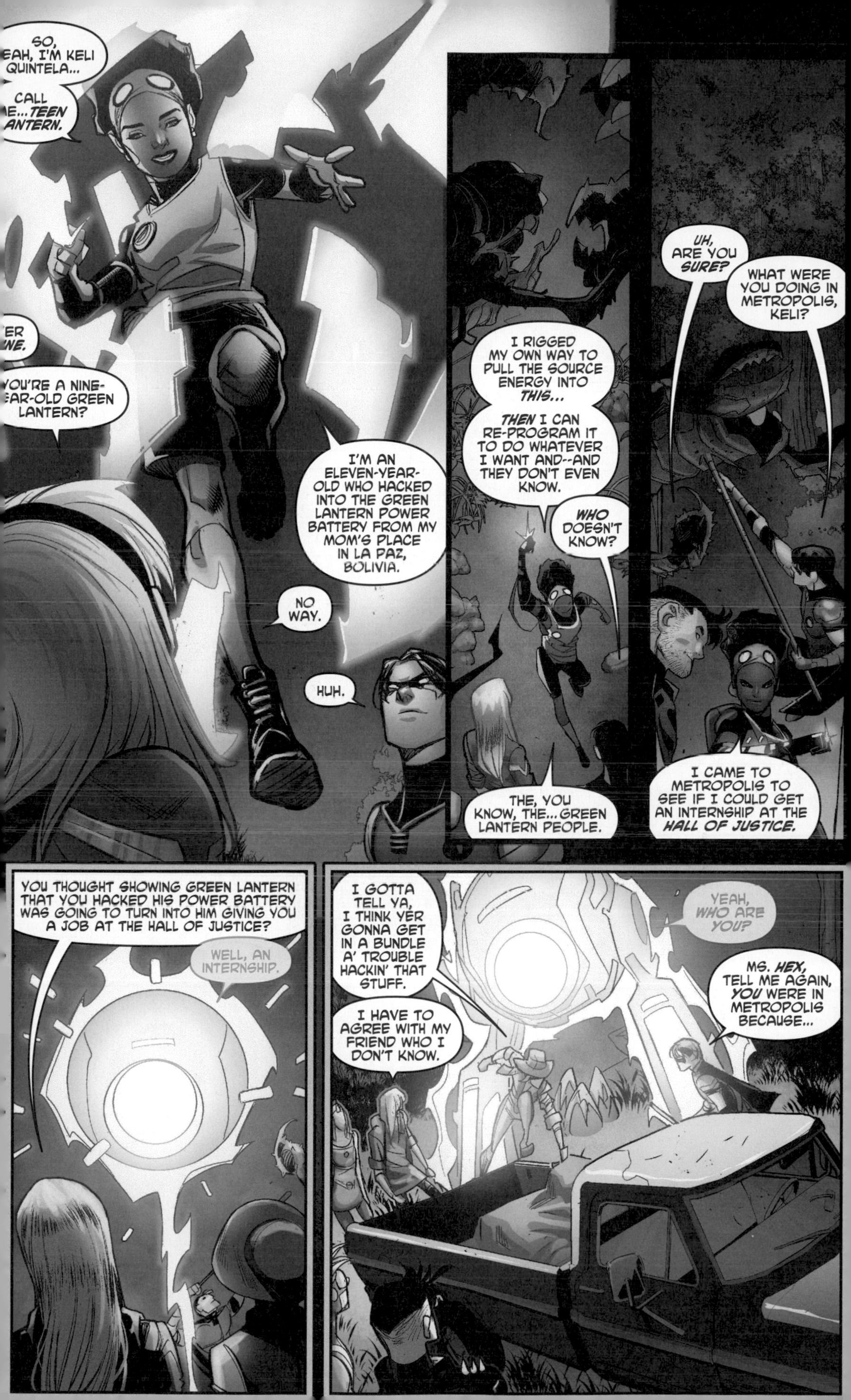
SO, EAH, I'M KELI QUINTELA...
CALL E...TEEN ANTERN.
ER NE.
OU'RE A NINE-EAR-OLD GREEN LANTERN?
I'M AN ELEVEN-YEAR-OLD WHO HACKED INTO THE GREEN LANTERN POWER BATTERY FROM MY MOM'S PLACE IN LA PAZ, BOLIVIA.
NO WAY.
HUH.
I RIGGED MY OWN WAY TO PULL THE SOURCE ENERGY INTO THIS...
THEN I CAN RE-PROGRAM IT TO DO WHATEVER I WANT AND--AND THEY DON'T EVEN KNOW.
WHO DOESN'T KNOW?
THE, YOU KNOW, THE...GREEN LANTERN PEOPLE.
UH, ARE YOU SURE?
WHAT WERE YOU DOING IN METROPOLIS, KELI?
I CAME TO METROPOLIS TO SEE IF I COULD GET AN INTERNSHIP AT THE HALL OF JUSTICE.
YOU THOUGHT SHOWING GREEN LANTERN THAT YOU HACKED HIS POWER BATTERY WAS GOING TO TURN INTO HIM GIVING YOU A JOB AT THE HALL OF JUSTICE?
WELL, AN INTERNSHIP.
I GOTTA TELL YA, I THINK YER GONNA GET IN A BUNDLE A' TROUBLE HACKIN' THAT STUFF.
I HAVE TO AGREE WITH MY FRIEND WHO I DON'T KNOW.
YEAH, WHO ARE YOU?
MS. HEX, TELL ME AGAIN, YOU WERE IN METROPOLIS BECAUSE...

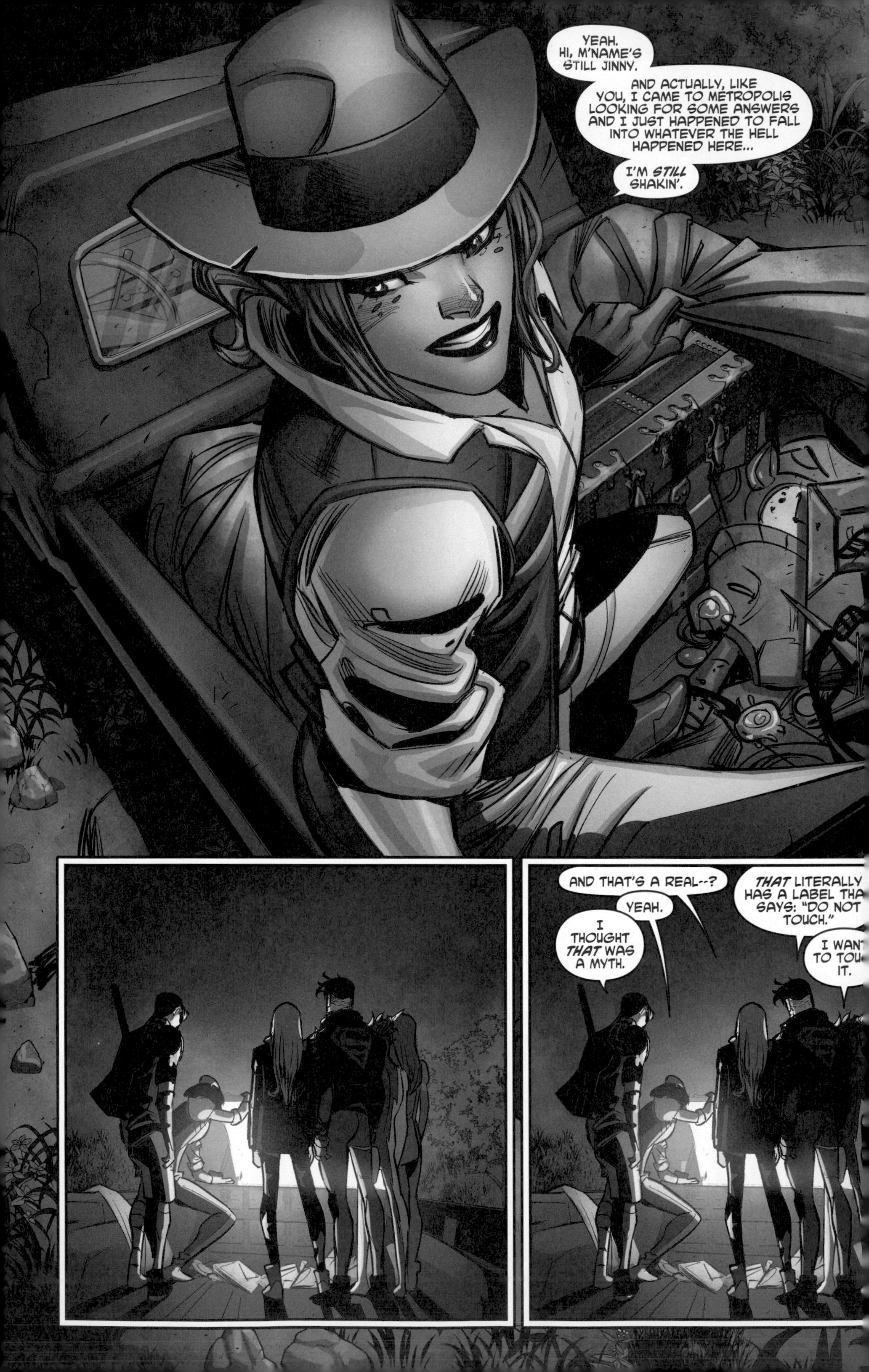
YEAH. HI, M'NAME'S STILL JINNY.
AND ACTUALLY, LIKE YOU, I CAME TO METROPOLIS LOOKING FOR SOME ANSWERS AND I JUST HAPPENED TO FALL INTO WHATEVER THE HELL HAPPENED HERE...
I'M *STILL* SHAKIN'.
AND THAT'S A REAL--?
YEAH.
I THOUGHT *THAT* WAS A MYTH.
THAT LITERALLY HAS A LABEL THA SAYS: "DO NOT TOUCH."
I WAN TO TOU IT.

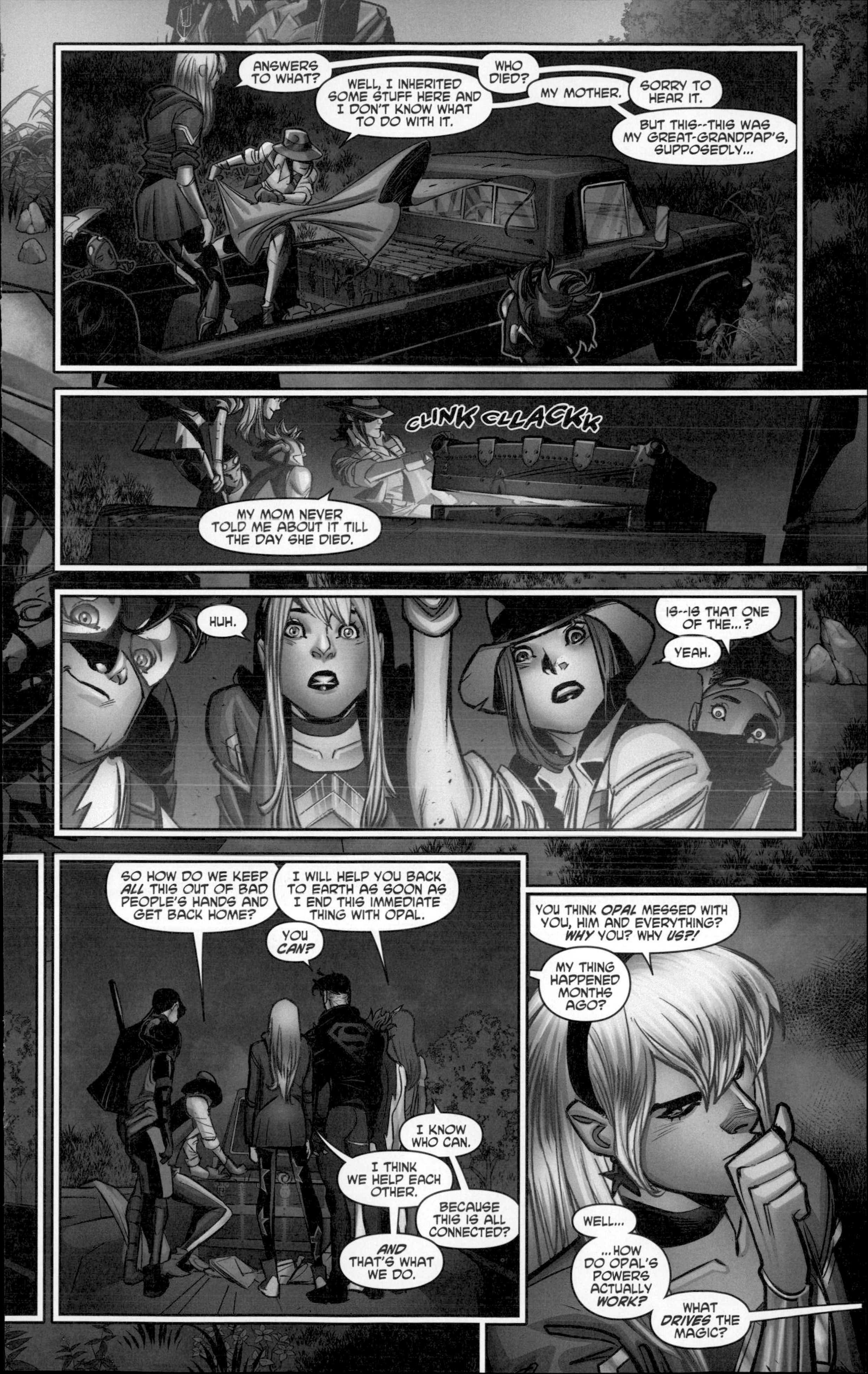
ANSWERS TO WHAT?
WELL, I INHERITED SOME STUFF HERE AND I DON'T KNOW WHAT TO DO WITH IT.
WHO DIED?
MY MOTHER.
SORRY TO HEAR IT.
BUT THIS--THIS WAS MY GREAT-GRANDPAP'S, SUPPOSEDLY...
CLINK CLLACKK
MY MOM NEVER TOLD ME ABOUT IT TILL THE DAY SHE DIED.
HUH.
IS--IS THAT ONE OF THE...?
YEAH.
SO HOW DO WE KEEP ALL THIS OUT OF BAD PEOPLE'S HANDS AND GET BACK HOME?
I WILL HELP YOU BACK TO EARTH AS SOON AS I END THIS IMMEDIATE THING WITH OPAL.
YOU CAN?
I KNOW WHO CAN.
I THINK WE HELP EACH OTHER.
BECAUSE THIS IS ALL CONNECTED?
AND THAT'S WHAT WE DO.
YOU THINK OPAL MESSED WITH YOU, HIM AND EVERYTHING? WHY YOU? WHY US?!
MY THING HAPPENED MONTHS AGO?
WELL...
...HOW DO OPAL'S POWERS ACTUALLY WORK?
WHAT DRIVES THE MAGIC?

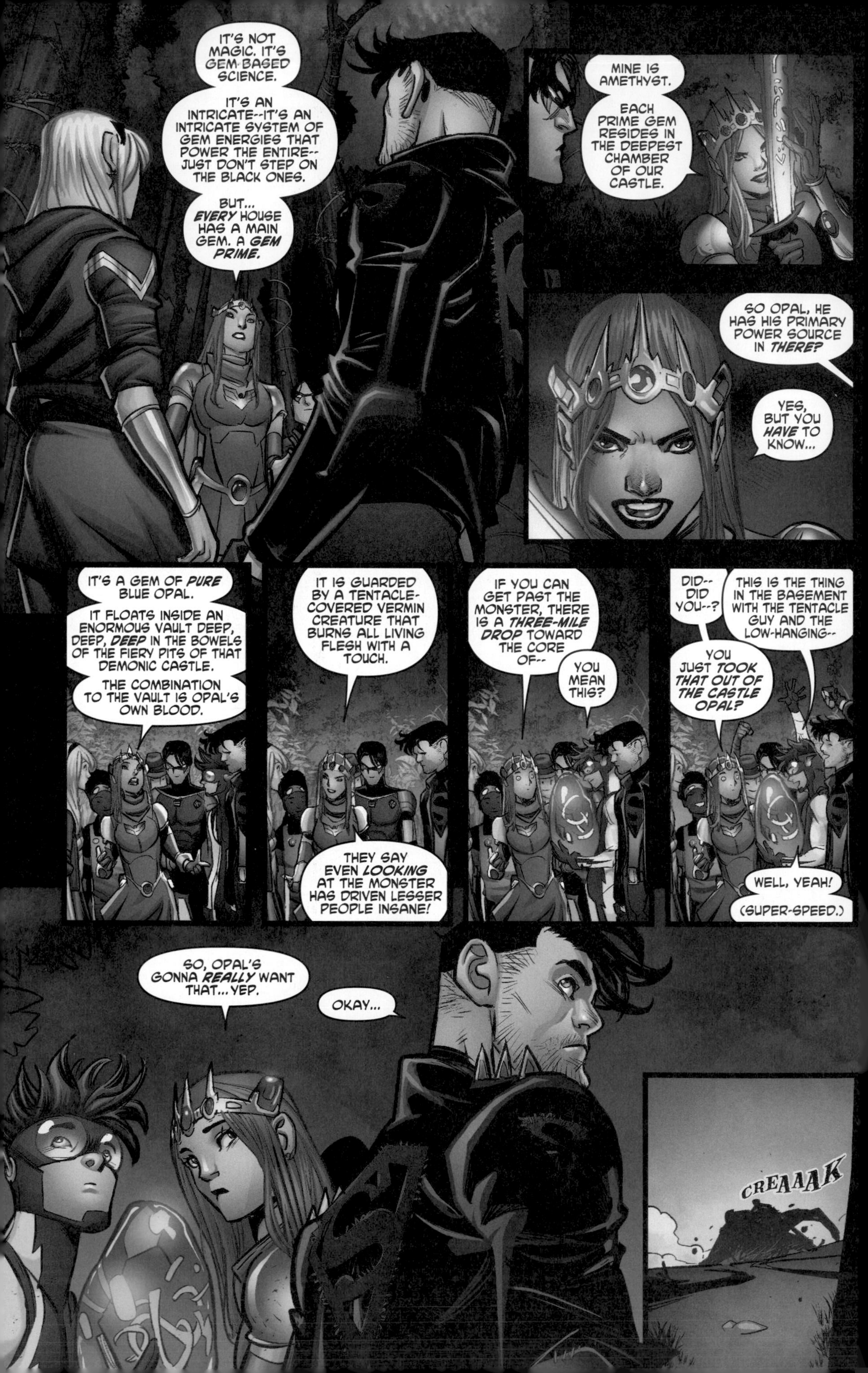
IT'S NOT MAGIC. IT'S GEM-BASED SCIENCE.
IT'S AN INTRICATE--IT'S AN INTRICATE SYSTEM OF GEM ENERGIES THAT POWER THE ENTIRE-- JUST DON'T STEP ON THE BLACK ONES.
BUT... EVERY HOUSE HAS A MAIN GEM. A GEM PRIME.
MINE IS AMETHYST.
EACH PRIME GEM RESIDES IN THE DEEPEST CHAMBER OF OUR CASTLE.
SO OPAL, HE HAS HIS PRIMARY POWER SOURCE IN THERE?
YES, BUT YOU HAVE TO KNOW...
IT'S A GEM OF PURE BLUE OPAL.
IT FLOATS INSIDE AN ENORMOUS VAULT DEEP, DEEP, DEEP IN THE BOWELS OF THE FIERY PITS OF THAT DEMONIC CASTLE.
THE COMBINATION TO THE VAULT IS OPAL'S OWN BLOOD.
IT IS GUARDED BY A TENTACLE-COVERED VERMIN CREATURE THAT BURNS ALL LIVING FLESH WITH A TOUCH.
THEY SAY EVEN LOOKING AT THE MONSTER HAS DRIVEN LESSER PEOPLE INSANE!
IF YOU CAN GET PAST THE MONSTER, THERE IS A THREE-MILE DROP TOWARD THE CORE OF--
YOU MEAN THIS?
DID-- DID YOU--?
THIS IS THE THING IN THE BASEMENT WITH THE TENTACLE GUY AND THE LOW-HANGING--
YOU JUST TOOK THAT OUT OF THE CASTLE OPAL?
WELL, YEAH!
(SUPER-SPEED.)
SO, OPAL'S GONNA REALLY WANT THAT... YEP.
OKAY...
CREAAAK

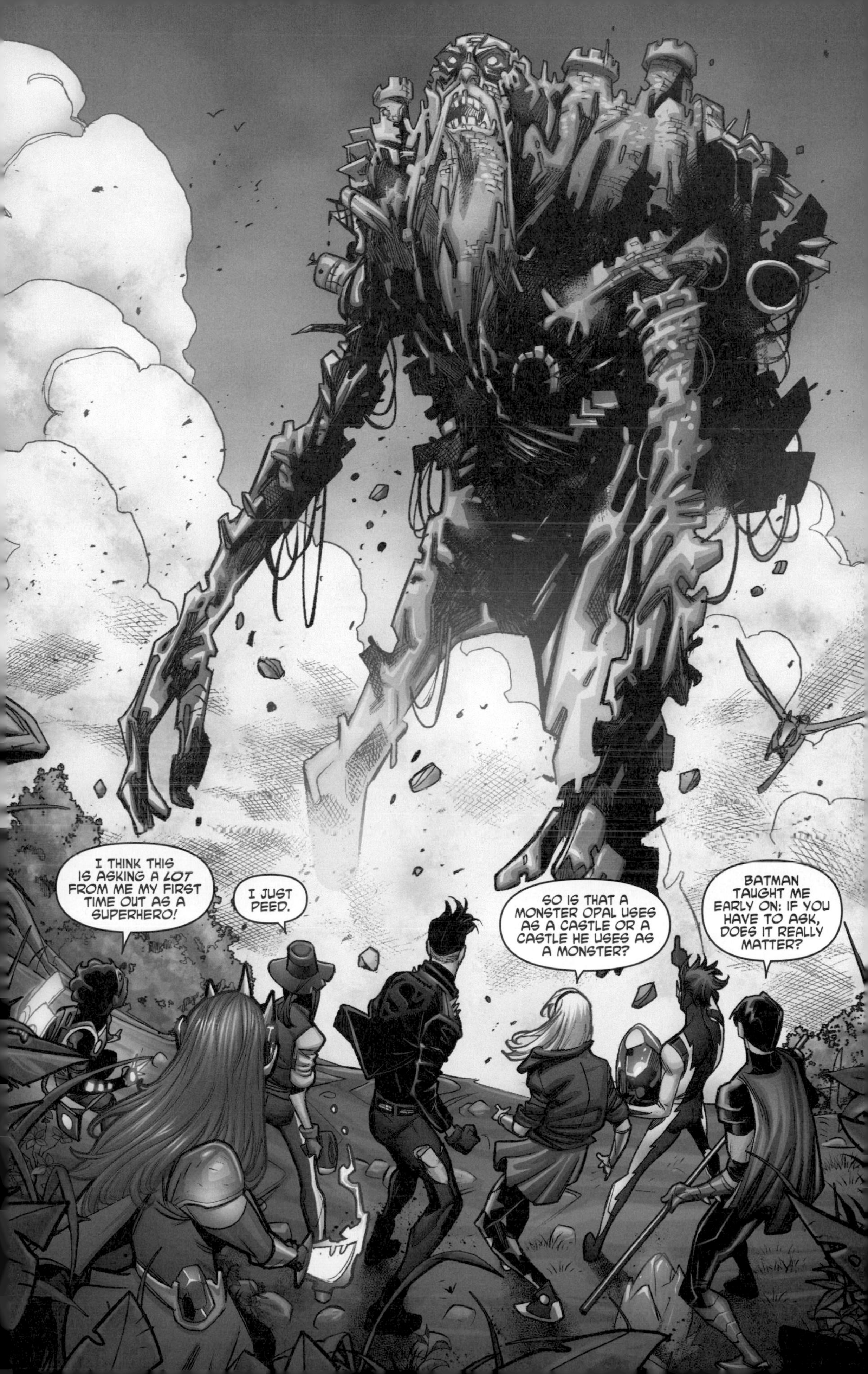
I THINK THIS IS ASKING A *LOT* FROM ME MY FIRST TIME OUT AS A SUPERHERO!
I JUST PEED.
SO IS THAT A MONSTER OPAL USES AS A CASTLE OR A CASTLE HE USES AS A MONSTER?
BATMAN TAUGHT ME EARLY ON: IF YOU HAVE TO ASK, DOES IT REALLY MATTER?

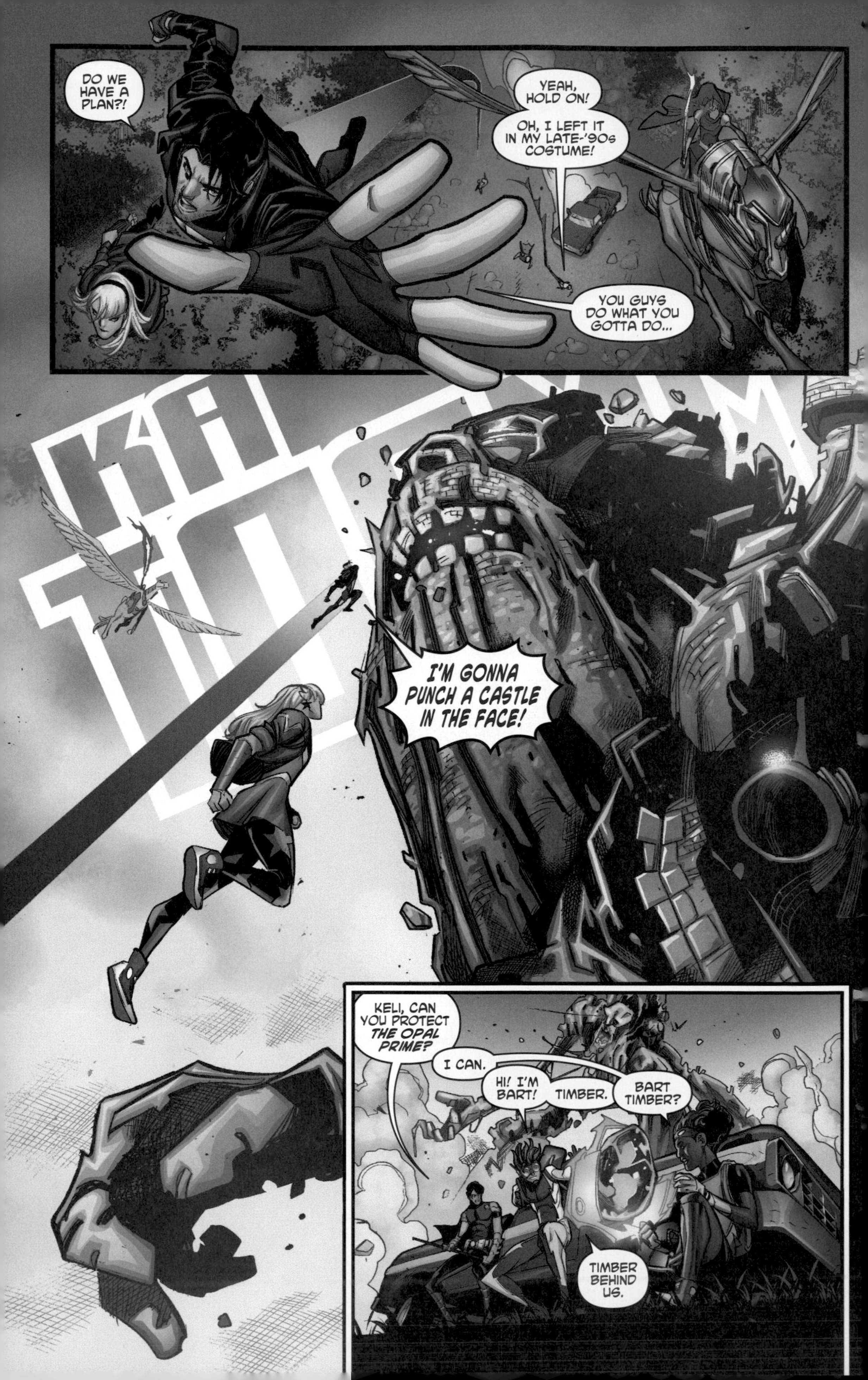
DO WE HAVE A PLAN?!
YEAH, HOLD ON!
OH, I LEFT IT IN MY LATE-'90s COSTUME!
YOU GUYS DO WHAT YOU GOTTA DO...
I'M GONNA PUNCH A CASTLE IN THE FACE!
KELI, CAN YOU PROTECT THE OPAL PRIME?
I CAN.
HI! I'M BART!
TIMBER.
BART TIMBER?
TIMBER BEHIND US.

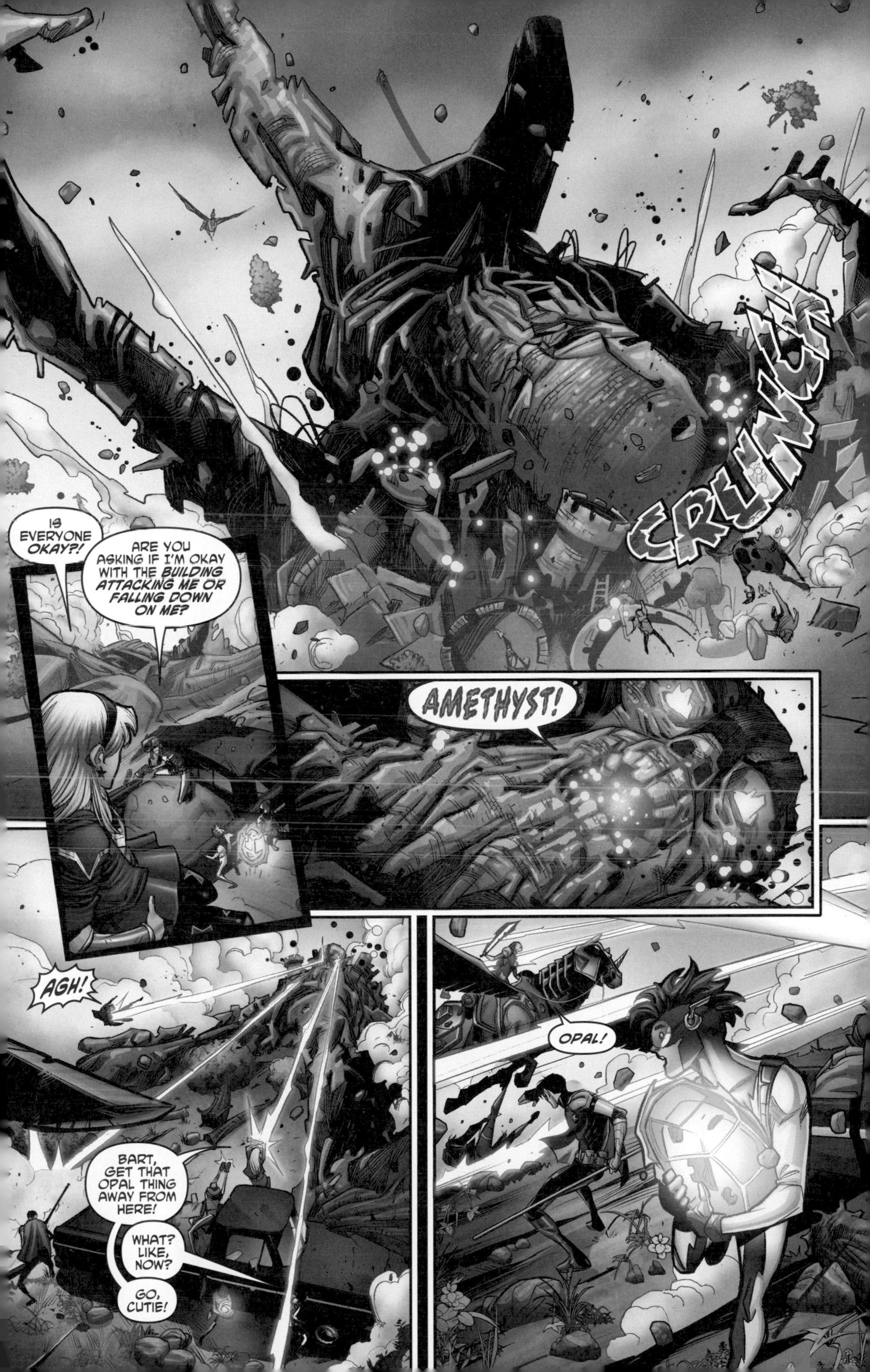
CRUNCH!
IS EVERYONE OKAY?!
ARE YOU ASKING IF I'M OKAY WITH THE BUILDING ATTACKING ME OR FALLING DOWN ON ME?
AMETHYST!
AGH!
BART, GET THAT OPAL THING AWAY FROM HERE!
WHAT? LIKE, NOW?
GO, CUTIE!
OPAL!

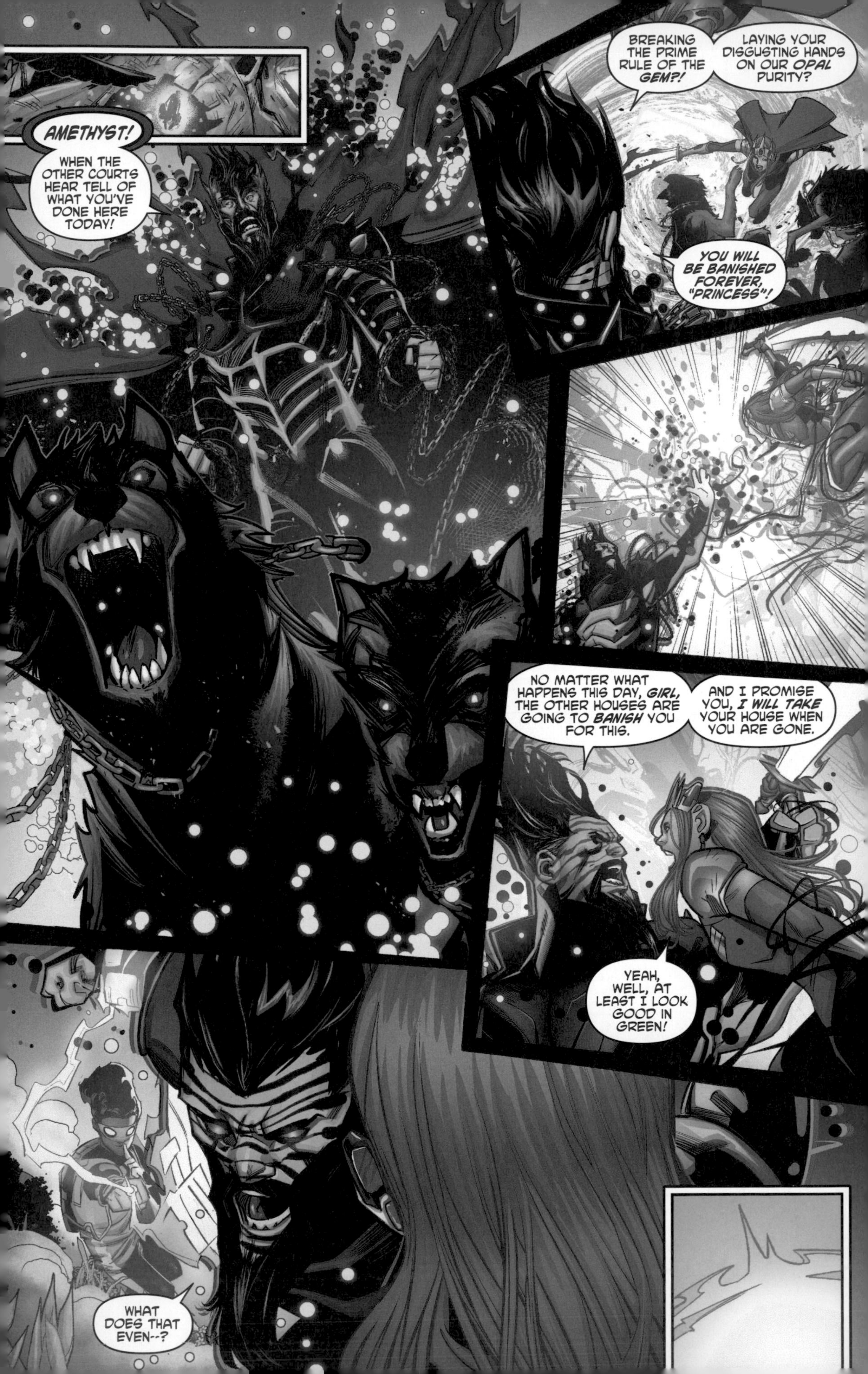
AMETHYST!
WHEN THE OTHER COURTS HEAR TELL OF WHAT YOU'VE DONE HERE TODAY!
BREAKING THE PRIME RULE OF THE GEM?!
LAYING YOUR DISGUSTING HANDS ON OUR OPAL PURITY?
YOU WILL BE BANISHED FOREVER, "PRINCESS"!
NO MATTER WHAT HAPPENS THIS DAY, GIRL, THE OTHER HOUSES ARE GOING TO BANISH YOU FOR THIS.
AND I PROMISE YOU, I WILL TAKE YOUR HOUSE WHEN YOU ARE GONE.
YEAH, WELL, AT LEAST I LOOK GOOD IN GREEN!
WHAT DOES THAT EVEN--?

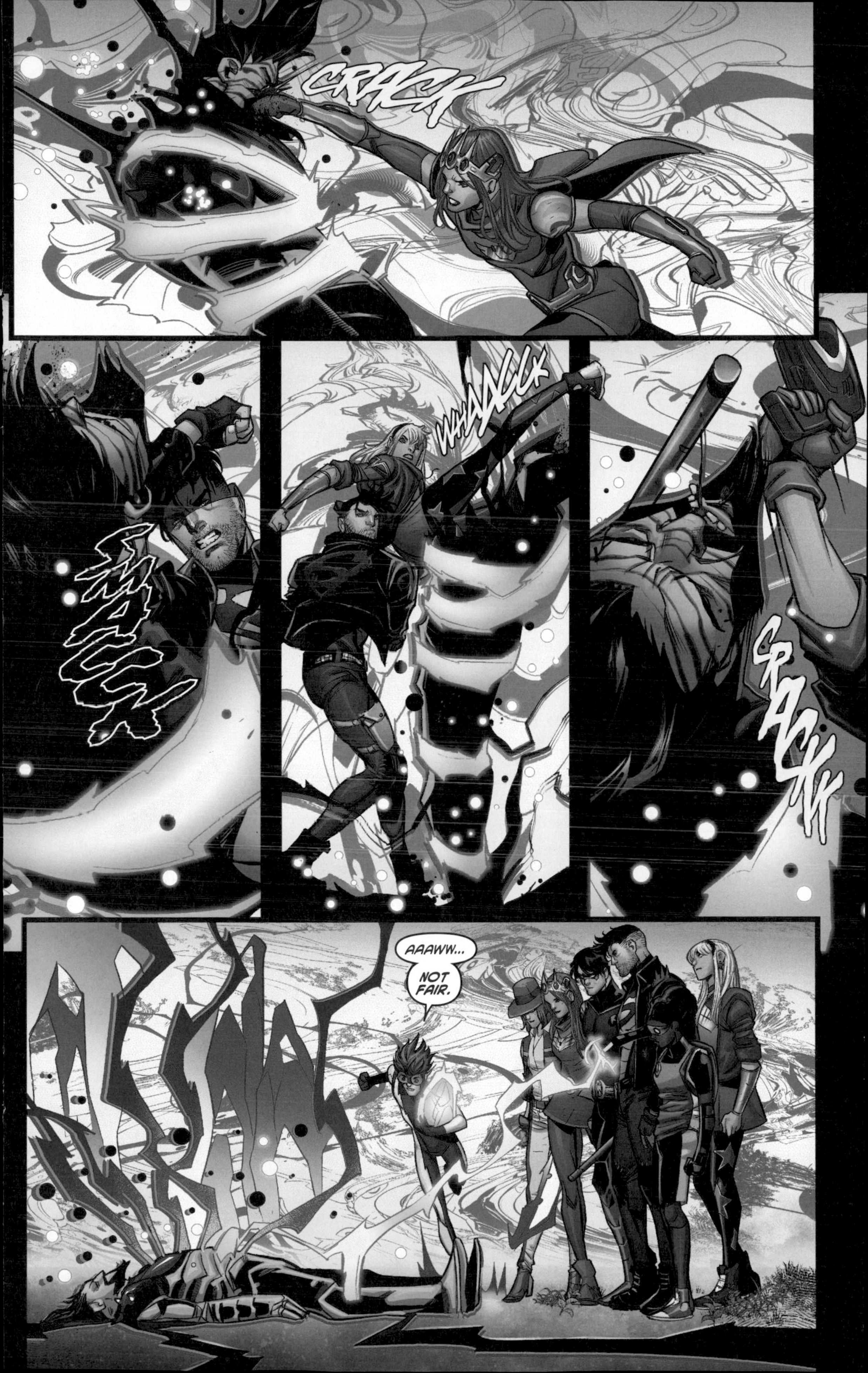
CRACK
SMACK
WHADUCK
CRACKK
AAAWW... NOT FAIR.

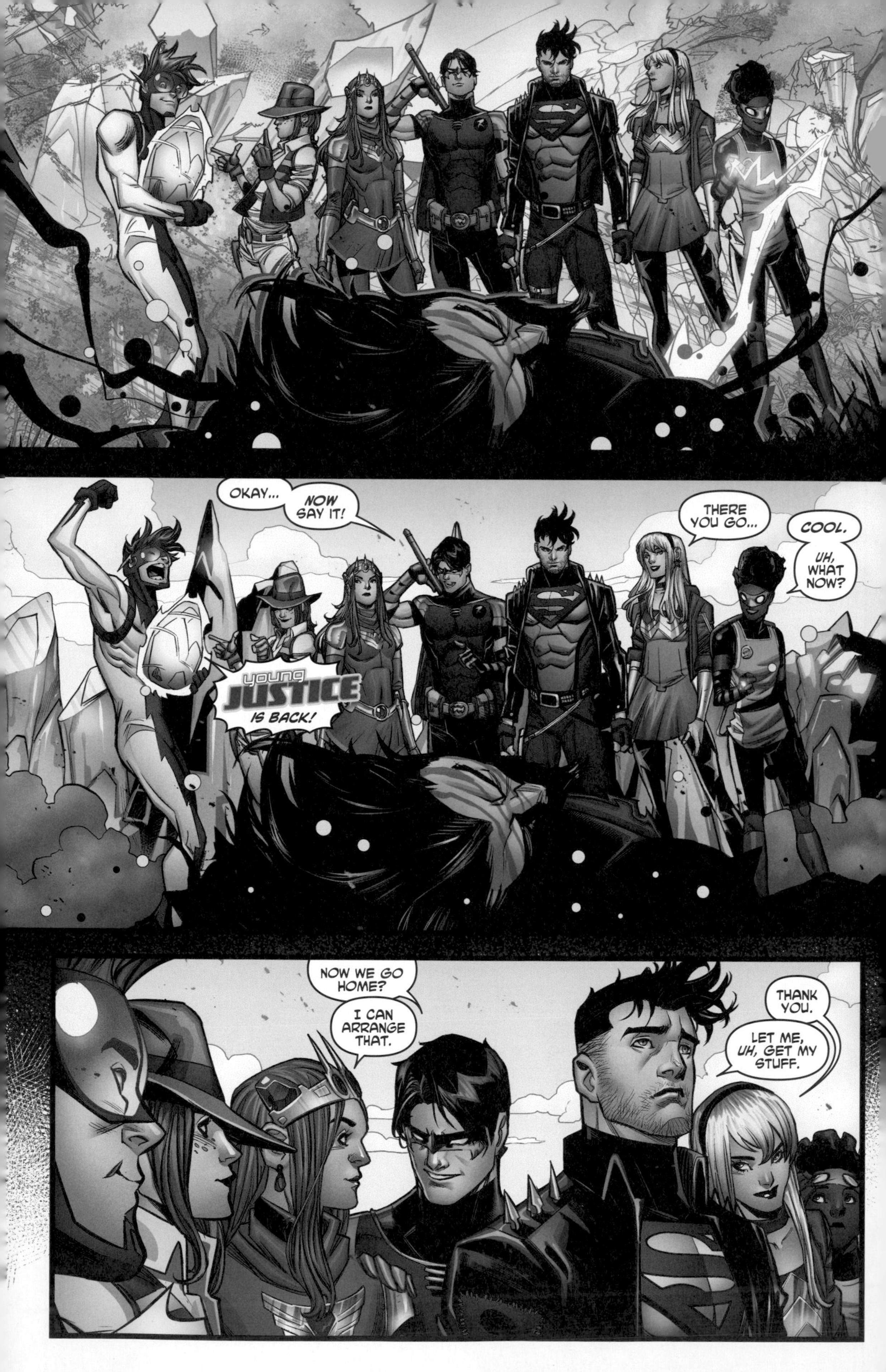
OKAY...
NOW SAY IT!
YOUNG JUSTICE IS BACK!
THERE YOU GO...
COOL.
UH, WHAT NOW?
NOW WE GO HOME?
I CAN ARRANGE THAT.
THANK YOU.
LET ME, UH, GET MY STUFF.

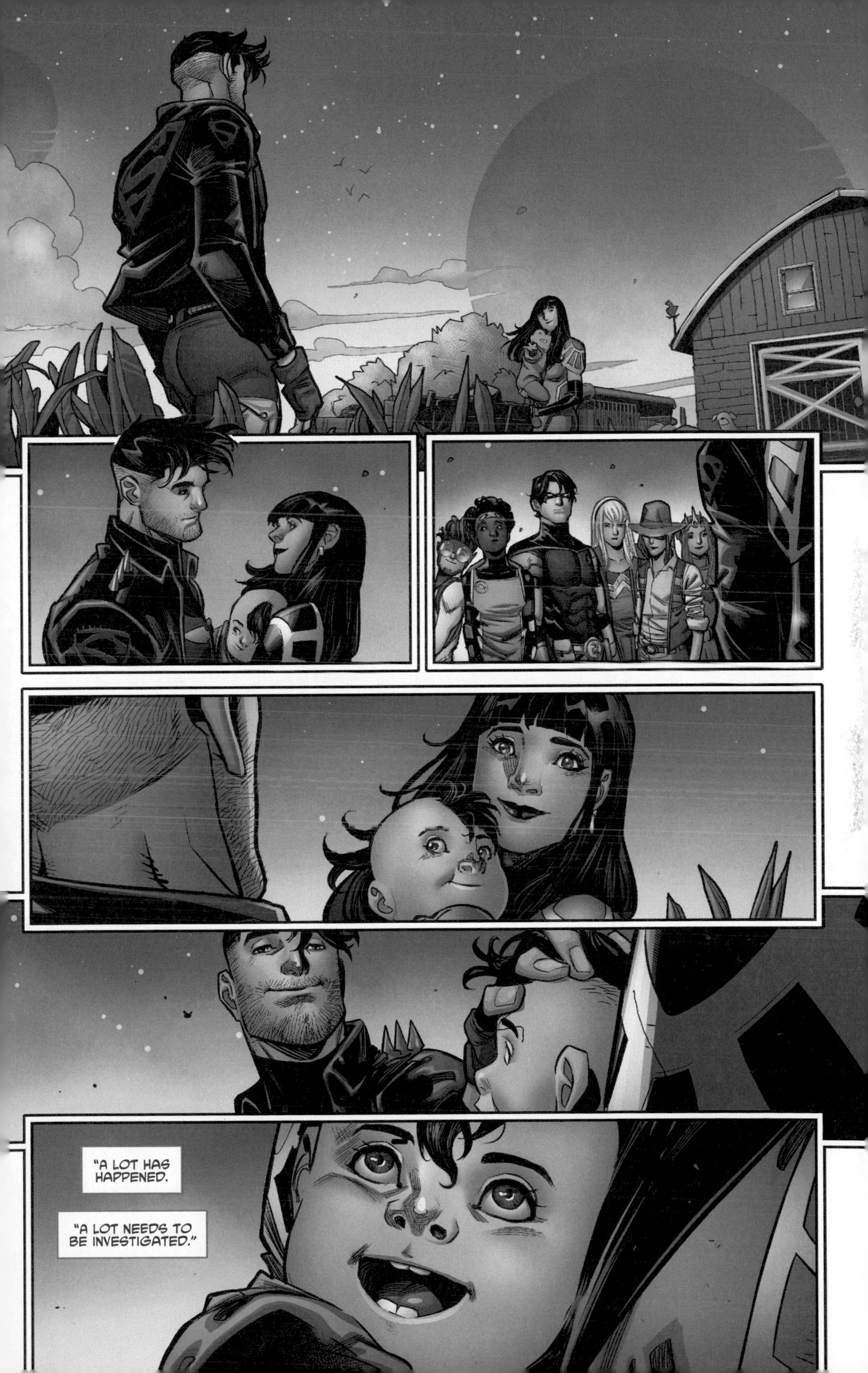
"A LOT HAS HAPPENED.
"A LOT NEEDS TO BE INVESTIGATED."

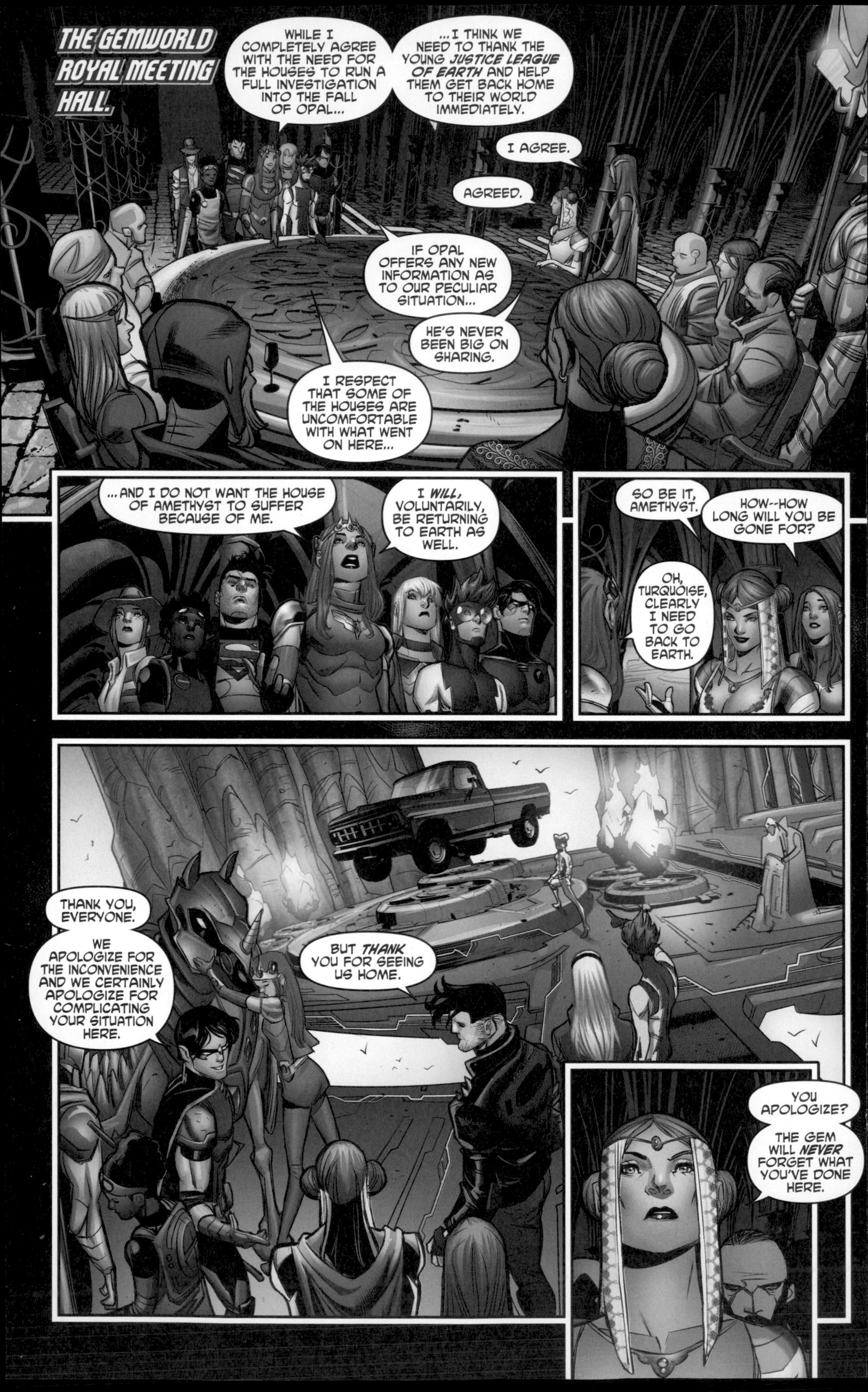
THE GEMWORLD ROYAL MEETING HALL.
WHILE I COMPLETELY AGREE WITH THE NEED FOR THE HOUSES TO RUN A FULL INVESTIGATION INTO THE FALL OF OPAL...
...I THINK WE NEED TO THANK THE YOUNG JUSTICE LEAGUE OF EARTH AND HELP THEM GET BACK HOME TO THEIR WORLD IMMEDIATELY.
I AGREE.
AGREED.
IF OPAL OFFERS ANY NEW INFORMATION AS TO OUR PECULIAR SITUATION...
HE'S NEVER BEEN BIG ON SHARING.
I RESPECT THAT SOME OF THE HOUSES ARE UNCOMFORTABLE WITH WHAT WENT ON HERE...
...AND I DO NOT WANT THE HOUSE OF AMETHYST TO SUFFER BECAUSE OF ME.
I WILL, VOLUNTARILY, BE RETURNING TO EARTH AS WELL.
SO BE IT, AMETHYST.
HOW--HOW LONG WILL YOU BE GONE FOR?
OH, TURQUOISE, CLEARLY I NEED TO GO BACK TO EARTH.
THANK YOU, EVERYONE.
WE APOLOGIZE FOR THE INCONVENIENCE AND WE CERTAINLY APOLOGIZE FOR COMPLICATING YOUR SITUATION HERE.
BUT THANK YOU FOR SEEING US HOME.
YOU APOLOGIZE?
THE GEM WILL NEVER FORGET WHAT YOU'VE DONE HERE.

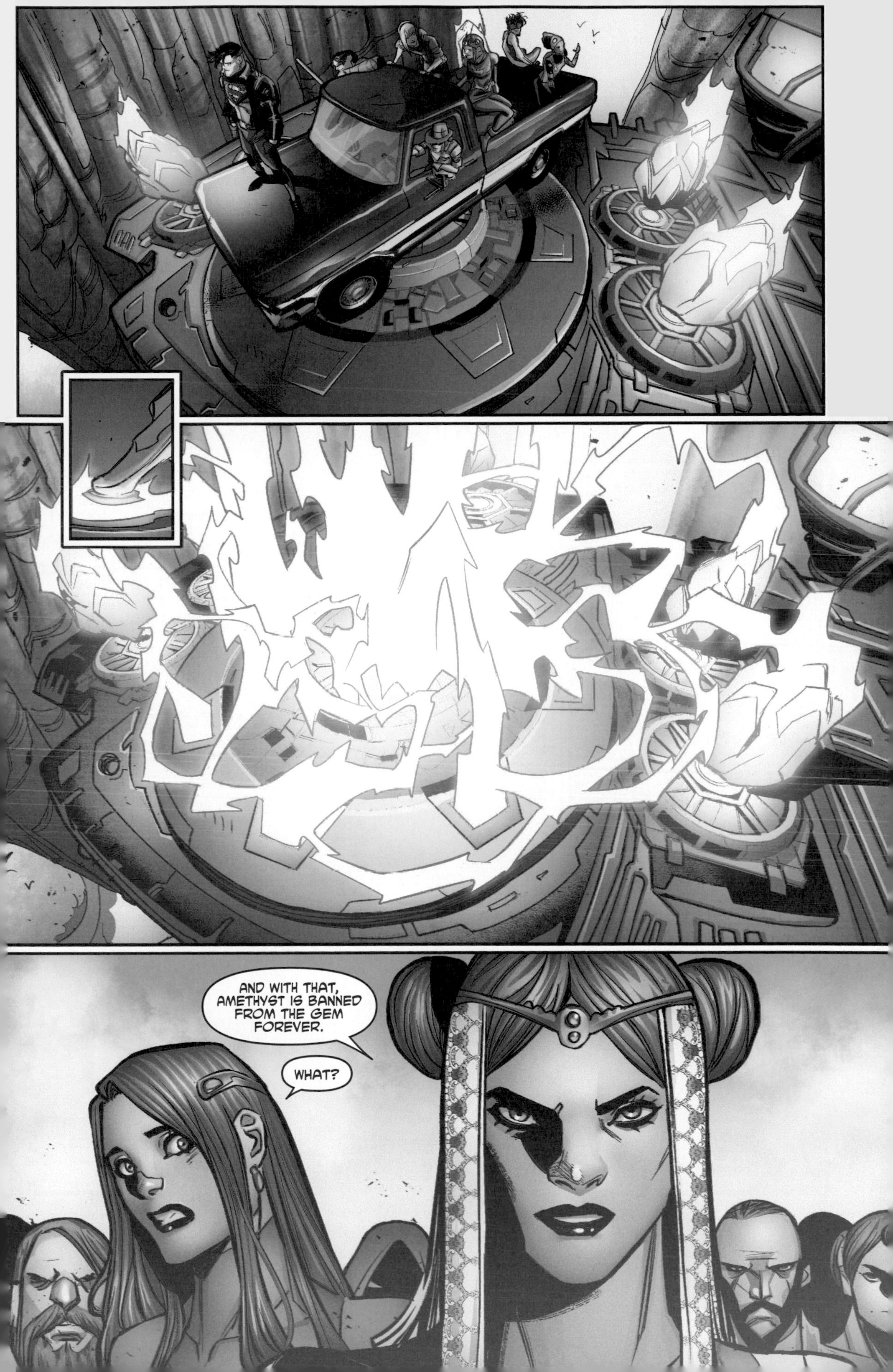
AND WITH THAT, AMETHYST IS BANNED FROM THE GEM FOREVER.
WHAT?

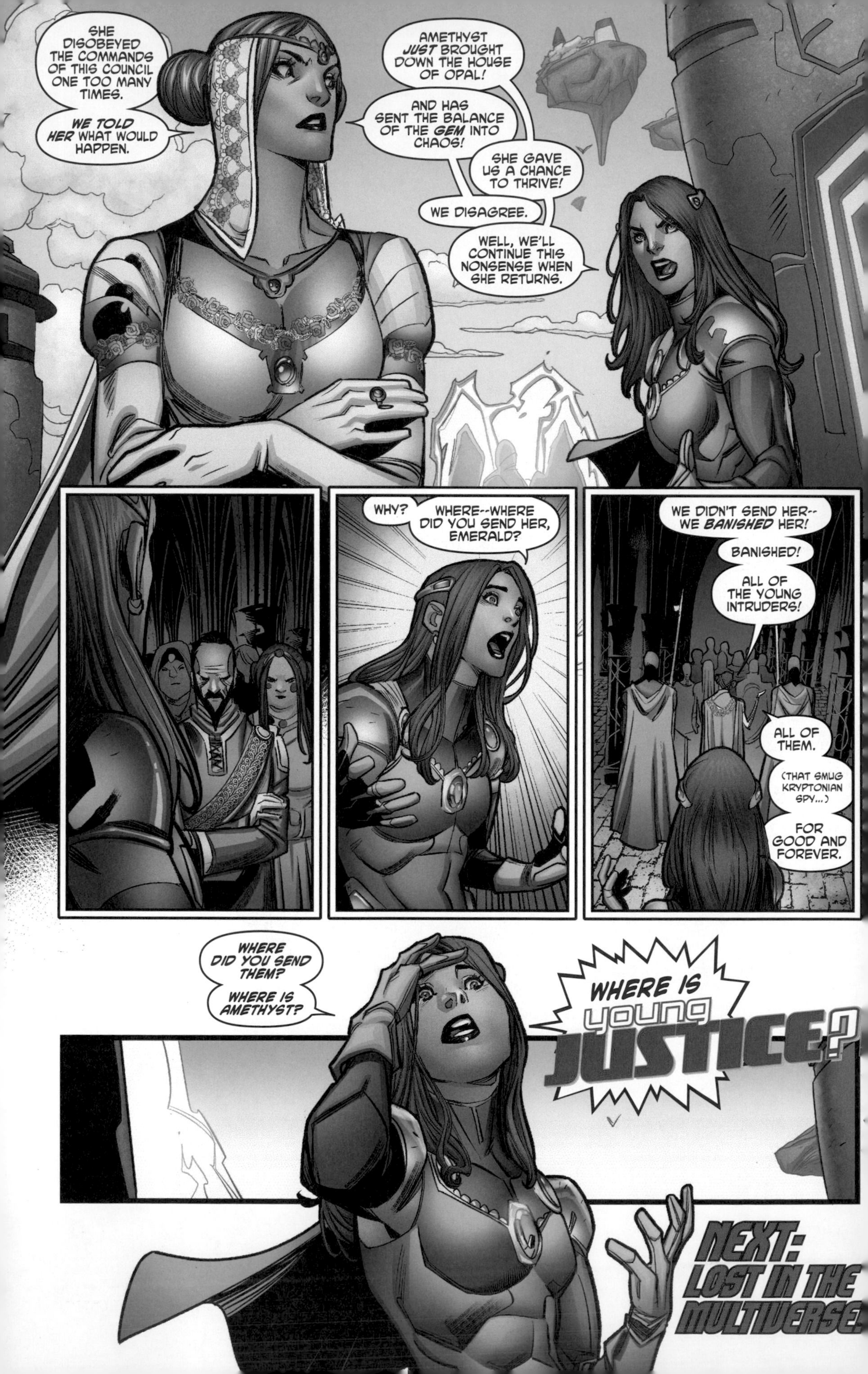
SHE DISOBEYED THE COMMANDS OF THIS COUNCIL ONE TOO MANY TIMES.
WE TOLD HER WHAT WOULD HAPPEN.
AMETHYST JUST BROUGHT DOWN THE HOUSE OF OPAL!
AND HAS SENT THE BALANCE OF THE GEM INTO CHAOS!
SHE GAVE US A CHANCE TO THRIVE!
WE DISAGREE.
WELL, WE'LL CONTINUE THIS NONSENSE WHEN SHE RETURNS.
WHY?
WHERE--WHERE DID YOU SEND HER, EMERALD?
WE DIDN'T SEND HER-- WE BANISHED HER!
BANISHED!
ALL OF THE YOUNG INTRUDERS!
ALL OF THEM.
(THAT SMUG KRYPTONIAN SPY...)
FOR GOOD AND FOREVER.
WHERE DID YOU SEND THEM?
WHERE IS AMETHYST?
WHERE IS young JUSTICE?
NEXT: LOST IN THE MULTIVERSE.

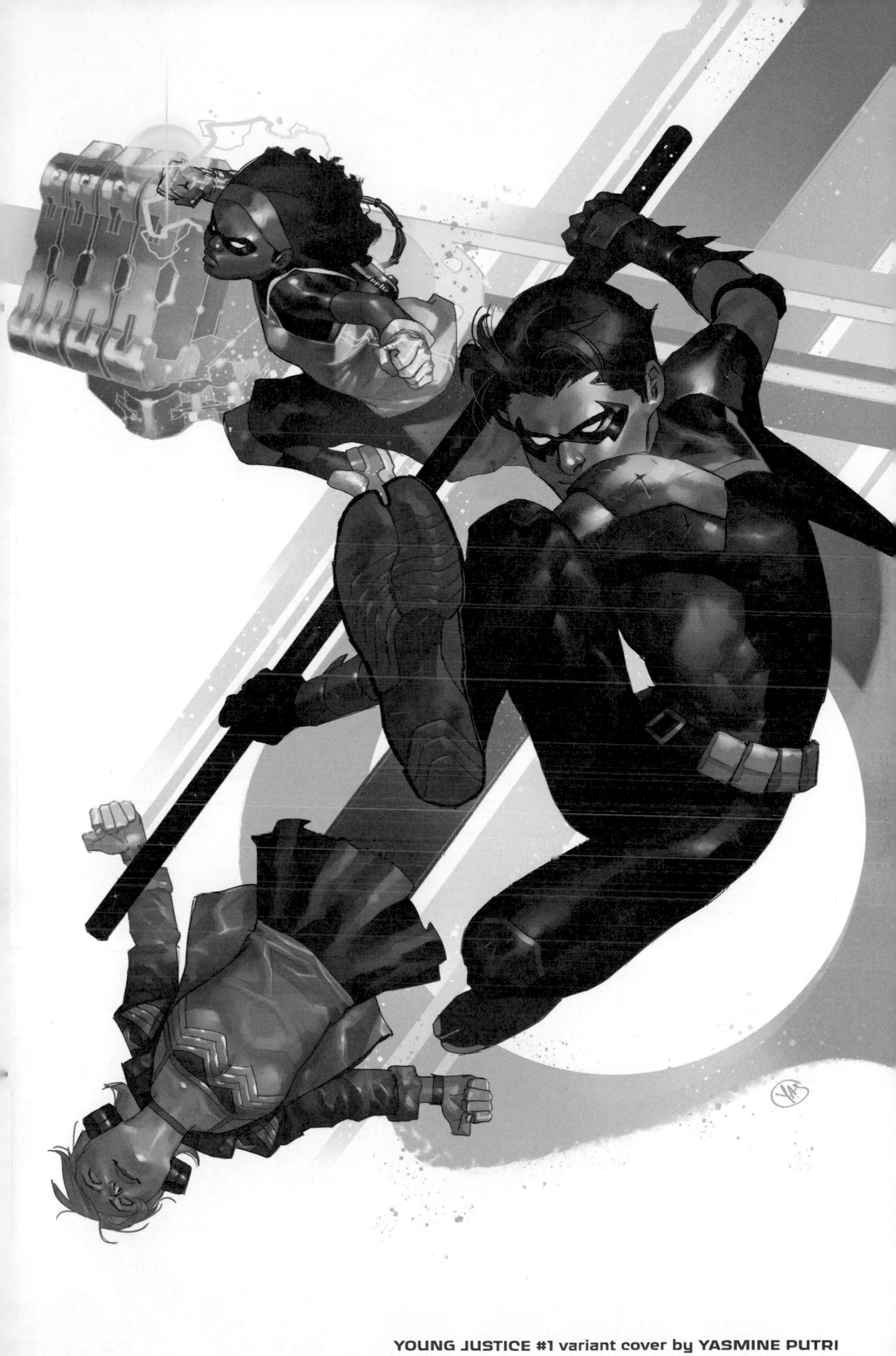

YOUNG JUSTICE #1 variant cover by YASMINE PUTRI

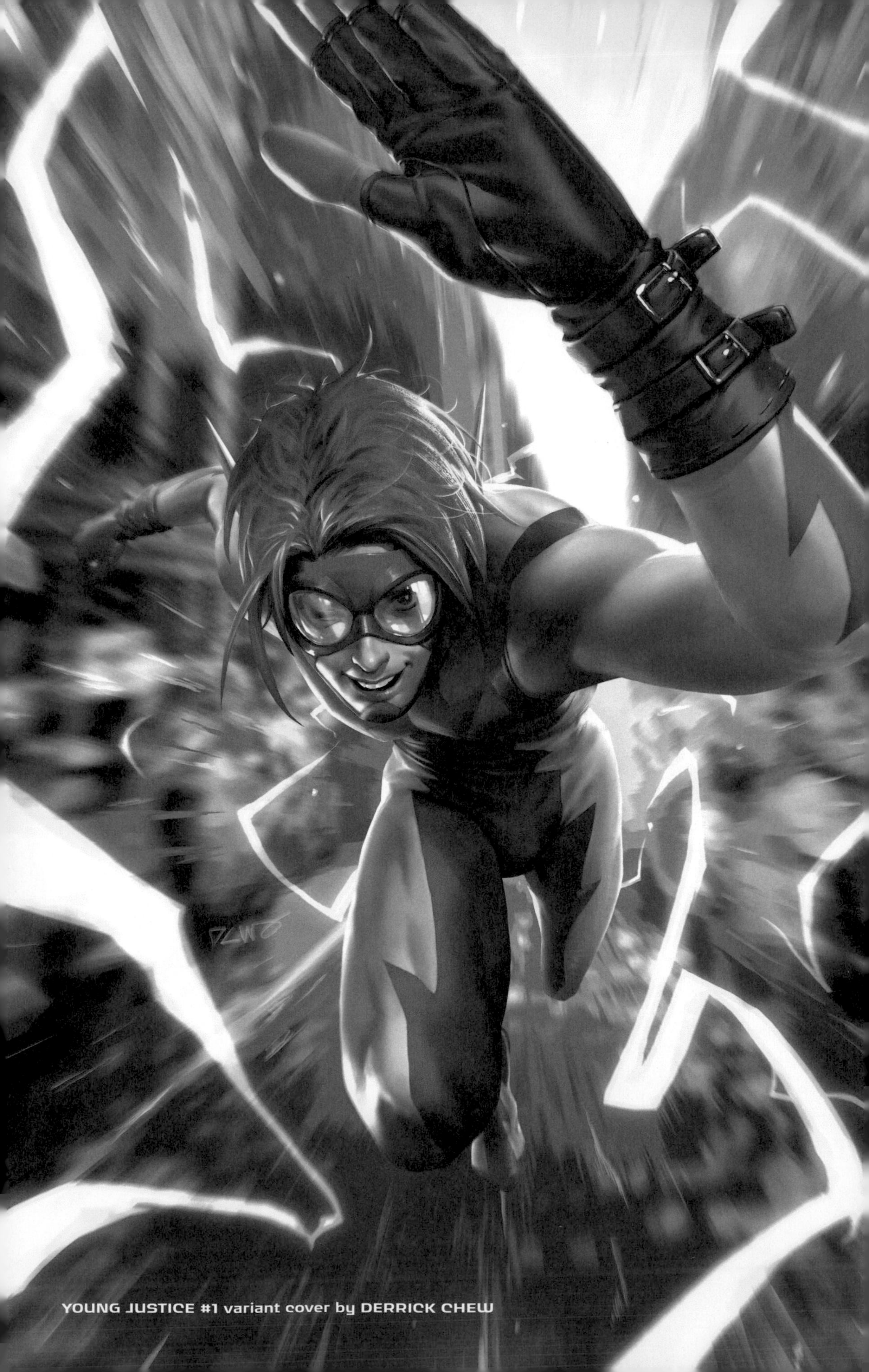

YOUNG JUSTICE #1 variant cover by DERRICK CHEW

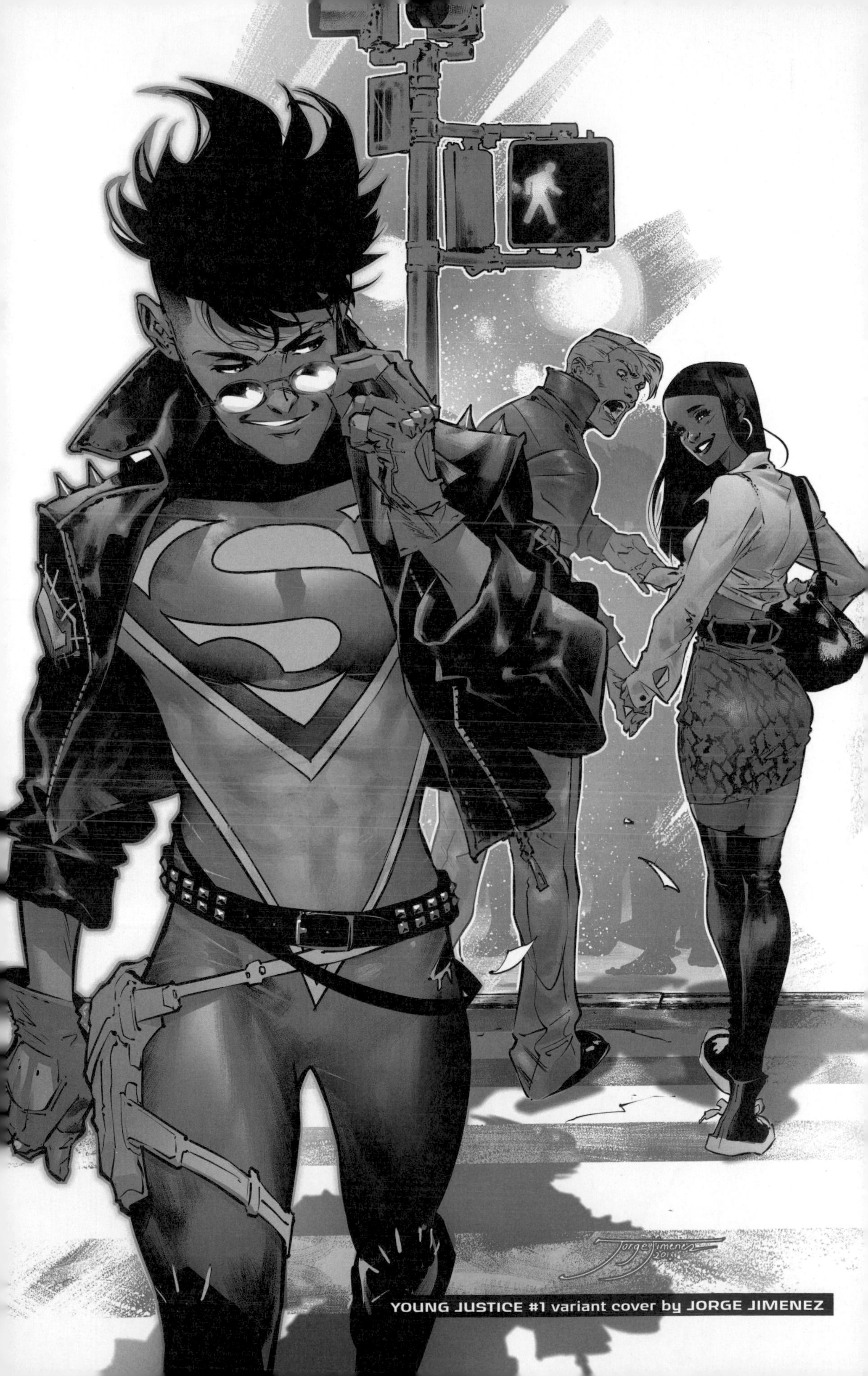

YOUNG JUSTICE #1 variant cover by JORGE JIMENEZ

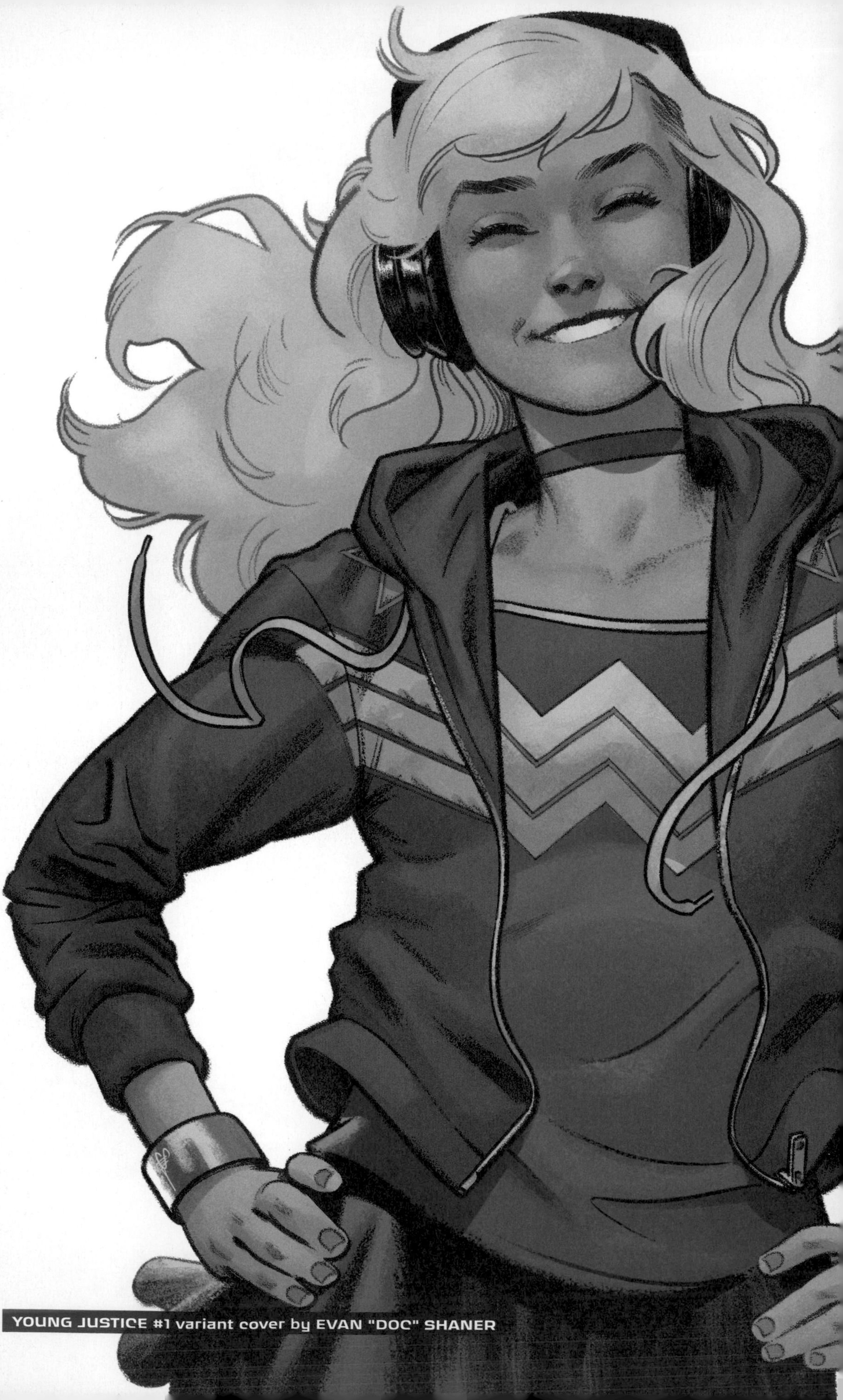

YOUNG JUSTICE #1 variant cover by EVAN "DOC" SHANER

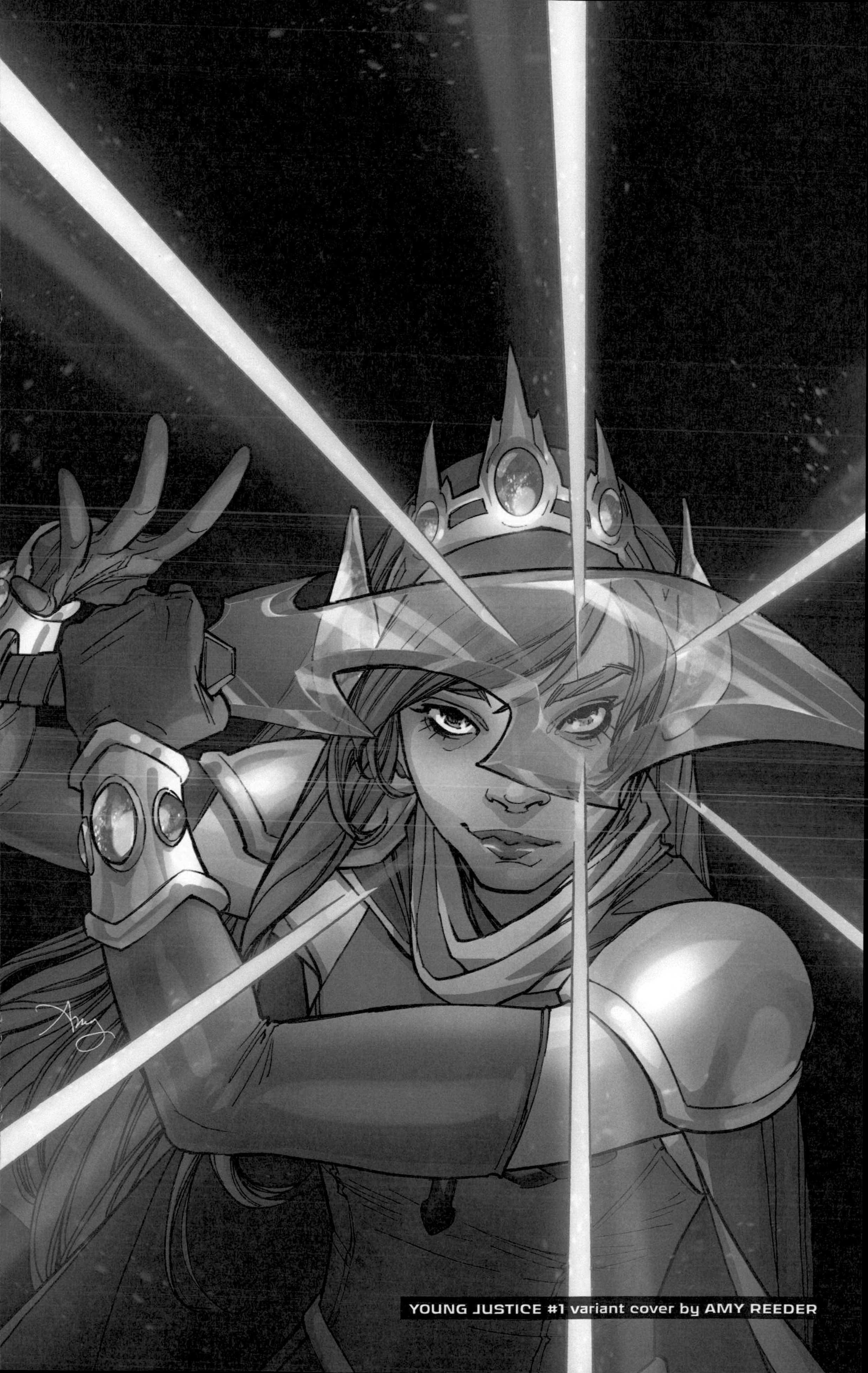

YOUNG JUSTICE #1 variant cover by AMY REEDER

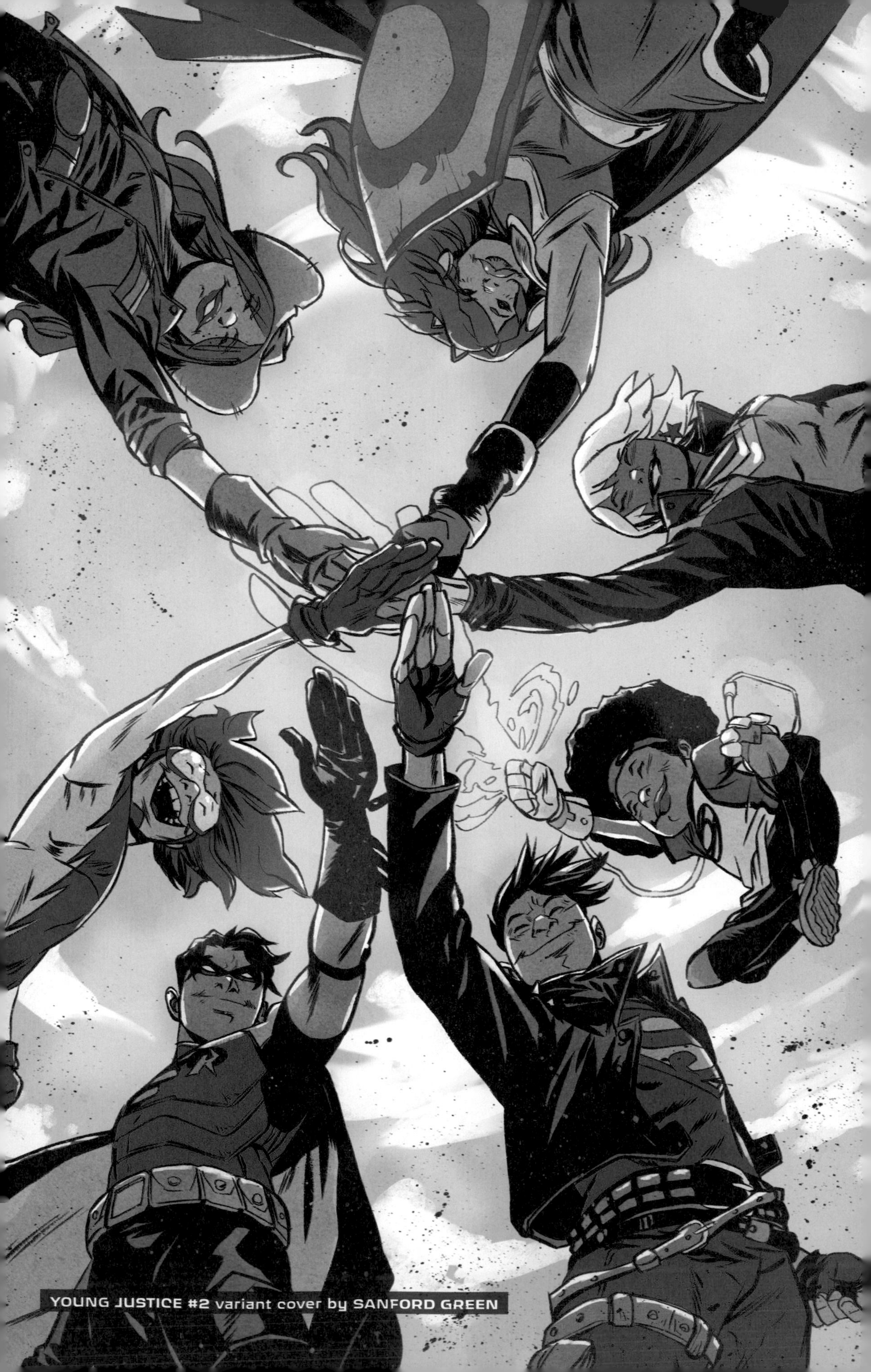

YOUNG JUSTICE #2 variant cover by SANFORD GREEN

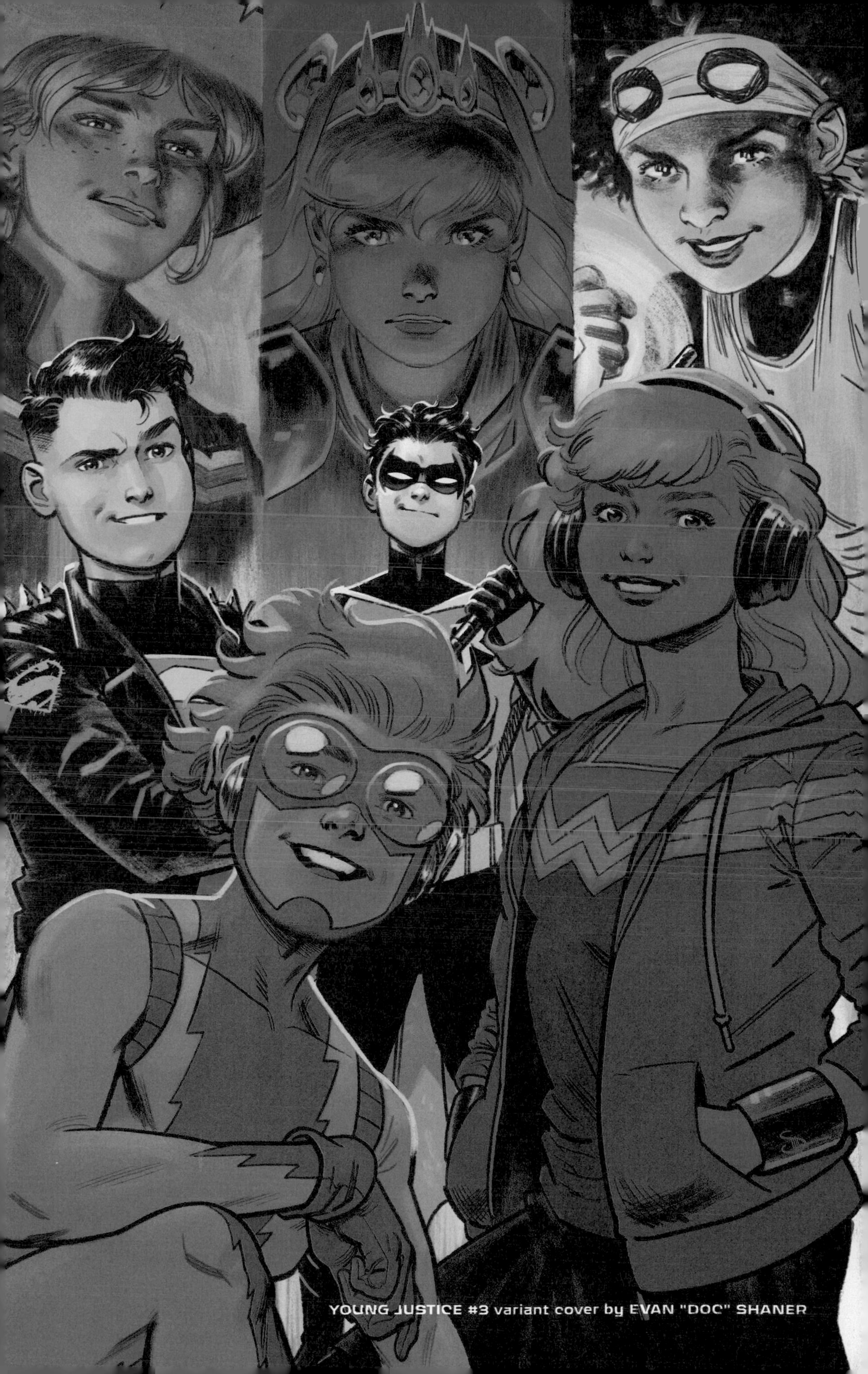

YOUNG JUSTICE #3 variant cover by EVAN "DOC" SHANER

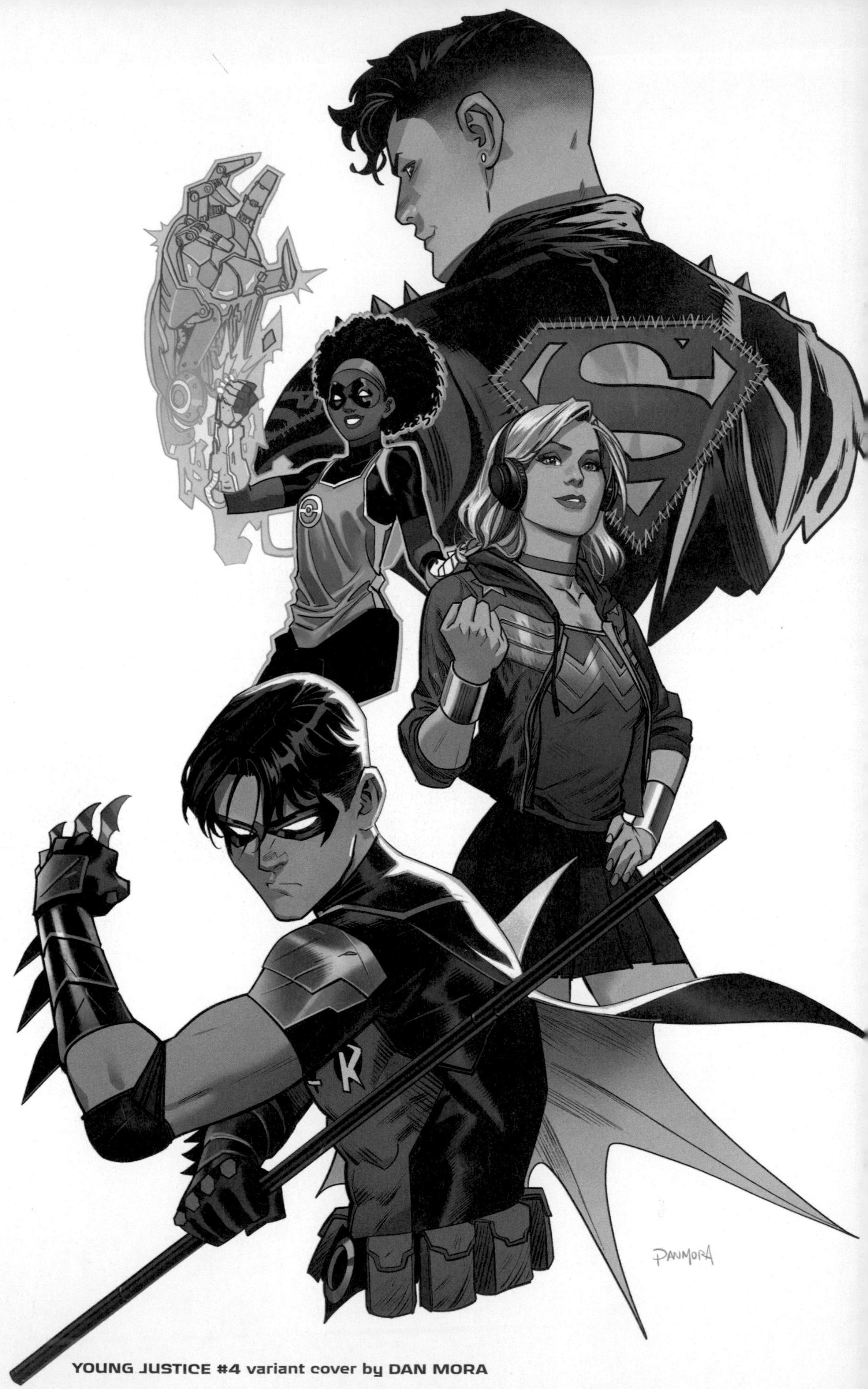
DANMORA

YOUNG JUSTICE #4 variant cover by DAN MORA

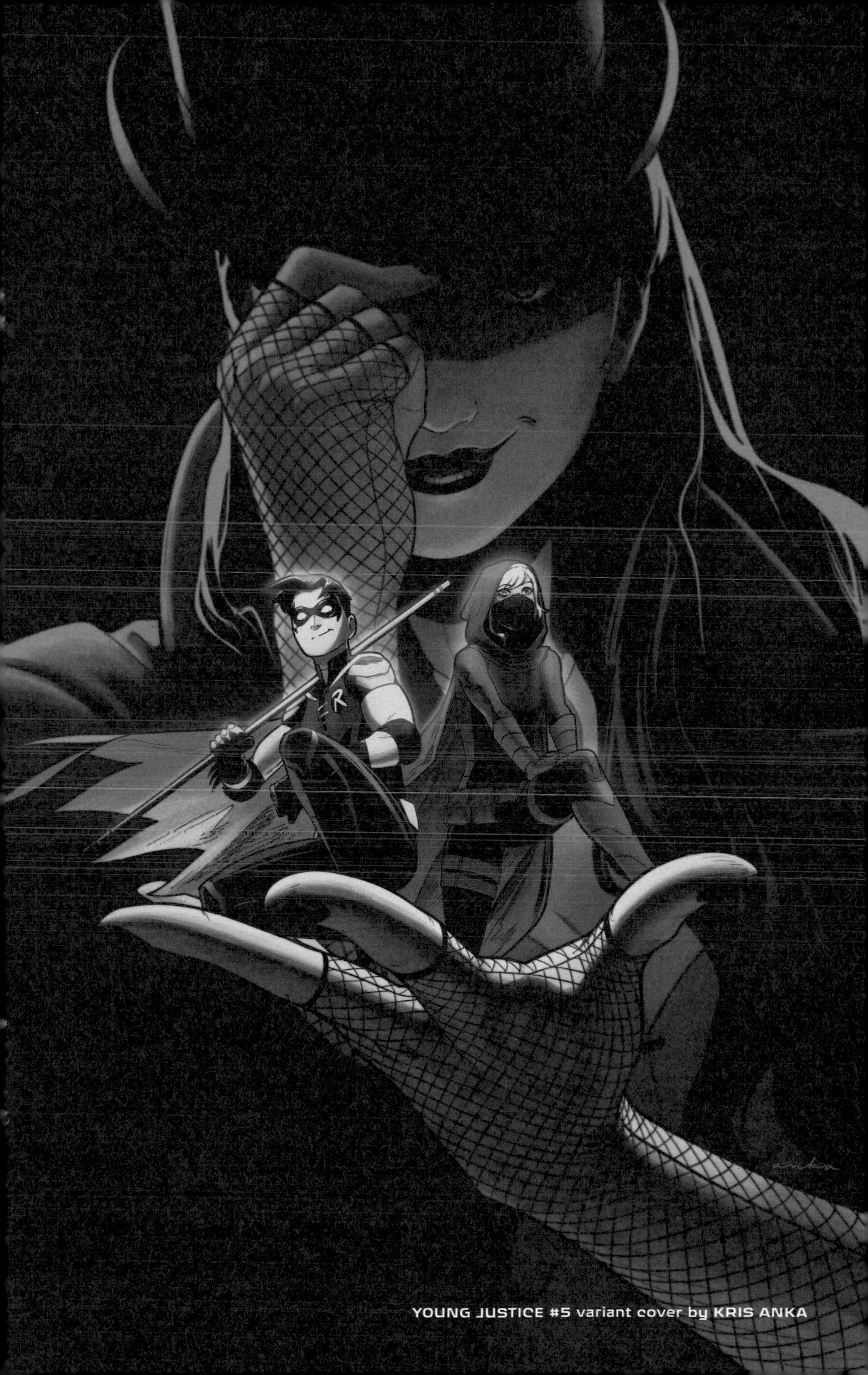

YOUNG JUSTICE #5 variant cover by KRIS ANKA

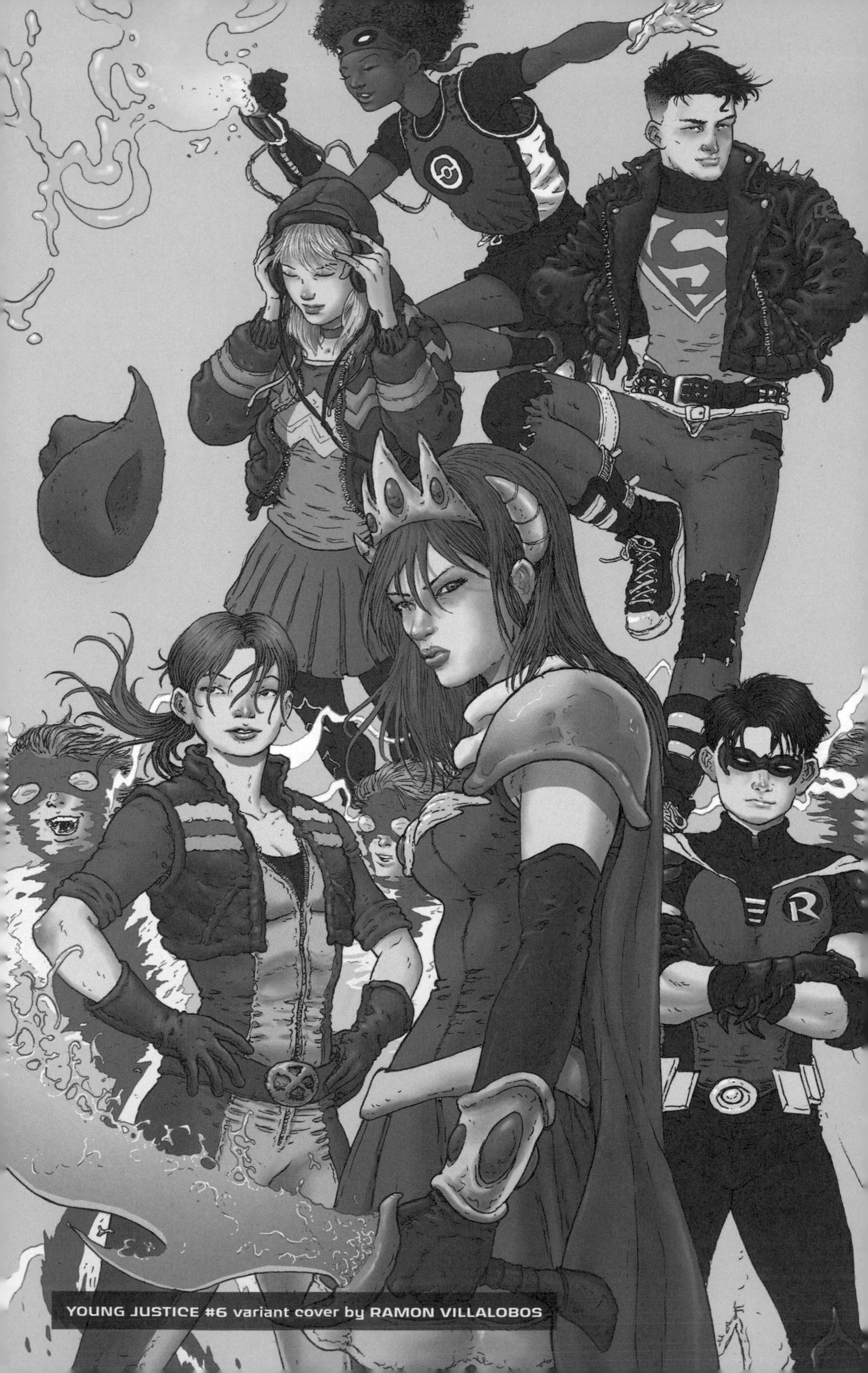

YOUNG JUSTICE #6 variant cover by RAMON VILLALOBOS

AFTERWORD

Hi! HEY! Welcome to Wonder Comics! I'm Brian Bendis, your imprint presenter! You just read the first collection of something we're very, very, VERY proud of. Why? What is it? Where did it come from?

Well, ever since I was old enough to know what they were I dreamed of being a comic book creator. First artist, then writer. I dreamed of seeing my name big on the cover of comics because I am short and that does it for me somehow.

But I never dreamed of "curating an imprint." Basically because when I was growing up there were no such things. There was Vertigo. The end. So when I first walked into DC Comics and sat down with publisher Dan DiDio, I was quite delighted and more importantly challenged by the offer. DC had already had some success with things like Young Animal, and Dan asked if I had anything to offer in that regard. Alisa, my wife and the publisher of our DC imprint Jinxworld, which houses all our creator-owned madness, thought about it. What would we do with an imprint?

I soon realized that the one creative energy in my life that I was really going to *really* miss at Marvel was what I got out of working on the Ultimate universe, on stories and characters at that magical moment when you need to grow the hell up and be the person you're supposed to be. Those kinds of stories have been a big part of what I write about. Why? Hopefully I'll find out one day!

I came back to Dan with the concept for a line of books *just* like the one you are holding. I picked titles like WONDER TWINS and DIAL H FOR HERO as, in my opinion, perfect examples of truly brilliant comic book ideas that belong only in the DC Universe. That speaks to the theme of what would be Wonder Comics.

I will write in depth about the other titles in their own volumes. I have lots of thoughts about those characters and those creators! Oh, the behind-the-scenes on WONDER TWINS!

But how does that get us to this? We all felt like the imprint would need an anchor book. A "big" book to hang the Wonder Comics theme on. Dan looked at me with big saucer eyes and said, "YOUNG JUSTICE."

It just so happened DC had been working on how to get YOUNG JUSTICE back in print, and here I was with a plan. Or the beginning of the beginning of a plan.

So we started the evil science experiments to bring the property back to life. At the same time, I was already working on ACTION COMICS and just having an amazing time working with Pat Gleason and Alejandro Sanchez. Unbeknownst to me, because I didn't know the guy, Pat'd had his eyes set on YOUNG JUSTICE long before this. Even though he would soon head for greener pastures, I'm so happy he helped us launch this book and set the perfect tone and tempo for the series.

So, the book itself. On top of having fan favorites like Conner Kent and Bart Allen come back to the fold, we wanted to include new characters...like every iteration of YOUNG JUSTICE has always done. Pat came to us with the awesome idea of Teen Lantern, which we filled out together, and at the same time I had co-created a new character over in BATMAN: UNIVERSE, with Nick Derington, called Jinny Hex. I couldn't wait to get her magical, mysterious Texan energy on the team.

YOUNG JUSTICE is filled with so many new and classic characters that people hadn't seen in a long time or hadn't met yet, I knew that we were going to have to do some special moments with each character to introduce them or reintroduce them to the audience. So we created this flashback narrative in some issues. *That* opened the book to other artists like Emanuela Lupacchino and Viktor Bogdanovic, whose voices gave each character their own energy and style along the way. It also, organically, got us to the amazing John Timms, who, by the end of the story, had become the official awesome artist of this book.

Alisa and I have been working with some of the best editors and creators in comics to launch Wonder Comics, and the love you feel on every page is a reflection of every person involved. This kind of love and affection doesn't just happen. It has to really be there. It has to be coming out of the people making the comics. It can't be faked. Read the credits. These are good people.

Hey, by the by, like I said before: if you collect the other trades in our Wonder Comics lineup (NAOMI, WONDER TWINS and DIAL H FOR HERO) (and wow, I think that's just a great idea), I will continue this behind-the-scenes look.

But for now...thank you.

BENDIS!
Portland, Oregon | 2019

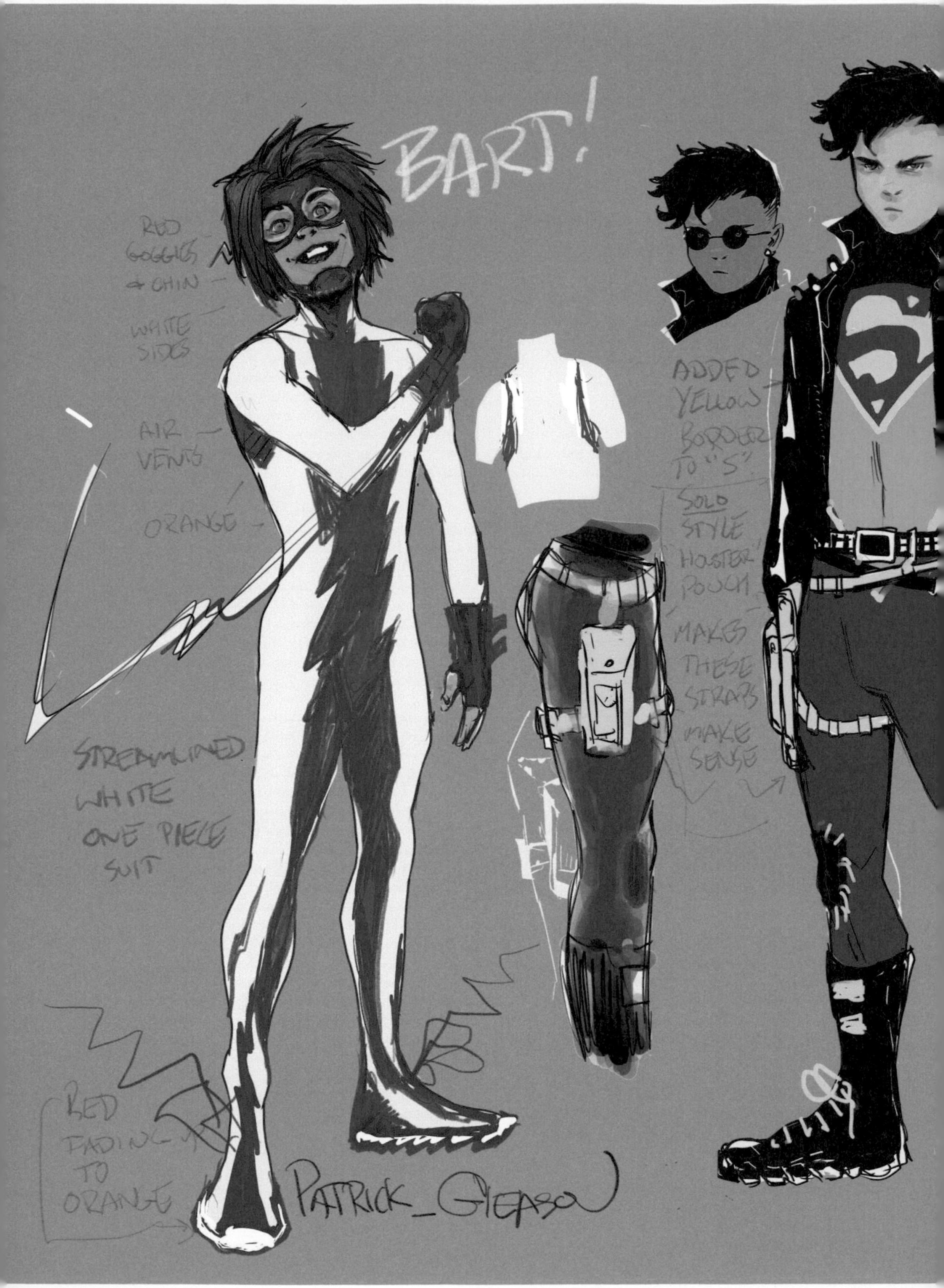
BART!
RED GOGGLES + CHIN
WHITE SIDES
AIR VENTS
ORANGE
STREAMLINED WHITE ONE PIECE SUIT
RED FADING TO ORANGE
PATRICK_GLEASON
ADDED YELLOW BORDER TO "S"
SOLO STYLE HOLSTER POUCH
MAKES THESE STRAPS MAKE SENSE

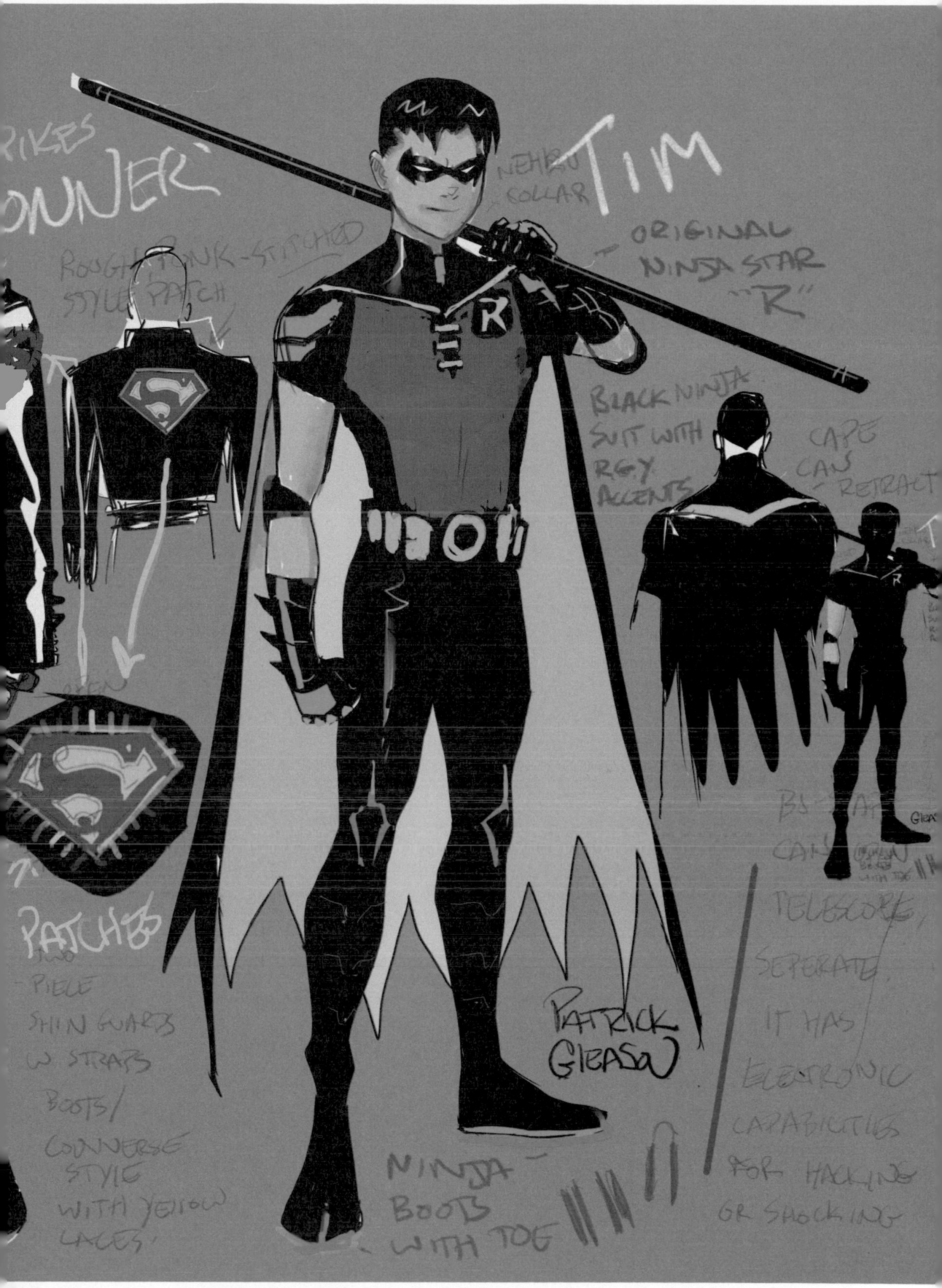
TIM
NEHRU COLLAR
ORIGINAL NINJA STAR "R"
ROUGH PUNK-STITCHED STYLE PATCH
BLACK NINJA SUIT WITH R.G.Y. ACCENTS
CAPE CAN RETRACT
PATCHES
TWO-PIECE SHIN GUARDS W STRAPS
BOOTS/ CONVERSE STYLE WITH YELLOW LACES
TELESCOPE, SEPERATE, IT HAS ELECTRONIC CAPABILITIES FOR HACKING OR SHOCKING
NINJA BOOTS WITH TOE
PATRICK GLEASON

IMPULSE, SUPERBOY and ROBIN character designs by PATRICK GLEASON

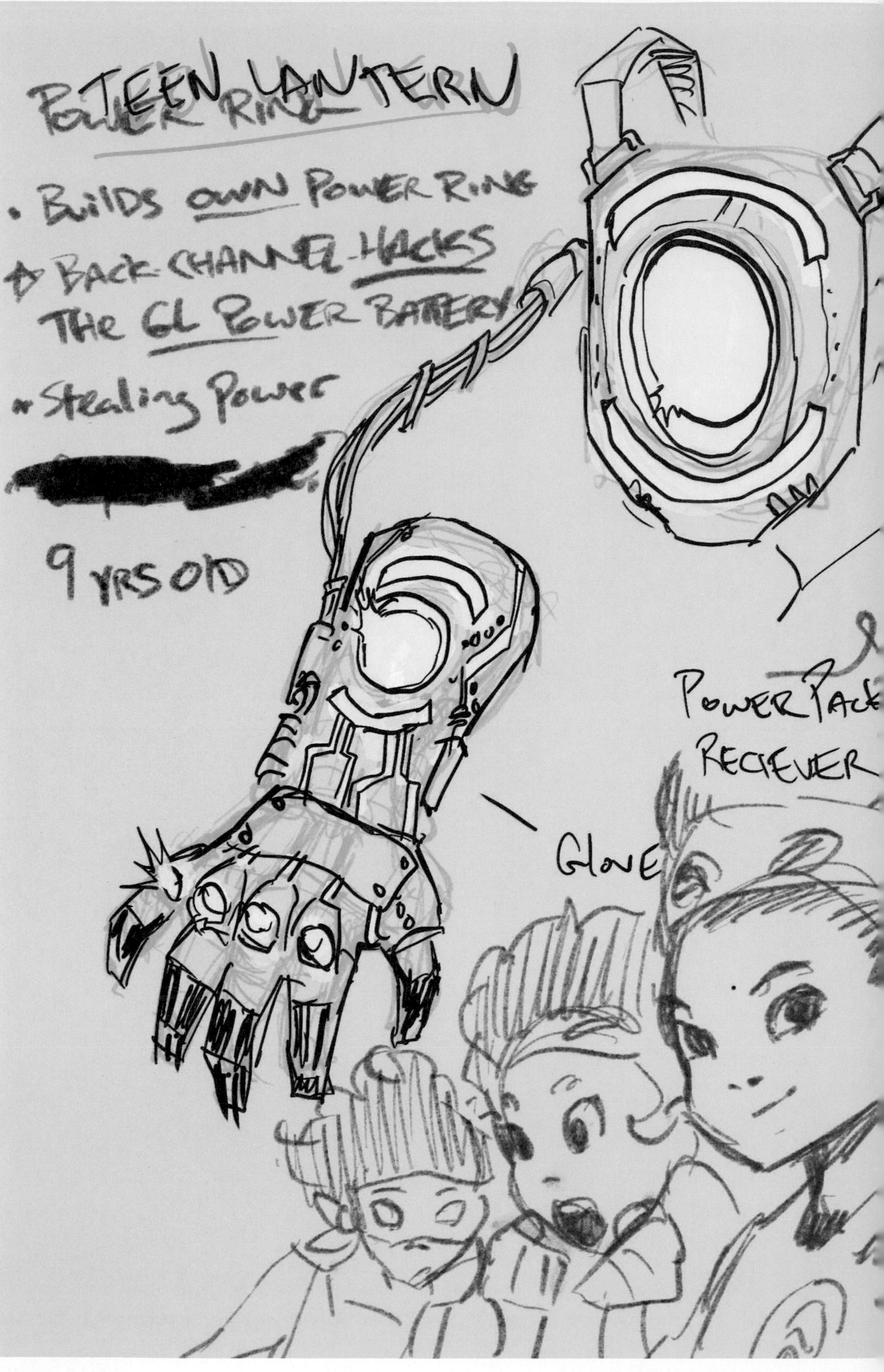
TEEN LANTERN
POWER RING
• BUILDS OWN POWER RING
☆ BACK-CHANNEL-HACKS THE GL POWER BATTERY
• Stealing Power
[redacted]
9 YRS OLD
POWER PACK RECIEVER
GLOVE

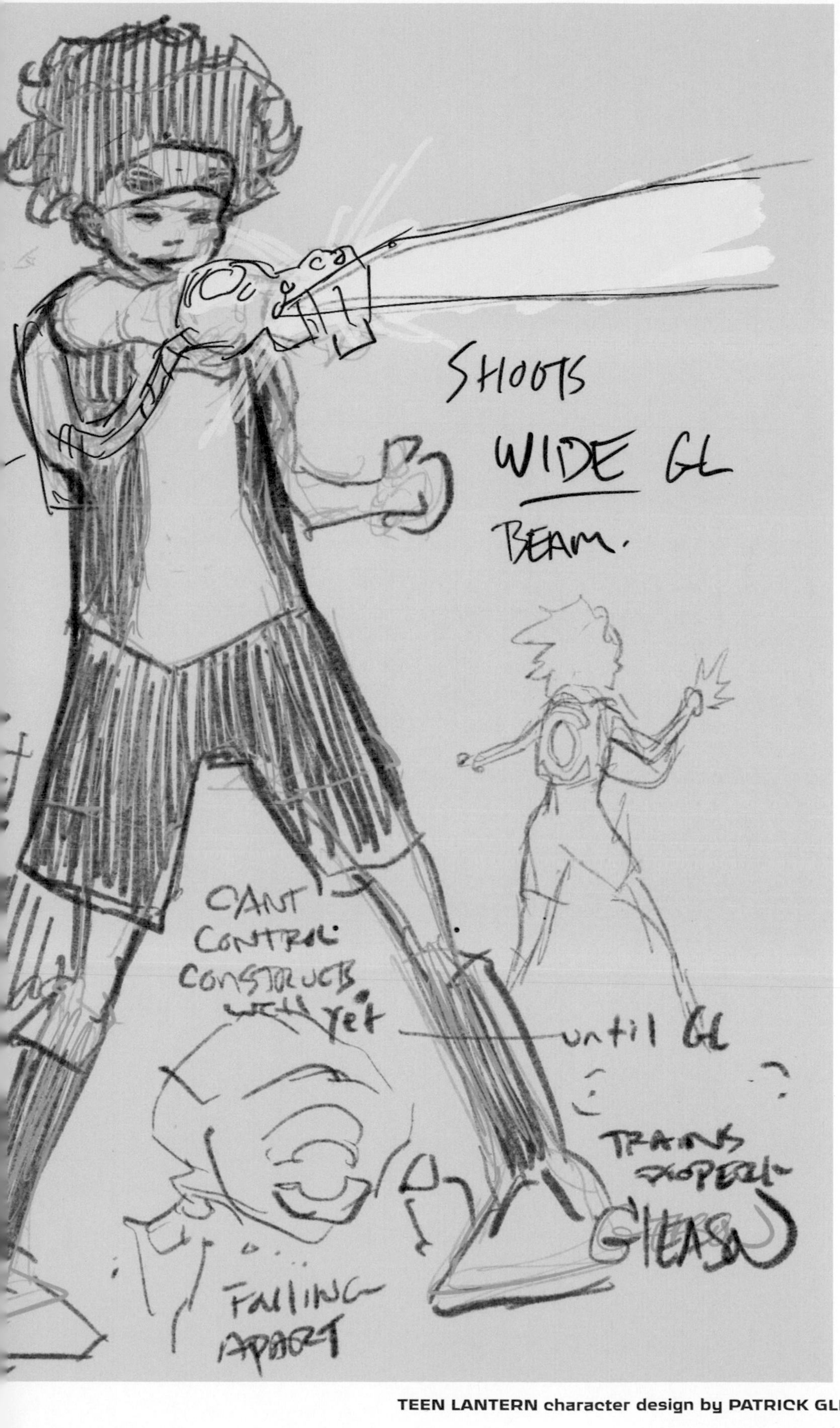
SHOOTS
WIDE GL
BEAM.
CANT
CONTROL
CONSTRUCTS
yet
until GL
TRAINS
PROPERLY
FALLING
APART
GLEASON

TEEN LANTERN character design by PATRICK GLEASON

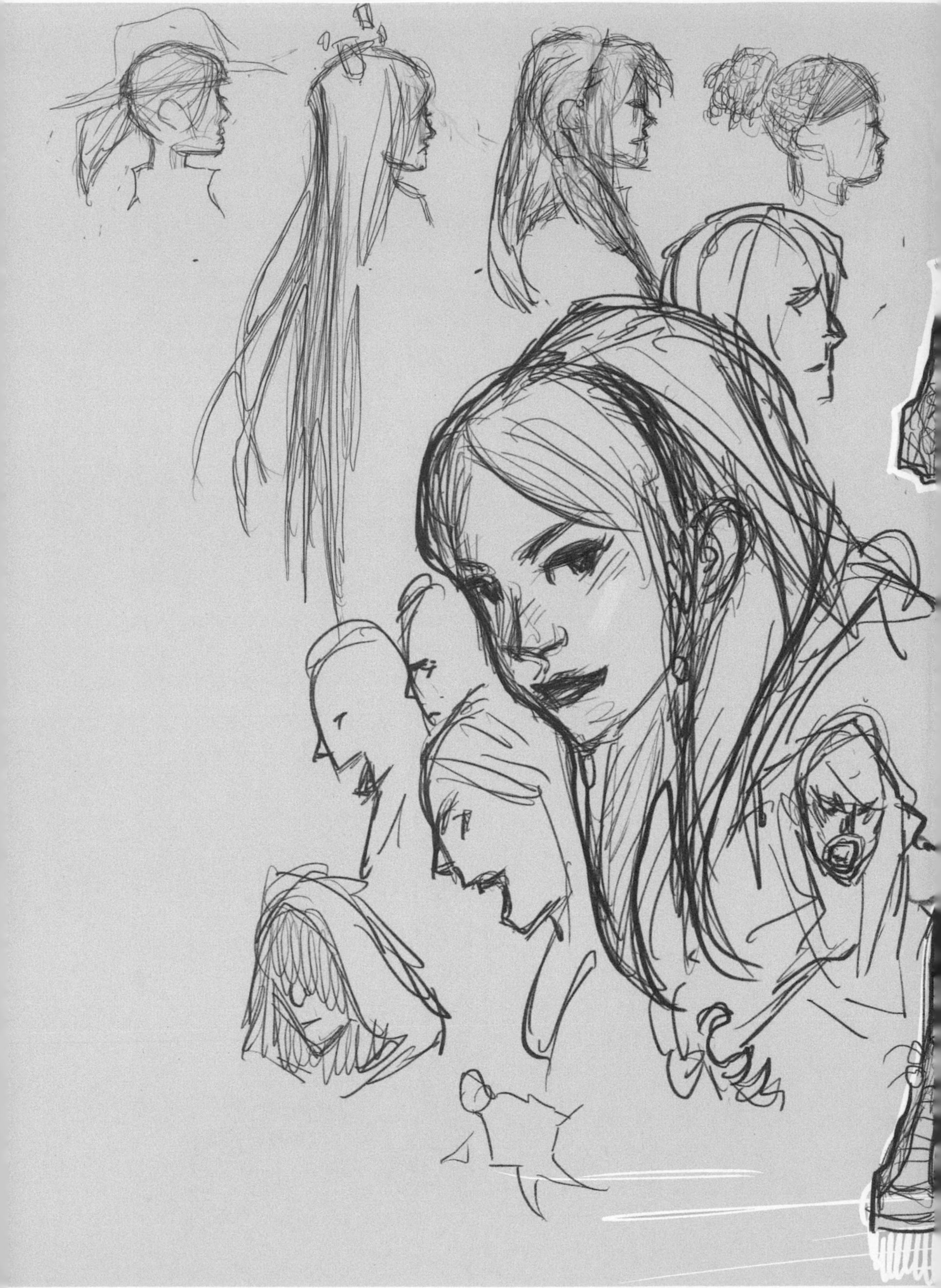

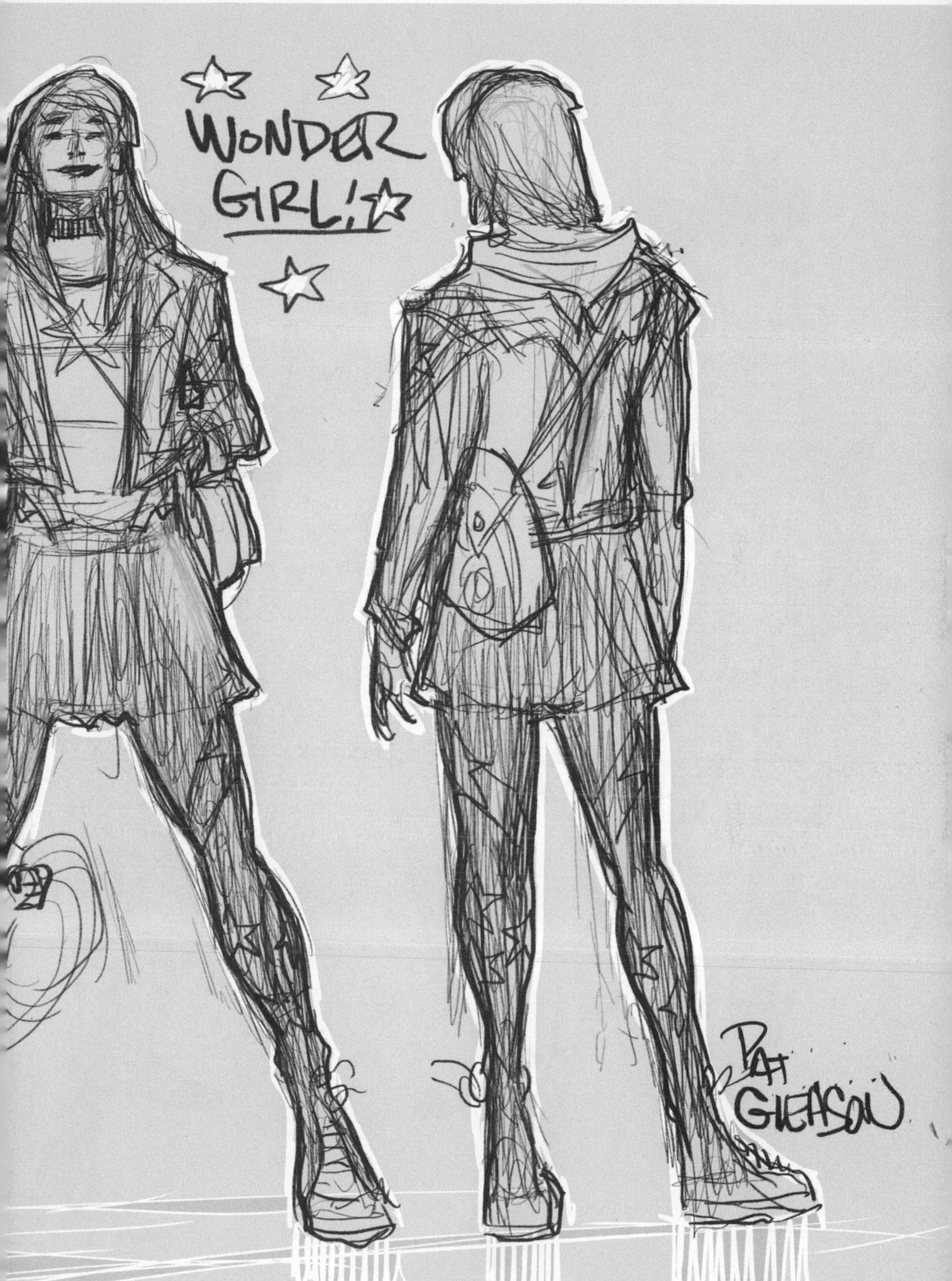
WONDER GIRL!
PAT GLEASON

WONDER GIRL character design by **PATRICK GLEASON**

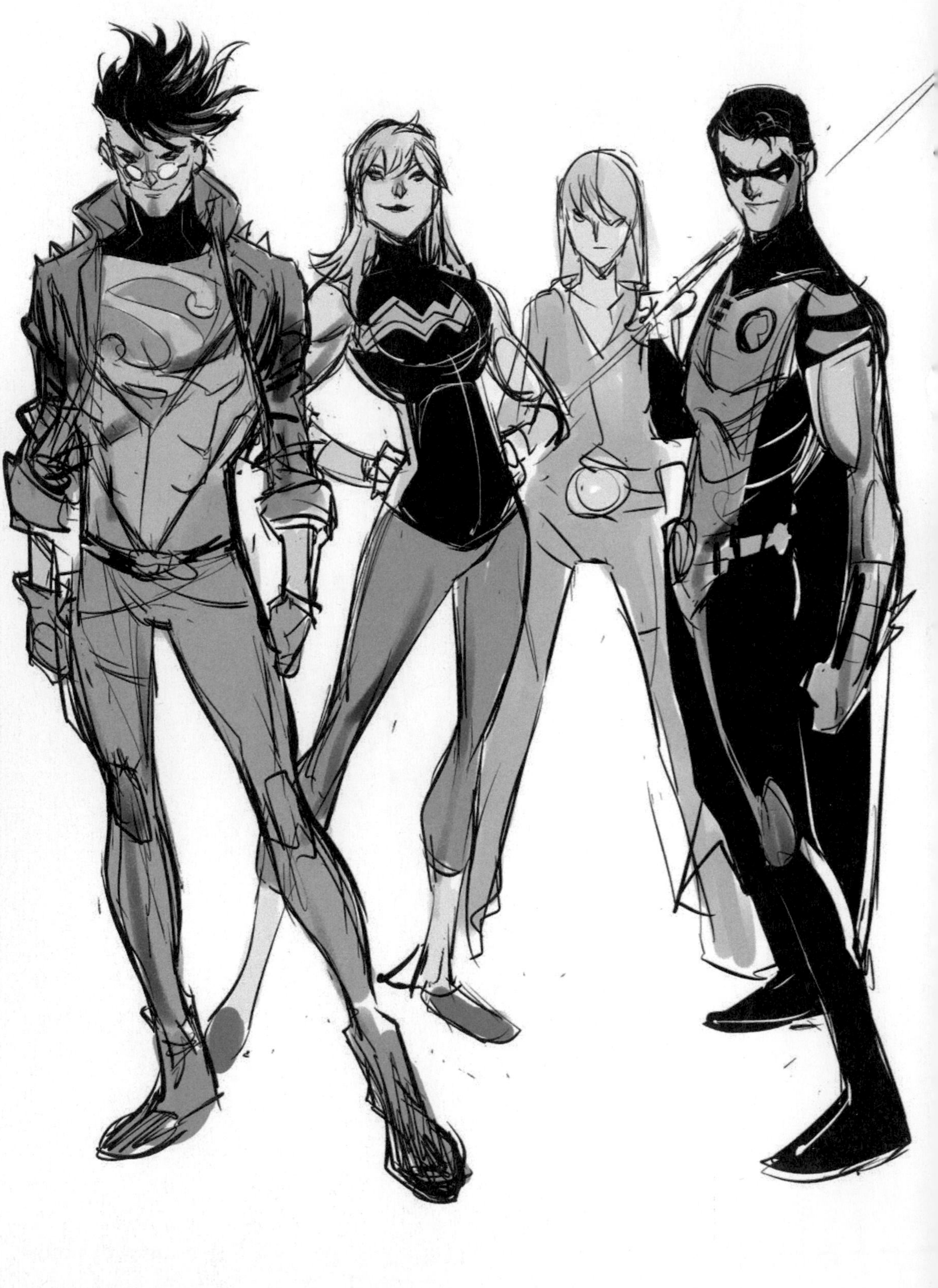

YOUNG JUSTICE sketch by JOHN TIMMS